Invisible and Inaudible in Washington

Edelgard Mahant
and Graeme S. Mount

Invisible and Inaudible in Washington: American Policies toward Canada

UBC Press / Vancouver and Toronto
Michigan State University Press / East Lansing

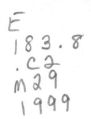

Published in the United States by Michigan State University Press.

Canadian Cataloguing in Publication Data

Mahant, Edelgard E. (Edelgard Elsbeth)
 Invisible and inaudible in Washington
 Includes bibliographical references and index.
 ISBN 0-7748-0702-4 (bound); ISBN 0-7748-0703-2 (pbk.)
 1. United States – Relations – Canada. 2. Canada –
Relations – United States. I. Mount, Graeme S. (Graeme Stewart), 1939-
II. Title.
FC249.M432 1999   327.71073   C99-910107-2
F1029.5.U6M332 1999

Library of Congress Cataloging-in-Publication Data

Mahant, Edelgard E. (Edelgard Elsbeth)
 Invisible and inaudible in Washington : American policies toward
Canada / Edelgard Mahant and Graeme S. Mount
 p. cm.
 Includes bibliographical references and index.
 ISBN 0-87013-525-2 (alk. paper)
 1. United States – Relations – Canada. 2. Canada – Relations –
United States. 3. United States – Foreign relations – 1945-1989. 4.
United States – Foreign relations – 1989- I. Mount, Graeme S. (Graeme
Stewart), 1939- . II. Title.
E183.8.C2M29   1999
327.73071 – dc21   99-22416
                                                CIP

UBC Press acknowledges the financial support of the Government of Canada through the Book Publishing Industry Development Program (BPIDP). We also acknowledge the support of the Canada Council for the Arts for our publishing program, as well as the support of the British Columbia Arts Council.

Set in Stone by Brenda and Neil West, BN Typographics West
Printed and bound in Canada by Friesens

UBC Press   Michigan State University Press
University of British Columbia   1405 South Harrison Road, Suite 25
2029 West Mall, Vancouver, BC V6T 1Z2   East Lansing, Michigan 48823-5202
www.ubcpress.ubc.ca   www.msu.edu/unit/msupress

To Joan and Parkash,
for their love, patience, and support

Contents

Acknowledgments

Many people and organizations helped us write this book. The United States Information Agency, Glendon College of York University, and Laurentian University all contributed money which made the travel affordable. Librarians and secretaries at Glendon and York, particularly Rose May Démoré, a secretary at Laurentian, proved indispensable. Colleagues at Glendon and York listened to our ideas, as did students on both campuses and Dr. Greg Inwood, of Ryerson Polytechnic University. Xavier de Vanssay, an economist at Glendon, gave invaluable advice for Chapters 5, 6, and 7, while graduate student Glenn Goshulak helped with the proofreading and formatting as only a PhD student could.

The staff at the presidential libraries we visited – LBJ in Austin (Texas), Gerald Ford Presidential Archives in Ann Arbor (Michigan), Jimmy Carter Center in Atlanta (Georgia) – proved particularly helpful, as did the people at the National Archives and Research Center in College Park (Maryland), where the Nixon Collection is housed, and at the National Archives of Canada (Ottawa). As usual, Paulette Dozois at the National Archives of Canada went out of her way to be helpful.

There were opportunities to receive feedback on parts of this book. In particular, we want to thank Professor Ged Martin of the University of Edinburgh, Scotland, for allowing a paper at the 1994 Canadian Studies Conference and Professor Doug Owram for his comments on that paper. In 1996, the Canadian Historical Association allowed us to constitute a panel based on parts of Chapters 3 and 5; to commentator Albert Desbiens, we are grateful.

Some of the people mentioned in this manuscript helped set us straight, correcting impressions left by the paper trail and filling gaps. Those who gave formal interviews include National Security Adviser Walt Rostow, Ambassador Jack Warren, and Secretary of State Dean Rusk. (Rusk granted the interview from a sick bed shortly before he died.) Previous conversations with participants – Ambassador Kenneth Curtis and External Affairs Ministers Paul Martin and Mitchell Sharp – proved helpful.

Above all, we would like to thank our advisors at UBC Press – Peter Milroy, Holly Keller-Brohman, Laura Macleod, Camilla Jenkins, and Jean Wilson – for having confidence in us and for making useful suggestions. To the anonymous reviewers they selected, we are also grateful. Finally, we thank our families who tolerated our absences from home and our involvement in the project when we were at home.

Abbreviations

ABM	Anti-Ballistic Missiles
AEC	Atomic Energy Commission
ASIS	Australian Secret Intelligence Service
BNS	Bank of Nova Scotia
BRUSA	Anglo-American signals intelligence sharing organization (later reorganized as UKUSA)
CFIUS	Committee on Foreign Investment in the United States
CIA	Central Intelligence Agency
Coco	Coordinating Committee for Multilateral Export Controls
CPC	Combined Policy Committee
CTV	Canadian Television Network
DEW	Distant Early Warning
DISC	Domestic International Sales Corporation (a type of export subsidy)
DND	Department of National Defence
DRV	Democratic Republic of Vietnam (North Vietnam)
ECOSOC	Economic and Social Council
EOKA	Greek Cypriot insurgents
FNLA	National Front for the Liberation of Angola
FTA	Free Trade Agreement
GATT	General Agreement on Tariffs and Trade
ICC	International Control Commission
ICCS	International Commission of Control and Supervision
ICSID	International Centre for the Settlement of Investment Disputes
IEA	International Energy Agency
IEP	International Energy Program (later, IEA)
IET	Interest Equalization Tax
IMC	International Materials Conference
ITO	International Trade Organization

LOS	Law of the Sea Conference
MNC	Multinational corporation
MPLA	Popular Front for the Liberation of Angola
NAFTA	North American Free Trade Agreement
NATO	North Atlantic Treaty Organization
NEP	National Energy Programme
NORAD	North American Air (later Aerospace) Defense Command
NSC	National Security Council
OAS	Organization of American States
OECD	Organization for Economic Cooperation and Development
OPEC	Organization of Petroleum Exporting Countries
PJBD	Permanent Joint Board on Defense
PPP	People's Progressive Party (British Guiana)
PQ	Parti Québécois
PRC	People's Republic of China
RCAF	Royal Canadian Air Force
ROC	Republic of China
RYAN	Soviet program that anticipated nuclear war
SAC	Strategic Air Command
SHAPE	Supreme Headquarters, Allied Powers Europe
SPR	Strategic Petroleum Reserves
SWAPO	South West African People's Organization
UDI	Unilateral Declaration of Independence (Rhodesia)
UN	United Nations
UNEF	United Nations Emergency Force
UNITA	National Union for the Total Independence of Angola
UNTCOK	United Nations Temporary Commission on Korea
UNTSO	United Nations Truce Supervisory Organization
UNYOM	United Nations Yemen Observer Mission
USAF	United States Air Force
USDIA	United States Direct Investment Abroad
USTR	United States Trade Representative
VC	Viet Cong

Invisible and Inaudible
in Washington

1

Canada As Seen from the United States

It is time for Canadians and Americans ... to recognize that we have very separate identities, that we have significant differences ... mature partners must have autonomous independent policies; each nation must define the nature of its own interests.

– President Nixon to the Canadian Parliament, 14 April 1972

What is required of the United States ... ? It must come to think of Canada ... not as a source of raw materials, not as a useful, if backward, annex to the domestic market, not as a *glacis* between itself and the Soviet Union, not as the great-out-of-doors ... not as a museum of old-fashioned qualities miraculously frozen in ice ... but as a country with its own problems, possibilities, desires.[1]

– Douglas LePan, Canadian academic and former diplomat, 1964

Academics and writers from all parts of the world have at times savagely denounced American foreign policy as imperialistic or exploitive. Others sycophantically praise the United States and its good deeds. Yet other studies fall between these two extremes. Many Americans do not realize it, but there is a large gap between what they say and what they do in their foreign policy, and an equally large gap between how they see their actions and motives and how others perceive these same actions and motives.

Perhaps no one has studied their country's relationship with the United States as obsessively as have Canadians. Yet we still do not know if there is or ever has been an American policy toward Canada. In fact, hardly anyone has ever attempted systematically to place American policies toward Canada in the general context of American foreign policy. To date there appear to be only two book-length studies of American policies toward Canada. Gordon Stewart's *The American Response to Canada Since 1776* gives an excellent and thorough analysis of the documentary record as it describes American policies during the nineteenth century, but it touches only briefly on a few major incidents during the first half of the twentieth century.[2] Lawrence Robert Aronsen's *American National Security and Economic Relations with Canada, 1945-1954* gives thorough coverage to resource issues and to the national security implications of the St. Lawrence Seaway.[3]

This book will try to identify and, where possible, analyze, some of America's Canada policies from 1945 to the end of the Cold War. Because so much has already been written about Canadian-American relations, there is no shortage of – Canadian – interpretations of American policy toward Canada. We shall analyze American policies toward Canada in relation to the overall objectives of American foreign policy. This book will, therefore, mention the familiar Canadian works on Canadian-American relations only occasionally. Because we are studying American policies, we shall try to rely on American sources, primary as well as secondary. Strange at it may seem, however, there are times when only interested Canadians have dug out the necessary primary sources to study American policies toward Canada.

A first question is the extent to which American policies toward Canada relate to American policies overall. Note the term "policies," not "foreign policy," because in the case of American-Canadian relations, the distinction between foreign and other governmental policies is increasingly blurred. This observation may have been less true in 1947 than today, although many bilateral issues have been of the "low politics" variety since at least the 1920s, when Canadians became concerned about American cultural influence on their country. No value judgment of the importance or prestige of one or the other type of policy is intended here, nor is there any intention to deny the link between the two types of policies. However, most studies do distinguish between traditional foreign policy or "high policy" issues (such as defence and security) and "low politics" issues (such as energy, culture, and resources), even though on resource issues at least, foreign and domestic politics tend to overlap.

Charles Doran, an American academic, suggests that Americans and Canadians may differ in the extent to which they emphasize "high" and "low" politics: "From the American foreign policy perspective, nothing exceeds the importance of the political strategic dimension; from the Canadian foreign policy perspective, this dimension is secondary to the economic and commercial dimension."[4] A 1978 document, prepared in the Carter White House for a meeting of world leaders, provides some support for Doran's distinction. The document lists ten issues that might have come up in discussions with Prime Minister Trudeau. Of the ten, six are of a multilateral nature, and of those, five have security and/or Cold War implications (the Belgrade Conference on Human Rights, the situation in southern Africa, the American withdrawal from the International Labour Organisation, the Law of the Sea Conference, and Caribbean economic cooperation).[5] The existence of such a list suggests that a number of general American policies may have Canadian implications. In this book, the high and low politics issues are discussed in separate chapters; the Cold War-related or strategic security issues are discussed in Chapters 2, 3, and 4; the "low" politics issues of resources, investment, and trade, in Chapters 5, 6, and 7. "High" and "low" issues are brought together in the concluding chapter.

For such American policies, at least two assumptions are possible: the United States government had general policies, and policies toward Canada constituted a subset of these policies.[6] Or the American government had policies, but specific policies toward Canada were not a part of these general policies. The papers of American presidents and secretaries of state are full of pronouncements, principles, and doctrines that describe American foreign policy in grand, idealistic terms. This book takes these general principles and attempts to identify to what extent these principles translated into policy toward one of America's closest allies.

Determining whether there was an American policy toward Canada and Canadian issues is a problem which can be approached in at least two ways. One way is to attempt to identify policy coordination across issue areas. Did American policies toward Canada represent specific applications of policies on such issues as access to oil supplies or foreign investment? Or were America's Canada policies ad hoc and *sui generis?* That is, are they afterthoughts or responses to momentary pressures not related to more general policies? Another way of determining whether there was an American policy toward Canada is to look at issues across time. Did American policies on issues such as the stationing of American weapons in Canada or trade with Canada reveal a pattern? Or was policy erratic, determined simply by the pressures relating to a specific "Canadian" issue as that issue arose?

The two types of policy coordination are not necessarily related to one another. It is possible to imagine – and indeed there were times when – as a result of able leadership, policies were coordinated across issues during the term of one president or secretary of state, but ceased to be so coordinated at a later date. It is also possible to imagine that a well-trained bureaucracy (say, in the Office of the United States Trade Representative) might coordinate policy from the administration of one president to that of the next one, but that bureaucracy might not bother to coordinate, or might deliberately avoid coordinating policy, with other central agencies of the American government. This second contingency is, however, less likely than the first one, because the American system of replacing senior bureaucrats as well as policy makers when a new president takes office makes coordination over time unlikely in all but the most entrenched bureaucratic environments.

Americans and Canadians often assumed that there was no US-Canada policy. In 1947, the then Canadian minister for external affairs and later prime minister, Louis St. Laurent, said of Canada and the United States, "Like farmers whose lands have a common concession line, we think of ourselves as settling, from day to day, questions that arise between us, without dignifying the process by the word 'policy.'"[7] In a follow-up letter to the 1965 Merchant-Heeney report, American diplomat Livingston Merchant wrote President Johnson to point out that at least twenty-three American government departments and agencies dealt regularly with their Canadian counterparts. He suggested naming an assistant secretary of state for Canadian affairs who would coordinate America's Canada policies. Eighteen years later, Kenneth Curtis, another former ambassador to Canada, made a similar suggestion with as little consequence.[8]

Canadians seem almost to enjoy citing examples of how Americans forget about them. John Holmes, in earlier days an ardent liberal-internationalist, said in a 1981 lecture, "The Americans have a galling habit of regarding us as a regional aspect of a national problem," and "one persistent problem is that the US forgets about us."[9] There are several instances of Canada's simply being forgotten in Washington; for example, President Nixon identified Japan as America's largest trading partner; a November 1975 document on economic recovery mentions the importance of France, Germany, and Japan – someone penciled Canada into the margin.[10] Even if *Foreign Relations of the United States* devotes many pages to Canada and Canadians, we would not always expect that from reading the history books. Some prominent American diplomatic historians totally ignore Canada's importance to the United States after 1945. Similarly, some recent books specializing in the twentieth century, or even in the United States since 1945 leave the impression that Canada was totally irrelevant to the United States.[11]

On the other hand, books by diplomatic historian Walter LaFeber frequently mention Canada.[12] In view of the vast nature of their subject – American foreign policy since 1900 – Thomas G. Paterson and his fellow researchers devote considerable attention to Canada.[13] Subjects of interest to American writers include Canada's contribution to nuclear technology, the Soviet spy ring exposed in Canada in 1945, and Canada's role as a founding member of the North Atlantic Treaty Organization (NATO).[14] Yet such issues as the withdrawal of Canadian forces from Europe at the end of the Second World War, their return after the outbreak of hostilities in Korea, Canadian thoughts about China, and even Canada's relevance to Korea and Vietnam (before 1960) have all attracted little attention from American writers.

There have been a few exceptions to this general forgetfulness about Canada in recent years. In their quasi-memoirs, President George Bush and National Security Advisor Brent Scowcroft write that Canadian prime minister Brian Mulroney was a person whose advice they valued. Bush welcomed Mulroney's judgment on international issues and used him as a messenger when dealing with other leaders. This relationship, if confirmed by the primary sources on the Bush presidency (which will become available as of 2005), would indeed be exceptional.[15]

Obviously, if Americans ignored Canadians when they made foreign policy, there would be little or nothing to write about here. The fact is not, however, that they had no policy on Canadian issues, but that they often had a number of policies on various issues. In many cases, the different departments of the American administration practised their own policies for whatever Canadian issues came their way. While it is true that the complex bureaucracies of contemporary governments often have difficulty coordinating their policies, this situation might be even more true of relations with Canada than of those with countries on America's crisis list. Canada also has not found its own niche in the State Department. Because it fits in with neither the Caribbean nor Latin America culturally or politically, Canada, since its independence from Britain, was appended to the State Department's European Office. (It remains there to this day, and as a non-European country, Canada receives relatively little attention there.)

As a result, only a few cases of linkage among Canadian issues come to mind: the exemption in 1962 from an investment tax in return for a double-taxation treaty (see Chapter 6) or a favourable deal in 1965 for the automobile industry in return for cooperation on Cyprus (see Chapter 3). Instead, different departments of the American government (such as the State Department or the Department of the Environment) might have various policies on issues relating to Canada. Such policies need to be examined individually, but the lack of linkage is itself evidence of a lack of an overall policy toward Canada.[16] As this book will show, this situation prevailed for most of the Cold War years. On only a few occasions – for example, when the Truman administration in 1947 set the policy guidelines to shape the geopolitical framework of American foreign policy; when Kennedy's "best and brightest" tried in 1962 to recast American foreign policy on rational foundations; and when Kissinger in 1974 tried to do likewise, albeit from a more geopolitical frame of reference – did the American central administration attempt to review its Canadian policy in its entirety. We shall try to determine the extent to which such guidelines translated into specific policies. General policy guidelines are the academic's *faux amis*. They may suggest, for example, that some American policy makers saw Canada simply as a great storehouse of resources, or as a country with no future as an independent state (as did George Ball, a former under-secretary of state), but such guidelines need to be translated into specific policies, and it is these specific policies that we shall be looking for.[17]

There is another way that the various policies of the American government departments could amount to a Canada policy. The various policies might result from a common mindset among officials in the various departments. While such a concordance of views cannot be ruled out, it seems unlikely. Most studies of American government policies in whatever domain have found a great variety of views and a lack of, not an excess of, coordination. It is also possible that a general policy existed on, say, the NATO allies, or America's energy supplies, but that policy was applied to Canada only in its role as one ally among others. In other words, American policy was applied to Canada as general policy, with no special provision for Canada as a neighbour or an ally with a longstanding special relationship with the US.

Now, of course, the rational policy-making model assumes that policies, especially foreign policies, are usually made from the top down, so that a general policy of alliance with some countries (for example, "the West") and hostility to others (for example, "the Communist bloc") is applied to the individual states constituting those blocs. A lack of policy precision, however, can result if the overall policies are applied rigidly, without adaptation to the individual states. Or if it is blithely assumed that all allies will always follow in the steps of the alliance hegemon, then no specific policy on the individual allied states may exist. According to Canadian academics Laura McKinsey and Kim Nossal, "The United States does not make a habit of consciously evaluating ... options in relating to Canada because of the tendency to assume almost automatic acquiescence in decisions made by the alliance leader."[18] In the case studies included in this book, we shall be looking to see if general policies were adapted for Canada and communicated to the Canadian government, or whether Canada was expected to fall into place once the general policy was implemented.

Here we tread a fine line. One would normally expect a general policy, for example, toward NATO allies not only to be applied to Canada but also to be adapted to Canadian circumstances. What we are looking for are such Canadian adaptations of American policies. Yet it is easy to fall into the trap of damning American policies whatever the Americans do. If America's Canada policy was made especially for Canada case by case, one could accuse the American administrations of not having a Canada policy. If other policies were expected to apply to Canada, willy-nilly, without any adaptive measures, one could accuse Americans of insensitivity and rigidity or of demoting Canada to the status of a satellite. Ideally, one could compare Canada to other allies. Was Canadian policy more ad hoc or more rational than policy on, say, Italy? But that goes beyond the topic of this book.

Some Canadians, especially those of a Marxist or other left-wing persuasion, might say that the term "ally" does not accurately describe the relationship between the US and Canada; that terms such as "satellite" or "peripheral dependence" might provide a more accurate description of the relationship. This question is another to which our cases may provide an answer. Was Canada an ally that supported American policy, and also contributed to that policy? That is, did Canada make a difference? Or did American policy makers expect Canadian "policy makers" to implement policies made in Washington with few questions asked? That is, did they treat Canada as a satellite? In our cases, we shall try to determine to what extent American policy makers considered Canada as a satellite.

Technical Issues

This book uses a simple analytical framework. The given, or the independent variable, is the policy of the American government. The topic to be studied, or the dependent variable, consists of the role, if any, Canada played within American policy; the focus is thus not on Canada as an actor, but on Canada as a subject of American policy.

We assume that there is such a phenomenon as American policy on most issues, even if there may not be a Canada policy. American policy may appear to consist of an amalgam of the interests of various groups, the Congress, the administration, and the president and his advisors. At the end of the day, there emerges from what has aptly been called the "foreign policy fudge factory" (or in our case, perhaps more accurately, the policy fudge factory) a recognizable series of pronouncements and/or actions that can be called American policy.[19] Our analysis is thus unabashedly and unashamedly state-centric. This approach does not mean that either author subscribes to a particular view about the endurance of the nation-state; it means only that for the purpose of this topic and for the time covered, the nation-state still constitutes a useful element of analysis.

The researchers' problem is to identify a national policy. Like Stephen Krasner, we have, therefore, relied on both State Department and White House documents and presidential papers, with a heavier emphasis on the latter, on the assumption that if there is one place where the policies of the American government are likely to be coordinated, that is the spot where it is most likely to happen. Krasner, who used the statist approach to study American raw materials policy during the early Cold War, relied largely on the policies of the White House and the State Department as "the pivot of the state."[20] But the State Department, much as it would have liked to be the coordinator of all things foreign in Washington, increasingly had to share that role with other central governmental agencies. We have therefore also sometimes needed to determine the policies advocated or implemented by other parts of the American government, most notably the Department of Defense, the Department of Energy, and the Office of the United States Trade Representative.

This book will deal with American policy as made in and carried out from Washington. What this means with respect to America's Canada policies is that we shall look at the policies as revealed by the documentation of the American government and as carried out by American diplomats and other bureaucrats. To that end, we will not always need to distinguish between policies that succeeded (that is, which elicited the desired response from Canada) and those that did not. Our primary purpose is to study not the outcomes, but the intended consequences, of American policy.

Obviously, such a perspective misses some aspects of American policy. This book takes American policy as a given. It does not delve into the interest groups and political pressures preceding the making of the policy. Nor does it look at many of the departmental archives, except for those of the State Department. The assumption is that there is an American state and that that state has a policy, which is that of the White House and the State Department.

The method used is case studies; that is, for the most part, the book deals with substance rather than process. Our means of finding out what role Canada was assigned and/or played in American policy will be to examine issues, such as the beginning of the Cold War, the Vietnam War, American concerns about supplies of raw materials, or American trade policy. In the case studies, we shall be particularly careful to identify which of the two governments initiated particular proposals. If few proposals came from the American government, that might help confirm that there really was little Canada policy on the part of the United States. We chose the cases as representative of major issues that would occupy the attention of the highest American decision makers. For the most part, this approach means issues that attracted a fair amount of public attention in the US or in Canada when they occurred. Thus, we had to include the Korean War, the Vietnam War, and the 1970s energy crisis, though only the last had an immediately evident Canadian component. Our second criterion for cases was that the issues involved should be expected to involve Canada. Otherwise, there obviously would not be a Canada policy. Canada is a major producer of energy, the most important trading partner of the United States, and a major destination of American investment. So policies on all three of these issues have a Canadian component. Other important issues in Washington (such as the arms limitation agreements with the USSR) involved Canada only marginally and were therefore not included.

That said, we could not deal with all the cases we might have liked to include, because in some instances (such as that of the Congo crisis of 1960-2) the documentary record simply did not reveal enough of an American policy toward Canada for there to be anything worth writing about. Canadians might believe that their contribution to peacekeeping would entitle them to some role in American policy on the Congo. But the documentary record, which by now appears to be fairly complete, does not reveal much evidence of such a policy. In other cases, such as that of

Yemen or Namibia, the documentary trail led us down roads we had not expected to travel. In the end, the cases were chosen by a combination of the first two rational criteria – representativeness and relevance – and the serendipitous – an adequate documentary record.

Most of the cases discussed in this book predate January 1981, when Ronald Reagan succeeded Jimmy Carter as president. We are aware that some of the most frightening years of the Cold War were those of the Reagan presidency. ABC featured the television program *The Day After*, which dramatized the possible outcome of nuclear war; Ronald Reagan referred to the Soviet Union as "the evil empire"; and the Soviets launched Operation RYAN (a Russian acronym for a program which anticipated nuclear war). Historian Christopher Andrew believes that Operation RYAN was the world's most dangerous event since the Cuban Missile Crisis of 1962.[21] The Reagan administration also conducted a military build-up, including the controversial Strategic Defense Initiative (SDI) or Star Wars. There were wars in Central America and the Caribbean, notably in Nicaragua and El Salvador. But, unfortunately, documentation on the Reagan presidency was not available as this book was being written. The focus of most of the cases therefore remains on events during the terms of office of earlier presidents. Indications are that the people in the Reagan White House did not like Prime Minister Trudeau's peace initiative and did not solicit Canada's help with or opinion on the 1983 invasion of Grenada. It also seems that Brian Mulroney, prime minister from 1984 to 1993, was anxious to adopt most of the policies advocated by the Reagan administration and that Mulroney and Reagan liked one another personally. But the kind of documentation available for the earlier years is not yet available for this later time period. We therefore had to omit many events of the Reagan and Bush years. The main exception is trade, where Canadian researchers have ferreted much about the origins of the FTA and the NAFTA, though the official records are not yet available.

Chapter 2 deals with the early part of the Cold War and includes eight case studies. The first case deals with Canada's strategic importance. The second and third cases discuss North American air defence and the role that nuclear weapons played in that defence in the early Cold War. The fourth and fifth cases deal with the early years of the United Nations and the founding of NATO. The sixth through eighth cases deal with the Cold War as it played itself out in the Far East: Canada's role in the Korean War, the consequences of the Communist takeover of China, and the International Control Commission, which made up part of the Geneva settlement by which the French withdrew from Vietnam. Canada participated in this commission; the US disapproved of the settlement.

Chapter 3 continues with the Cold War since 1961 and includes seven case studies. The first case is that of the controversy over the stationing of nuclear weapons in Canada. The second deals with the Vietnam War and Canada's various roles as that tragedy played itself out. The third case is Cuba, from the time of the Cuban Revolution and the Cuban Missile Crisis to the continuing problem of the American trade embargo against Cuba. The fourth case concerns Cyprus and the role Canada played in helping the United States deal with that problem and its Cold War implications. The fifth case concerns the admission of China to the UN, and the sixth the Soviet invasion of Afghanistan and the various attempts by the Carter and then the Reagan administration to obtain the support of allied governments for American policies designed to oppose the Soviet intervention in that country. The seventh case concerns the possibility of Quebec independence (after the 1976 elections in that province) and the American administrations' thoughts on the effect Quebec's separation from the rest of Canada might have on North American defence.

Chapter 4 looks at post-colonial and North-South issues, and includes eight case studies. The first two cases consist of a review of American and Canadian roles in the Middle East, first in the 1956 Suez crisis and then in Yemen. The third and fourth cases consist of two Latin American issues: the 1965 invasion of the Dominican Republic and the negotiation by the Carter administration of the 1977-8 Panama Canal Treaties. The fifth case is technically not Latin American; it concerns Guyana, where both Americans and Canadians had major investments. The sixth case deals with the Law of the Sea conferences, where North and South clashed on issues such as the international control of resources and the rights and obligations of multinational corporations. The seventh case in this chapter concerns Africa, where Cubans and Soviets opposed Americans in Angola, and a final case examines the Iranian Revolution, where Canadians helped Americans.

Chapter 5 discusses resources, which have been a topic of American policy toward Canada in both the nineteenth and the twentieth centuries. In 1908, President Theodore Roosevelt told Prime Minister Sir Wilfrid Laurier, "The progress of the people of the United States obviously depends on the availability of resources, and it is evident that natural resources are not limited by the boundary lines which separate nations."[22] Americans have continued their interest in Canada's resources, and that interest has been heightened by external events such as the Second World War, the Cold War, and the 1970s energy crisis. This chapter consists of four case studies. The first deals with the need for resources and the control over mineral resources as part of American strategy from 1945 to 1960. The second case describes the oil shortage that followed the Middle East War of 1973 and recurred in the early 1980s. The third case provides a brief explanation of natural gas policies. The fourth case study traces the history of atomic energy, from its discovery at the end of the Second World War, through the fears in the 1970s of a worldwide energy shortage, to the 1980s, as the star of atomic energy waned.

Chapter 6 deals with American investment and the extent to which American policy supported American-based multinational firms. While resources have been primarily an American interest, Canadians have shown great concern about American investment in Canada. Americans have replied by insisting on the right to invest without restriction. At the same time, Americans faced much more serious challenges to their overseas investment in Latin America and the Middle East than they did in Canada. The chapter will relate American policy on investment in Canada to American policy on foreign investment generally. The first topic is monetary policy and the relationship between American monetary policy and the Canadian dollar. The 1971 American dollar crisis and the consequent attempt to put an end to exemptionalism is of special importance in this respect. The second topic is direct investment by the US in Canada, which has at times been the subject of a major public debate among Canadians. The third topic is that of the various American attempts to impose export controls on American-owned corporations in Canada, a subject that is closely related to direct investment.

Chapter 7 deals with American trade policy. Whether to protect or trade freely has been a controversial topic in American politics since the founding of the American Republic. After all, British efforts to control American trade formed part of the background to the American Revolution. Because Canada was the largest trading partner of the United States for most of the period after 1945, it will be interesting to see to what extent Canada fit into American trade policy overall. The first case deals with various attempts to create some kind of a free trade system between the two countries, from 1947 to 1975. The second case deals with the slide away from multilateralism and the negotiations leading to the 1988 Canada-US Free Trade Agreement. Was it an American or a Canadian initiative – or both? The next case deals with the NAFTA. How, if at all, did Canada fit into this policy, whose focus was primarily directed at Mexico? The last case demonstrates the extent to which trade between the two countries is managed rather than free. It is an examination of the 1965 Autopact and its revisions by the FTA and NAFTA.

The methodology is simple and analytical. Each chapter begins with a brief summary of the major outlines of American policy on the relevant issues during the time period in question. The chapter then examines specific American policies on the issues selected and attempts to determine the role, if any, Canada was assigned or undertook in the making and implementation of these policies. Each chapter concludes with summary answers to questions posed earlier in this introductory chapter.

In the concluding chapter, we attempt to determine if there has been an

American policy toward Canada, especially insofar as issues affecting Canada may have been coordinated. Overall, we found little evidence of such a coordinated policy. Surprisingly, much of America's Canada policy originated with stimulus from Washington, but beyond that simple fact there was little in the way of a pattern to that policy. Instead, we identified three different policy patterns in America's Canada policy: times when Canada played the role of a strong and independent ally, able to influence American policy; times when Canada was treated differently from other allies (exceptionalism); and times when Canada was treated like a satellite or dependent state. There were also occasions when Canada was just forgotten or ignored. No single policy pattern predominated, a fact which leaves us with a long and varied story to tell.

This book builds on the work of its predecessor in the field, Annette Baker Fox's *The Politics of Attraction*.[23] Fox described the relations between the US and four of its middle-power allies – Australia, Brazil, Canada, and Mexico. Her study is based on the writings of scholars and the statements of officials from the four middle powers. She did not focus on American policies or on the thinking of the White House, the State Department, and the National Security Council, which are the central concerns of this book.

2
The Cold War,
Part I (1945-60)

During the first fifteen years of the Cold War, successive American and Canadian governments agreed on most important issues. Officials in Washington and Ottawa feared Soviet aggression and saw the Soviet Union as the major threat to world peace, international security, and the survival of the United States and Canada. Differences of opinion were relatively minor – what restrictions should be on American nuclear weaponry at Goose Bay or what role Canadian forces should play in Korea. That nuclear weapons had a role to play in the defence of the Western world or that South Korea should be defended was not seriously in dispute. Canadian politicians and most Canadian voters appreciated American leadership on Cold War-related issues, and the major point of contention was the kind of support Canada should offer. Under the circumstances, bilateral controversies – although they did exist – were minimal.

The Second World War was barely over when Americans were shocked to see their erstwhile allies, the Soviets, seize control of one East European country after another. Soviet troops occupied Poland and allowed Stalin to impose a pro-Soviet government there. Soviet-style Communists took control of Bulgaria, Yugoslavia, and Albania. They were well on their way to complete domination of Hungary and Romania. Soviet armies occupied North Korea and the eastern part of Germany. A Communist takeover of Czechoslovakia appeared probable.

By the end of 1947, the Communist takeovers of Hungary and Romania were complete, and Czechoslovakia fell in February 1948. Even the Norwegian government feared that Norway, like Finland, might have to surrender some of its sovereignty to the Soviet Union. According to Norway's foreign minister, Halvard Lange, Norway had little with which to defend itself, because German occupiers had destroyed most of the equipment Norway needed for self-defence.[1]

Americans reacted by halting demobilization and preparing for what became the Cold War. Their suspicions about a Soviet-led Communist plan to dominate the world seemed to be confirmed when the Communists won the Civil War in China in 1949 and when Communist North Korea attacked US-backed South Korea in 1950. It appeared that only Latin America and Africa were spared, for the time being. Until Fidel Castro's Cuba clearly entered the Soviet orbit in 1960, Latin America remained a low priority, seemingly far removed from the Soviet menace, despite the catastrophic riots of 1948 in Bogotá and the appearance in 1953-4 of a Guatemalan government that seemed to have socialist overtones. Africa – most of it still ruled by Western European nations and their expatriates – was an even lower priority.

American foreign policy during these fifteen years was thus dominated by the search for security, and security was seen as threatened primarily by the Soviet-led Communist bloc which was seeking to dominate Europe and Asia. These two continents, therefore, became the focus of a security-dominated (some would say obsessed) American foreign policy.

Throughout this period, the Truman and Eisenhower administrations considered Canada an important ally. Secretary of State James Byrnes (1945-6) portrayed the United Kingdom and Canada as two of his country's principal allies, partners in developing nuclear weapons.[2] Canada was one of only five foreign destinations (Potsdam had been another) for President Truman. President Eisenhower made Canada his second (after Mexico) foreign destination. After his state visit of 13-14 November 1953, when the Liberals held office, he returned to greet Conservative prime minister John Diefenbaker (8-11 July 1958) and to open the St. Lawrence Seaway in the spring of the following year. While he met British prime minister Harold Macmillan in Bermuda a couple of times, Eisenhower did not make a presidential visit to the United Kingdom until late summer 1959, on a trip that also took him first to West Germany and subsequently to France.

This chapter will assess the extent to which Canada fit into American strategy during these early Cold War years. Was Canada an ally or simply an appendage, a large piece of territory that would give the US armed forces time to prepare if the Soviet Union attacked? Was it an exceptional ally, somewhat more important than Great Britain or France? Or was it just another ally, so reliable that it required little attention?

Canada's Strategic Importance
The Joint Chiefs of Staff – the individuals ultimately responsible for advice on the security of the United States – realized that the United States needed allies, and Canada was for most purposes one ally among others. On 29 April 1947, the Joint Strategic Survey Committee of the Joint Chiefs of Staff ranked Canada as the eighth most important nation to "the national security of the United States," after Great Britain, France, Germany, Belgium, the Netherlands, Austria, and Italy. (Evidently, the numbers and

industrial potential of the Western European countries counted for more than Canada's geographical location.) Canada ranked ahead of the more vulnerable Greece and Turkey, all of Latin America, and Spain – let alone Japan, China, Korea, or the Philippines, ranked in that order.[3] The Joint Chiefs of Staff were fully aware that areas of traditional American interest – the Western Hemisphere, the Philippines, Australia, and Greenland ("tradition" in these last two cases dating only to the Second World War) – included 40 percent of the world's surface area and only 25 percent of its population. By themselves, these areas could not withstand a unified challenge from Europe, Asia, and Africa. At the very least, the United States needed "allies on the eastern side of the Atlantic," and realistically, the Western European nations were capable of the most meaningful assistance. The two world wars had demonstrated "the interdependence of France, Great Britain, and the United States."[4]

By 1947, the United States and the Soviet Union were adversaries. While the Joint Chiefs of Staff did not anticipate an actual war between the two superpowers, they did want to be prepared.[5] As pro-Soviet governments came to power in Europe, American authorities regarded the United Kingdom and Canada as their most reliable allies.[6] Americans, British, and Canadians had fought together in the Second World War, and they shared a political tradition and a language. Canada remained a military associate of the United States through the Permanent Joint Board on Defense, created in 1940 by President Roosevelt and Prime Minister Mackenzie King and still in existence today. Australia, New Zealand, and South Africa – the other English-speaking allies of the Second World War – were smaller and less vital to the defence of the United States. Like the United States, Canada had enjoyed a privileged position outside the war zone and was able to assist the war-ravaged peoples of Europe. As one of the non-permanent members of the United Nations Security Council, and elected to a two-year term in 1947, Canada could assume roles not open to the United States. Washington hoped that in those roles Canada, because of its shared outlook with the United States, might help to fulfil American goals at the United Nations, in the Middle East, and in Korea.

Sometimes American policy makers remembered how sensitive their neighbour to the North could become about its status. In 1946, George Kennan and a General Lincoln made a secret trip to Ottawa to enlist Canadian support for America's "Russian policy" and to help persuade the Canadians "to agree to a further development of the defense arrangements under the Ogdensburg Agreement, and [to make] them feel that we were taking them into our confidence."[7]

Strategically, Canada was probably most important to the United States in the 1940s and 1950s. In 1951, when the Joint Chiefs of Staff envisaged possible scenarios "under which the US will accept war ... a Soviet attack against the continental US – including Alaska and Canada" was the first of six possible situations they envisaged.[8] The State and Defense Departments considered the Soviet Union to be the chief threat to American security, and Canadian cooperation was vital for Soviet containment. Until late in the Eisenhower presidency, most aircraft lacked the capacity to fly non-stop from American territory (other than Alaska) to targets in the Soviet Union or across the Atlantic Ocean. Bases at stops in Canada increased the range of the United States Air Force. After 1960, the development and deployment of long-range aircraft and of intercontinental ballistic missiles would reduce the need for Canadian cooperation.

The Permanent Joint Board on Defense remained active. In the words of Dean Acheson, then the under-secretary of state, "Our military authorities are naturally intent on closing the gap between Alaska and Greenland."[9] On 6 May 1946, President Truman formally approved the board's 35th Recommendation, which provided for personnel exchanges between the armed forces of both countries, standardization of equipment, provision of military facilities by each country to the armed forces of the other, and other ongoing cooperation.[10] President Truman told Prime Minister Mackenzie King that technological advances no longer allowed North America the luxury of relative isolation from conflict and that, within five years, both countries "must be prepared to meet major enemy capabilities."[11] The Soviet Union was, of course, the potential enemy against whom American authorities felt they must be on guard. To that end, Truman and his military advisors sought to strengthen the American air base at Goose Bay, Labrador (not then formally a part of Canada).[12] Also in 1947 Truman's secretary of war, Robert P. Patterson, deemed military cooperation between the United States and Canada as "vital." Military training and equipment for other countries of the Western Hemisphere, thought Patterson, would strengthen the "national security of the United States." He favoured congressional approval of the Inter-American Military Cooperation Act, which would apply to Canada as well as to the Latin American republics: "In the case of Canada, on the northern flank, there cannot be the slightest doubt as to the value of the proposed legislation. We already have a program under way with Canada for standardization of equipment, training, and organization, and the proposed bill will implement and facilitate this program."[13] The Joint Chiefs of Staff agreed. One year later, they advised Patterson's successor, James Forrestal, "that in implementation of the Canada-United States Basic Security Plan, Canada should receive first consideration among the other American states."[14]

There was never the slightest doubt that Canada appeared indispensable to the security of the interdependent France, Great Britain, and the United States. This was no mere theory, agreed the Joint Chiefs of Staff, but a fact confirmed in the two world wars. "In the light of this past experience the burden of proof is on anyone who opposes the interdependence of these four countries," said the document.[15]

In 1947, Canada was also militarily important to the United States not only as part of the North Atlantic quadrilateral but also for its economic capability. Since the defeat of Germany and Japan, noted an ad hoc committee to the State-War-Navy Coordinating Committee, only the United States and the Soviet Union could reliably produce "modern complicated military arms and munitions in large quantities."[16] The United Kingdom had fallen behind the two superpowers in military capacity; four other nations were considered important to the defence of the US – Sweden, France, Belgium, and Canada. Canada could pay its own bills, thought the strategists, but Canadians and Americans ought to adopt "common designs and standards in arms, equipment, organization and training methods," and the United States ought to assist Canada in the acquisition of whatever equipment it wanted.[17]

Undoubtedly, the survival and continuing relevance of the Permanent Joint Board on Defense helped to keep Canada in the eye of the State Department. As for the president, Truman biographer Roy Jenkins notes that long before he was a Congressman, Truman had been a tourist in Canada, a place he could afford to visit, and the president also enjoyed his 1947 visit. In the words of his daughter, "We spent a really delightful three days there."[18] According to Jenkins, the British and Canadian prime ministers, Clement Attlee and Mackenzie King, were the statesmen whom Truman most enjoyed on a personal basis, because they spoke English.[19]

There was also the matter of intelligence gathering. In September 1945, Soviet cipher clerk Igor Gouzenko defected from his country's legation in Ottawa and revealed many Soviet secrets to the RCMP. In turn, the RCMP forwarded the information to the FBI, which found Gouzenko's revelations very useful in the search for Communists and Soviet agents.[20] Canadian intelligence proved useful in another way. Before the arrival of satellites and high-flying long-range aircraft, there were "blind spots" where Americans simply could not eavesdrop. Allies could collect information not readily available to Americans, and, because of its location, Canada hosted monitoring sites for the electronic surveillance of Siberia and much of Asia, including Vietnam. Canadians at Whitehorse, Churchill, and Alert became the eyes and ears of the United States. In 1944, Canada and Australia became full members of BRUSA, the Anglo-American signals intelligence sharing organization, which New Zealand joined and which reorganized to become UKUSA in 1947. The FBI shared information with the RCMP as well as with the British domestic intelligence agency, MI5, but the CIA – formed in 1947 – did not liaise with the RCMP until 1955, when the RCMP and the CIA sent officers to each other's capital. The only ally whose intelligence contribution exceeded those of Canada and of Australia – which in 1950 created the Australian Secret Intelligence Service (ASIS) to conduct human intelligence (as distinct from signals or electronic intelligence) in Southeast Asia – was the United Kingdom.[21]

North American Air Defence[22]

In 1951, the US National Security Council predicted that after 1954 the USSR would have the capacity to inflict a "devastating" nuclear attack on Canadian and American targets.[23] Only close cooperation with Canada could forestall such an event. Late in 1950, President Truman promised British prime minister Clement Attlee to "keep [him] ... informed at all times of developments which might call for the use of atomic weapons." Said the State Department's Carleton Savage, "This has been informally extended to the Canadians. As we should need to use British and Canadian bases for atomic strikes in case of global war, we should keep in touch with the British and Canadians concerning respective estimates of existing and developing situations which might call for the use of atomic weapons."[24]

This position was not enough for the Canadian government, which continued to insist on some say in Canada's foreign and defence policies, a fact which annoyed some Americans. In view of the seriousness of the perceived Soviet threat, some officials in Washington thought that Ottawa should forget about Canadian sovereignty in the interest of increased efficiency, as the following examples illustrate.

Given the limited range of fighter aircraft in 1951, the United States Air Force base at Goose Bay, Labrador was of critical importance, and Goose Bay was the one base on Canadian territory leased by the *Canadian* government (as distinct from bases in pre-1949 Newfoundland leased by the *British* government) to the United States for military purposes.[25] The lease, signed in 1952, had a lifespan of twenty years. (In March 1949, Newfoundland with Labrador became a part of Canada; shortly thereafter, the Permanent Joint Board on Defense began talks on the bases.[26]) In all matters except nuclear ones, the Canadian government was prepared to allow any reconstruction the Strategic Air Command (SAC) wanted. The St. Laurent government, however, demanded consultations on the storage of nuclear weapons at Goose Bay, overflights of Canadian territory by SAC aircraft carrying nuclear weapons, and SAC takeoffs from Goose Bay to bomb the USSR with nuclear weapons.[27]

This demand created differences that lasted for months. The American government argued that "the vital security interests of the United Kingdom and Canada are akin to those of the United States ... developments which would jeopardize the survival of one as a free nation would likewise jeopardize the others.[28] The Canadian government did agree that "in the event of Soviet armed attack anywhere on the North American continent ... the United States should launch immediate retaliation by any and all means and from any and all available bases."[29] Although "by any and all means" undoubtedly meant "by nuclear weapons, if necessary," the State Department found this assertion too vague and sent Gordon Arneson to Ottawa for discussions with Canadian officials. After all, as early as 10 September 1948, the National Security Council had in its possession a recommendation that the American government maintain its legal right to use nuclear weapons whenever it thought the situation required them. There should be no legally binding international (even bilateral) restrictions on this right.[30] Arneson thought that SAC aircraft at Goose Bay should have virtually automatic permission to use nuclear weapons in the event of a Soviet attack on any NATO country. The Canadian government agreed. Arneson then raised the matter of a Soviet attack on American forces anywhere in the world; this issue proved more difficult. Arnold Heeney, Canada's under-secretary of state for external affairs, warned that if the Canadian government had to give an immediate answer, it would have to be negative for political reasons. Canadian and American authorities agreed to leave the matter of Goose Bay and hypothetical Soviet attacks on American forces outside the NATO area to a series of meetings between Paul Nitze, director of the State Department's policy planning staff, and Canadian ambassador Hume Wrong.[31] Secretary of State Dean Acheson agreed that additional pressure on Ottawa for a blank cheque to permit SAC take-offs for nuclear strikes, overflights of Canadian territory by SAC aircraft with nuclear weapons, and the ongoing deployment of nuclear weapons on Canadian soil "would not yield the desired results."[32] After meetings of Nitze, Wrong, and others,[33] the Canadian embassy reported:

> Requests of the Government of the United States for permission to make use of facilities in Canadian territory for the deployment of atomic weapons (both with and without their nuclear components) and for the conduct of operations involving the use of such weapons, or to overfly Canadian territory with such weapons are to be addressed to the Canadian Government through the Canadian Embassy in Washington, and the reply of the Canadian Government is to be through the same channels. As much advance notice as possible will be given by the Government of the United States, and on its part the Government of Canada will seek to answer such requests promptly.

Talks on these and other matters continued[34] because Acheson remained less than satisfied. On 6 August 1951, he told the Joint Chiefs of Staff that "we have been trying to get agreement with Canada to use their bases *as if they were our own*, which we had not been able to do." The Canadian government held firm, and American authorities had to live with Canadian intransigence.

Similar problems arose over the questions of a deputy commander for the Northeast Command. The United States Air Force (USAF) assumed that the Joint Chiefs of Staff would not want a Canadian officer as deputy commander, although the area of responsibility for the Northeast Command included Canadian territory. "Therefore, the role of the Canadian officer would have to be carefully defined and limitations would have to be placed on his authority. The Air Force feels that he might be used in bringing about an integrated US-Canadian air defense system for the Island of Newfoundland. They also consider that the Canadian officer might be used by the Northeast Command as a channel of communication with Ottawa for getting Government permission for certain projects, for keeping the Canadian Government informed, and for handling civil defense and other important matters." If the USAF saw a Canadian officer's role as part messenger boy, part lobbyist, the US Navy found the very idea of a Canadian deputy commander of the Northeast Command to be "embarrassing." The Navy conceded that a Canadian officer might be part of the planning staff of the Northeast Command, but to the dismay of American defence planners, the Canadian government sought an "important and active" role in the Northeast Command.[35]

By 1952, a series of radar lines seemed to be a good way of protecting North America from Soviet air attacks. The shortest route from the Soviet Union to the United States was across the Arctic Ocean and Canadian air space, and the farther north the radar lines, the greater would be the chances of destroying incoming enemy aircraft before they could do much harm.

That radar defence was desirable was not in doubt. Where it should be located was another matter. In 1952, some strategists suggested a distant early warning or DEW system across Canada's Arctic, but for technical and political reasons, the US Army, Navy, and Air Force preferred a line near the 60th parallel. Canadians would help to build a line near the 60th parallel but would not assist in the Arctic. In either case, "their cooperation is indispensable."[36] Talks with Canadian authorities began right away.[37]

In their efforts to persuade the Canadians, American authorities dangled the carrots of investments and jobs in Canada. In October 1953, one State Department official wrote his superior about a military study group's recommendations to build radar lines in Canada. The equipment for those lines would be developed and manufactured in Canada, and that was considered "a very important point in getting Canadian approval for the project as a whole." Even then, Canadian resistance to a DEW system in the Arctic continued. Some Canadians feared that an American occupation of arctic Canada might compromise Canadian sovereignty in the area.[38]

The idea of a formal American-Canadian structure for the defence of North America appears in a memorandum of 7 May 1954 from Sterling

Cole, chair of the Joint Congressional Committee on Atomic Energy, to Charles Wilson, Eisenhower's secretary of defence.

> I suggested in a recent public speech that we enter into a mutual continental defense pact with Canada ... which would represent a continental defense equivalent of the NATO agreement ... My thought was that such a pact would establish a North American Continental Organization, to which Army, Navy, and Air Force units from our two nations with continental defense responsibilities would be assigned in a manner akin to the land, sea, and air forces now reporting to SHAPE [Supreme Headquarters, Allied Powers Europe] headquarters. My further thought was that such an organization would be headed by a Supreme Commander, whose responsibility and authority in the field of continental defense would parallel those now exercised by General [Alfred] Gruenther in his capacity of Supreme Commander of the Allied Powers in Europe.[39]

The Eisenhower administration apparently did not care to share responsibility for the defence of the United States. While it would support the European allies in Europe, it did not care to share information about defence plans, the Strategic Air Command, or other vital data, even with allies. A separate alliance with Canada for the defence of North America would eliminate the need to treat all allies on an equal basis, and Canada would learn what was happening only on a "need to know" basis.[40]

Shortly before its defeat in 1957, St. Laurent's Liberal government agreed to such a structure, the North American Air Defense Command (NORAD), and the newly elected Conservative government of John Diefenbaker concluded the arrangement. Both Eisenhower and Diefenbaker agreed to the deployment of nuclear weapons targeted on incoming Soviet aircraft, the weapons to be located at North Bay, Ontario, and La Macaza, Quebec. Such weapons would protect Toronto and Montreal, as well as population centres in the United States.

The Diefenbaker government's 1958 decision to acquire nuclear weapons for the defence of North America initially created problems for the National Security Council (NSC). What sort of precedent would this decision set for American relations with other NATO allies? An NSC authority recommended that Canada merited a "special status" because of "the peculiarities of geography, the defense structure which we have established, and purely defensive role of the weapons under consideration, and the partnership of the United States and Canada in this defense undertaking."[41]

Before the bases could become operational, however, Diefenbaker would have second thoughts and provoke a first-class row with the Kennedy administration. In April 1963, the Liberals – by this time led by Pearson – defeated Diefenbaker's Conservatives; they authorized the installation of nuclear weapons. They also accepted the nuclear strike role for the Royal Canadian Air Force (RCAF) which Diefenbaker's government had negotiated.[42] This story, however, belongs in the following chapter.

An example of supposed American imperialism much cited by the Canadian Left deserves mention here. A 1992 book by Palmiro Campagna suggests that Secretary of State John Foster Dulles and his brother Allen, head of the CIA from 1953 to 1961, played a critical role in the destruction of the Avro Arrow, the pride of the RCAF and the Canadian aviation industry until February 1959. Of all the world's aircraft at the time, notes Campagna, only the Arrow could fly as high as the CIA's U-2, thought essential for aerial surveillance of the Soviet Union. Security in Canada might not be adequate, and the Soviets might learn how to make the Arrow and thus disrupt the U-2 program. To prevent this outcome, the Diefenbaker government ordered that all existing Arrows along with their blueprints be destroyed. Campagna, an employee of the Department of National Defence (DND) in Ottawa and an engineer, drew these conclusions after a thorough investigation of DND files at the National Archives of Canada in Ottawa and of Canada-related papers at the Eisenhower Archives in Abilene, Kansas.[43] A recent biographer of Diefenbaker's, Denis Smith, agrees that official Washington wanted an end to the Arrow. According to Smith, Diefenbaker – anxious to save money – willingly complied with Washington's defence plans without asking questions.[44] Campagna's speculation is inconclusive, but it merits serious consideration.

The United States, Canada, and Nuclear Weapons

During the Second World War, the United States began to experiment with nuclear energy, with explosions near Alamogordo, New Mexico, on 16 July 1945, and then over Hiroshima and Nagasaki, Japan, on 6 and 9 August respectively. British and Canadian scientists also engaged in nuclear research.[45] When President Roosevelt and Prime Minister Churchill met at Quebec City in 1943, they agreed to share uranium from the Belgian Congo (later Zaire, now the Democratic Republic of Congo) and from any other sources.[46] On 16 November 1945, their successors, President Truman and Prime Minister Clement Attlee, agreed in writing "that there should be full and effective cooperation in the field of atomic energy between the United States, the United Kingdom, and Canada."[47] However, after the war, American scientists wished to acquire as much data as they could from the British and Canadians while giving them as little as possible in return.[48] In the end, Canada's principal role became that of a supplier of uranium to the United States nuclear program. When McGeorge Bundy, who became national security advisor to Presidents Kennedy and Johnson, wrote about postwar nuclear diplomacy, he failed to mention Canada as a factor for the years when he worked at the White House. However, he described "the significant role of the Canadians as a friendly third party with uranium mines" in the 1940s, and he praised Canadian efforts at limiting the spread of nuclear weapons during that decade.

> Canada was the first country to decide clearly that it would not itself become a nuclear weapons state ... in 1945. The Canadians had everything at hand – the uranium, the science, and the technical head start – everything but the desire. In 1946 Canada became a member of the UN commission that eventually became the forum for debate on international control ... There have been differences between Washington and Ottawa over the years. They have usually been resolved, and on balance what is impressive is that on this troubling subject the habit of self-respecting cooperation between Canadians and Americans has endured.[49]

Ironically, it was this same McGeorge Bundy who wrote a memo in 1963 that challenged the credibility of the Diefenbaker government's nuclear weapons policy.[50]

That Canadians did not want a major nuclear role was probably just as well for the sake of harmonious Canadian-American relations. Because of the intense Anglo-Canadian relationship, American authorities feared to share nuclear technology with Canada in case the knowledge would reach the British. Some Americans feared that the United Kingdom's geographical location was too close to the Soviet-occupied part of Europe.[51] Although American authorities realized that the situation of 1947 was not as desperate as that of 1940 when the *Wehrmacht* had occupied France and the Low Countries, the Red Army was nevertheless too close for comfort.[52] Repeatedly, United States authorities begged their British counterparts to transfer their scientists and nuclear facilities to Canada.[53] (See Chapter 5.)

There was also a well-justified perception in Washington that the more widespread the knowledge of nuclear technology, the greater the danger that it would fall into the wrong hands. Senator Burke Hickenlooper (Republican-Iowa), chair of the Joint Congressional Committee on Atomic Energy, feared "a swing to the left by the British."[54] While this swing did not happen, Donald Maclean, first secretary at the British embassy in Washington and one of the key players in Anglo-American nuclear liaison, forwarded nuclear secrets to the Soviet Union.[55] Although Americans did not know that, they did know that he was frequently requesting information that might be useful "to the construction of a large-scale atomic energy plant in Britain."[56] Had General Andrew McNaughton, chair of the Canadian section of the Atomic Energy Board, known about Maclean, he would have been less vehement about the one-sided nature of the exchange.[57] Canada was giving nuclear information to the United States but receiving nothing in exchange. As it was, the McMahon Act of 1948 limited American nuclear cooperation with the United Kingdom and Canada.[58]

Between 1945 and 1948, the other key Western nation in the nuclear equation was Belgium. Until 1960, Belgium controlled the Belgian Congo, principal source of uranium for the United States.[59] Canada did not become a major supplier of uranium until the next decade. American diplomats saw their country as a competitor against the United Kingdom and Canada for the world's apparently limited supply.[60]

Some State Department officials thought that the greatest advantage for the United States lay in American opportunities to learn from, even to hire, British scientists, but this opportunity turned out to be a mixed blessing. Early in 1950, one of the scientists co-opted from the United Kingdom by the Atomic Energy Commission (AEC), Klaus Fuchs, pleaded guilty to charges of forwarding American nuclear secrets to the Soviet Union.[61] Because of the Fuchs revelations, official Washington had such reservations about the British and Canadians that it suspended nuclear talks with America's erstwhile partners.[62] In 1951, the Joint Chiefs of Staff reported, "There are now no US commitments to other governments which limit the President's freedom of action in arriving at a determination to use atomic weapons."[63] Defense Secretary Louis Johnson worried about the nature of the nuclear technology which the AEC had already forwarded to Canada's nuclear facility at Chalk River. Was any of it relevant to the production of nuclear weapons? When Robert LeBaron, deputy to the secretary of defence on atomic energy matters, inquired about the desirability of using the Chalk River facility, the acting chair of the AEC said that on occasion the scientists could save "valuable time" by doing so. Whether or not they would do so in future, however, would have to depend on a case-by-case study.[64]

While United States authorities sought new sources of uranium in South Africa,[65] the United States and the United Kingdom agreed on a division of the limited supply of uranium. By 1950, uranium was available from American and Canadian sources as well as from the Belgian Congo. Notwithstanding the ambitions of politicians in Pretoria, American and British authorities agreed that South Africa's role should be that of a supplier of uranium, like Belgium, not that of a partner, like Canada.[66] Indeed, Canada's role as a supplier of raw materials for nuclear technology assumed unprecedented importance in 1950 when the State and Defense Departments accepted a Canadian proposal "to buy all plutonium in excess of Canada's research requirements." For its part, the State Department authorized the export of uranium rods to Chalk River.[67]

Canada and the United Nations
At the United Nations, the State Department sought an active role for Canada. Lester Pearson, at that time Canadian ambassador to the United

States, was its favourite candidate in 1946 for the position of secretary-general.[68] Belgium's Paul-Henri Spaak spoke no English, and Norway's Trigve Lie, who spoke no French, also came from a country located close to the Soviet Union and thus was potentially vulnerable to Soviet pressure. Although Pearson himself knew otherwise, Secretary of State James Byrnes thought that Pearson "spoke French well." The Soviets' favourite candidate for the post was Ambassador Simic of Yugoslavia, and although they expressed personal admiration for Pearson, Ambassador Andrei Gromyko found him unacceptable. With the United Nations' physical location in New York, argued Gromyko, a secretary-general from Canada would give the United Nations too North American an orientation.[69] At least one American diplomat thought a Soviet veto of Pearson as reasonable and as predictable as an American veto of Simic, whose country was still a Soviet ally.[70] In the end, everyone accepted Lie, three years before his country became a founding member of NATO.

The State Department also sought a non-permanent (two-year) term for Canada on the Security Council. It seemed reasonable that the non-permanent seats should be apportioned among Western Europe, Eastern Europe, Latin America, the British Commonwealth, and the rest of the world. In 1946, Australia and Canada were the contenders for the British Commonwealth seat, and Washington preferred Canada because of its membership in the Atomic Energy Commission.[71] Other members of the General Assembly disagreed and supported Australia; Canada had to settle for a seat on ECOSOC, the Economic and Social Council. In 1947, Canada did win a seat on the Security Council, as Australia's successor.

Between 1945 and 1949, the American and Canadian governments worked together on many issues on the UN agenda. In March 1947, when the American government temporarily suspended the shipment of weapons to Chiang Kai-Shek's army in China, the British and Canadian governments followed suit.[72] Later that year, the United States ended its arms embargo and Canada did likewise.[73] Shortly thereafter, Chinese Communists specifically targeted Canada and Belgium for special criticism because they had followed the "lead of American imperialism by sending munitions and planes to China."[74] Before the Jewish-Arab confrontation in Palestine erupted into full-scale war in 1947, Canada had gained its coveted seat on the Security Council. In private conversation, Canadian envoys "said very emphatically they would support anything on which [the] US and [the] UK agreed."[75] One Canadian diplomat at the United Nations, George Ignatieff, worked closely with the American and British delegations to minimize the violence.[76] Like Secretary of State Marshall, the American delegation at the United Nations, and officials at the State Department in Washington,[77] the Canadian delegation at the United Nations felt "double-crossed" by President Truman's announcement of

14 May 1948 that when Israel declared its independence a few minutes later, American recognition would be instantaneous.

Yet, American officials continued to hold frequent conversations with counterparts from Canada and other friendly countries. The Economic and Social Council (ECOSOC) had eighteen members, including the United Kingdom and Poland, whose terms expired 31 December 1950; France, whose term lasted an additional year; and the United States and Canada, whose terms ended 31 December 1952. The State Department sought support from the British, French, and Canadians to prevent the election of an Eastern European country as successor to Poland. Given American opposition to a People's Republic of China (PRC) presence at the United Nations, official Washington appreciated a motion sponsored by Australia and Canada to study (and thus postpone) that controversial issue.[78]

On substantive matters as well, American and Canadian envoys managed to collaborate. In September 1950, they drafted a resolution on united action against aggression.[79] A few days later, Canadian envoys had an opportunity to examine an Anglo-American document entitled "Uniting for Peace."[80] Canada then worked with Haiti, Peru, and Syria to make a Soviet counterproposal more acceptable to the United States.[81] When that failed, Canadian officials (R.G. Riddell and Charles Ritchie) joined Henry Cabot Lodge (Republican senator from Massachusetts and a member of the American delegation at the United Nations) as well as diplomats from the United Kingdom and Mexico at Lake Success, where they hammered out another response.[82] Other friendly countries joined the talks over the next few days.[83] The pages of *Foreign Relations of the United States* make clear the importance of Canada as a like-minded partner at the United Nations in 1950;[84] indeed, one American delegate lamented that he had spent so much time consulting British, French, Australian, and Canadian diplomats that he had had to neglect many others – who then voted contrary to American wishes.

Yet Canada did not play the role that Washington would have wished. The Canadian government informed the State Department that it did not want an invitation of any sort to the Rio Conference of 1947.[85] The Canadian government still thought in terms of the Commonwealth and the North Atlantic, not in terms of the Western Hemisphere. In a hope (which was not realized until 1990) that Canadians would become more committed, Secretary of State George Marshall persuaded delegates at the Interamerican Conference of 1948 to name their newly created secretariat the Organization of American *States*, not the Organization of American *Republics*.[86]

Canada's Position among the Allies

Several events in 1949 affected Canada's position as an American ally. The creation of the Federal Republic of Germany and the signing of the NATO defensive alliance by twelve West European governments (though not that of Germany), the United States, and Canada, demonstrated that Americans had other important allies. In September, the USSR exploded its first nuclear weapon; October saw the birth of both the People's Republic of China and the German Democratic Republic (East Germany, conterminous with the former Soviet Zone of occupation in Germany). These events changed the emphasis of American foreign policy with respect to Canada.

France moved into a close relationship with the United States, approaching or replacing Canada in most matters except nuclear technology. There were good reasons for this shift, including France's geographical location, large population, and advanced level of development. Ties between the United States and France had been strong since the War of Independence (1775-83), sufficiently so to withstand tensions arising from the Second World War. With the establishment in 1949 of the People's Republic of China, the Truman administration decided to help France defeat the Communist Viet Minh in neighbouring Vietnam. American reservations about European imperialism were minor considerations in comparison with the possibility of yet another Communist victory in Asia.

There is considerable evidence for the increasing importance of France. On 29 December 1949, the State Department's R. Gordon Arneson prepared a memorandum on the international control of atomic energy. One consideration was, "Is [sic] the procedure and solution acceptable to our closest friends, particularly the United Kingdom, Canada, and France?"[87] One week later, the deputy under-secretary of state, Dean Rusk, wrote to George Kennan, one of the State Department's leading authorities on the Soviet Union: "I see very serious objections to new bilateral discussions between ourselves and Russia on atomic energy, unless such discussions resulted from consultation with and agreement by the United Kingdom, France, and Canada."[88]

In connection with the same subject (international control of atomic energy), John D. Hickerson, assistant secretary of state for United Nations affairs, saw "the importance of keeping the United Kingdom, Canada, and France fully informed of what we are doing."[89] In 1949, Canada provided Hickerson with one of four "colleagues" at the six power talks on arms control; the other colleagues came from the United Kingdom, France, and Nationalist China. Hickerson indicated that the US needed a "meeting of minds" first with the British, then with the French, "while it appeared necessary only to tell the Canadians and Chinese that these talks had taken place."[90] On 17 January 1950, American, British, Canadian, and French envoys met at the United Nations to discuss arms control.[91] On 5 April, Hickerson said that the United States must discuss certain diplomatic military matters with "our principal allies, certainly the United Kingdom and France, and perhaps Canada."[92] In 1951, the State Department coordinated arms control proposals with the British Foreign Office alone. The British and American governments then planned to give simultaneous advance notice of the proposals to the governments of France and Canada – as well as Australia, New Zealand, and South Africa. Informing the Commonwealth governments would be a British responsibility;[93] State Department officials subsequently took steps to inform the French, Canadian, and Nationalist Chinese governments of their intentions.[94] Canadian and French delegates worked alongside American and British delegates on the Collective Measures Committee.[95]

For one moment in spring 1950, it appeared that Canada might replace China as a de facto member of the Big Five. Arms control was a concern for the permanent members of the Security Council, where Chinese participation had become an obstacle. While the United States would not negotiate with a representative from the PRC, the Soviet Union refused to bargain with a subordinate of Chiang Kai-Shek. Dean Rusk suggested a face-saving formula for breaking "the procedural deadlock." In November 1945, Rusk noted, the Canadian and British prime ministers had visited Washington where they and President Truman signed a proposal for the establishment of a United Nations Atomic Energy Commission. Now, the American, Canadian, and British governments could invite the French and Soviets (but not the Chinese Nationalists) to join them for further talks.[96] As this formula also proved unacceptable to the Soviets, Hickerson then recommended that the Americans, British, and French negotiate with the Soviets, without the Canadians or Chinese.[97]

Although Canadians would not sit at the bargaining table, American officials would listen to their opinions.[98] Nor would Canada be simply one of several more or less friendly countries to which the United States would politely listen. In December 1950, Australian and United States officials discussed the creation of a special United Nations committee on disarmament to consist of the current members of the Security Council, plus Canada and Australia. Canada would take a seat because of its membership on the Atomic Energy Commission, Australia as sponsor of the enabling legislation in the General Assembly. Australia quickly withdrew its candidacy, but Canada remained on the list. Frank Nash of the United States delegation appreciated the Australian withdrawal, because it meant that those who had supported Australia might transfer their support to Canada and prevent victory by a less desirable country.[99] On 13 December, the General Assembly voted that the members of the Security Council plus Canada should "consider and report to the next regular session of the General Assembly on ways and means whereby the work of the Atomic Energy Commission and the Commission for Conventional Armaments may be coordinated."[100]

Nevertheless, in some aspects of security and national defence, France could not compete with Canada (and Great Britain). On 20 July 1948, Defense Secretary James Forrestal wrote to the National Security Council that while standardization of equipment among American allies was desirable, "a somewhat closer standardization may be expected to develop between the United States, Britain and Canada than with the continental powers."[101]

A State Department memo of 8 February 1950 read:

> Our commitments and risks are so extensive and important that Canada in a military sense must be considered as if it were an integral part of the United States. It is as important to our security to protect Canada as it is to protect California. Canada is the most logical avenue for a large scale attack on the United States. Even if it were not for the commitments in the Atlantic Pact [NATO] and the extension of the Monroe Doctrine to Canada, it would be necessary to protect Canada instantly from any threat.[102]

In April of that year, the National Security Council submitted to President Truman a report which mentioned "the likelihood of attacks ... with atomic weapons ... against targets in Alaska, Canada, and the United States.[103] On 25 August, with the Korean War at its nadir, the National Security Council noted the Soviets' "capability of initiating limited-scale air raids on the United States and Canada."[104] To cope with these dangers, President Truman approved recommendations of the Permanent Joint Board on Defense to increase the effectiveness of the bases in Newfoundland,[105] and the National Security Council's policy planning staff recommended that Canada and the United Kingdom undertake a military build-up. The United States should persevere in its defence commitments to Western Europe, said the Policy Planning Staff, but only inasmuch as those commitments did not adversely affect the defence programs of Canada and the United Kingdom. This recommendation was considerably more restrictive than a pre-Korean War document of 31 August 1949, which had envisioned "'substantial' military aid" for a limited number of allies, specifically the Benelux countries (Belgium, Netherlands, and Luxembourg), Canada, France, and the United Kingdom.[106] In 1951, a senior State Department official said that no country had received quicker action on its requests for military aid than Canada, and the runner-up was neither Great Britain nor France but Liberia![107]

Canada was at least as important as France, in some ways more so, insofar as American policy toward some of the less fortunate nations was concerned. The State Department wanted to march in step with the British, Australians, and Canadians in policies toward minor Axis countries that had become Soviet satellites – Bulgaria, Hungary, and Romania.[108] Then, after Tito's break with Stalin, official Washington sought to maintain Belgrade's distance from Moscow. To that end, Washington sought to support the Yugoslav economy with assistance from the United Kingdom, Canada, and France.[109] Although Canada did not want to cooperate until and unless Yugoslavia's problems were handled in a multinational forum such as the United Nations or NATO,[110] within months the State Department was praising Canadian generosity to needy Europeans and Asians in forty-three countries, including Yugoslavia. Later, Acheson contrasted Canada's early payment in full to the United Nations Reconstruction Agency with the slow progress of the necessary legislation through the United States Congress.[111] As 1949 began, the Joint Chiefs of Staff considered Canada and the Brussels Pact nations to be the only allies capable of "substantial" military aid.[112] At the same time, the Soviet Union "and its satellites ... [were] the only nations ... with whom any likelihood of war exists,"[113] and such a war appeared "improbable" before 1953. However, authorities in both the United States and its "substantial allies" wanted to prepare for the worst, and thereby prevent the worst.

As mentioned, the United States sought to contain Soviet expansionism in Europe by becoming a founding member of the North Atlantic Treaty Organization (NATO). NATO members assumed an obligation to consider an attack on one member as an attack on all members and to take appropriate measures to defend each other's territory in Europe and North America. Canada and other founding members (the United Kingdom, France, the Benelux countries, and Norway), helped persuade the US to assume an unprecedented peace-time commitment in Europe.[114]

In February 1948, the very month of the coup that turned Czechoslovakia into a Soviet satellite, Great Britain, France, and the Benelux countries formed a military alliance, the Brussels Pact. By March, American, British, and Canadian negotiators were considering an enlarged "pact of mutual defense against aggression to which the US (and Canada) would finally adhere."[115] Delegates from the United States, the United Kingdom, and Canada proposed "a Security Pact for the North Atlantic Area, plus an extension of the Brussels agreement."[116] In the United States, the United Kingdom, and Canada, government officials and diplomats took Canada's participation for granted. Mackenzie King's government had refused to let the Royal Canadian Air Force participate in the Berlin air lift. Even after St. Laurent succeeded King as prime minister, Canada did not participate in the air lift.

On 3 January 1949, the six "substantial allies," including Canada, approached the State Department with a formal proposal for a military alliance, a proposal which the Truman administration accepted.[117] On 4 April 1949, those seven countries, plus Norway, Denmark, Iceland, Portugal, and Italy, signed the North Atlantic Treaty.[118]

Some minor disagreements and ambiguities remained. In the interest of harmony, Canada quickly swallowed any initial doubts about whether Italy was a "North Atlantic" nation,[119] although it did insist on Article II: "The Parties will contribute toward the further development of peaceful and friendly international relations by strengthening their free institutions, by bringing about a better understanding of the principles upon which these institutions are founded, and by promoting conditions of stability and well-being. They will seek to eliminate conflict in their international economic policies and will encourage economic collaboration between any or all of them."[120] Such an article, according to Hume Wrong, Canada's ambassador in Washington, was vital for political reasons in Canada. A purely military alliance would not attract a broad base of support. Acheson feared that Article II might create problems in the US Senate, which would have to approve any treaty, but he eventually agreed to its inclusion.[121]

At first, some American planners thought that the United States, the United Kingdom, France, and Canada should constitute NATO's inner executive council,[122] but the Canadians had no strong feelings in the matter, and the Joint Chiefs of Staff recommended in favour of simplicity – a three-nation rather than a four-nation directorate. Canada's role would be on the sidelines rather than in NATO's inner council.

Once hostilities had begun in Korea, the NATO allies wondered whether Stalin was testing their resolve. Would he support other proxy wars as well? Dean Acheson favoured a military build-up in Europe and he wanted Canadian help. With regard to NATO commitments, the newly appointed American ambassador to Canada, Stanley Woodward, noted that "Canada's effort has fallen short as compared with [the] UK and other countries." Pearson discussed this perception with Woodward in the summer of 1950, for the matter was by no means academic. Lewis Douglas, American ambassador in the United Kingdom, sensed that despite their dislike of Soviet Communism, continental Europeans were defeatist and unwilling to fight. Ambassador David Bruce in France recommended a solution: the United States and the United Kingdom "and if possible ... Canada ... [should] increase ... [the number of] combat troops on the continent."[123] Secretary of State Dean Acheson noted that the Europeans agreed. At a September 1950 meeting of the North Atlantic Council, Dutch, French, and British delegates called for a troop build-up so that any confrontation with the Soviets would occur "as far east in Germany as possible." The Dutch and French representatives specifically called for more troops from the United States, the United Kingdom, and Canada.[124] In 1951, Canadian forces arrived in Europe to supplement the British and American forces already there.

Canada proved a useful ally in other ways. Ambassador Lewis Douglas saw yet another psychological advantage in Canadian participation. British governments might be torn between their love of the Commonwealth and their NATO obligations.[125] With Canada in NATO, they could serve both at the same time. In 1951, Pearson made a number of constructive suggestions for the reorganization of NATO,[126] and the Canadian government did not insist on its doubts about NATO membership for Greece and Turkey. The military commitment was widening. From Western Europe and North America, the obligation had expanded to include Greece and Turkey.

The Eisenhower administration also found Canada to be a "sound and reliable ally."[127] Support for NATO was not a partisan matter, and in the words of one Canadian expert in the State Department: "The Canadians are almost always with us on the major issues in NATO and in the UN (most notable exception Korea), in GATT, and multilateral trade matters and in bilateral defence and economic collaboration."[128]

Aware of the political objections to conscription in Canada, at least one official saw Canada's value to NATO as a source of strategic materials and weapons rather than as a supplier of uniformed personnel.[129] In 1955, the American delegation at the North Atlantic Council's ministerial meeting cabled from Paris that the United States and Canada were both essential "to effective Atlantic defense."[130]

Korea

The most serious differences of opinion between Washington and Ottawa in the early years of the Cold War arose over Korea.[131] At the end of the Second World War, Japanese forces in Korea surrendered to the Soviets north of latitude 38, and to the Americans south of that parallel. In 1947, the United Nations created the United Nations Temporary Commission on Korea (UNTCOK) to establish a civilian government on the peninsula, and the General Assembly chose Canada as one of nine members. Canadian prime minister Mackenzie King did not want this honour and presented his arguments to Ray Atherton, the American ambassador in Ottawa. Canada's priorities lay in Europe, said the prime minister, and there was a limit as to what Canadians could do.[132] As Canada was already a member of UNTCOK, albeit without the consent of the Canadian prime minister (Mackenzie King had been on a trip to Great Britain at the time of the vote), President Truman himself intervened. Canada's proposed withdrawal from UNTCOK aroused official Washington in a manner that Canada's initial election never did. Although it was the busy Christmas season, a lengthy personal appeal from the State Department to the prime minister urged the Canadian government to be more obliging. Canada *must* have some talented person who could work with UNTCOK, the Americans argued, and Canada had historic ties to Asia. The world would regard a Canadian refusal to participate in UNTCOK as a serious vote of non-confidence in the United States.[133]

Early in 1948, the Americans became aware of differences within the Canadian government, especially between the prime minister and his minister of external affairs, Louis St. Laurent. On 3 January, Canada's then under-secretary of state for external affairs, Lester Pearson, who had moved to that position from the ambassadorship in Washington in October 1946, told State Department officials of the split in the Canadian cabinet. According to Pearson, the prime minister believed that because UNTCOK was doomed to failure, Canada should not be part of it. Acting Secretary of State Robert Lovett warned Pearson that the credibility of Canada as a new member of the Security Council and a diplomatic partner as well as the credibility of the United Nations would suffer if UNTCOK did not attempt to function. Moreover, argued Lovett, even if UNTCOK established a government limited to the American-occupied zone of Korea, that alone would be an achievement.[134] President Truman sent a personal appeal to Mackenzie King,[135] and King capitulated. Truman then sent the prime minister a note of appreciation.

As a member of UNTCOK, Canada continued to disagree with the Americans. The Canadian government did not like the idea that in the event of a Soviet refusal to cooperate with UNTCOK north of latitude 38, UNTCOK should proceed with elections south of latitude 38.[136] By mid-February, the American political advisor in Korea was complaining to Washington that Canada, Australia, India, and Syria constituted an "anti-American bloc" on UNTCOK. Both he and Ambassador Atherton attributed Canadian recalcitrance to British influence and the Canadian government's desire to demonstrate to the Canadian electorate that Canada was no lapdog of the United States.[137] From Seoul, Lieutenant-General John R. Hodge complained to the secretary of state that the Canadian and Australian positions were hopelessly naive. The Canadian-Australian argument that "civil liberties and freedom in South Korea are not on a par with stable Canada and Australia, therefore it is impossible to hold any elections" failed to take account of Cold War hostilities, complained Hodge.[138] Hodge labelled Dr. G.S. Patterson, Canada's envoy to UNTCOK, as "the number one outspoken apologist for Soviet Russia and for communism that I have encountered for many months."[139] American officials accused Patterson of trying to "sabotage the election in South Korea,"[140] and of making "continuing attempts to impede the progress of the Commission." Patterson had had years of experience in Asia as missionary, YMCA worker, and diplomat (including a tour of duty at the Canadian embassy in Nanking).[141] Nevertheless, his statements became so controversial that Hume Wrong, Canada's ambassador in the United States, had to go to the State Department to listen to a litany of complaints.[142] Secretary Marshall told Warren Austin, the American ambassador at the United Nations, that UNTCOK's work should not be hampered by "a disgruntled minority, and [the] Canadian member in particular."[143] UNTCOK took advantage of Patterson's absence to vote for elections in South Korea if necessary, despite the fact that Patterson had left a telephone number where he might be reached should any important matter arise.[144] In June, Hodge complained of "more foot-dragging and vacillation tactics, wherein the Australian-Canadian-Syrian stand" had gained support from the French and Indians.[145]

Canada's role in UNTCOK proved such a diplomatic irritant to Americans, from President Truman and Secretary Marshall to soldiers and diplomats in Seoul, that in Korean matters Canada suffered a decline in influence. When the South Koreans did hold elections, Pearson asked that their newly elected government claim to be no more than the government of South Korea and not "the National Government of Korea."[146] No one in Washington took this idea seriously.

Despite disappointments over the Canadian performance on UNTCOK, Canada was one of the countries which the Truman administration consulted when North Korean forces invaded South Korea on 25 June 1950.[147] Truman wanted as many allies as possible to share the burden.[148] Canada's minister of external affairs, Lester Pearson, applauded the American decision to defend South Korea against military aggression and promised Canadian support.[149] That support, however, turned out to be less than what official Washington wanted, and as far as the Truman administration was concerned, the Canadian government was excessively eager to grasp at straws of conciliation offered by India and not eager enough to get on with the war.

In mid-July 1950, only weeks after hostilities began, the Joint Chiefs of Staff asked for Canadian troops to fight under the United Nations banner with forces from the United States, South Korea, and other UN countries.[150] The St. Laurent government quickly dispatched combat aircraft and ships of the Royal Canadian Navy but considered the deployment of Canadian ground troops most unlikely.[151] American authorities wanted Canadian ground troops, and the Canadian government reluctantly agreed to send them,[152] but not in the numbers nor at the speed the State Department and certain American generals thought appropriate. On 7 August 1950, the St. Laurent government agreed to send a brigade (5,000 men and 2,100 reserves) to Korea, but it would go to the front only when battle-ready. There would be no repeat of the 1941 disaster at Hong Kong, where almost 2,000 Canadian troops were sent to defend the colony from Japanese attack, only to die in battle or become prisoners of war. On 15 February 1951, the Canadian brigade took its place with the other combat forces who, without Canadian help, had stopped the southward thrust of the Chinese forces on 24 January.[153] The Canadians did, however, help to push the Chinese northward. Canadian battle deaths numbered 312; ninety-four other Canadians had died from "non-battle causes."[154] The US lost 33,629 in battle, and 20,617 to "other causes" such as accidents and friendly fire.[155] Lester Pearson's biographer, John English, has suggested that pressure from the American Right affected Truman and Acheson. *Their* reaction, in turn, affected relations between Acheson and Pearson. Truman and Acheson wanted a military victory. Fearing a wider war, Pearson urged restraint.[156]

Not surprisingly, then, the Truman and Eisenhower administrations hardly felt an obligation to grant the Canadian government a veto over their war policies. After Eisenhower assumed office on 20 January 1953, he all but ignored Canada as he took advantage of Stalin's death and negotiated a cease-fire with his Communist adversaries. The Canadian government made several attempts to communicate its ideas, but official Washington appears to have been deaf.[157] When their thoughts did turn to Canada's war effort, members of the Truman administration had to contend with Canada's limited war goals. Recalling the Second World War, General Douglas MacArthur and American political leaders hoped for the annihilation of the enemy, North Korea. They also resented the role of the Chinese province of Manchuria as an enemy sanctuary, beyond the range of UN bombers. From Nanking, site of Canada's last embassy on the Chinese mainland, Canadian diplomat Chester Ronning warned that the PRC might intervene if UN troops continued to approach the Korean-Chinese border and that the immediate admission of the PRC to the United Nations would moderate the Chinese government's behaviour.[158] Dean Rusk, assistant secretary of state for Far Eastern affairs, minimized this threat.[159]

In his memoirs, Secretary of State Dean Acheson made no secret of his contempt for Canadian, British, and Indian efforts at finding a negotiated settlement to the Korean conflict. The president of the United Nations General Assembly (1950-1), Iran's Nasrollah Entezam, joined India's Sir Benegal Rau and Canada's Pearson in trying to discover some common ground with the Chinese. They failed, and Entezam announced that failure on 2 January 1951. "Not content with this rebuff," wrote Acheson, "the British, Canadians, Indians and others produced another bid to the Chinese."[160] As president of the General Assembly (1952-3), Pearson maintained a diary of his problems with Acheson.[161] Acheson lamented, "Not yet despairing of persuasion, I made one more attempt to win the British and Pearson."[162]

Certainly, Canadian enthusiasm for the war was limited. Canadian diplomats warned the Truman administration that the costs of carrying the war into Manchuria would outweigh any benefits.[163] In 1951, Canadian strategists argued that from a purely logistical standpoint, it made more sense to fight the war along the current battlefront – more or less the present frontier between North and South Korea – than farther north at North Korea's narrow neck. Battles at the neck "would lengthen UN supply lines and shorten those of the Communists and would bring UN forces within closer range of the Communist radius of air strikes."[164] In other words, the Canadian government preferred holding what United Nations forces already held to launching a military offensive.

Meanwhile, Canada repeatedly forwarded news and ideas from India. Undaunted by the fact that neither Canada nor India had had ground troops in Korea when the enemy twice captured Seoul, Canadian authorities forwarded news[165] and supported proposals from New Delhi. President Truman despaired that his British, French, and Canadian allies were willing to strike too soft a deal with the enemy.[166]

There is little evidence that these Canadian efforts bore fruit. For reasons of their own, the Truman administration and the Joint Chiefs of Staff did not want the Korean War to become a war against China. They did not need Canadian diplomats to remind them to keep away from China. As General Omar Bradley, chair of the Joint Chiefs of Staff, said, "It would have been the wrong war, at the wrong time and in the wrong place."[167] Troops – American, Canadian, or of any other nationality – sent to Asia would not be available to defend Western Europe against a Soviet invasion – which was a higher priority. Despite the political risks, with the support of the Joint Chiefs of Staff, President Truman dismissed General MacArthur as commander of the United Nations forces in Korea before MacArthur could provoke an all-out Sino-American war.[168] Yet, before that happened, the Truman administration had downplayed Canadian advice and allowed MacArthur to advance to the Chinese border. To its peril, it had also ignored Canadian diplomat Ronning's warnings about Chinese intervention.

This is not to say that the Truman and Eisenhower administrations resented the limited Canadian war effort and the accompanying deluge of advice. Eisenhower gave no special status to his Canadian ally. But on 19 March 1953, he and the Joint Chiefs of Staff discussed their "final position" in connection with the armistice talks with the five Commonwealth belligerents – the United Kingdom, Canada, Australia, New Zealand, and South Africa.[169] The combined Commonwealth troops in Korea were but a small fraction of the total United Nations command. However, they did constitute a majority of those from outside South Korea and the United States, and Eisenhower thought it appropriate to give their diplomats some of his time.[170]

Yet neither he nor Secretary of State John Foster Dulles paid very much attention to the Commonwealth allies, even collectively. When Hume Wrong, Canada's ambassador in Washington, went to the State Department with his British and Australian counterparts on 21 July 1953 for talks with Dulles on "the status of the Commonwealth forces in Japan," they seized the opportunity to raise the matter of a joint policy declaration on Korea. Even at that late date, it was the visiting Commonwealth dignitaries – not Dulles or his subordinates also in attendance – who mentioned Korea.[171] It would appear that American officials, like some subsequent American historians, minimized the significance in the Korean War of the military contributions of other United Nations allies. Joseph C. Goulden's authoritative history of that war makes no mention of Canada,[172] and if Canadian diplomacy was at all relevant to the 1953 cease-fire, as Lester Pearson indicated in his memoirs, Eisenhower's biography fails to even mention it.

China

For more than two decades after the Korean War, the United States and Canada had policy differences over China. The American government apparently did not want Canadian diplomats in the PRC, even if they could provide information. On 17 December 1950, Pearson was to comment that "but for [the] US view," Canada would have recognized the PRC.[173] American pressure prevailed, and Ronning and other Canadian diplomats still in China returned home. Canada's role was to be that of partner, not intermediary. Almost three years later, when the Eisenhower administration *did* want news from Beijing, the PRC's capital, it relied on Swedish diplomats. Canada was more useful to the United States as an agreeable ally than as an intermediary, a role which the Swedes could safely assume.

When Chiang Kai-Shek's Nationalists fled the Chinese mainland in 1949 and established a provisional government at Taipeh on the island of Taiwan, they maintained a state of war with the People's Republic of China. Still calling their government the Republic of China (ROC), Chiang and his ministers promised to break out of their island fortress and to liberate the mainland. Besides Taiwan itself, the ROC controlled the Pescadores (a group of islands between Taiwan proper and the mainland, roughly some 100 miles distant), as well as Quemoy, Matsu, and adjacent islands. Quemoy itself was within sight of the mainland province of Fujian, and guns on Quemoy could block the PRC port of Amoy. Throughout the first half of 1955, guns from the mainland lobbed shells into Quemoy and Matsu, and their satellite islands. The ROC sought to keep these islands as springboards for the liberation of the Chinese mainland, and the Eisenhower administration supported the ROC – up to a point.

The St. Laurent government in Canada did not. Canada accepted ROC control of Taiwan and the Pescadores; indeed, the ROC maintained an embassy in Ottawa, and the Canadian ambassador in the Philippines was also accredited to Taipeh. However, the Canadian government thought the ROC presence in Quemoy and Matsu a provocation. It was unreason-able, thought official Ottawa, to expect the PRC not to use Amoy and to tolerate hostile islands so close to its territory.[174] In 1955, Dulles visited Ottawa, and Pearson asked him "to get out of Quemoy and Matsu." Dulles disagreed. It would be difficult, he advised the State Department, to per-suade the ROC to leave the islands, and the loss of Quemoy and Matsu would remove obstacles should the PRC fulfil *its* proclaimed intention of capturing Taiwan.[175] Canada was not the only close ally to disagree with Dulles. The United Kingdom, which already had formal diplomatic rela-tions with the PRC, agreed with the Canadians.[176] However, Eisenhower felt sufficiently strongly about Canadian lack of support for American policy on this issue that he mentioned it in his memoirs.[177]

In 1958, the PRC resumed its bombardment of Quemoy and Matsu. Prime Minister Diefenbaker discussed this aggression with West German chancellor Konrad Adenauer and with Malayan prime minister Tunku Abdul Rahman, but evidently not with Eisenhower.[178]

Vietnam

The International Control Commission (ICC) was the creation of an inter-national conference that convened in Geneva early in the summer of 1954. The diplomats met because the terms of the Korean Armistice of 1953 required a meeting to attempt the unification of Korea. Vietnam was almost an afterthought. The French and their Viet Minh (Communist) adversaries managed to negotiate a cease-fire at Geneva, but they needed an international team to monitor its enforcement. The truce supervisory team in Korea offered one model – two Western-leaning neutrals (Sweden and Switzerland), and two countries with pro-Soviet governments (Poland and Czechoslovakia), with India as chair. Experience had demonstrated a five-nation team to be unwieldy; three, it appeared, would perform as well. As in Korea, India could remain the chair of the supervisory body – to be called the International Control Commission – and a Communist country (Poland) could protect Soviet-bloc interests. However, if a Soviet-bloc country was going to do that, Western diplomats wanted a NATO country, not Sweden or Switzerland, to represent Western interests on the ICC. Belgium seemed an appropriate candidate for the job.

However, the Viet Minh rejected the nomination. Belgium, they thought, might be subject to pressure from France, their old adversary. Canadians, like Belgians, spoke French and had a well-trained army. Nor did Canada appear particularly vulnerable to pressure from France. Because Canada was acceptable to the Soviet Union, China, and the Viet Minh, and because it did not want the fragile peace formula for Vietnam to unravel, the Canadian government agreed that Canadian soldiers and diplomats would serve alongside Indian and Polish representatives on the ICC.

At first, the ICC's tasks were clear-cut. It could oversee the French evacuation of Hanoi by 20 October 1954 and of its port, Haiphong, six months later. As the French withdrew their forces from Vietnam north of the seventeenth parallel and as the Viet Minh withdrew theirs from south of that parallel, the ICC should guarantee the free movement of civilians who might want to go with them. The ICC should also supervise nationwide elections in 1956 to establish a government for all of Vietnam.[179]

Because American authorities, particularly Secretary of State John Foster Dulles, thought that France had made too many concessions at Geneva, the United States did not sign the Geneva Accord. Demoralized and frustrated after almost a decade of war against the Viet Minh, the French government washed its hands of Vietnam, south as well as north of the 17th parallel, and recalled its troops. President Eisenhower sent hundreds of advisors to train police and establish a viable non-Communist government and army south of the seventeenth parallel. The seat of government for that territory would be Saigon, and the popular name for the country was South Vietnam. Neither the South Vietnamese nor the American government believed that fair pan-Vietnam elections were possible in 1956, and because neither had signed the Geneva Accord, neither felt an obligation to honour that commitment. Hence, Vietnam's 1956 election never took place.[180] Yet the ICC remained in place, supposedly to monitor violations of the 1954 cease-fire terms in Vietnam, as well as in neighbouring Laos and Cambodia.

Throughout the Eisenhower presidency (that is, until 20 January 1961), no major differences over Vietnam-related issues appear to have separated American and Canadian authorities. Early in 1955, the American consul in Hanoi, capital of Communist North Vietnam where the Viet Minh had formed the government, cabled the State Department: "We had the impression that Canadians always friendly but sometimes overcautious about offending Viet Minh had taken extra pains during Christmas season to demonstrate friendliness for American consulate." On 10 March, the American special representative or quasi-ambassador in Vietnam wrote: "Canadians, long intent on strict neutrality, now appear leaning to this side."[181]

Less than two weeks later, Secretary Dulles discussed Vietnam with Canada's minister of external affairs, Lester Pearson. They speculated on the possible outcome of the pan-Vietnam elections negotiated at Geneva and agreed that if those elections never took place, the blame should appear to fall on the Viet Minh, who had become the rulers of North Vietnam.[182] Later in 1955, Dulles again travelled to Ottawa for talks with Pearson, this time on Laos,[183] and in late 1955 and early 1956, American officials in Vientiane (capital of Laos) and in Washington expressed approval of the way Canadians were thinking and voting on matters related to Laos. Eisenhower's government planned to defy the Geneva agreement if defiance proved the only way to prevent a takeover in Laos by the pro-Communist Pathet Lao. It therefore accepted the likelihood of differences with France (the former colonial power), the United Kingdom (the Western co-chair of the Geneva Conference), and Canada (the Western member of the ICC), but it hoped that any ill will would be minimal.[184] At any rate, Washington did not target Canada for special criticism but saw it, along with France and the United Kingdom, as another Western country with interests in Southeast Asia.

Conclusions

At the end of the Second World War, because of its economic importance and territorial size and location, Canada was a foremost ally of the United States, almost as important as Britain. As such, American officials consulted Canadians on most major issues of defence and Cold War strategy. As the two allies began to make more detailed plans for the defence of North America, this harmonious picture changed. Americans, especially the Joint Chiefs of Staff, wanted to treat Canada as simply an extension of the United States. The Canadian government resisted, insisting in particular that it be consulted about the use and storage of nuclear weapons. On the related issue of nuclear know-how and raw materials, American policy changed over the early Cold War years. While Canada at first played an important role in the development of atomic energy and was one of three governments (British, Canadian, and American) that sat on international committees dealing with this issue, the revelation of a number of spies – several of them of foreign origin – caused Americans to become more secretive and to leave their Canadian allies out of the picture.

At the United Nations in its early years, Canada was one of America's favourite and most reliable allies. The American government supported Canadians for several important positions within the UN, because Canadians could be relied on to speak for Americans. Other factors, such as the spread of the Cold War to Asia and the beginnings of reconstruction in Western Europe, reduced the importance of Canada in relative terms. While still an important ally in the founding of NATO, Canada mattered less than did the European partners. Indeed, Americans could almost take Canadians for granted.

The issue of Korea clearly demonstrates the shift in American policy toward Canada. After the Second World War, the American administration went to great lengths to recruit Canada as a member of UNTCOK. American leaders wanted Canada, not just any minor ally, as a member. But when war broke out and Canadians continued to insist that they play a mediating role, Americans were not interested and conducted *their* war while ignoring Canadian offers of help and advice. Canadians might have thought that they were playing a significant role, but the Americans had no particular role for them in their policy. The situation was similar with respect to China. Americans were not interested in listening to the more "liberal" Canadians, and indeed they successfully persuaded the Canadian government not to accord diplomatic recognition to the government of the People's Republic of China. The situation was somewhat different with respect to Quemoy and Matsu, where the Canadian government bluntly told the American that it disagreed with the latter's policy. In this case, Canada had the support of several of the West European allies. But the American government refused and scorned the advice, treating Canada less as a liberal internationalist ally than as a *peripherally dependent* minor power. On Vietnam, however, Canada as a member of the ICC was one ally among others, a substitute for Belgium.

On the strategic and security issues discussed in this chapter, almost all American policy on Canada was policy initiated by the United States. For the most part, Canada was one ally among others, except where its geographical position (air defence, stationing of nuclear weapons) made a difference. There were few exceptions. If the suspicions of Campagna about the Avro Arrow are correct, Canada was clearly reduced to the status of a peripherally dependent ally on this issue. On China, Canada was forced to cling more closely to the American line than were the British. We also found only one instance where Canada made a difference in American policy: inclusion of Article II of the NATO treaty. One should not exaggerate that particular Canadian "success": although included in the charter, Article II has had next to no impact.

3
The Cold War, Part II (since 1961)

In contrast with Chapter 2, this chapter deals with a period of the Cold War when Canada was not as consistent an ally as it had been. Canada's politicians responded to Canadian public opinion which, as international tensions lessened, could afford to have doubts about certain key American policies. Forces opposed to nuclear weaponry gained in numbers, became more prominent, and gave the politically conscious Diefenbaker government sober second thoughts. During the period covered by this chapter, the Cold War entered Latin America with a vengeance. As American policies in Vietnam, Cuba, and China often seemed less than successful, many Canadians wondered about their merits. However, when Canada could play a useful role, as in Cyprus, or when Soviet aggression was blatant, as in Afghanistan, Canada rallied to the Western, US-led cause. Another factor that differentiates this chapter from Chapter 2 is the Quebec issue. Before 1960, the question of Quebec's secession from Canada was almost unthinkable. In the years covered by this chapter, it became a possibility.

Canada was a less important ally in the later stages of the Cold War for several reasons.[1] There were more differences of opinion than there had been. President Kennedy and Prime Minister John Diefenbaker disliked each other, as did President Nixon and Prime Minister Pierre Trudeau. Members of the Johnson administration thought that Canada was not carrying its share of the defence burden.[2] Fifteen years after the Second World War, the European allies had recovered, and the Federal Republic of Germany (West Germany) had become an ally, joining NATO in 1955. Its economy, along with those of France and the United Kingdom, outstripped Canada's. Japan, too, became an economic giant. Long-range aircraft and intercontinental balistic missiles rendered air bases on Canadian territory less significant than they had been. In 1963, as the United States Air Force retired its B-47s and deployed B-52s, the Strategic Air Command (SAC) withdrew from Churchill, Manitoba, and Frobisher Bay (now Iqaluit) on Baffin Island. Although ground forces remained at some Canadian sites, including Goose Bay, by 1973 the only SAC base outside the United States was on the US-owned island of Guam.[3] Satellite technology rendered Canada and the United Kingdom less essential to the retrieval of American intelligence data, at a time when Communists and supposed Communists raised questions about the reliability of the Canadian and British intelligence services. Given the role of Canada's Herbert Norman and Great Britain's Kim Philby as key players, many Americans preferred self-reliance to cooperation with leaky or potentially leaky partners.[4] A recent diplomatic history by Henry Kissinger – President Nixon's national security advisor who became secretary of state to Presidents Nixon and Ford – makes no mention of Canada as a factor between 1945 and 1981, but repeatedly refers to the special relationship between the United Kingdom and the United States.[5]

Yet, the stability of NATO remained a serious American concern, as did Communist takeovers in Vietnam, Cuba, and Afghanistan. Hostility between Greeks and Turks was to threaten the viability of the Western Alliance on the borders of Bulgaria, a Warsaw Pact country, and of the Soviet Union itself. An estimated 58,151 Americans died fighting Communist forces in Vietnam.[6] In October 1962, the United States and the Soviet Union came closer to direct conflict over Cuba than they had over any other issue. Local resistance to the 1979 Soviet invasion of Afghanistan would prove so costly in terms of men, money, and morale that it became a major factor in the disintegration of the Soviet Union a decade later.

Air defence remained of primary importance. On 8 December 1964, Secretary of State Dean Rusk wrote to Canada's ambassador in Washington "regarding overflights of Canadian territory by aircraft of the Strategic Air Command carrying atomic weapons in an ongoing series of training exercises calculated to develop an emergency alert capability." The American government sought permission for "up to twenty-eight flights daily" until 30 June 1965.[7] In March 1966, the Joint Chiefs of Staff issued "Instructions for Reporting Vital Intelligence Sightings." To be carried in aircraft, these instructions required flight crews to report unusual sightings in land, sea, air, and space (along with supporting evidence) to NORAD commanders in Colorado Springs or North Bay, or to Air Command at Canadian Forces Base, Winnipeg.[8] A State Department paper of April 1967 notes: "The only absolutely essential [defence] requirement we would have to levy on the Canadians would be use of their air space. Everything beyond this would appear to be a bonus."[9]

Because of the nature of Canada's army in the case of Vietnam and Cyprus and the nature of the Canadian economy in the case of Cuba and Afghanistan, successive American administrations chose to consider Canada and possible Canadian reactions as they planned their strategies. Canada's army could be effective in a mediating role and was too small to appear a threat to any anxious potential host; many Canadian factories were American-owned branch plants of American corporations that produced goods almost identical to those produced by the American parent. When Ottawa responded as Washington wished, the American-Canadian relationship was harmonious. When the Canadian government pursued policies of its own, as at times it did with respect to Vietnam and Cuba, American reactions ranged from tolerance to a measure of understanding to outright anger.

Some Americans realized that a more sensitive treatment of Canada might bring results closer to those desired by the US. A paper on Canada prepared for McGeorge Bundy during the Kennedy years begins by stating that "Canada's economic resources and potential ... and its forward strategic position ... [formed] the basis for a closer identification of its national identity with ours." However, the paper continues, Canadians' "inferiority complex with respect to the US" and their "growing nationalism" led them to want to "promote a Canadian national identity" while believing themselves "entitled to a privileged relationship with the US."[10] Unfortunately, as this chapter will show, American leaders did not always see the need for a more sensitive treatment of Canada.

Walt Rostow, President Johnson's national security advisor from 1966 to 1969, has said that after the Cuban Missile Crisis of 1962, few policy makers in Washington seriously anticipated a major war between the United States and the Soviet Union.[11] There would be skirmishes here and there, but not a major conflict. This belief allowed the administrations of Gerald Ford and Jimmy Carter to focus on other situations and to overlook Canada. Even the possibility that the province of Quebec might secede, causing Canada to disintegrate, does not appear to have alarmed the Ford or Carter White House.

Kennedy, Diefenbaker, and the Nuclear Weapons Controversy

Whatever the challenges for the two governments responsible for North American defence in the nuclear era, the bad interpersonal relationship between President Kennedy and Prime Minister Diefenbaker made matters worse. From retirement, Kennedy's secretary of state, Dean Rusk, remembered that relations between Kennedy and Diefenbaker were bad "right from the start."[12] Documentary evidence indicates that relations between the two men were bitter indeed, although there might have been an interlude of harmony. Diefenbaker was the first foreign head of government to visit Washington after President Kennedy's inauguration; they met in Washington on 20 February 1961. On 8 March, Livingston Merchant – the American ambassador to Canada – went to the White House and discussed the visit with President Kennedy, and the memorandum of their conversation reads: "The President said that he liked the Prime Minister and gained the impression that on any really important issue he would be on our side." For his part, Merchant said that he considered the visit "a great success."[13]

Yet, on 14 May 1961, days before President Kennedy paid a return visit to Ottawa, Secretary Rusk had doubts about the general direction of Canadian foreign policy and the personal values of Diefenbaker's minister of external affairs, Howard Green. Rusk recommended that in Ottawa, Kennedy should speak frankly about Green's "neutralist tendencies." Green, complained Rusk, seemed less than supportive of NATO than he should have been at a recent meeting of NATO foreign ministers, and more interested in a general reduction of nuclear tensions than in bolstering the Western cause. Green also failed to support the adversarial nature of American policy toward Castro's Cuba; instead he tried to maintain a business-as-usual approach with the Havana regime. Although the Poles on the International Control Commission (ICC) gave their full support to Soviet diplomacy in Vietnam, Canada – like Poland a member of the ICC – saw itself as an impartial observer rather than as a partisan of the Western cause. Rusk also found that Green exhibited "relative indifference" to the Western cause in Laos.[14] Unfortunately for Rusk, he had to deal with Green in connection with nuclear weapons, Cuba, and Southeast Asia.

When Kennedy went to Ottawa, Diefenbaker appears to have raised the matter of statements attributed in the press to Howard Green. Green had reportedly expressed a willingness "to mediate between Cuba and the United States." Diefenbaker denied that Green had made such a statement and said that he too "wanted nothing to do with it."[15] The matter of nuclear weapons, which the Diefenbaker government had persuaded the Eisenhower administration to locate at North Bay, Ontario, and La Macaza, Quebec, was more difficult to resolve. Having asked for the Bomarc-B missiles, which required nuclear warheads, Diefenbaker was unwilling to receive the warheads once the missile sites were otherwise operational, as domestic opposition to nuclear weapons was stronger than he had realized. As these sites replaced missile bases that could have been built in the United States, there was a gap in North American air defence, and American cities, thought Kennedy, were more vulnerable to Soviet air attack than they should have been. According to a memorandum of conversation, "The President again expressed perplexity at the fact that the difficulties were so great for Canada in taking this step" (that is, in accepting the nuclear warheads).[16]

Diefenbaker did not budge, and on 26 February 1962, Ambassador Merchant wrote to Secretary Rusk: "As you know, [the] greatest single outstanding problem between [the] US and Canada is Canadian failure to face up to [the] question [of] nuclear weapons." Merchant referred to the Bomarc-B warheads that Diefenbaker and Kennedy had discussed nine months earlier, but he also noted the Honest John rockets for ground troops in Europe, which were linked to a similar defence concern.[17]

Before Howard Green had become minister of external affairs, Diefenbaker's minister of defence, George Pearkes, had arranged for the acquisition of Honest John rockets, which also required nuclear warheads. By 1962, Canadian soldiers in Europe had their Honest John rockets, but without the warheads which might have made them more than ornamental. Diefenbaker's indecision was thus responsible for a second gap in Western defence capacity.

Merchant also regretted that Diefenbaker's government, like St. Laurent's until 1957, would not allow the United States Air Force and the United States Navy to store nuclear weapons on Canadian soil.[18] A statement of Diefenbaker's to the effect that he was in no hurry to receive nuclear weaponry in either Canada or Europe struck Merchant as "nothing more than dismaying since they represent irresponsible treatment of [a] subject of vital importance to both Canada and the US."[19]

The State Department in Washington was prepared to be somewhat more patient. Guidelines for relations with Canada prepared in March 1962 recommend:

> [the US] should continue to encourage the Canadian Government to prepare the Canadian public for a decision to accept nuclear weapons under US custody and for use by Canadian and US forces in Canada ... While continuing to press for such arrangements, we should avoid heavy-handed pressure, which would probably be counter-productive, and we should realize that some time may be required for the Canadian Government to take this step.[20]

This advice to be patient did not, however, improve relations between the Kennedy and Diefenbaker administrations.

In May 1962, as Merchant's term as American ambassador to Canada was ending, he made what was supposed to have been a courtesy visit to Prime Minister Diefenbaker. Diefenbaker angrily raised the matter of a memo written by Walt Rostow, which Kennedy had inadvertently left in Ottawa in May 1961. In its margin, Kennedy had made a reference to the "OAS," the Organization of American States, but Diefenbaker read Kennedy's handwriting as "SOB." Diefenbaker threatened to release the document and the presidential suggestion that he was a son of a bitch during the Canadian election campaign which was in full swing. He hoped that he might win votes by claiming that he had won Kennedy's enmity by his zealous defence of Canadian interests. Merchant reported the conversation to his immediate superior, Under-Secretary of State George Ball, who replied: "You should go back to [the] Prime Minister and ... indicate your own personal reluctance [to] report to Washington anything which could be construed as a threat to publish private communication directed to President US by one of his staff officers. Such publication would cast grave shadow over public attitudes between our two countries and make difficult future relations between President and Prime Minister."[21]

Merchant did as instructed, and Diefenbaker did not use the memorandum in his campaign. Nevertheless, the damage was done. Kennedy and his White House did not trust Diefenbaker, and correspondence between Washington and Ottawa dwindled to a minimum. Diefenbaker lost his majority in the 1962 election, and with Canada's pending acquisition (or non-acquisition) of nuclear weapons very much an issue during the Cuban Missile Crisis of October 1962 and into 1963, National Security Adviser McGeorge Bundy effectively torpedoed the minority Diefenbaker government. On 30 January 1963, the State Department released a statement written by Bundy that ridiculed Diefenbaker's refusal to accept the nuclear warheads.[22] Within a week, three of Diefenbaker's cabinet ministers (including the minister of national defence and the associate minister of defence) resigned over the issue, and his minority government lost a vote of confidence in the House of Commons. The Liberal party led by Lester B. Pearson assumed office after the election of 8 April 1963, and fulfilled the nuclear commitments Diefenbaker had made two years earlier.

Vietnam

Dean Rusk, secretary of state from 1961 to 1969 when the Vietnam War was at its height, commented that Canada was guardian of Western interests in Vietnam and "Canada did not do a good job representing the West."[23] Rostow has said that Canadian policy on Vietnam was "not diplomatically reputable." Canada pretended to take its commitments to the International Control Commission (ICC) seriously, but the ICC was "a farce." From the first day, the Communists violated the 1962 agreements on Laos, but the ICC took "weak positions."[24] In his year-end report for 1963, Walton Butterworth, American ambassador to Canada, complained that Canadian governments "feel a high degree of compulsion to demonstrate that Canada is not an American satellite. Thus, in the Gaza Strip, for example, where the quarrel is between Arab and Jew, [Canadians] can be and have been impressively objective. When, however, as in the Control Commissions in Laos, Viet-Nam, and Cambodia, we need a solid Western posture to balance the Communist third of a *troika*, we find the Canadians continually edging toward the centre position regardless of the merits or demerits of the issue of the moment."[25] What evoked such negative appraisals? Were they justified? Was the 1970 assessment by the CIA's Chester Cooper that Canadian diplomacy in Vietnam was "of considerable value" and "sensible" at all justified?[26]

American contempt for and disappointment over Canada's Vietnam policies may surprise many Canadians. In the words of retired Canadian diplomat Arthur Andrew: "Many Canadians thought [Canada's] role in Indochina did it no credit. There were allegations that while ostensibly serving the cause of international peace, we were in fact acting as agents of the United States: carrying their messages and bringing back intelligence, blindly defending American interests within the International [Control] Commission ... and selling arms to a belligerent country contrary to our own arms export policies. There was enough truth in the allegations to make it difficult to issue a blanket denial."[27] Yet, what Canada did was not what the White House wanted and expected.

The basic problem lay in Article 34 of the Geneva Accord. Negotiated in haste to meet a 20 July deadline – French premier Pierre Mendes-France had promised the National Assembly an end to the hostilities by that date – Article 34 was ambiguous. What role were the members of the International Control Commission supposed to play? Were they to serve as impartial jurists responsible for enforcement of the Geneva Accord? Or were Canada and Poland representatives of Western and Soviet-bloc interests respectively? The critical words were: "An International Commission shall be set up for the control and supervision of the application of the provisions of the agreement on the cessation of hostilities in Vietnam. It shall be comprised of the following states: Canada, India and Poland. It shall be presided over by the Representative of India."[28] If the wording seems clear, the context raised some legitimate questions. Canada's counterparts on the Korean Armistice Commission of 1953 had been Switzerland and Sweden, neutrals with a Western orientation. Western diplomats at Geneva wanted a bona fide NATO country to balance Poland, which had represented Soviet-bloc interests in Korea as well as in Vietnam. The ambiguity led to deep tensions between the Johnson administration in Washington and the Pearson government in Ottawa.

John Kennedy's Vietnam policy remained that of his immediate predecessors – to maintain a viable, non-Communist South Vietnam. As a Democrat, he could have repudiated such a goal as a Republican mistake, but he chose to pursue it with unprecedented vigour.[29] He increased the number of uniformed Americans in South Vietnam from fewer than 1,000 at the time of his 1960 inauguration to 16,300 at the time of his 1963 assassination.[30] Financial assistance increased from US$209 million in fiscal year 1960, Eisenhower's last year, to US$376 million in fiscal year 1963.[31] Kennedy despatched the Green Berets, and he recruited the advisors whom Lyndon Johnson inherited on 22 November 1963.

Despite President Kennedy's personal dislike of Prime Minister Diefenbaker,[32] Canada remained relevant to United States policy in Vietnam for two reasons – its membership in the International Control Commission (ICC) and its aid to South Vietnam. To Americans, Canada appeared the most reasonable member of the ICC, more sympathetic than India to

American concerns. By one count, between 1954 and 1965, Poland and India voted the same way forty-three times, Canada and India forty-two times. Canada and Poland rarely united against the Indians. Canada supported South Vietnam in 53 percent of votes; Poland supported Communist North Vietnam in 84 percent of votes.[33] Although some have accused Canadian members of the ICC of strong partiality toward the official American position in Vietnam,[34] the record shows otherwise. Canadians on the ICC were certainly more sympathetic to the US than were their Indian or Polish counterparts, but the White House and the Pentagon could not depend on their support.

In the early days of the Kennedy administration, the American embassy in Saigon referred to the "excellent, close working relationship we have with [the] Canadian ICC delegation."[35] There was good reason for such enthusiasm. Canadians told the embassy what happened at ICC meetings,[36] and when they returned from Hanoi to Saigon, they were known to tell the American embassy what they dared not include in their official reports. On 6 January 1961, for example, the embassy in Saigon advised the secretary of state:

> Canadians ... have told us that they will not reveal in ICC their observations of ... Soviet planes at Hanoi airport because such disclosures would lead to further restrictions on Canadian movement in North Vietnam to [the] detriment [of] intelligence needs of both US and Canada. They point out that they have no right under accords to station observers at Hanoi airport ... and DRV [Democratic Republic of Vietnam; that is, North Vietnam] has already established requirement for 48-hour prior application for permission [to] visit airport and at present permits only Indian traffic officer [to] make such visits. Under these circumstances we can no longer hope that ICC will find DRV guilty of procedural violation of [Article] 17 (E) [of the Geneva Accord].[37]

The Canadian members shared many of the American frustrations. They knew that they were much better able to observe American and South Vietnamese violations of the Geneva Accord than any violations on the part of the North Vietnamese. Canadians too did not trust Gopala Menon, the Indian chair of the ICC.[38] The Canadians disliked the overt partisanship of the Poles on behalf of the North Vietnamese government.[39]

Soon, however, relations between the American government and the Canadian members of the ICC began to deteriorate. Before the discovery that South Vietnamese Colonel Hoang Thuy Nam had drowned, there was a widespread perception that the Viet Cong had kidnapped him. Polish members of the ICC refused to condemn the kidnapping, and, without the Poles, the Indians did not want to do so. Canadian members did express disapproval, but the American embassy staff in Saigon believed that the ICC was a weak reed on which to lean if it could not agree to condemn a crime such as a suspected case of kidnapping.[40]

The second problem was that of exceeding the number of military personnel and equipment imposed by the Geneva Accord. Secretary of State Dean Rusk believed that Communist violations justified less than total compliance by the United States and South Vietnam.[41] President Kennedy raised the matter when he visited Ottawa in May 1961, but Diefenbaker was "cautiously negative."[42] A State Department official wrote: "We cannot hope to defeat the fast moving Viet Cong if we are required to seek multilateral consultation and concurrence prior to every move." He recommended:

> Parallel US and Vietnamese diplomatic conversations with the British, Canadians and Indians to inform them that the Vietnamese Government considers that the Geneva Cease Fire has been flagrantly violated and this situation plus the flood disaster has created a situation in which the Government of Vietnam has decided to ask increased US assistance in the flooded area. We should not indicate what form our assistance may take. It would be unconvincing to cite only the flood as a reason for bringing in US troops. The purpose is to give the ICC powers some private, advance notice of our views and intentions.[43]

The South Vietnamese, thought the official, should explain that they were requesting American forces to assist with flood relief so that South Vietnamese troops might concentrate on military matters and "defend their country." In no way, the official continued, was the government of South Vietnam to imply dissatisfaction with the ICC. "It considers the situation has gone beyond minor infractions of the cease-fire which the ICC was designed to control. Regretfully, it can no longer voluntarily observe Articles 16 and 17 of the Geneva Accords controlling the importation of men and equipment. It is prepared to resume observance as soon as the DRV ceases to violate them."[44] Hence, when the Kennedy administration decided to shake off the Geneva restrictions and augment the number of American forces in South Vietnam, Canada had a special status – of sorts. Its government would not be consulted, but it would be one of three governments (along with the United Kingdom and India) to receive some advance warning.

In Saigon, American ambassador Frederick Nolting had no faith in the ICC and was sarcastic about its Indian and Canadian members. He agreed that the United States should tell the Indians and Canadians of its intention to increase its Military Assistance Advisory Group (MAAG) in South Vietnam above levels allowed by the Geneva Accord. However, it should do so "bilaterally (not through formal ICC channels ...)," and it should be cautious with the arguments it advanced for doing so. Nolting said that the wrong arguments would make the increase "harder to sell [to the] Indians and therefore [to the] Canadians," as though the Canadians slavishly followed the Indian lead. Nolting also discussed the "eventual publicity which we might undertake after establishing 3,500 justifications with Indians and Canadians."[45]

Yet, the State Department retained some faith in the ICC's Canadian and Indian members. Late in October 1961, the department wanted the South Vietnamese government to be patient with the Polish members of the ICC in case their expulsion from South Vietnam might lead to a shutdown of ICC operations there.[46] On 9 February 1962, Secretary of State Dean Rusk expressed confidence that "Canadians and Indians" would recognize Communist aggression in South Vietnam and the need for a strong United States response – if only they were properly briefed. It "would be damaging," said Rusk, if the ICC were to criticize American and South Vietnamese violations of the Geneva Accord but ignore violations by the North Vietnamese and their allies in the South, the Viet Cong.[47]

The imbalance of criticism was a problem for the Canadians and Indians. They knew that the North Vietnamese were violating the Geneva Accord, and in February 1962 Canada's high commissioner in New Delhi proposed that whenever the ICC investigated a Communist complaint, it should also investigate a South Vietnamese one. An Indian official explained to American embassy officials in New Delhi that American violations of the Geneva Accord were so brazen and so open that the ICC could not pretend not to see them. The Communists, by contrast, were more subtle.[48]

The Diefenbaker government did give Kennedy's Vietnam policy some support. On 15 March 1962, Canadian diplomat Saul Rae told American officials in Washington that "Canadians understand and have real sympathy for US objectives in Vietnam."[49] Arnold Heeney, Canadian ambassador in Washington, told one State Department official that he "shared ... US anxieties about Vietnam." Heeney said that "if the United States thought the only way to save Vietnam was to bring personnel and material above the limits set by the Geneva Accord, then he would be willing to accept this judgment. He would bless any attempt to save Vietnam."[50]

With some reason, however, American officials regarded Canadian policy on Vietnam during the Diefenbaker era as one of "hypocrisy."[51] Because members of the Kennedy administration assumed that Communist violations of the Geneva Accords justified American counter-violations, they wanted the International Control Commission to agree.[52]

Heeney thought that that argument would hold no credibility in Ottawa. It would be preferable, thought Heeney, if the Americans would commit their violations outside Saigon, where ICC officials could ignore or pretend not to notice them.[53] It was particularly embarrassing, the Canadians thought, to have American ships unload helicopters at the dock opposite Saigon's Majestic Hotel.[54] Unfortunately, Saigon had the best deep-water port in South Vietnam, the only port capable of handling large ships with heavy equipment, and Canadian sensitivities were inconvenient from the American government's standpoint.[55] Despite this complication, American officials hoped that Canadian members of the ICC might persuade their Indian colleagues of the merits of American actions.[56]

With regard to the legality of American actions, Under-Secretary of State George Ball, himself a critic of the enhanced American war effort in Vietnam, proposed discussions "with Canadians in first instance and Indians later."[57] Subsequently, even the American embassy in Saigon saw hope. In May 1963, the embassy told the State Department that the chairs of the Indian and Canadian delegations were likely to accuse all parties – Communists, the South Vietnamese government, and the United States – of violations of the Geneva Accord. However, it added, a Canadian minority report would probably attribute the American and South Vietnamese violations to the necessity of dealing with Communist violations.[58] When the ICC issued its report a month later, it complained of lack of cooperation from authorities in both North and South Vietnam. Polish members dissented, and the Indians refuted the Poles' arguments.[59] Canadian members decided not to issue a minority report but to leave any explanations to the political leadership in Ottawa.[60]

After President Johnson replaced Kennedy, the US and Canada had no major disagreements about Vietnam for a year and a half. When President Johnson won the presidential election of November 1964, Pearson phoned his congratulations, and the two men had a warm and friendly conversation.

"I've been too late in telling you that you carried Canada," joked Pearson.

"Well, you don't know how much your friendship means to me, and I'm glad you called," said the president.

"Nice to think we're going to work together," responded Pearson.

"It'll be a great pleasure to me," continued Johnson.[61]

In January 1965, the Pearsons, accompanied by Minister of External Affairs Paul Martin, Sr., spent a weekend at the LBJ Ranch, President Johnson's home in the hill country near Austin, Texas.[62] Only delegations led by Mexican president Gustavo Diaz Ordaz and West German chancellor Ludwig Erhard had received similar hospitality.[63]

But differences over the Vietnam War soon clouded this friendly picture. According to some commentators, there was far too much cooperation.[64] One Canadian scholar, Douglas Ross, suggests that Canada played a useful role in preventing a wider conflict, even nuclear war.[65] Another, Robert

Bothwell, states that Pearson and Johnson came to physical blows over Vietnam.[66] American documentation supports Bothwell.

At first, Lyndon Johnson's government found Canada most useful as a diplomatic intermediary with North Vietnam. American officials wanted the North Vietnamese government to have a clear understanding of American determination *not* to allow a Communist takeover of South Vietnam, and they thought that a Canadian intermediary from the ICC would be the best intermediary. As ICC officials, Canadian diplomats travelled to Hanoi, and, in the words of Under-Secretary of State George Ball, "We believe we can count on their discretion."[67] Nevertheless, somebody's indiscretion led to a leak, and on 7 June 1964 Canada's House of Commons discussed the activities of Blair Seaborn, the Canadian who became the intermediary.[68] Despite this revelation, Seaborn continued his search for common ground. One of his tasks was to pursue hints from North Vietnam's consul in Paris, Mai Van Bo, leaked to an American diplomat in the French capital, Edmund Gullion.[69] Seaborn was to determine whether Bo really reflected the views of the men at the top in Hanoi and to clarify certain ambiguities arising from what Bo had said.[70] Unfortunately, Seaborn was unable to report any response from the leadership in Hanoi that would satisfy the Johnson administration, and the war escalated. Seaborn's trips to the North Vietnamese capital ended in mid-1965 when publicity rendered his efforts futile.[71]

The first ominous portent of disagreement between Washington and Ottawa came on 28 May 1964, when Johnson met Pearson at New York's Hilton Hotel. The Canadian prime minister attached little importance to the occasion and barely mentioned it in his memoirs,[72] but American sources are more explicit. Both leaders deplored the possible use of nuclear weapons in Vietnam as recommended by the probable Republican presidential nominee, Arizona senator Barry Goldwater. Regarding escalation of the conflict Pearson said – and Johnson agreed – that it might be all right to bomb "a bridge or an oil tank [but not] to shower bombs on a village full of women and children."

Less than a month later, William H. Sullivan of the State Department was complaining that Canada's Department of External Affairs had ignored a request for military aid for fighting the Vietnam War. There was, wrote Sullivan, a "political requirement for ... third country assistance."[73] By July, the American embassy in Vientiane was forecasting "serious complications with British and Canadians, on whom we depend for co-chairman and ICC help," because of the war effort in Laos.[74] By August, William Bundy, who had succeeded Sullivan as assistant secretary of state for Far Eastern affairs, was lamenting that Canada and the United Kingdom were siding with the Soviet Union, France, and India in promoting a peace conference he considered premature.[75] By December, the United Kingdom (which never had any troops in Vietnam), as well as Australia, New Zealand, and the Philippines (which would supply them), appeared on a list of "key allies," but Canada did not. The document referred to Canada, India, and France merely as "key interested governments."[76] President Johnson told Ambassador Maxwell Taylor in Saigon that he hoped for "military and political cooperation" from governments of Thailand, the Philippines, Australia, New Zealand, and the United Kingdom,[77] but evidently he had given up on or forgotten Canada. Later that month, President Johnson and his advisors gave diplomats from Great Britain, Australia, and New Zealand "the whole picture" on Vietnam, while Canadian diplomats received "slightly less." On 18 February 1965, William Bundy expressed the fear of "the Soviets – or even the Canadians – sounding us out on whether we would stop our attacks in return for some moderation in VC [Viet Cong] activity. This is clearly unacceptable, and the very least we should hold out on is a verified cessation of infiltration (and radio silence) before we stop our attacks."[78] During 1965, large numbers of American conscripts began to arrive in Southeast Asia. It was also the year of the Temple University affair.

Philadelphia's Temple University awarded Pearson its World Peace Award, and the White House sent its congratulations.[79] The president even invited the prime minister for lunch at Camp David after his trip to Philadelphia to make a speech and receive his award. Pearson used his speech to appeal to the American government for a pause in its aerial bombardment of North Vietnam. As John English, Pearson's biographer, has indicated, the speech was a "turning point" in the relationship between Johnson and Pearson, and, by extension, between their two countries.[80] Johnson was furious. Criticism of American policy was tolerable, but not in a speech delivered to an American audience inside the United States.[81]

When he returned to Ottawa, Pearson thought that he ought to write a letter of explanation. National Security Adviser McGeorge Bundy drafted a warm presidential reply which began "Dear Mike." The president, however, changed the opening to the more cursory "Dear Mr. Prime Minister." It was only late in 1966, when Johnson was sick and Pearson sent him best wishes for a speedy recovery, that the president finally wrote to "Dear Mike."[82]

Pearson wanted to show his Canadian critics that his Vietnam policy was substantially different from that of the president's. In 1965, he sought permission to publish Johnson's written request for Canadian combat forces. The president denied such permission and Walton Butterworth, American ambassador in Ottawa, gloated that if the Canadians wanted to use their ICC membership as a pretext for refusal, they could certainly provide more non-military aid than they were giving.[83] Assistant Secretary of State William P. Bundy said that the ICC was totally ineffective but that the American government might suggest that the Poles, Indians, and

Canadians discuss among themselves what they might do to be helpful. "Certainly Hanoi would not play," said Bundy, but "at least, it would ... give Mr. Pearson an outlet for his peacemaking energies, and just might lead to some discussion of other matters that would not be harmful to us."[84]

After 1965, personal contacts between Johnson and Pearson were minimal and brief. Dean Rusk wanted the president to go to Ottawa in mid-1966 to meet Pearson and to address a joint gathering of both houses of Parliament. Instead, the two leaders met on Campobello Island to launch an international park. In March 1967, Pearson suggested that he might stop in Washington for lunch as he returned from a Caribbean vacation, and Johnson agreed to receive him – with a condition. Walt Rostow, who had succeeded McGeorge Bundy as Johnson's national security advisor on 31 March 1966, insisted to Edgar Ritchie, Canada's ambassador in Washington, that in exchange for lunch at the White House, Pearson must promise not to make any public comments on the Vietnam War while he was in the United States. Pearson accepted the condition. Rostow thought that President Johnson could use the session to encourage Pearson to be generous with food aid and to discuss the law of the sea.[85] That visit never took place because Governor General George Vanier, Canada's head of state, died and Pearson had to make a hasty return to Ottawa for the funeral.[86] On 25 May, Johnson made a visit of a few hours to Montreal's World Fair, Expo 67, and to the Canadian prime minister's country home at Harrington Lake. That visit was short, at least in part because another Arab-Israeli war was imminent, and the presidential party believed that it belonged in Washington.

Ambassador Butterworth's 1967 report ridiculed any advice from Pearson and Martin on Vietnam. Martin, he thought, had "decided that there was a groundswell of public demand for taking stances which would not necessarily please Washington and for advertising them openly."[87] This maintained the tone set by Rostow. "Just for fun," Rostow sent President Johnson a piece by the *Toronto Telegram's* right-wing columnist, Lubor Zink, who found Canadian policy in Vietnam to be silly, dishonourable, and without merit.[88] However, as acting secretary of state in mid-April 1967, Nicholas Katzenbach thought that in response to a "curious" peace proposal of "good, bad, and indifferent" ideas from Paul Martin, Sr., Canada's minister of external affairs, the United States and South Vietnam should announce a willingness to restore the area between North and South Vietnam as a demilitarized zone, provided that North Vietnam agreed.[89] However, nothing seems to have come of this suggestion.

In 1966, the American government reluctantly accepted Canadian diplomat Chester Ronning as an intermediary between itself and the North Vietnamese government. The initiative for this journey lay with the Canadian government. With the Johnson administration's approval,

Ronning travelled to Hanoi to identify any common ground on which a cease-fire agreement might rest. After Ronning's return, Rostow complained that Martin was exaggerating Ronning's achievements. "Martin," said Rostow, "without revealing any substance, is trying to keep us hemmed in on the grounds that the channel is 'still open.'"[90] Almost thirty years later, President Johnson's defence secretary, Robert McNamara, would write that the administration should have taken the Ronning mission more seriously than it did.[91] Yet, even in 1966, Secretary Rusk felt an obligation to inform the government of Canada that the US was planning to undertake military action in the demilitarized zone between North and South Vietnam. Other than London, Ottawa was the only capital privy to such information.[92] (At the time, Canadians on the ICC were doing what they could to facilitate mail between American prisoners of war and their families.[93])

Pearson and Johnson did not meet again after the Expo visit, nor did Johnson meet Pearson's successor, Pierre Elliott Trudeau, who assumed office in April 1968 and won a decisive election victory in June. *Globe and Mail* reporter Lawrence Martin as well as Professors Granatstein and Bothwell claim that Trudeau deliberately kept his distance from the lame-duck Johnson administration.[94] However, declassified documents tell another story. On 29 June, Johnson invited Trudeau to the White House, and exactly two months later, the president received word that the Canadian prime minister was willing to come. By then, President Johnson had lost interest. The president had already indicated that he "did not care anything about the proposed Trudeau visit," and the writer of the memo suggested that if President Johnson still felt that way, Walt Rostow "certainly can and will turn this project off." The memorandum ended with a question: "Shall we turn it off?" Johnson ticked the "Yes" box, but scrawled: "Do easily without hurting his feelings." Somebody else scrawled that Rostow then received instructions to do just that.[95]

It is certainly understandable that President Johnson did not want to spend any part of 1968 with a Canadian prime minister, amiable or otherwise. That was Johnson's last full year as president, and it was a calamitous one. It included such horrors as North Korea's seizure of the US Navy spy ship, Pueblo, the Tet offensive in Vietnam, the assassinations of Martin Luther King and Robert Kennedy, race riots in Washington, the Warsaw Pact invasion of Czechoslovakia, and a presidential election from which Johnson withdrew his candidacy.

President Johnson's successor, Richard Nixon, had so little regard for Prime Minister Trudeau that on one occasion he referred to him as an "asshole."[96] Yet, when Nixon's national security advisor, Henry Kissinger, and North Vietnam's Le Duc Tho negotiated what they claimed to be a cease-fire and what Nixon termed "peace with honour" in January 1973, the

American government wanted Canadian troops to remain as part of the new supervisory system, the International Commission of Control and Supervision (ICCS). This time, there would be four umpires instead of three: Poland and Hungary from the Soviet bloc, Canada and Indonesia to represent "the West."[97] Jaundiced by past experience, India refused to take part, as chair or in any other capacity. Evidently, the performances of Poland and Canada over the previous nineteen years had been sufficiently acceptable to all concerned that their sponsors called them back for an encore.

Both the Canadian government in Ottawa and Canadians in Vietnam realized that the cease-fire was a charade, but they reluctantly agreed to play along for six months as American combat forces withdrew from South Vietnam and the US and North Vietnam exchanged prisoners of war. The Canadian government decided that it should play the game so that American prisoners of war could return home and American combat forces could leave Vietnam, but the Canadian government realized that this was no "peace with honour." It agreed to serve for a period of three months, and then agreed to one extension of two months, on the condition that there would be no further requests. At the time of the extension, Prime Minister Trudeau told President Nixon:

> I hope that the assurances I was able to provide in our telephone conversation Tuesday morning regarding the Government's decision to continue Canadian participation on the International Commission of Control and Supervision in Viet Nam for a further two month trial period have served to meet the concern which you have expressed in this regard in your letter to me of March 22nd.
>
> Your words of commendation for the part which Canadian members have so far played in establishing and activating the I.C.C.S. were much appreciated, and due note was taken of your views regarding the possible consequences of our withdrawal. As your people will no doubt have noted from the statement made by Mr. Sharp [Mitchell Sharp, Canadian minister of external affairs] on March 27 announcing this decision in the House of Commons, I would be less than frank if I were not to say that I and my colleagues in the Cabinet find it difficult to share fully your confidence that the I.C.C.S. can become an effective instrument for controlling and supervising the implementation of the 27 January 1973 agreement on Vietnam.[98]

When the Canadian forces were about to leave, Kissinger found it difficult to replace them. Kissinger contacted American diplomats in Brazil, Turkey, Austria, Malaysia, and Singapore to approach those governments for troops to serve on the ICCS, but none of them wanted to put their forces into the line of fire. Finally, Kissinger managed to persuade the Shah to send Iranian troops.[99] Thus, in 1975, when North Vietnamese forces overran South Vietnam, Iranians and not Canadians had to scramble for safety.

Cuba

In July 1993, after the collapse of the Soviet bloc, when Cuba was one of a few countries that still had Communist governments, the Clinton administration concerned itself with the Canadian connection. Telephone service between Cuba and the United States had deteriorated to the point where American entrepreneurs were offering telephone service via Canada – albeit at prices more than nine times those charged by ATT. Callers in Miami or New York would be linked first to a Canadian exchange, and then to Havana. The Clinton administration threatened fines of US$500,000 and prison terms of ten years against violators of the communications embargo, particularly those who advertised the Canadian telephone route to Havana.[100] In so doing, the Clinton team was pursuing the policies of its various Republican and Democratic predecessors of the previous three decades, and beyond. Cuba remained one of the major problems in American-Canadian relations.

Official American anger and frustration over Canadian-Cuban relations began in mid-July 1960, during the Eisenhower presidency. By then it was obvious that Castro's Cuba would not be a democracy, although that in itself should not have been a problem. The Eisenhower administration had befriended other authoritarian governments in Latin America. However, in January 1960, Anastas Mikoyan – deputy premier of the Soviet Union – visited Cuba and concluded a trade agreement. In May, Cuba and the Soviet Union established diplomatic relations. In June, Castro expropriated American-owned oil refineries in Cuba. On 12-13 July, three members of President Eisenhower's cabinet – Secretary of State Christian Herter, Secretary of Defense Thomas Gates, and Secretary of the Treasury Robert Anderson – journeyed to Ottawa for the third regular meeting of the Canada-US Ministerial Committee on Joint Defense. This meeting, they thought, would provide an opportunity to explain the Soviet threat that Castro represented to both Canada and the United States, and they sought Canadian cooperation.[101] In this objective, they were unsuccessful, and their failure began the tensions between Ottawa and Washington over Cuba.

On 25 July, State Department officials expressed disapproval of a Mexican idea forwarded by Canada's minister of external affairs, Howard Green, the previous day. That is, Mexico, Canada, and Brazil would offer their services as mediators of Cuban-American differences.[102] Conventional wisdom in Washington was that the Mexicans were so obsessed with their own revolutionary experiences that they could not appreciate the evils of Cuba's revolution. Brazilians were in the midst of a presidential election campaign, and President Juscelino Kubitschek would have to pander to left-leaning politicians. Canadians in their ignorance, the State Department continued, insisted that Castro and his associates were Cuban politicians reacting to Cuban pressures and dealing with Cuban problems.[103]

Alleged Canadian ignorance of Cuba appalled the Eisenhower administration, whose members then concluded that opinions of Canadian government officials were of little value. The very morning after the Ottawa meetings ended, Secretary Anderson told the secretary of state about a Canadian who had said "that nobody [in the Canadian government] knows anything about Latin America, except Green who was there once."[104] Under-Secretary of State Douglas Dillon told the National Security Council that the Canadians had "the presumption to tell us that ... they had received reports from their diplomatic sources which did not agree with ours. When we asked them about the reaction they had got in Central America, the Canadians had had to admit that they had no representative in the area."[105] That Canada had had a legation or embassy in Havana since 1945 and that Canadian bankers had been active in Cuba since 1899 appear to have made little impression in Washington.

By October 1960, Castro had seized without compensation additional American-owned property in Cuba and strengthened his ties with the Soviet Union. The Eisenhower administration responded with a trade and communications embargo, which remains in effect to this day. If the embargo were to be effective in weakening the Cuban economy and hastening the overthrow of Castro, America's allies would have to cooperate because their products would be almost as useful as American ones. As Canadians could supply more or less the very products Americans were refusing to supply, Canadian cooperation was vital.[106]

However, such cooperation was not forthcoming. Representatives of Canadian Prime Minister John Diefenbaker told their American counterparts "that the US was preoccupied with communism. They stated that they could not imperil the free right of their banking institutions and businesses to take up any slack that might be created by US economic sanctions." One State Department official, Robert H. Johnson, termed Canada's Cuban policy "disturbing."[107] Diefenbaker forebade American suppliers from sending goods to Cuba via Canada, and he limited Canadian sales to non-strategic goods, but that was not good enough for the American government.[108]

The Bank of Nova Scotia is one example of a Canadian company that played a role in the Castro government's economic survival. Treasury Secretary Anderson claimed that in order to put its currency reserves beyond American control, the Cuban government by mid-summer 1960 had "moved most of its funds to ... Canada" through the Bank of Nova Scotia, one of the Canadian banks with years of service in Cuba.[109] Any attempt

to freeze Cuban funds in an effective way would require Canadian cooperation. Treasury Secretary Anderson thought "that it was inconceivable
that the Canadians would not cooperate with us in the matter of Cuban
assets in Canada."[110]

Anderson was wrong. Canadians did not pretend to agree with American policy, let alone follow the American lead. At a meeting of the
National Security Council in October 1960, Secretary of State Herter targeted Canada as the least cooperative ally regarding the embargo. Herter
wanted to investigate the Federal Reserve Board's supply of $100 bills to
the Bank of Nova Scotia, which could then forward them to Cuba.[111] He
also expressed anger that Canadian General Motors was "thinking of sup-
plying spare parts to Cuba." Under-Secretary Dillon, however, saw reason
for hope – of sorts. Dillon noted that many Canadian companies were only
branch plants of American corporations and, thus, the American government could pressure them. The State Department lauded Continental Can
of Canada for threatening to boycott a Canadian steel company if it sold
any steel to Cuba.[112]

Until their differences over Cuba, Eisenhower and Diefenbaker had had
a friendly relationship.[113] However, the bitterness over Canada's Cuban
policy soon became obvious. In October 1960, as the American embargo
began, the State Department considered severing diplomatic relations
between Cuba and the United States. Great Britain, the first country
approached for informal discussions about representing American interests in Cuba, did not want the job, but suggested Canada. The State
Department rejected that idea at once. Canadians, a memo said, "should
be ruled out because of the way ... [they] are acting about our export control policy." Besides, if asked, the Canadian government would probably
refuse the role of protector of American interests in Cuba for fear that such
a role would interfere with Canadian economic opportunism.[114] When the
break with Cuba did come in January 1961, the Eisenhower administration turned responsibility for American interests over to Switzerland.

Rusk also threatened to invoke the Trading with the Enemy Act to stop
American-owned companies with factories in Canada from selling to
Cuba, regardless of what the Canadian government might do.[115] Chief
executive officers in the United States could face fines or imprisonment if
they allowed their Canadian branch plants to do business with Cuba. On
24 April 1961, the Kennedy administration's deputy advisor on national
security, Walt Rostow, suggested to Defense Secretary Robert McNamara
that when President Kennedy visited Ottawa the following month, he
might publicly urge Canada to join the Organization of American States.
Once a member, Rostow argued, Canada would have no choice but to
cooperate in the effort against Castro.[116] Secretary McNamara and President Kennedy accepted that advice, which deeply offended Diefenbaker.

The following month, Rusk and Green had a heated debate over Cuba when NATO foreign ministers met in Oslo.[117]

To members of the Kennedy administration, opinions of Diefenbaker and his cabinet were inconsequential during the Cuban Missile Crisis. Canada was within range of the Soviet missiles in Cuba. Canada was a partner of the United States not only in NATO but also in NORAD. The Royal Canadian Navy played a significant role in anti-submarine warfare against the Soviets in the North Atlantic.[118] Commercial aircraft travelling from the Soviet Union to Cuba refuelled in Newfoundland. The Strategic Air Command would overfly Canada on its way to targets in the Soviet Union. While American and Canadian military officers communicated with each other, at no time during the crisis did an American cabinet minister telephone, let alone visit, his Canadian counterpart. President Kennedy was, by contrast, frequently in contact with British prime minister Harold Macmillan, and sent a special envoy to President de Gaulle of France.[119] But Diefenbaker and his ministers, it seems, were either ignored or forgotten.

Thirty-one years later, one of the authors interviewed Dean Rusk. "May I have your thoughts on Howard Green, Diefenbaker's minister of external affairs?" he asked.

"Green did not play much of a role in my life," replied the former secretary of state.

"He *was* minister of external affairs during the Cuban Missile Crisis," countered the author.

"My mind is fairly blank when it comes to Green," responded Rusk.[120] The passage of time and the accumulation of events had erased from Rusk's memory his memorandum of 14 May 1961 to President Kennedy. Nevertheless, Rusk's reply confirms that Green played no significant role in the diplomacy of the Cuban Missile Crisis. That Rusk would have remembered. Perhaps the Kennedy administration thought the cooperation of Diefenbaker and Green quite unnecessary, given that Canadian and American military officers communicated with each other and worked together throughout the crisis. Or perhaps they did not think about Canada at all.

The Kennedy and Johnson administrations remained less than satisfied with Canada's Cuba policy, even after Diefenbaker's departure from office in April 1963. When Prime Minister Pearson visited President Kennedy at Hyannisport the following month, a briefing paper for President Kennedy noted: "Canada has not broken diplomatic relations with Cuba nor placed a total embargo on trade with it. We prefer a stronger Canadian attitude, although there has been some important cooperation with US policy." Canada, the paper noted, had established an embargo on strategic goods to Cuba and refused to be an entrepôt for American goods that might circumvent the embargo. Canadian trade with Cuba in 1962 was only one-third of what it had been in 1961. However, Canadian suppliers continued to send "critical spare parts to Cuba," and a branch of the Royal Bank of Canada in Mexico City provided the Castro government with one of its few links with the Western world.[121] Early in the Johnson presidency, one official thought that an outboard motor from Canada propelled a boat full of weapons from Cuba to Venezuela, where it was to be used to over-throw the constitutional government. Moreover, despite official Canadian policy to the contrary, chemicals and machinery of American origin were still finding their way to Cuba via Canada.[122] By September 1964, the White House was concerned that Canada remained Cuba's largest free-world trading partner.[123]

During the Ford administration (1974-7), Canada's ties with Cuba continued to bother official Washington. In January 1976, the very month when Canadian Prime Minister Trudeau shouted to a crowd in Cienfuegos, Cuba, "Viva el Primer Ministro Comandante Fidel Castro!"[124] the White House expressed fear that DC-8 aircraft manufactured in the United States might acquire a Canadian home and then join the fleet of Cubana Airlines. The White House was prepared to contact Trudeau advisor Ivan Head on the matter.[125] Yet the following year, Trudeau was a welcome guest at America's bicentennial celebrations.

Canada's business as usual approach toward Castro's Cuba has continued to be a contentious issue in American-Canadian relations, even after the Cold War. In 1996, years after the end of the Cold War and the withdrawal of Soviet or Russian support for Castro's government, the Helms-Burton Act threatens penalties against foreign (including Canadian) executives of companies involved in transactions with expropriated American property. Named for its sponsors, Senator Jesse Helms (Republican-North Carolina) and Representative Daniel Burton (Republican-Indiana), the Helms-Burton Act would probably never have become law if Castro's air force had not shot down aircraft – piloted by Miami Cubans – approaching Cuban air space. The pilot's purpose was to harass Cuba. Castro's planes should not have fired at them when they were still over international waters. Given the influence of the Miami Cubans, President Clinton could not afford to veto Helms-Burton in an election year. However, his failure to do so has created disharmony not only with Canada but also with Mexico and with Canada's G-7 partners. Clinton, in return, has not implemented several sections of the Helms-Burton Act.

Cyprus

In 1830, much of mainland Greece seceded from the Ottoman Empire and won international recognition as an independent kingdom. Cyprus, however, remained within the Ottoman Empire until 1878, after another round of fighting in which, once again, the Ottoman Turks fared badly.

The Great Powers of Europe met at the Congress of Berlin (1878) to redraw the map of southeastern Europe, and the Congress of Berlin (1878) awarded Cyprus to Great Britain, which sought a naval base near the northern end of the Suez Canal. About 80 percent of Cypriots were ethnic Greeks, most of the rest Turkish.

From 1950 to 1960, Greek Cypriot insurgents (best known by the Greek acronym EOKA), rebelled against British authority on the island. British officials had to consider not only their strategic interests in connection with the Suez Canal but also the position of the Turkish Cypriots. For many in EOKA, the goal was not Cypriot independence but *enosis,* or political union with Greece. Turkish Cypriots opposed this idea. Nor did it help that ethnic Greeks and ethnic Turks had had an adversarial relationship for more than 500 years. In 1960, Great Britain transferred authority (outside military bases which Great Britain would retain) to a government led by Archbishop Makarios, the head of the Greek Orthodox Church in Cyprus. The British government insisted on constitutional guarantees for the Turkish Cypriot minority and a pledge that Cyprus would remain independent and not unite with Greece.

Late in 1963, the two Cypriot communities were resorting to violence against each other, and Washington feared that Greece and Turkey would intervene in support of their respective Cypriot communities. The possibility of war between two NATO allies that shared common borders with the Soviet Union and its Bulgarian ally was a serious concern. The British, with their residual military rights, seemed unable to mediate.

The one ray of hope came from the Cypriot president, Archbishop Makarios. His government would allow troops under United Nations auspices to separate the Greek-Cypriot and Turkish-Cypriot adversaries. Unfortunately, there was no stampede of countries to volunteer forces. One of the conditions was that every nation sending troops to Cyprus would have to pay its own expenses, until President Johnson promised that the United States would meet 35 percent of the costs. Even then, there was a shortage. Finally, the president resorted to the telephone and to his famous skills of persuasion.[126] Among those with whom he spoke was Lester Pearson, but Pearson has said that his government had decided to send troops even before the president's call.[127] (Paul Martin claims that it was he, not Lyndon Johnson, who persuaded other countries to follow Canada's lead and send soldiers.[128]) At any rate, those countries besides Canada who sent soldiers to Cyprus included the United Kingdom, Austria, Australia, Denmark, Finland, Ireland, and Sweden – four of these being neutrals, in no military alliance with the United States. As far as the Johnson White House was concerned, Canadian participation in Cyprus was "essential."[129]

The first Canadians arrived in Cyprus on 15 March 1964, and their areas of responsibility were those of maximum tension. These areas included the green line between Greek and Turkish parts of Nicosia, the capital, as well as other parts of the island. Canadian forces stood – and indeed lived – between the hostile Greek-Cypriots and Turkish-Cypriots. At times, both Cypriot factions shot at the Canadians as well as at each other, especially during the Turkish invasion of 1974. At that time, two Canadians died and seventeen suffered injuries, and Canadian forces fired at Greek-Cypriots.[130] Canadian troops remained in Cyprus for almost thirty years. By 1993, 30,000 Canadians had served, and twenty-eight had lost their lives in the course of duty.[131] When the Canadians departed, only British and Austrian forces remained. However, Canadian soldiers had helped prevent a major conflict in Cyprus.

Cyprus represents an instance where a relatively small problem could have caused a major division within the Western world and left American interests exposed to Soviet penetration. Given the many centuries of hostility between Greeks and Turks, the following scenario was certainly conceivable. Ethnic fighting on Cyprus might well have led to the intervention of Greece, on behalf of the Greek Cypriots, and Turkey, on behalf of the Turkish Cypriots. The result would have been an international war between two NATO members in a vulnerable part of the world. Turkey bordered on the USSR, Greece on the USSR's most reliable satellite, Bulgaria. It is little wonder that President Johnson sought to contain the problem while it remained a small concern, and that he was grateful to Canada for helping him to do so. Professors Stephen J. Randall and John H. Thompson suggest that the highly profitable (for Canada) 1965 Autopact was Canada's reward for cooperation in Cyprus.[132]

China

Publicly, the Kennedy and Johnson administrations still treated the People's Republic of China as an international outcast, not worthy of American recognition. Behind the scenes, however, the Kennedy administration had been prepared to treat China as a participant in the international system and to use Canada and Australia as instruments of American policy to that end. When these two countries started selling wheat and other agricultural products to China, two high-level Kennedy advisors suggested that such sales might be a means of influencing Chinese foreign policy. In February 1962, Chester Bowles wrote Kennedy: "This administration should give urgent and intensive study to the key role which may be played by US agricultural resources, as well as those of Canada and Australia, in meeting the China food crisis, either through direct commercial transactions or – in return for a relaxation of Chinese pressure in Southeast Asia and elsewhere."[133] A month later, Walt Rostow wrote to George

Ball, the under-secretary of state, that Canada and Australia (but not the US which, presumably, would keep its hands clean of such dealings) "should be asked to communicate to the Chinese Communists that provocative Chinese actions will influence the willingness of countries of the West to sell grain to Communist China."

During the Johnson presidency, the People's Republic of China was still anathema in the United States. In his memoirs written decades later, Dean Rusk would say that reconciliation at a later date made sense but that during his time in office, "the Chinese Communists didn't seem interested in improving US-Chinese relations." Moreover, American recognition of Communist China and that country's admission to the United Nations would have been highly controversial with the American electorate.[134] What Rusk did not say in his memoirs was that the Johnson administration feared that the Canadian government of Lester B. Pearson (1963-8) would recognize the PRC and lobby for its occupying the China seat at the United Nations. This outcome would be particularly inappropriate, thought the Americans, while the PRC was aiding the North Vietnamese in their war against the South Vietnamese and the Americans.[135]

American concerns about Canada were twofold: first, that Canada would support Communist China's entry into the United Nations,[136] and second, that Ford of Canada was about to sell trucks to China. As Pearson visited Johnson at the LBJ Ranch in January 1965, a briefing paper advised the president that the next United Nations vote to unseat the Chinese Nationalists and receive the Chinese Communists would probably be very close: fifty in favour, fifty-four opposed, and ten abstentions. The United States was including Canada as one of the fifty-four in opposition. "We wish to keep in close touch with Canada on the China problem," said the briefing paper.[137] At the same time, Paul Martin had made Communist China's admission to the United Nations one of the high priority goals he wanted to accomplish during his tenure as Canadian minister of external affairs.[138]

Moreover, the Johnson administration invoked the Trading with the Enemy Act. (See Chapter 6.) As a result, although it was legal under Canadian law for Ford of Canada to sell trucks, and the sales would have benefited the Canadian economy, Ford's corporate directors at Detroit forced Ford of Canada to cancel the deal. With regard to the United Nations, Martin in 1966 suggested – to Washington's dismay – that the PRC have seats in the General Assembly and the Security Council, while Nationalist China would have a seat in the General Assembly under the designation "Taiwan." That idea failed, and Martin in 1967 abstained on the Albanian resolution to admit Communist China. He still thought China's admission a good idea, but he did not want to antagonize Washington.[139]

Even when the American and Canadian governments shared similar views on China, there were problems. In 1970, Prime Minister Trudeau's government established diplomatic relations with the PRC. According to Professors Granatstein and Bothwell, that action "may have represented a watershed in China's relations with the West."[140] President Nixon and his national security advisor, Henry Kissinger, also wanted to end the PRC's isolation and to normalize the relationship. However, the Nixon White House was furious at the Canadian action. "Future contacts or channels with the Chinese," the president said, "could take place anywhere except Ottawa."[141] The declassification of additional documents may well reveal that Nixon did not dislike Trudeau's actions but rather his timing. Trudeau upstaged him. Secretary of State Kissinger was about to commence his own secret contacts with the Chinese.

There was a bitter dispute in 1976, during the Ford presidency, by which time the United States had established de facto but not de jure relations with the PRC. When athletes from Taiwan arrived at the Canadian border on their way to the 1976 Summer Olympics in Montreal and claimed to represent "The Republic of China" (ROC), the government of Prime Minister Trudeau refused them entry. Trudeau, who did not want to disturb Canada's relationship with the PRC, said that he could not admit athletes from one place (Taiwan) who claimed to come from another (China). The Ford administration was disturbed, to say the least, because it still recognized the ROC as China's legitimate government. Communications Officer David Gergen prepared for the president a possible answer to a hypothetical question:

Q: Why did you put so much pressure on the United States Olympic Committee and the International Olympic Committee to force Canada into allowing Taiwan to compete in the Olympics?

A: My concern in this matter was not to champion Taiwan or to criticize Canada, but *to see that the Olympic movement did not yield a fundamental principle that politics should not interfere in the participation of athletes in the Games.*[142] [italics added]

In brief, China was a source of ongoing differences between the United States and Canada. From Eisenhower to Ford, administrations disagreed with the China policies of successive Canadian governments. On China, Canada was not the reliable ally the Americans sought.

Afghanistan

Throughout most of Jimmy Carter's presidency (1977-81), the Cold War did not appear ominous. The Soviet Union and the United States negotiated a second Strategic Armaments Limitations Treaty (SALT II). Relations between the United States and Communist China continued to improve, while China's relations with the Soviet Union remained strained. Until the

Soviet Army invaded Afghanistan in December 1979, the Soviet government preferred to operate through Cuban surrogates in some Third World countries. Cuban soldiers, not Soviets, went to the assistance of friendly governments in Angola and Ethiopia, and Cubans offered moral and material support to Nicaragua's Sandinistas who, in 1979, ousted a government that had enjoyed extensive support from the United States. Such Cuban activities were tolerable, not major threats to the security of the United States, and even Soviet aggression in Afghanistan was relatively peripheral. Afghanistan in itself was not important to the United States, unless it became a highway for Soviet penetration of the oil-rich Middle East. Yet the invasion, after nearly ten years of detente, led to seriously strained superpower relations for the next several years.

In the aftermath of the Soviet invasion of Afghanistan, President Carter established an embargo on wheat sales to the Soviet Union and called for a boycott of the 1980 Summer Olympics, scheduled for Moscow. On 20 January 1980, President Carter warned that if Soviet forces did not leave Afghanistan within thirty days, the United States would not send a team to the Moscow Olympics.[143] Within a week, Prime Minister Joe Clark announced that if Soviet forces were not out of Afghanistan by 20 February, the Canadian government would not provide financial assistance to Canadian athletes who did go to Moscow.[144] Despite initial reluctance on the part of Pierre Trudeau, whose Liberals regained office in the 18 February 1980 general election, Trudeau endorsed the boycott, but not, it would appear, because of pressure from Washington.[145] Rather, the Canadian public shared President Carter's conviction that attendance at the Moscow games in the face of clear-cut Soviet aggression would be inappropriate. Ironically, however, the American boycott of the Moscow Olympics saw a complete reversal of the American and Canadian roles. In 1976, the Ford administration had wanted Trudeau to keep politics out of the Olympics; in 1980, the Carter administration wanted Trudeau to use the Olympics to make a political statement. Evidently what had been "a fundamental principle" for some Ford advisors was of little relevance to the Carter people.

With regard to the wheat embargo, President Carter asked the governments of the world's other major wheat-producing nations – Canada, Australia, and Argentina – not to fill the shortfall created by the American embargo; he did not ask them also to embargo their countries' sales. Joe Clark and Australian Prime Minister Malcolm Fraser agreed not to replace American shipments, but there were some problems with Argentina's military rulers, with whom the Carter administration had ongoing problems because of their human rights record. However, the suspension of wheat sales turned out to be more damaging to American farmers, who needed the markets, than to Soviet consumers. Early in 1981, the newly elected Reagan administration resumed wheat sales to the Soviet Union.[146]

Quebec Independence and North American Defence

Since 1940, when President Franklin D. Roosevelt and Prime Minister Mackenzie King signed the Ogdensburg Agreement, which created the Permanent Joint Board on Defense (PJBD), the United States and Canada had cooperated in the defence of North America. When the United States and Canada became charter members of NATO in 1949 and formed the North American Air Defense Command (NORAD) in 1957, the cooperation became more formal. The possible secession of the province of Quebec from Canada would necessarily complicate defence arrangements for North America. At the very least, agreements would require approval from three governments instead of two. The secession of Quebec might also bring a challenge to the Monroe Doctrine. A premier of Quebec, Jacques Parizeau (1994-5), thought that an independent Quebec could actually blackmail the United States. Given the sanctity of the Monroe Doctrine, any American government would, according to Parizeau's logic, rush to recognize an independent Quebec before France could establish a sphere of influence there.[147] Despite these arguments, successive American governments exhibited a fair measure of complacency in the face of possible Quebec independence.

The year 1967 witnessed the birth of the Parti Québécois (PQ), pledged to bring about Quebec independence. The PQ's leader was a charismatic ex-cabinet minister, René Lévesque. In November 1976, days after the defeat of President Ford by Jimmy Carter, the PQ won a provincial election and Lévesque became premier of his province. In spring 1980, Lévesque held a referendum on independence (which he euphemistically labelled "sovereignty-association"). Neither the Ford nor the Carter administration appears to have taken the possible disintegration of Canada seriously.

In fact, the possibility that Quebec might secede from Canada had been a matter of some concern more than a decade before the Ford presidency: as early as *1964*, even before the de Gaulle visit and the birth of the Parti Québécois. On 1 April 1964, Ambassador Butterworth advised the State Department that Canadian anglophones, tired of Quebec's demands, were taking a "go-to-hell" attitude toward Quebec. This lack of sympathy, Butterworth feared, would produce "even deeper resentment in Quebec." That the disintegration of Canada was contrary to the interests of the United States struck Butterworth as "self-evident truth," and he urged his government to "stand clearly and scrupulously aloof from this major internal problem." Unfortunately, as far as Butterworth was concerned, an American policy of detachment was not likely to last because Quebec nationalists tended to regard Americans as well as Anglo-Canadians among those who had exploited them. Butterworth also feared that if New York moneylenders continued to meet the borrowing demands of the Quebec government, Quebec would find itself less dependent than ever on the financial resources of the rest of Canada and "we [Americans] may soon find ourselves in unwilling collaboration with forces tending to dismember Canada." At the same time, warned Butterworth, the United States "must not give any appearance of discriminating against Quebec."[148] Despite Ambassador Butterworth's concern, Quebec failed to maintain the attention of the White House.

Prime Minister Trudeau has written that he and President Ford "became good friends."[149] In 1976, the Ford administration invited Canada to join the G-7, which had organized the previous year as the G-5 association of the democracies with the strongest economies: France, West Germany, Japan, the United Kingdom, and the United States. (At the request of France, Italy joined at the same time as Canada.) National Security Adviser Brent Scowcroft established an excellent working relationship with his Ottawa counterpart, Ivan Head, as well as with the Canadian embassy in Washington.

President Carter's national security advisor, Zbigniew Brzezinski, Polish by birth but a one-time resident of Montreal and a graduate of McGill University in that city, often refused to meet visiting Canadians, even important ones. Among those whom he declined to meet was Jean Chrétien, then Trudeau's ranking cabinet minister from the province of Quebec, who was in Washington for talks on trade with Vice President Walter Mondale.[150] (Mondale handled American-Canadian relations for the Carter administration.) Another was Maurice Strong, president of Petro-Can (a large oil company owned by the Canadian government) and the former head of the United Nations Environment Program, who visited Washington shortly before Mondale's trip to Ottawa and Edmonton.[151] (Brzezinski was on a first-name basis with Trudeau's special adviser, Ivan Head, whom he met a few times.[152]) On 1 October 1977, when Brzezinski agreed to a television interview with three senior journalists from the Canadian Television Network, his interviewers – Henry Champ, Michael Maclear, and Peter Trueman – sought his opinions on Quebec independence. When Brzezinski replied that he had not seriously studied the matter, the interviewers were incredulous. An independent Quebec, they said, might affect NORAD. Surely Brzezinski must have thought of that. The national security advisor replied that if the journalists could see the flow of paper across his desk, they would understand the reasons for his not thinking about Quebec.[153]

There is further evidence of Brzezinski's indifference. Less than a month before President Carter's proposed trip to Ottawa and less than a year before Quebec's long-promised sovereignty referendum of 1980, Brzezinski refused to meet the newly appointed American ambassador to Canada, Kenneth Curtis. Aides explained that his schedule was "too crowded."[154] The Carter presidential library has a transcript of an interview given by

Brzezinski and key aides on 18 February 1982, a little more than two years after their departure from public office. They discussed at length the Panama Canal treaties, Middle East problems, events in Iran, the establishment of diplomatic relations with Communist China, the SALT talks, and the Soviet invasion of Afghanistan. However, in ninety-one pages of single-spaced type, there is no mention of Canada, let alone Quebec.[155] In December 1977, Mondale and Brzezinski had met to discuss "Increasing Canadian Participation in the Inter-American System."[156] Canada's lack of response seems to have ended whatever interest in Canada Brzezinski had.

On 15 September 1996, when the Cold War was long over, Tom Campbell, a Republican member of the House of Representatives – raised the subject of Quebec independence before a house subcommittee. Campbell believed that the disintegration of Canada would jeopardize American interests, not least because of NATO and NORAD. Would Quebec be a member of either or both? If not, would Canada's contributions be less than they had previously been? Would navigation on the strategically important St. Lawrence Seaway operate under different rules?[157] If these issues were important in 1996, they should have been of greater significance during the Cold War. In any event, most of Campbell's colleagues on the subcommittee in 1996 shared Brzezinski's earlier indifference. When the matter of possible Quebec independence came to the top of the agenda, most of them left the room to handle what appeared to be more important matters. The American media shared the representatives' indifference. Most, if not all, of the journalists in attendance were Canadians.

Jean-François Lisée's book, *In the Eye of the Eagle*, gives the impression that Quebec was a serious concern of the Carter administration.[158] We have no quarrel with Lisée's facts, and admire his determined research. However, Lisée went out of his way to study American interest in Quebec, and interviewed many people keen on that subject. Accordingly, he may have left the impression that Americans as a whole were more interested than they were in Quebec independence. Admittedly, a briefing paper prepared for Mondale at the time of Jean Chrétien's 1977 visit summarizes the Carter administration's Quebec policy: "We believe that a strong and unified Canada is in the best interest of the United States, but the future of Quebec is a Canadian internal domestic issue which must be resolved by Canadians themselves."[159]

Professors Granatstein and Bothwell agree with Lisée that initially President Carter and his colleagues were concerned about the possibility of Quebec independence, but they say that any concern evaporated early in the administration when the Canadian prime minister visited Washington. Trudeau's assurances on this subject were so credible that his hosts may have decided that it was safe to ignore Quebec and concentrate on more urgent problems.[160]

It is obvious that the Carter White House did not give much thought to Canada as an ally. All references to Canada in President Carter's memoirs deal with Canadian support for American positions in multilateral forums – at the Tokyo G-7 meeting of 1979 and the Venice G-7 meeting of 1980, in dealings with Iranians and Soviets. Every instance is from 1979 or 1980, most of them during Joe Clark's brief prime ministership (June 1979 until February 1980), and not one reference deals with a bilateral issue. It is obvious that in critical situations, President Carter felt that he could count on Joe Clark and, to almost the same degree, on Pierre Trudeau. Few other allies were as consistently reliable.[161]

At an earlier stage of the Cold War, difficulties over NORAD might have been a cause for concern, if not reason for a trip to Ottawa, by a high American official. While there was little doubt that both American and Canadian governments would agree to extend the life of NORAD, there were problems. Granatstein and Bothwell have suggested that by the time of its scheduled renewal in 1980, NORAD appeared less important than it had been. By that time, it seemed implausible that the Soviets might use aircraft (rather than missiles) to launch a surprise attack on North America, and Soviet-American agreements on anti-ballistic missiles (ABMs) had lessened the chances of interceptions above Canada or the perceived American need for ABMs stationed on Canadian territory.[162] In the end, the Carter administration agreed to NORAD's temporary extension for a maximum of twelve months, but it was only after President Reagan visited Ottawa in March 1981 that the Canadian minister of external affairs, Mark MacGuigan, and Reagan's secretary of state, Alexander Haig, signed a new five-year agreement. That agreement took into account the new technological realities: NORAD would henceforth stand for North American *Aerospace* Defense Command.[163]

The saga is ongoing. In 1985, the Reagan administration in Washington and Brian Mulroney's government in Ottawa signed the North American Air Defense Modernization Accord. There would be 52 radar sites (47 of them in Canada). "Canada was assigned responsibility for designing and constructing the short-range radar stations [39 of the stations, 36 of them in Canada], procuring the system's communications, and providing the total system integration of sites in Canada. It was agreed that Canada would pay roughly 12% of the total modernization bill."[164] Even if the danger from across the pole had lessened or disappeared, rogue states from other parts of the world (such as Libya and Iraq) might threaten North America with isolated attacks. Just one bomb, even if not a nuclear bomb, could destroy considerable life and property, and American and Canadian military strategists have an obligation to prevent such an event. The return to office in 1994 of a Parti Québécois government pledged to the independence of Quebec and the narrow victory for a united Canada in

Quebec's 1995 referendum can hardly be pluses as far as continental defence is concerned and may help explain President Clinton's interest in Canada's survival as one country at the time of Quebec's 1995 referendum. In a recently published book, James Blanchard, US ambassador to Canada from 1993 to 1996, claims to have played an active role in keeping Canada united during the weeks before the October 1995 referendum. He tried to persuade members of the Clinton administration to do what they could to ensure a federalist victory. Notably, Prime Minister Chrétien and his closest advisors were able to consult Blanchard and experts in Washington on short notice.[165]

Conclusions

American policy during the latter Cold War is harder to analyze than for the early years, when the world, and thus American policy, seemed relatively simple. The controversy over nuclear weapons, intense as it was at the time, does not add much to our understanding of America's Canada policy. Canada had requested these weapons, and the US which, after revising its defence plans to accommodate the Diefenbaker administration, insisted that it had the right to station them at the agreed sites. One could argue that the American government's insistence on stationing the nuclear warheads, whether or not the Canadian government would accept them, smacks of a determination to treat Canada as a satellite, but given the divisions within Canada and even within the Diefenbaker cabinet, such an interpretation would be unfair. The whole situation can be attributed to the state of disintegration of the Diefenbaker government. Given a consistent and united Canadian decision not to accept nuclear weapons, perhaps the American government would not have been as persistent as it was.

When the United States first became involved in Indochina and Canada agreed to serve on the International Control Commission, Canada, the ever helpful ally, was willing to observe the peace and do some minor mediating, as in the Seaborn mission. But as American concern over Indochina and especially Vietnam deepened, the American administration was no longer willing to have Canada play the role of independent mediator. Instead, it pressured the Canadian government not only to support whatever the US did, but also to gather information for the US in North Vietnam. At the same time, Canada's status as a member of the ICC gave it a special role in America's Vietnam policy. Americans often consulted or informed Canadians of their impending actions when few other governments were similarly advised.

As the war in Vietnam intensified, so too did Canadian opposition. The Johnson administration would not tolerate opposition toward the war from such a close ally, when the honour and credibility of the United

States seemed at stake. So what little Canada policy there was during these years consisted of American reactions to Canada's perceived meddling, until toward the end of the war, when the Canadian government agreed to serve, for nine months only, on the International Commission of Control and Supervision. Canada showed its independence by withdrawing before the war was over. So the cycle of American policies had come full turn. From being considered a respected and helpful independent ally, Canada was downgraded to a despised meddler, then again became a respected ally. On Indochina, Canada, along with India, Australia, and the United Kingdom, always had a special status in American policy, but the nature of that status varied. At times, Canada showed its independence, but its policy made no difference to what the US did.

With respect to Cuba, the Eisenhower and Kennedy administrations began the embargo and other policies designed to counter Castro's Cuba with high hopes for cooperation from Canada. The expectation that Canada, America's "foremost ally," would surely go along constitutes an example of Canada as an ally that is taken for granted. But when Canadian cooperation was not forthcoming, American administrations began to ignore Canada and turned hostile. Indeed, American attempts to impose American laws on Canadian branches of American firms constitute a clear example of attempted extraterritorial jurisdiction; that is, treatment of Canada as a satellite. During the Cuban Missile Crisis, however, Canada was all but forgotten.

In Cyprus, Canada played the role of good friend and ally by sending peacekeepers to a spot where the Americans were especially anxious to prevent war. Whether it was the Canadian or American leaders who persuaded others to send troops, the Canadian example seems to have persuaded others to join. Canada, as a special friend and ally, could be relied on to rally when others were reluctant.

On China, the Canadian government of Lester Pearson tried hard to play a constructive role, but the Americans were not playing the same game. They maintained their hard line on the PRC, and as a result gave Canada no special role. In a final irony, when Canada *did* establish diplomatic relations in 1970, President Nixon became annoyed that Canada had done so before the United States. Then, after the Soviet invasion of Afghanistan, the Canadian government almost meekly acquiesced in whatever measures the Carter administration asked it to take. Yet, there is no evidence that the American government asked more of the Canadians than of its other allies.

As for the threat of Quebec separation from Canada and its implications for the defence of North America, the Ford and Carter administrations again seemed to see *no need for a policy* on Canadian issues, even faced with such a momentous change as the potential break-up of Canada. Instead, the two American presidents pursued other priorities and seemed to give Canada barely a thought.

Changes to NORAD and modernization of the North American defence infrastructure could be considered exceptional because they applied only to Canada. However, because these changes came at a time when the American government was also pushing other governments to modernize their defences and to accept more up-to-date American weapons, one could also speak of a Canadian policy in which Canada was one ally among others.

In summary, this chapter has found that for much of the 1960s and 1970s, the Canada policies of the various American administrations were inconsistent or non-existent. With the exception of the Quebec issue, all of the issues discussed in this chapter caused the American government to initiate policies that included Canada among other allies. Even trouble north of the border – the likelihood of the break-up of Canada – did not shake American administrations out of their forgetfulness toward Canada. On political and foreign policy issues, Canada was little more, sometimes less, than one good ally among others.

4
North-South Issues

One of President Ford's advisors, Arthur Burns, wrote in the mid-1970s: "Canada has a special relationship with the Third World which can be useful to us. It has no colonial history, and has played a leading role in peacekeeping operations. As a bilingual country, it has ties with both the Commonwealth and the francophone Third World. It is the world's sixth largest aid donor."[1] The purpose of this chapter is to determine the extent to which successive American governments actually found Canada a useful partner in Third World issues during the Cold War years.

Americans entered the Cold War with a glow of idealism toward the countries of Asia, Africa, and the Pacific. They believed that as former colonials themselves they understood the peoples there better than did the European colonialists, and, unlike most Europeans, the American government advocated political independence for most of these colonies, if not immediately, then at least within the foreseeable future. In the late 1940s and 1950s, Americans also had an almost naive faith in economic development. They believed that with relatively small amounts of economic aid and technical assistance, most of the countries of Asia, Africa, and Latin America could soon begin to "take off" into rapid economic development and a consequent improvement in their standard of living. Americans were somewhat less idealistic in their policies toward the Western Hemisphere, which they had seen as essential to their security since the Monroe Doctrine of 1823, and where Americans had long held economic interests. There was thus a marked contrast between American policy toward Guatemala, where the State Department suspected Communist influence when the government tried to nationalize unused foreign land in 1953, and the policy toward the Suez Crisis, which the Eisenhower administration saw largely as a manifestation of European colonialism. That same Eisenhower administration favoured the withdrawal of British and French forces from Egypt, site of the Suez Canal, but an ongoing military presence in Panama.[2] Our case studies illustrate this difference in attitude.

The continuation of the Cold War, however, and the hot war in Vietnam, led to a waning of America's anti-colonialist ardour. Americans began to see Soviet and Chinese influences in various parts of the Third World, not just in Latin America. They perceived a need to counter such influences in most of Africa, in the Middle East, and in India. It also soon became evident that the process of economic development was long and complicated, and that even fairly large amounts of economic aid were not enough. So Americans became disillusioned about giving, and by the late 1960s, most of the American so-called foreign aid consisted of assistance to potential Cold War allies who were believed to be especially vulnerable to Soviet influence or were threatened by Soviet surrogates (for example, Israel and Pakistan). Thus, North-South issues overlapped with East-West issues, and in some cases became extensions of Cold War quarrels.

This chapter includes several cases where the North-South factor seemed to predominate. The Arab-Israeli conflict and certain differences between Latin Americans and United States citizens predated the Cold War and would have continued with or without the Cold War. They are not primarily Cold War issues, even if the Cold War influenced the outcome of certain crises.

Arab-Israeli Relations

As tensions developed between Israel and its Arab neighbours in 1956, the United States sought help from American allies. The Eisenhower administration wanted Israel to survive – in large measure because Jewish Americans had votes – but Secretary of State John Foster Dulles and his subordinates wanted Great Britain, France, Italy, and Canada to supply Israel with weapons. There were several reasons why the United States did not want to be Israel's principal supplier of armaments. Dulles thought that the Soviet Union would be more tolerant of arms sales to the Israelis by other NATO countries than of arms sales by the United States. If the United States were to sell, the "Soviets might redouble their efforts to arm Arabs ... and [an] arms race might result." Second, wrote Dulles, the Arabs would be "less excited" if the vendors were allies of the United States rather than the United States.[3] Moreover, as Dulles told Abba Eban, then the Israeli ambassador in Washington, "The US would imperil what remaining influence it had with the Arab states if it were to become an important supplier of arms to Israel."[4]

Canada's role was particularly vital because Canadair of Montreal could sell the Israeli Air Force F-86 aircraft. Once Israeli pilots learned to fly Canadian F-86s, they would be able to fly US-made F-86s when the moment was opportune to sell them.[5] According to Pearson, the American government was prepared to land some fifty or sixty F-86s in Israel on short notice in an emergency, but Israel would need pilots already trained to fly them.[6] The Canadian government – like the British, French, and Italian – was hardly overjoyed at the prospect of doing for the United States what Americans chose not to do for themselves. Canadians, too, had reason for concern about their relations with the Arab states. Apart from the need for oil for Eastern Canada, Paul Martin, Sr. – then Canada's minister of health and welfare who assisted Pearson at external affairs – foresaw that Canada might be able to play a "potentially useful mediator role with Arabs in various upcoming issues in [the] UN involving [the] Arab bloc."[7] American officials realized that they had to tread with some delicacy, for the Liberal government of Prime Minister Louis St. Laurent did not want to look like an American puppet.[8] In the end, the American government reluctantly agreed to a public announcement that the US would allow the Israelis to purchase helicopters and "scout cars"; thus, Canada would not appear to be Israel's sole benefactor.[9] As soon as the American government made its announcement, Pearson agreed that Canadair would sell twenty-four F-86s. However, none had been delivered before Israel's 29 October 1956 invasion of Egypt, and the Canadian government cancelled the deal.[10]

With regard to the Suez crisis of late October and early November 1956, it was Lester Pearson and United Nations Secretary-General Dag Hammarskjold who provided the initiative.[11] Pearson proposed that United Nations forces separate Egyptians and Israelis and replace the Israelis' British and French allies. Dulles approved of what Pearson was doing, and Canada proved a very useful diplomatic ally. Pearson won the Nobel Peace Prize, defused a touchy situation, and served the interests of many people in many countries, including the United States. The settlement of November 1956 was very different from that of the F-86 sales, for in the arms sales, Washington had plans that Canada reluctantly and temporarily agreed to fulfil. In the post-Suez crisis diplomacy, Pearson had plans with which Dulles and others concurred. Canada definitely proved more useful to the United States in the second instance.

Canada was not so helpful, however, in the case of the Arab-Israeli war of 1967. Disputes over the distribution and ownership of the limited fresh water supply in the Jordan River valley, combined with Arab humiliation over earlier military defeats, led Egyptian president Gamel Abdul Nasser to order United Nations troops out of Egypt. Egyptian forces then occupied Sharm-el Sheik, at the tip of a peninsula on the Sinai coast of the Red Sea, and closed the Strait of Tiran to Israeli shipping. Because Nasser would not allow Israelis to use the Suez Canal, they would have been forced to depend exclusively on the route around the Cape of Good Hope for any commercial transactions with the Far East, the Persian Gulf, and through the Indian Ocean. To avoid such a fate, early in June 1967 the Israeli armed forces launched a pre-emptive strike. Within six days, they managed to defeat Egypt, Syria, and Jordan, and to occupy some of their territory.

By then, Pearson was prime minister of Canada and Paul Martin was minister of external affairs. As war in the Middle East approached, Pearson found himself hosting a luncheon for President Lyndon Johnson and members of his staff, including National Security Adviser Walt Rostow. The occasion was US Day at Montreal's World Fair, Expo 67. Until the morning of the trip to Montreal and to Harrington Lake, the prime minister's country home near Ottawa where Pearson was to host the luncheon, the Americans were not certain whether they would be able to leave Washington. Rostow later explained, "We wanted to go, but we were concerned about the pending war in the Middle East. We did not want to be away from Washington when it started."[12]

After observing the necessary formalities at the Expo site, the dignitaries took a helicopter to Harrington Lake. Martin wanted to use the occasion for serious discussions. President Johnson, however, had other ideas. He wanted to sleep, and he did.[13] Given the international situation, Pearson insisted that they talk about the Middle East over lunch,[14] but Johnson's advisors did not appreciate Pearson's expertise on the region. Although they did discuss the Middle East, Rostow later described the lunch as "amiable" but without discussion of matters of substance.[15] Secretary of State Dean Rusk, who did not go to Montreal, said years later, "We didn't take Canada's views into account. Canada played a very small role in US Middle Eastern policy. We heeded the Israelis and the Arabs."[16]

Pearson died in 1972, and evidence that Canadian diplomacy was an important consideration before or after the 1973 Middle East War does not appear to exist.

Yemen

One of the Kennedy administration's major concerns in the second half of 1962 and throughout 1963 was Yemen, an Arab country that Secretary Rusk considered a "backwater."[17] That Yemen should command so much attention when the Cuban Missile Crisis took place, when the Soviets were threatening (or appearing to threaten) Western interests in Berlin – when China was occupying Indian territory, and when coups overthrew governments in Syria and Iraq – all indicate its perceived importance in Washington.[18] In September 1962, Yemeni rebels overthrew that country's monarchy and established a republic. The Egyptian government of Colonel Abdul Gamel Nasser supported Yemeni republicans, while the Saudi Royal Family backed the royalists. Nasser sent soldiers and aircraft to Yemen, while Saudi forces went to the Yemeni-Saudi border. The Egyptian air force bombed villages in Saudi Arabia, and Egypt and Saudi Arabia suspended diplomatic relations.

Because of its oil reserves, Saudi Arabia had become a vital American interest. Official Washington feared a serious Saudi-Egyptian war that might involve the Soviets, Nasser's principal outside supporters at the time. Already the Soviets and the People's Republic of China were sending weapons and technical advisors to Yemen.[19] Given the importance of Saudi Arabia and the relative unimportance of Yemen beyond the fact that it bordered on Saudi Arabia, the Kennedy administration promoted a cease-fire and the stationing of United Nations forces along the Saudi-Yemeni border. By April 1963, the principal parties to the dispute agreed that a United Nations Yemen Observer Mission (UNYOM) would patrol a demili-tarized zone twenty kilometres from each side of the Saudi-Yemeni border.[20]

Canada had no direct interests in Yemen. Weeks after the republican takeover, Howard Green sent a telegram to several Canadian embassies which stated: "We are almost entirely dependent on UK and USA sources for information as to the actual situation in Yemen." Green was also con-cerned that the longer the conflict continued, the greater the likelihood that the Soviets and Egyptians might increase their influence in Yemen.[21] It was his intention to recognize the Yemeni Republican government immediately after the United States did so,[22] and that is what happened. The Kennedy administration recognized the Yemeni Republicans 19 December 1962, and Canada followed suit two days later. Nevertheless, the initiative to send Canadian service personnel to Yemen came from the United Nations, not from Canada, and it did not happen until late spring 1963. By then, Lester Pearson's Liberal government had replaced the Con-servative government of John Diefenbaker, and Paul Martin had replaced Howard Green as minister of external affairs.

At the time, the United Nations had two military operations in the Middle East, the United Nations Truce Supervisory Organization (UNTSO) in Jerusalem and the United Nations Emergency Force (UNEF) along the Israeli-Egyptian border; Canadians were part of both operations. United Nations Secretary-General U Thant requested the transfer of some person-nel and equipment from UNTSO and UNEF to the Saudi-Yemeni border for four to six months,[23] and Paul Martin agreed. On 13 June 1963, Martin told the House of Commons that Canada would be sending troops to Yemen, and leaders of the three opposition parties expressed approval.

By autumn 1963, it was obvious that six months were not sufficient. If the United Nations forces were to leave, chaos might descend on the area. Because Yemen was of little interest to Canadians, Pearson and Martin did not jump at the opportunity for further service there. However, the Kennedy administration wanted the Canadian soldiers to stay, and Wash-ington's will prevailed. Robert W. Komer of the National Security Council summarized events in a letter of 19 October 1963 to his boss, McGeorge Bundy: "We finally got [Adlai] Stevenson [American ambassador to the United Nations] to beat up Paul Martin on keeping Canadians in UNYOM (I've been threatening to urge JFK [to] write Pearson if State didn't get off the dime.) Canadians have agreed if Yugoslavs will stay, plus certain other conditions not yet clear. But we told Canadians [the] President had braced Tito, and this greatly impressed them with JFK interest. As you know, Tito said he'd certainly consider it and JFK drove point home by asking Tito to let us know pronto."[24]

In this case, Canada was a helpful ally, one which took political (and life-threatening) risks for its American neighbour. The United Kingdom had interests in neighbouring Aden and was reluctant to embrace the Yemeni republicans for fear that such an action might strengthen Egyptian influence. As Parliament met in January 1963, Under-Secretary of State for External Affairs Norman A. Robertson prepared Green for a possible hostile question about Canada's recognition of the Yemeni Republic "while a friendly power principally concerned in the area, the United Kingdom, has continued to withhold recognition."[25] While Diefenbaker's Conservatives, best remembered for conflict with the Kennedy administration, fully supported Kennedy's policies in Yemen, it was the Liberal government that required some prodding from Washington. The last Canadians left Yemen on 4 September 1964, but the war continued for another three years.[26]

Panama

In January 1964, Prime Minister Pearson, External Affairs Minister Martin, and other ranking Canadians travelled to Washington for an official visit – Pearson's first after President Kennedy's funeral. Less than two weeks earlier, tens of thousands of Panamanians had rioted along the border separating the US-controlled Panama Canal Zone from the Republic of Panama, and between 9 January and 13 January, twenty-four Panamanians and four American soldiers died in the violence. More than 200 Panamanians as well as eighty-five Americans were wounded.[27] The morning of 22 January, Paul Martin, Charles Ritchie – Canada's ambassador in Washington – and other Canadian officials met for talks with Under-Secretary of State George Ball, with Walton Butterworth – the American ambassador to Canada – and others. According to State Department notes, Paul Martin brought little knowledge and few strong opinions to the talks. He began by asking if "it were true that a crisis in Panama arises periodically." Ball replied that the last eruption had taken place in 1959 and then lectured him on the differences between the Suez and Panama Canals and the need for ongoing American control in Panama.[28] Paul Martin had so little interest in the subject that he did not mention it in his voluminous memoirs. Neither did Lester Pearson, who arrived late for those particular talks, nor had John Diefenbaker, Canadian prime minister at the time of the 1959 eruption. As for George Ball, his memoirs fail to mention Canada in connection with Panama or with any other subject.[29]

In the aftermath of the January 1964 riots, the Johnson administration began negotiations for a new canal treaty with Panama. These negotiations continued throughout the Nixon and Ford administrations and came to fruition in 1977, the first year of Jimmy Carter's presidency. To add credibility to the two treaties he managed to negotiate with the Panamanian government of Omar Torrijos, and to raise the stakes so that the United States Senate would feel a moral obligation to give the necessary two-thirds vote of approval, President Carter invited heads of government from most Western Hemisphere nations (other than Cuba) to witness the formal signing.[30] Canada's Pierre Elliott Trudeau received an invitation and went. However, when the Canadian prime minister met President Carter, Panama was not on the list of topics for discussion.[31] Whether Trudeau's presence, among those of dozens of others, may have swayed a few votes in the Senate, where the treaty squeaked through by only two votes, is doubtful. At any rate, Panama does not appear to have been a matter of serious concern to Trudeau.

The Dominican Republic

The Eisenhower and Kennedy administrations wanted Canada to become an active member of the Organization of American States (OAS),[32] but events in the Dominican Republic – among others – delayed Canadian membership. Ottawa saw little point in involvement in controversies between the Dominican people and the United States. With regard to the Dominican Republic, successive Canadian governments pursued policies out of step with American policies. There was no desire on Canada's part to be helpful or supportive. There was definitely no special relationship.

Information reaching Ottawa suggested White House support for the dictatorship of Rafael Leonidas Trujillo as late as 1960. In January 1960, a Canadian businessman anxious to do business in the Dominican Republic advised the Canadian government that, according to Vice President Richard Nixon, Trujillo was an ally in the struggle against Communism who ran a government that was sympathetic to the cause of multinational corporations. Nixon was cited as having said: "That there is a great necessity for North Americans to encourage leaders of governments, such as General Trujillo, to build up stability in their countries ... to remember that these people are defenders of free enterprise; that they are friends; that their people on the whole are well treated and that, although they may appear to us to be dictators, nevertheless they are defenders of our way of life and we should encourage them."[33]

Members of Canada's business community evidently agreed with this approach. According to the British embassy in the Dominican Republic, the Bank of Nova Scotia (BNS) – which had branches in that country and thus was more vulnerable than the Canadian government to pressure from Trujillo – had made some questionable loans to the dictator in 1959. "It is believed," said the British embassy report of 9 February 1960, "that the Bank of Nova Scotia had taken the risk of being involved in a political scandal should the present Dominican Government collapse." A Royal Bank official in Ciudad Trujillo – then the name of that country's capital city – estimated that the BNS loan approximated $50 million. According to the same official, the BNS had physically removed the "monetary gold reserve of the Dominican Central Bank" to Canada for safekeeping.[34]

By contrast, documents from Canada's Department of External Affairs demonstrate that the department became disgusted with the regime of Trujillo (1930-61) before Nixon, Eisenhower's vice president, did. The Canadian embassy in Ciudad Trujillo reported that Trujillo's days were probably numbered and rightly so. His government deserved no support on either moral or financial grounds. On 19 November 1959, an official at the Department of External Affairs warned that support for Trujillo would create ill will for Canada "throughout the rest of Latin America," and said: "Surely you do not give a high credit-rating to a prospective borrower, however apparently well-off now, who is in serious danger of losing his job and whose indebtedness his successor may not recognize!"[35]

Later in 1960, the Eisenhower administration finally realized that if it wanted support from other Latin American governments in the OAS against Fidel Castro's tyranny in Cuba, it had to withdraw support from Trujillo's tyranny in the Dominican Republic. The double standard was not justifiable, especially when Castro's domestic policies were more defensible than Trujillo's. Highlighting the comparison was the presence of the deposed Cuban leader Fulgencio Batista, Castro's predecessor, in Ciudad Trujillo, where he had fled. To make matters worse, in 1960 Trujillo was part of (probably instigator of) a plot to assassinate the elected president of Venezuela, Romulo Betancourt (1958-63). Members of the OAS considered the evidence against Trujillo's involvement so persuasive that all agreed to impose diplomatic and economic sanctions against the Trujillo regime.

The Canadian government, by contrast, continued a business as usual policy, at least up to a point. As early as 26 January 1959, less than a month after Castro's triumph, Canada's minister of trade and commerce, Gordon Churchill, announced refusal of a permit to export twelve aged Vampire jets to the Dominican Republic. According to W.B. McCullough, Canadian chargé d'affaires in the Dominican Republic, the Trujillo regime was "shocked" that Canada would leave the Dominican Republic so exposed to possible Cuban aggression.[36] Yet, aware of OAS pressures to sever relations with Castro's Cuba, the Diefenbaker government regarded compliance with the OAS decision on the Dominican Republic as "a dangerous precedent."[37] Others might have sanctions, economic and diplomatic, against the Trujillo regime, but Diefenbaker's Canada would have no part of them. Under-Secretary of State for External Affairs Norman A. Robertson advised the minister, Howard Green, that an OAS committee had "formally condemned" the Trujillo regime with "the denial of free assembly and of free speech, arbitrary arrests, cruel and inhuman treatment of political prisoners, and the use of intimidation and terror as a political weapon." Green, however, had a simple reply. "There was to be no change in Canadian representation in [the] Dominican Republic with whom we have no quarrel."[38] There is no evidence of any American attempt to persuade Canada to change these policies.

Government by Trujillo and other members of his family ended in 1961 when gunmen assassinated Trujillo. President Kennedy then sent warships within sight of the Dominican capital. Various Trujillos who had held positions of authority fled into exile, and the American embassy helped to organize elections. Ciudad Trujillo reverted to its previous name, Santo Domingo, and in December 1962 the Dominican electorate chose as president Juan Bosch, an idealist who had spent the Trujillo years in exile. The Canadian government did not participate in any of these activities.

Despite the presence of the Bank of Nova Scotia and the Royal Bank of Canada, and the interest of Falconbridge (a Canadian mining corporation), the Canadian government continued to maintain a low profile in the Dominican Republic. Conspirators ousted Bosch in 1963 within a few months of his inauguration, and both the United States and Canada recognized the junta that replaced him and maintained their embassies. (President Kennedy ordered his ambassador home, but shortly after the Kennedy assassination, President Johnson sent another in his place.) Both American and Canadian embassies remained in Santo Domingo until April 1965, when Bosch supporters attempted to restore the elected president so that he could complete his term in office.

At that point, President Lyndon Johnson sent US Marines to the Dominican Republic, ostensibly to protect the lives of American citizens but also to prevent the Dominican Republic from becoming another Cuba – pro-Soviet and Communist. Because many Americans thought that the White House was exaggerating the Communist threat to the Dominican Republic,[39] the Johnson administration appreciated whatever international support it could muster. For example, in an attempt to make the military intervention appear international, the administration asked other members of the Organization of American States (OAS) to supply troops for the Dominican Republic, and some did. Because Canada did not belong to the OAS, it neither received an invitation nor volunteered to send any forces. To the contrary, in his memoirs Paul Martin, Sr., said that the Dominican invasion was a deterrent to more extensive Canadian involvement in Latin America,[40] and in his year-end report, Ambassador

Butterworth – never one to err on the side of optimism – referred to "private reservations over the initially unilateral action of the US in Santo Domingo," but he seems not to have asked for Canadian support. Also, the American embassy in Ottawa noted considerable doubts in the Canadian media. In 1966, Juan Bosch and Joaquín Balaguer – the last figurehead president under Trujillo – challenged each other in another presidential election, and Balaguer won. "Re-elected" honestly or otherwise at four-year intervals, he remained president of the Dominican Republic (except between 1978 and 1986) until 1996.

After Pierre Trudeau replaced Pearson as prime minister, he and his government considered the possibility of Canadian membership in the OAS. The State Department took due note of that fact and of the opposition to membership on the part of Diefenbaker's successor as Conservative leader, Robert Stanfield. It did not, however, try to influence the Canadian decision, and the Trudeau government did not pursue this question. Richard Nixon became president of the United States and supported Balaguer as he had Trujillo. The Canadian mining corporation Falconbridge Limited invested almost $200 million in an operation at Bonao in the Dominican Republic. Of that sum, $20 million came from yet another Canadian bank, the Canadian Imperial Bank of Commerce. In 1971, Falconbridge Dominicana became operational.[41]

In 1969, the Trudeau government had decided to close its embassy in Santo Domingo – not because it found the Balaguer government repulsive, nor on any matter of principle, but for reasons of financial and political expediency. If it closed Canada's embassies in the Dominican Republic, Ecuador, and Uruguay, the government could open new ones at the Vatican and in certain French-speaking countries of Africa. Canada's embassy in Caracas, Venezuela, would look after Canadian interests in the Dominican Republic. At the same time, Canada would maintain its embassy in Haiti, where Canadian interests were less substantial but where the ruling class spoke French. As it formulated policy on the Dominican Republic, the Trudeau government thought more about opinion in Quebec than about Washington.

In 1990, when George Bush was president of the United States and Brian Mulroney, prime minister of Canada, Canada *did* join the OAS. Its entry all but coincided with President Bush's invasion of Panama and capture of its military strongman, Manuel Noriega. The kind of unilateral American military action in the Dominican Republic that had disturbed Paul Martin was a matter of relative indifference to Brian Mulroney. Canadian, not American, priorities had driven Canadian policies toward the Dominican Republic, but in the case of Panama, the Canadian government of the day lacked strong convictions.

British Guiana

British Guiana on the South American mainland was another problem. Since 1953, British authorities had been allowing elections for the colonial legislative assembly, and the winner each time was the People's Progressive Party (PPP), led by the pro-Soviet Cheddi Jagan. Other British colonies in the area, most notably Jamaica and Trinidad in 1962, had received their independence, and the British did not want to prolong colonial rule indefinitely in British Guiana. Yet the American and British governments did not want British Guiana to receive its independence while Cheddi Jagan was prime minister and the PPP formed the government.[42]

Canadians, like Americans, had extensive investments in British Guiana – most notably in aluminum, banking, and life insurance. Despite policy differences over Cuba (see Chapter 3), Canadians could not afford to be indifferent to a Communist British Guiana, and it was hardly surprising that British Guiana was on the agenda when Johnson and Pearson met in Washington in January 1964. President Johnson's staff thought Paul Martin, who was also present, to be hopelessly naive about Jagan. Rusk and Martin had discussed British Guiana on 4 December 1963, less than two weeks into the Johnson presidency. At that time, Martin had told Rusk that the Canadian government was contemplating sending an envoy who would assess the situation. Then Canada might open a mission in Georgetown, British Guiana's capital, and Paul Martin himself might visit. The Johnson White House thought it appropriate for Canada to open an office in Georgetown, but it did not want Paul Martin or any other senior Canadian official to visit British Guiana and enhance Jagan's prestige. The Americans claimed to have known since 1961 that Jagan was a Soviet surrogate. The issue seemed sufficiently critical that despite the Christmas season, the State Department summoned officials of the Canadian embassy in Washington for talks, and American embassy officials in Ottawa discussed British Guiana with the Department of External Affairs. These talks went well from the American point of view, and by the time Johnson and Pearson were about to meet, the Johnson White House was fairly confident that neither Martin nor "any other high-ranking Canadian" would visit British Guiana. On 15 December 1963, Martin had told the American embassy in Ottawa that he did not want "a second Castro in the region."

The Johnson/Pearson summit resolved any differences over British Guiana quickly, quietly, and amicably. Canada would send its own "commissioner" to British Guiana, Milton Gregg, a former minister of labour in the government of Louis St. Laurent. (Because Canada and British Guiana both were parts of the Commonwealth, they could not exchange ambassadors, and because British Guiana was still a colony, Gregg would not be a high commissioner like Canada's heads of mission in London, Canberra, and Wellington.) According to the memorandum of conversation, George Ball, the under-secretary of state, "repeated that the United States thought it was a good idea for Canada to be represented there."[43]

In the end, however, the British and American governments "resolved" the British Guiana problem without Canadian help. They changed the voting system to one of proportional representation, so that Jagan's arch-rival, Forbes Burnham, could win the election of 1964. Henceforth, Guyanese would vote like Israelis, not like Britons. The entire country would be one vast constituency, and each party's share of the seats in the legislature would be proportional to that party's share of the popular vote. In 1966, the British Labour government of Harold Wilson allowed British Guiana its independence under Burnham's leadership. Over the next two decades, Burnham – chosen over the pro-Soviet Jagan – nationalized British, American, and Canadian companies, all but eliminated the private sector, rigged elections, imposed tight foreign exchange controls, and forged closer relations with Communist China, Cuba, and North Korea. But his party did keep Jagan out of power until 1992, by which time the Cold War had ended.

Law of the Sea

The quarrel between the United States and Canada over the extent of territorial waters – an ongoing issue throughout the twentieth century[44] – became more heated after the Second World War. In 1950, the State Department included Canada in a list of twenty-two countries – the rest of which were in Europe, Asia, and Latin America – that it considered guilty of "the illegal and unwarranted seizure of United States commerce on the high seas or the shooting down of United States planes in the air column above the high seas."[45] In 1951, a State Department paper noted "numerous issues with Canada concerning jurisdiction over territorial waters."[46] That same year, the State Department specifically rejected the "sector theory," that Canada and other arctic nations owned a pie-shaped piece of the Arctic Ocean between their arctic coastlines and the North Pole.[47]

According to international law at the time, waters within three miles of the coastline were part of the territory of the adjacent country. Beyond the three-mile limit, waters were international, open to ships and fishermen of all nations. Left to themselves, this law was what most Americans wished to preserve, so that the United States Navy might have the maximum area in which to conduct operations[48] and New England and Pacific coast fishermen maximum access to the world's best fisheries. In 1951, more than a year before Eisenhower's election to the presidency, a State Department policy statement clearly said: "The US Government does not recognize the sector claims of the Soviet Union and Canada in the areas north of their accepted territorial limits."[49] The statement made clear that ownership of land areas was no problem, but that any Canadian or Soviet claims to a pie-shaped swath of ocean from their respective mainlands to the North Pole could not stand.

Desirable as it might appear, the status quo seemed unlikely to last very much longer. Iceland wanted control over the fishing grounds off its shores.[50] The Philippines and Indonesia wanted sovereignty over the waters that separated their islands. Some nations that had achieved independence in recent years appeared to want change for its own sake.[51] At the first Law of the Sea (LOS) Conference, held in 1958, pressure for extension of the territorial waters beyond three miles was so strong that the Eisenhower administration realized that it would have to make a strategic retreat. Even such allies as the Philippines, South Korea, and Nationalist China – whose survival might depend on the United States Navy – disliked the three-mile limit.[52] Failure to agree on a new LOS, the American government feared, might result in unilateral proclamations of twelve-mile limits by many countries and then potential hostilities between them and the United States Navy.[53] Some compromises seemed advisable, and at times Canada offered what appeared to be the best compromises.

The first Canadian compromise was a three-plus-nine formula. Three miles would remain the limit for a country's territorial waters, but the country could enforce its fishing regulations for the next nine miles. Such a formula would have some negative impact on American fishermen and a much stronger negative impact on Portuguese fishermen who for centuries had fished off the Canadian coast, but it would not restrict the US Navy.[54] That Canadian proposal failed to attract the two-thirds vote necessary for approval and died.[55] Over the next two years at successive LOS conferences, Canada put forth other proposals, which drew mixed reactions from American authorities. In April 1958, when Canada was promoting a six-plus-six mile formula, the American delegation to the conference on the LOS lamented "the completely selfish attitude of Canada."[56] Yet, within eighteen months a six-plus-six idea had become the joint "Canadian-US proposal" and the American government was seeking British support.[57] In the end, however, the coastal states failed to agree on any changes to the LOS.[58] As far as the Eisenhower administration was concerned, Canada was an erratic ally of limited utility on LOS matters.

Whatever frustration the Eisenhower administration had felt with Diefenbaker and Green over the LOS paled into relative insignificance over the next few years. The Kennedy and Johnson administrations took a strong stand over the Pearson government's decision that the Gulf of St. Lawrence was an inland Canadian waterway, as Canadian as Lake Athabaska and equally off limits to foreign commercial fishermen and navies. When Kennedy and Pearson met at Hyannisport in May 1963, they discussed the problem, but agreement proved impossible. Subsequent talks proved equally fruitless.[59] Aware that this issue might set a dangerous precedent for the United States Navy in other parts of the world and limit the waters open to American fishermen, Secretary of State Dean Rusk was furious. The State Department made its position clear to Paul Martin in 1964,[60] and put the issue onto the agenda when Pearson visited the White House in January 1964, again when the president and the prime minister met in September 1964 for the signing of the Columbia River Treaty, and yet again when the prime minister visited the LBJ Ranch in January 1965. Before the Texas rendezvous, Dean Rusk advised the president:

> The Canadians propose to enclose the Gulf of St. Lawrence and other large contiguous bodies of water as "internal waters." This would give the Russians, Indonesians and others an invaluable precedent to harden their claims to nearby waters and thereby greatly impair security operations such as those of our Polaris submarines. We doubt that Pearson has been given a clear picture of the very important security problems involved. If he raises this subject, you should (a) make clear the firmness of our opposition, (b) assure him that we remain ready to explore any realistic solutions he may suggest, and (c) tell him that, in the absence of a solution which protects our security interests, we will have no alternative to taking the matter to the International Court of Justice.[61]

A White House briefing paper for the Texas meeting argued that the United States had already made several concessions to Canada. It had "acquiesced" when Canada extended its claims to sovereignty from three to twelve miles "provided US fishing rights are maintained," agreed not to oppose Canadian claims to Hudson Bay provided "the other proposals were not pursued," and offered military help to Canada against Soviet trawlers in disputed waters. The US had also refrained from discussions on the topic with other parties, the paper noted, but it would deal with others if Canada proceeded to claim the Gulf of St. Lawrence.[62]

Nevertheless, in 1967, three years after initial American objections, the Pearson government proclaimed sovereignty over what Ambassador Butterworth called "portions of international waters along the coasts of Newfoundland and Labrador." Butterworth took comfort that the area claimed in 1967 was smaller than that claimed in 1964, and he credited American pressure for the difference.[63] His superiors at the State Department warned that the United States would not recognize "the validity of these lines ... and planned formally to object ... to the Government of Canada."[64] The Johnson administration left office with the Gulf of St. Lawrence issue unresolved. Since then, the issue has not resurfaced.

The Nixon administration had so little regard for Canadian sensitivities on arctic and environmental matters that on occasion it treated Canada almost as an adversary. To the Nixon administration, access to the Northwest Passage was a matter of national security. If it recognized Canadian sovereignty over the waters of the Canadian archipelago, it might be setting a dangerous precedent for the US Navy in the waters of the Indonesian and Philippines archipelagos, or even in the Straits of Gibraltar. Like other American administrations of the twentieth century, Nixon's wanted a minimum area of the oceans defined as territorial waterway and a maximum declared to be high seas.

In 1969, Humble Oil refitted a supertanker, the *Manhattan,* and sent it from New York to Prudhoe Bay, Alaska, via the Northwest Passage. There, the supertanker was to fetch a symbolic barrel of oil and carry it back to New York. Canadian authorities were not concerned about the *Manhattan* as such. Humble Oil, its owner, was a responsible company, and the *Manhattan* was reinforced to withstand the arctic ice. But the precedent mattered. If Humble had the legal right to traverse the Northwest Passage without Canadian permission, so would a less seaworthy vessel, chartered perhaps in Liberia or Panama, and owned by a profiteer. If the ice crushed that ship, the resulting oil spill could ruin the ecology for the Inuit and others who lived in the region, and the consequences would be catastrophic. The oil slick might kill the wildlife on which the Inuit depended for food, and Canadian taxpayers would then have to relocate the Inuit, with all the social and psychological upheaval involved, which might last for generations. Moreover, as long as the Inuit – Canadian citizens – lived in the Arctic, Canada had clear claim to the land (as distinct from the water). If the Inuit moved south, the Canadian Armed Forces would have to wave the flag – again at considerable expense. Under the circumstances, the Canadian government – backed strongly by popular opinion argued that permanently frozen water might be in a somewhat different legal category from liquid water. The dispute resolved itself for the moment in 1970 when, after a second trip to the Arctic, Humble Oil decided that the Northwest Passage was more trouble than it was worth.

The *Manhattan* was not the only challenge. In 1971, the Nixon administration relocated its underground nuclear test site from Nevada to the Aleutian island of Amchitka. A test had rocked a building in Las Vegas owned by Howard Hughes, the billionaire, and Hughes had sued the federal government. Howard Hughes owned no real estate in the Aleutians, but there were other hazards. A blast might well trigger an earthquake which could create a tidal wave. Because the tidal wave might hit the British Columbia coast, the Trudeau government asked Parliament to protest the forthcoming test. Ambassador Peter Towe went to the White House with the message, but he failed to make much of an impression. White House advisor Peter M. Flanigan reported:

At a meeting with Peter Towe of the Canadian Embassy, he indicated the extreme sensitivity of the Canadians to the proposed Amchitka tests. They understood why the US might consider it necessary to move ahead with the test. However, he pointed out that Trudeau has resisted political pressures to make public statements urging the US to abandon the test.

In the interest of rebuilding cordial relations between the president and Trudeau, he urged acknowledgment, perhaps in a letter, be given of Trudeau's restraint, and if possible some advance notice when a final decision is made.[65]

When a member of the British Columbia Legislative Assembly, Dennis G. Cocke, wrote a letter to President Nixon, another White House official said that "public safety considerations are given the greatest weight in connection with underground testing which you know is directly related to US national security requirements including the fulfilment of our mutual defense commitments to our allies."[66] In spite of Canadian protests, the tests took place.

The issue of Canadian sovereignty over the Northwest Passage resurfaced during the Reagan presidency. The Soviet Union and the United States had come to depend on submarine-launched ballistic missiles as the primary deterrent against a surprise attack. Cameras in satellites made the location of land-based missiles impossible to hide, and by 1985, strategically placed technology allowed NATO countries to monitor the movement of Soviet submarines into the Atlantic. Only in arctic waters could Soviet submarines find a place to hide, and there also the US Navy wanted to know where they were. As neither the Reagan administration nor the Canadian government of Brian Mulroney wanted a quarrel over Canadian sovereignty, both parties reached a *modus vivendi* in January 1988. While silent on issues of sovereignty and submarines, the temporary arrangement obliged American-owned surface vessels to obtain Canadian permission before passing through the Northwest Passage.[67] Nevertheless, serious issues are unresolved. (That they remain unresolved is more than hypothetical, given that the US Navy remains active in the Arctic after the end of the Cold War.[68]) As far as the Law of the Sea is concerned, the American-Canadian relationship remains adversarial rather than allied.

Southern Africa

Before Pearson's Temple University address, the Johnson administration thought that Canada could interpret America's Commonwealth policy to other members of the British Commonwealth. As Prime Minister Pearson prepared to leave Ottawa in July 1964 for a meeting of Commonwealth prime ministers, Secretary of State Rusk asked the American embassy in Ottawa to forward its thoughts on India-Pakistan relations and the strategic importance of Malaysia. Rusk also had ideas on British Guiana, Nigeria, Southern Rhodesia, and South West Africa which he wanted the Canadians to convey. "[It] would be useful if occasion arises for Canadians [to] stress immediacy and importance [of the] South West Africa issue," Rusk wrote.[69] Indeed, it would be in South West Africa where Canada would be most useful to the United States, but not until the Carter administration more than a decade later.

One of the Carter administration's concerns was southern Africa. Only people of European descent could vote or hold political office in the Republic of South Africa, the largest and most powerful nation in the area. By the time President Carter took the oath of office, there was war in three of South Africa's neighbours: South West Africa, on the Atlantic Ocean; Rhodesia (formerly Southern Rhodesia), across the Limpopo River from the South African province of Transvaal; and Angola, until 1975 a Portuguese possession to the north of South West Africa. South Africa had influence in all three situations. Long simmering, these conflicts had come to a boil during the Ford presidency.

The 1885 Congress of Berlin, which partitioned most of Africa into European colonies, awarded South West Africa to Germany. With Germany's defeat in the First World War, South West Africa became a League of Nations mandate, with South Africa as the mandate power. South Africa defied United Nations attempts to terminate that trusteeship, and some black Africans formed the South West African People's Organization (SWAPO) to challenge South Africa's control of the territory. Until 1975, SWAPO did little. However, events in neighbouring countries were to improve SWAPO's chances.

In 1965, Southern Rhodesia was home to 219,000 Europeans, most of them British (many of them Scottish) and some Boers from South Africa.[70] Only 3 percent of the population, they were firmly in control of the self-governing British colony. The first European settlers arrived in 1890, but by 1923, they had achieved internal self-government. Voters elected deputies to a legislature that met in Salisbury, and the leader of the party that won a majority of the seats would become prime minister. The prime minister selected ministers among the deputies of his own party, and the ministers directed transportation, health services, education, and agriculture. The United Kingdom remained responsible for little more than foreign policy and defence, and in that regard, Southern Rhodesians contributed more to the British war effort in the two world wars than the British contributed to Southern Rhodesia.

While no laws specified racial requirements for voters or elected politicians, restrictions based on wealth and education guaranteed a largely European electorate. Until a constitutional reform in 1962, no black African managed to win a seat in the legislature. From 1953 until 1963,

Southern Rhodesia was the most economically advanced British colony in the Federation of Rhodesia and Nyasaland, but that federation disintegrated when black Africans in the other two colonies – Northern Rhodesia and Nyasaland – persuaded British authorities that Southern Rhodesia's European community was dominating them. In 1964, the United Kingdom granted independence to Northern Rhodesia as Zambia and Nyasaland as Malawi. Given Northern Rhodesia's name change, Southern Rhodesia became simply Rhodesia.

Harold Wilson's government, whose Labour party had won the British parliamentary election of 1964, refused independence to Rhodesia without some guarantee of eventual African majority rule. Rhodesia's European electorate was outraged. By every standard of measurement, Rhodesia was more highly developed than Zambia or Malawi. Moreover, the European community was better educated, more skilled than Rhodesia's African majority. Europeans knew how to farm, how to operate hospitals, how to maintain British-style government. Africans, they feared, would not. Determined to halt an emigration of Rhodesians who feared that African majority government was inevitable, Rhodesia's prime minister, Ian Smith, issued on 11 November 1965 what he called the Unilateral Declaration of Independence (UDI). Henceforth, Rhodesia would consider itself independent, no longer a British colony, regardless of British government policy. Harold Wilson's government countered with sanctions against Rhodesia.

For almost ten years, the sanctions had little negative impact on Rhodesia and UDI seemed a success. Rhodesian farmers continued to export their surpluses, although those who packaged those commodities labelled them as originating in South Africa or Mozambique. Neither the Portuguese nor South African governments cooperated in the sanctions, and Rhodesians were able to buy most of what they wanted from one of these neighbours. The formidable Zambezi River between Zambia and Rhodesia limited insurgent activities from the north.

In 1974, Portugal had a revolution, and the new Portuguese government granted independence to Angola and Mozambique in 1975. Three factions sought control of Angola: the Popular Front for the Liberation of Angola (MPLA), the National Front for the Liberation of Angola (FNLA), and the National Union for the Total Independence of Angola (UNITA). MPLA, the strongest faction, was Marxist, supported by Fidel Castro, and the Ford administration sought to prevent its triumph. South Africa sent forces into Angola to help the FNLA and UNITA, and Angola's MPLA government called on Fidel Castro's Cuba for further assistance. Castro obliged, and Cuban soldiers arrived in Angola.[71]

Meanwhile, the Portuguese situation destabilized Rhodesia. Rhodesia lost its outlet through Mozambique to the Indian Ocean and became totally dependent on South Africa. Insurgents from Zambia and Tanzania could enter Mozambique to cross the Zambezi River and then enter Rhodesia. The level of warfare escalated. The possibility that Cubans, even Soviets, might enter the fray appeared "dangerous" to Secretary of State Cyrus Vance.[72] In his memoirs, Vance accused the Ford administration (and particularly Ford's secretary of state, Henry Kissinger) of facilitating Cuba's entry into Angola by his tacit approval of South African support for the FNLA and UNITA. Vance did not want to repeat the error in Rhodesia.[73]

The destabilization of white-ruled Rhodesia as well as a change of government in Britain led to a solution of the Rhodesian problem. Democratic elections were followed by the creation of the state of Zimbabwe. However, the US and Canada were only marginally involved in these events. They were approving bystanders, and little more than that.

The Carter administration had other factors to consider. President Carter could not have won the 1976 presidential election without the overwhelming support of Afro-American voters, and he would need that support again in 1980. Afro-Americans would appreciate efforts to bring African majority rule to southern Africa. Moreover, human rights, including those of Africans, were an important moral concern for Carter and his administration.[74] The Carter administration worked closely with British authorities to bring African majority rule to Rhodesia, known as Zimbabwe after independence in 1980.[75] It sought, and received, Canadian help to achieve similar results in South West Africa.

Andrew Young, the Carter administration's first ambassador to the United Nations, suggested in 1977 that the United States might co-opt the other four Western members of the Security Council (the United Kingdom, France, West Germany, and Canada). These countries, thought Young, could negotiate with South Africa to leave South West Africa and, if necessary, exert considerable economic pressure (including the threat of sanctions) on South Africa. The four Western governments, including Canada's, obliged. Later in 1977, when President Carter invited Prime Minister Pierre Trudeau to witness the signing of the Panama Canal treaties negotiated with the government of Panama, southern Africa was one of the problems on their agenda.[76] When President Carter was planning his trip to Ottawa two years later, he intended to thank the Canadian Parliament for Canadian efforts in South West Africa.[77]

However, it would appear that (apart from the failure of the negotiations) those efforts were, by and large, undistinguished. Secretary Vance's memoirs mention the impact of his British, French, and German colleagues,[78] but he mentions Canada only in connection with Andrew Young's nomination of Canada as one of the Western five.[79] A compilation of United Nations documents and South African responses published by the South African government indicates that Canada's delegate to the

Security Council consistently voted with his American, British, French, and German colleagues, but, even when that delegate was External Affairs Minister Don Jamieson, Canada made little impression.[80] In the end, Canada's low diplomatic profile probably made little difference to the outcome. South West Africa remained an unresolved issue, and Cuban troops remained in Angola. Even the presence of United Nations forces (including Canadians) in South West Africa did little more than limit the conflict until 1990, when the South African government of President F.W. de Klerk granted independence to South West Africa (henceforth, Namibia). Both Canada and the United States contributed observers and Canada also contributed police to supervise Namibia's first elections. But this issue, like Rhodesia, did not become a subject of bilateral relations.

Iran

The best-known example of Canadian assistance to the United States during the Carter administration is undoubtedly that given in Tehran. In November 1979, six American diplomats in Tehran who escaped capture by Iranian militants hid with Canadian embassy officials who, in January 1980, helped them flee that revolutionary country. One hundred and forty-two members of Congress signed a letter of thanks and delivered it to Peter Towe, Canada's ambassador in Washington and the United States Senate passed Resolution 344 to commend Canada. The initiative in this instance lay with the American diplomats in Tehran, not with the State Department. They had sought Canadian help. The CIA did, however, work closely with Canadian officials, both in Tehran and in Ottawa, to facilitate the diplomats' escape.[81]

The memoirs of Secretary of State Cyrus Vance (1977-80) refer to Canada in only two contexts: as the helper in the embassy affair in Iran, and as one of the helpful allies in South West Africa.[82] When Vance left the Carter cabinet over his unwillingness to support the attempted rescue of the remaining hostages in Iran, his letter of resignation (and of support for other government policies) summarized his achievements while in office. None of these – negotiation of SALT II with the Soviet Union, completion of the Panama Canal treaties, conclusion of the peace agreement between Israel and Egypt negotiated at Camp David, the establishment of diplomatic relations with Communist China, even the settlement of the conflict in Rhodesia (now Zimbabwe) – had involved Canadian negotiators. (Trudeau had indicated in a letter to President Carter that he strongly approved the establishment of formal ties between China and the United States, but he did so in approval of a fait accompli.) Evidence that Vance's successor, Edmund Muskie, gave much thought to Canada as a Cold War ally is lacking. As secretary of state, he never even visited Canada.[83] Canadian assistance in Iran, spontaneous and effective, was not part of a larger strategy.

Conclusions

On the North-South issues discussed in this chapter, Canada's role in American policy was clearly less important than in the strategic security issues discussed in earlier chapters. In the Middle East, Canada was prepared to sell weapons to the Israelis that the Americans wanted the Israelis to have but did not want to sell themselves – clearly an example of functioning as a satellite or surrogate. Then came the Suez Crisis of 1956, in which Canada mediated, and thus became an ally that made a difference. But it was a brief, glorious moment. During the next two Middle Eastern wars, in 1967 and 1973, Canada played no role. In Yemen, Canada was somewhat more useful. Canada was part of the United Nations peacekeeping team in Yemen for its first two years. Canadians had gone there at the request of the United Nations secretary-general, but stayed on at the request of the Americans.

In Latin and South America, Americans are often more insistent on support from their allies than they are on other issues, as is obvious from the preoccupation of recent American administrations with Cuba. Yet on Panama, the American government saw no need for any particular policy to gain Canadian support, desirable as such support might be. On the Dominican Republic, the Americans had no need for a policy on Canada as long as the Conservative government in Ottawa was more supportive of the Trujillo regime than were the Americans themselves. Later, in 1965, when US Marines invaded the Dominican Republic, there seems to have been no effort to seek Canadian support, in spite of the presence of Canadian companies in the country. When one Canadian government considered joining the OAS in 1969, and another, in 1990, finally did so, these policies seem to have been entirely Canadian ones, not influenced by the US. In short, there seems to have been no particular American policy to include Canada in either the Dominican invasion or the OAS.

The situation was different with respect to British Guiana, where Canada had significant investments, and the Johnson administration saw the colony's choice of government as a Cold War issue, on which Canadians had to toe the line. Thus, when Canada sought American advice on its role in British Guiana, it was encouraged to send an envoy to Georgetown while the Marxist administration of Cheddi Jagan reigned, but it was told not to send higher-level officials. When the British and Americans thought of a way of resolving the Guiana problem, Canada again played no role. On the Latin and South American issues, several American administrations saw no need for a Canada policy. The only brief exception occurred in Guyana, during 1963 and 1964, where Americans foresaw a limited role for Canadians.

The Law of the Sea differs from the other topics examined in this chapter, because it involved direct American and Canadian clashes of interest.

When the Law of the Sea Conference met, Canada often found its position to be closer to that of the Third World countries than it was to that of the US. However, the resulting Canadian actions met with American hostility. American policy on the Law of the Sea was to treat Canada as it would any other country with which it disagreed; that is, to demand concessions and to negotiate. This approach was true of the Gulf of St. Lawrence, the arctic waters, and the waters between Alaska and British Columbia. In short, while no particular Canada policy developed on these issues, special American-Canadian policy measures did occur. Instead of sending a fleet or a warship to support an American claim, Americans sent oil tankers or diplomatic notes. And the three different outcomes on the three issues show that Canada was not treated as a dependent ally. Canada asserted control over the Gulf of St. Lawrence, the US ignored Canadian protests over the atomic tests under the Aleutian Islands, and they agreed to disagree over the Arctic.

On southern Africa, Americans asked Canadians to represent American interests with the Commonwealth and to maintain contacts in South West Africa. The Canadians did what they were asked, but in the end, their efforts made little difference, because outside events – such as the Portuguese revolution and the end of the Cold War – led to the independence of Zimbabwe and Namibia and the end of apartheid in South Africa. Again, Canada played a very limited role in American policy.

The predominant American policy approach to Canada on North-South issues, therefore, was no policy at all, with just the occasional bit of liberal internationalism when Canada was seen to have a special role (that is, in the Commonwealth) or where Canada had major interests (as in Guyana). With three exceptional cases (as surrogate for arms sales to Israel, as envoy to British Guiana, and as messenger to the Commonwealth), and a fourth case in which Canada was an independent and helpful ally (Suez), Canada was all but ignored on most of these issues.

5
Canada As a Source of Natural Resources

After introducing the historical attitudes of American policy makers to resource issues, this chapter explores the role Canada played in American resource policy during the Cold War. Four cases are presented: the security of mineral supplies in the immediate postwar and early Cold War years; oil and then natural gas policy from the 1973 Middle East War to the 1982 OPEC price increase; and uranium from the first atomic bomb to the end of the Cold War.

Since the turn of the century, if not earlier, Americans had begun to realize that their supply of natural resources was limited and that they would need to look outside their boundaries for some of the materials on which a modern industrial economy depends.[1] Between the two world wars, left-wing theories of imperialism as well as fascist claims that nations had a right to natural resources led to many a discussion of the role that access to raw materials might play in a peaceful, prosperous world – even as, during the Great Depression, raw-material-producing countries and communities suffered greatly from the collapse of the price and lack of a market for these materials. Yet, for the most part, access to raw materials was not a major concern of American foreign policy before 1939.[2]

The Allies' first declaration of war aims, the Atlantic Charter of August 1941, promised all states, "great or small, victor or vanquished ... access on equal terms to the trade and to the raw materials of the world which are needed for their economic prosperity."[3] By 1945, the Allies' war aims were beginning to sound less idealistic, especially after the use of the first nuclear weapons gave some American government officials the illusion that they could almost rule the world. General Leslie Groves, in charge of American atomic energy policy throughout the Second World War and into 1946, thought that the United States should try to control all the world's uranium and thorium. Nor was Groves's attitude unusual. Six years later, in a July 1951 address, William Thorp, the State Department's assistant secretary for economic affairs, listed three objectives of American foreign economic policy. The second objective was "the intelligent development and utilization of the resources of the *entire free world* through international cooperation" [emphasis added].[4] Groves wanted to control all materials related to nuclear energy, whereas Thorp included all resources but limited himself to the so-called free world.

In 1944 and 1945, the United States also made an attempt to include the marketing of raw materials and the concept of "intergovernmental commodity agreements" in the charter of the abortive International Trade Organization. The American intent in this case was not to assure an American supply of resources but rather to avoid "burdensome surpluses" and "wide spread" distress. This policy appears not to have been pursued after the war.[5]

Even after the Cold War, with again only one military and economic superpower, it is difficult to imagine the degree to which the United States dominated the world in 1945. It not only had a monopoly of atomic weapons, it also produced half of all the world's goods and services and owned two-thirds of the monetary reserves.[6] As the Second World War became the Cold War with scarcely a pause for demobilization, the years 1946 to 1947 marked a transition from one war effort to another.

In 1946, for example, the American government amended the 1939 Stockpiling Act. Under the terms of this act and later legislation, the American government continued to acquire and administer a "strategic stockpile" of as many as seventy (later expanded to ninety-three) materials. A stockpiling program remained in operation until the end of the Cold War.[7] The 1947 National Security Act, which created the National Security Council and the Central Intelligence Agency, also established the National Security Resources Board, consisting primarily of civilian administrators. In 1948, another study, commissioned by the Joint Chiefs of Staff, assumed that Western Hemisphere, Australian, New Zealand, and South African resources would be available in the event of war.[8] By 1950, the year of the outbreak of the Korean War, the US imported half of the minerals and one-eighth of the petroleum it needed. That year, the government adopted the National Defense Production Act, which attempted to establish an allocation of scarce materials controls similar to that which had existed during the Second World War. The act gave the president the authority to ration raw materials and consumer goods and to control wages and prices. In October 1950, the Canadian and American governments signed a "Statement of Principles for Economic Cooperation" whose operative sentence read, "The two countries shall, as it becomes necessary, institute coordinated control over the distribution of scarce raw materials and supplies." These principles appear not to have been invoked.[9]

In January 1951, the president appointed a commission to study the availability of raw materials, the President's Materials Policy Commission (also known as the Paley Commission, after its chair William S. Paley, the head of the Columbia Broadcasting System; see page 106). The commission's wide mandate included not only the raw materials availability in the United States and for American industries, but also "the needs and resources of the nations with which the United States was cooperating closely on military security and in economic matters."[10]

By 1952, the American administration had spawned an overlapping network of boards, committees, and agencies, all designed to deal with real or perceived materials shortages. There was, for example, the Vital Materials Coordinating Committee working under the authority of the Defense Production Administration, an Interdepartmental Stockpile Committee, a Defense Materials Operating Committee, as well as the National Security Resources Board (reporting to the National Security Council). By one count, 68 national agencies and committees were involved in the stockpiling program by the end of the Korean War, not counting the 22 industrial advisory committees (with their 35 subcommittees).[11]

The Korean War, however, was not the Second World War. An International Materials Conference (IMC), which the American, French, and British governments created in 1951, consisted of a series of uncoordinated committees on materials such as "manganese, cobalt and nickel" or "cotton and cotton linters." Each committee could recommend but not legally enforce quotas. By 1952, most of the quotas proved unnecessary, and by October 1953, the IMC put itself on standby basis. In short, most raw materials were in abundant supply while the Korean War was still raging.[12]

Americans returned to the comfortable feeling that resources were in plentiful supply. An expert study published in 1963 came to the conclusion that as far as the United States was concerned, "there is no general resource shortage problem for the balance of the century," though the situation might be different in other parts of the world.[13] The Vietnam War of 1963 to 1973 caused another drain on raw materials, but not to the extent of previous wars. For most materials, some prices increased but no shortages developed. In 1970, Congress adopted the National Materials Policy Act, which stated among its other purposes "to anticipate the materials requirements of the Nation and the world," but the act seems to have resulted in only a study, no executive action.[14]

Another event, the 1973 Middle East War, put the question of raw materials supplies on the world's, not just the Americans' political agenda. In the US, the partial embargo on oil supplies imposed by most OPEC members kept American dependence on imports on the government's agenda for the next eight to nine years. Then the OPEC effort started to crumble and oil prices began to drop. The oil problem caused some American policy makers to turn their attention to other raw materials, especially uranium, but there was little sense of crisis or urgency. Studies prepared for the Ford administration concluded that because the United States was both an importer and an exporter of commodities, it made no sense for the US to side with one of these groups, and that there was no need for special measures such as commodity agreements or buffer stocks.[15]

At the same time, the Law of the Sea Conference offered the possibility of an abundant supply of many resources for years to come. If only people could harvest the minerals that lay at the bottom of the ocean, the minerals so found could support America's lifestyle for generations to come. (On the Law of the Sea, see Chapter 4.)

Interest in American access to scarce raw materials revived briefly during the early years of the Reagan administration, partly in response to the Afghanistan War and the Iranian Revolution, but mostly as part of a renewed emphasis on defence issues. However, changes in technology (which have greatly diversified the number of materials on which a modern economy depends), the realization that a nuclear war might not last long enough to create a shortage of materials, and, much later, the end of the Cold War eclipsed this interest.[16]

It is important not to see American policy simply as the search for access to raw materials. American leaders saw their task not only to obtain such materials, but also to obtain them at the lowest possible price. They were, in other words, striving for economic well-being as well as security. In a study of American raw materials policy during the interwar and immediate postwar years, Stephen Krasner found that increasing competition among suppliers was as important a goal as simple access.[17] Any analysis must look not only for concerns about access to Canadian resources, but also for policies that would assure a plentiful supply at a low price.

There is one other aspect of American raw materials policy. The United States is an important producer, even an exporter, of many raw materials. While presidents and their advisors advocated policies of long-term security of supply, domestic producers were asking for protection, often on the grounds that domestic production was the most secure strategy and should be protected at almost any price.[18]

The Search for Mineral Security

During the Second World War, the American and Canadian economies had functioned as almost one unit. Industrial raw materials and manufactured goods were allocated by the two governments to users in both countries. In January 1946, the two governments dissolved the Joint War Production Board, but left in place the consultative Permanent Joint Board on Defense. As the United States continued large-scale purchases of raw materials, many of which Canada also imported, administrators perceived the need of another joint institution. In 1949, the two governments created the Joint Industrial Mobilization Planning Committee, consisting of senior administrators from both governments. A 1950 bilateral agreement defined the committee's tasks: to "institute coordinated controls over the distribution of scarce raw materials and supplies." These controls were, however, not mandatory and required the consent of both governments. Though it preceded the Korean War, the committee seems not to have survived it for long.[19]

This joint Canadian-American committee formed part of a larger American effort to conserve and accumulate apparently scarce minerals, an effort to which the Cold War seemed to lend some urgency. During the Second World War, Canada had produced a major share of the mineral supplies of the Western Allies, as much as 94 percent of the nickel, 75 percent of the asbestos, and 20 percent of the zinc.[20] The first two postwar secretaries of the interior, Harold Ickes and Julius Krug, were especially keen advocates of stockpiling.[21]

Thus from 1946 until the end of the Cold War, various parts of the American government built up and administered an elaborate series of stockpiles of various industrial raw and some semi-finished materials. This program was not a system of rationing or allocation of materials, but a system of holding materials which industry, the military, and in some cases the civilian population might need in case of war or scarcity. The authority for this program derived from the 1946 Stockpiling Act, the stated aim of which was "to decrease and prevent wherever possible a dangerous and costly dependence of the United States upon foreign nations for supplies of ... materials in times of national emergency."[22] Even at the height of the stockpiling program, at the beginning of the Korean War, the program was fuelled by a mixture of economic and security motives. The Paley Commission had made it clear that security meant not simply access but also the lowest cost consistent with security.[23]

Over time, the stockpiles became less closely associated with military needs and started to fulfil more clearly economic functions, such as the maintenance of domestic and in some cases foreign industries, the support of friendly governments, the disposal of agricultural surpluses (American food in exchange for other nations' minerals or tropical raw materials), or even the control of prices. That is, the American government would sell material from the stockpile when prices were high, reducing the costs of American industry, and buy when prices were low, assisting American producers.[24] The stockpile at times included ninety or more materials, everything from feathers and silk to copper and manganese. The military was careful to specify that the feathers were needed for arctic quality sleeping bags and the silk for "powder bags for large guns."[25]

Yet the stockpile was not an important factor in American policy after the Korean War. At the beginning of that war, it was only two-fifths full; by the middle of 1951, the stockpile was in worse shape, with no supplies at all in some categories, minerals being the least adequately stockpiled. By 1952, the stockpile began to replenish, and by 1954 the program mainly aided domestic producers. When the president appointed the Committee on Mineral Policy in 1953, he referred to the depressed condition of the *domestic* industry. The committee reported what it was expected to report; that is, that the stockpile be expanded, even though the Joint Chiefs of Staff thought there was no need to do so. During the 1960s, the stockpile was used only three times: once for nickel (to counter an INCO strike in Sudbury, Ontario; that is, to deal with a Canadian problem); once for copper (to dampen rising prices); and a third time for quinine (to supply American soldiers in Vietnam).[26]

The increased demand for raw materials during the Vietnam War followed by the Arab oil embargo of 1973-4 again led to concerns not so much about shortages of minerals but about their unavailability at the price to which American users had become accustomed. The president's economic advisors found such fears to be unfounded. In 1973, President Nixon reduced the stockpile guidelines so as to allow for supplies for a one-year rather than a three-year major war. In February 1975, President Ford's advisors assured him that "market forces ... appear adequate to deter price gouging or cartel-like action."[27]

That may have been the view of the president's advisors, but in 1976 a National Commission on Supplies and Shortages recommended an international convention on export controls and stockpiling for *economic* rather than against strategic purposes.[28] Despite the increasing tendency to view the stockpile as an economic tool, the 1979 Stockpiling Revision Act insisted on the strategic purpose of the stockpile, and instructed the president to maintain a stockpile sufficient to support a three-year war and mentioned a dangerous and *costly* dependence on foreign sources of supply.[29] A study commissioned by the next president, Jimmy Carter, found that of all the non-fuel minerals its economy and defence effort required, the United States faced a possible supply problem of only one, ferrochromium, a mineral for which Canada is not an important source.[30] In 1980, Congress adopted the National Materials Policy, Research and Development Act, which required the president to submit a plan to coordinate national minerals policy. By the time the deadline for that plan was reached, a new president, Ronald Reagan, with new priorities was in office. In 1981, yet another congressional study listed eight minerals it considered to be both "strategic" and "critical." Canada was not the lead supplier for any of the eight, and supplied a significant proportion of only one, titanium.[31]

One of the problems in determining whether the US had a minerals policy with respect to Canada lies in the fact that American governments were themselves ambivalent about having any kind of policy on such economic issues. "Raw materials problems were expected to fall into place" within the overall multilateral system. Despite occasional talk of a national minerals policy (especially in Congress), Congress did not commit itself to such a policy until 1980. Even then, Congress found that without presidential cooperation, it could not make or implement a policy.[32] If there was no minerals policy, a Canadian minerals policy could not have existed. Researchers therefore need to deduce policy from individual government activities.

Canada played two roles in the stockpiling program. In some cases, it continued to be almost a part of the American economy. In 1951 and 1952, for example, Congress agreed to allow Canadian lead, zinc, and copper destined for the stockpile to enter the US without paying tariffs or excise duties.[33] In 1954, Canada was assigned a part of the American copper stockpile at a time of high prices, and spokespersons for the American military referred to Canada as a source as safe as a domestic one. At an October 1953 meeting of the National Security Council, President Eisenhower said that "we would be idiots" to try to duplicate in the United States Canada's aluminum-smelting capacity at Kitimat. Secretary of State Dulles added that the US would run into "embarrassing difficulties" if it treated Canada as less secure than the US. In an April 1954 letter to Arthur Flemming, the supervisor of the stockpile program, Eisenhower ordered the stockpilers to consider "Canada, Mexico and comparably accessible nearby areas" as reliable wartime sources; later that year the National Security Council expanded the definition of the areas considered secure to include all Caribbean countries and Central America.[34] This decision did not lead to the anticipated result, which was higher purchases of lead and zinc from domestic producers. The Office of Defense Mobilization then set special higher purchase quotas for lead and zinc, but it continued to include Canada and Mexico as secure sources, a formula that amounted to special treatment for these two countries. At the same time, the American government asked Canada to limit its exports of lead and zinc to the US. The Canadian ambassador protested, citing "hemispheric defence considerations." The State Department threatened that congressional votes on other trading issues of interest to Canada might be lost. After this unseemly exchange among allies, the Canadian government conveyed the request for export restraints to Canadian producers.[35]

There were other cases in which Canada became a foreign country like any other. In 1944, a study published in the US Armed Services Forces Manual foresaw the possibility of American military action to secure the nickel mines of Northern Ontario.[36] In 1948, the Strategic Materials Committee, an interdepartmental committee that advised the administration about the stockpiling program, decided to rank all foreign countries according to degrees of security; that is, the likelihood that supplies from that country would continue to be available in wartime. Canada was judged just a little more secure than Mexico, and much more secure than all other foreign countries. This judgment, however, was questioned by the Department of the Interior which wanted to rank Canada as somewhat less secure. This judgment did not result from any doubts about access to Canada but rather because a lower ranking for Canada would have meant that a larger proportion of the stockpile would come from American mines.

In 1950, after the outbreak of the Korean War, the National Security Resources Board named Canada as an important supplier of half the minerals and strategic materials the US imported. However, the accompanying table showed that, in an emergency, the US would need to rely on Canada for more than 10 percent of its supplies for only five materials: aluminum, nickel, palladium, asbestos, and platinum.[37] Later that year, another interdepartmental committee found Canada and Mexico to be as safe as the US, "except for materials whose production was especially vulnerable to sabotage or bombing." These materials were not specified. Though it might appear that in this case Canada was in fact treated as equivalent to the US, the committee justified its decision with an apparently objective formula that judged the security of foreign sources according to four criteria: accessibility and security of shipping, political dependability, concentration of supply, and contiguity. For most materials, Canada would score high on all four counts.[38]

In 1952, the Paley Commission report, which Canadian nationalists love to hate, simply treated Canada as one foreign source of supply among others. The commission also wondered about the security of Western Hemisphere sources of minerals, stating that insufficient attention had been devoted to their "military vulnerability." Only a year later, the American ambassador in Ottawa suggested that Canada "be regarded less as a source of military manpower than as a source of economic strength for NATO in raw materials and in manufactured goods."[39]

In 1953, the National Security Council ordered the Office of Defense Mobilization to take special security measures to ensure that some important foreign-owned sources of raw materials did not fall into hostile hands, such measures to include CIA surveillance. The list included cobalt in the Belgian Congo, nickel in Canada, bauxite in Surinam and petroleum in the Dutch Caribbean. American-owned facilities were on a separate list that did not include any facilities in Canada.[40]

Nickel was a mineral for which Canada was the main supplier and of which the Americans had little. In 1960, an American military officer wrote that as far as nickel supplies were concerned, Canada could, for most purposes, "be treated as equivalent to a domestic source."[41] However, the American government was more concerned about its reliance on a single firm, INCO (most of whose mines are in Canada), than about its reliance on a friendly neighbour, Canada. To reduce that dependence, the government bought nickel from INCO's Canadian competitors, Falconbridge and Sherritt-Gordon, and encouraged American firms to develop Cuba's nickel deposits, a development that ironically led to greater vulnerability for American industry.[42] Yet other American experts suggested that even Canadian nickel might not be secure in time of war.[43]

During the early postwar years, American mineral policy included few examples of exceptionalism, in which Canada was given a special status as neither foreign nor domestic. Instead, American policy makers swung between two points of view: Canada as a foreign country and Canada as practically a part of the US. Canada benefited from the stockpiling program, almost regardless of which point of view prevailed in Washington. Those, such as Senator George W. Malone (Republican-Nevada), who favoured an almost isolationist reliance on Western Hemisphere sources of minerals, naturally included Canada as an especially secure source.[44] Others, such as the Paley Commission, which favoured purchases of low cost foreign materials, also saw Canada as a good source.

The kinds of materials the American government stockpiled provides further evidence of how secure a source Canada was considered to be. Minerals for which Canada was a major supplier (nickel, iron ore) were either not stockpiled or stockpiled only briefly during the postwar years. In 1964, Secretary of the Interior Stewart Udall referred to Canada and the United States together as "a great vault of resources, a storehouse ... We should not allow national boundaries to inhibit our effort to achieve maximum economic strength." (One of his advisors warned him of the "extremely delicate nature" of such statements.[45])

More than ten years later, when Americans feared the formation of producer cartels that might hurt their economy as well as their military security, President Ford's advisors thought they could count on Canada not to participate in such groupings. But could they be certain? They would have preferred assurances from the Canadian government, but they feared that the Canadians might find a request for such a bilateral assurance offensive. Their solution was to leave such requests for the upcoming multilateral trade negotiations. In 1981, when Ronald Reagan was president, military considerations once again dominated. A congressional committee pointed out that in emergencies, metals, which could not easily be airlifted because of their weight, could be shipped by rail from Canada or Mexico. The committee also found that of the two countries, only Mexico suffered from – unspecified – "disadvantages" as a supplier.[46]

One other aspect of American mineral policy involved Canada during the early years of the Cold War. From Secretary of the Interior Harold Ickes in 1945 to the Paley Commission and President Truman in 1952, and the Joint Chiefs of Staff and the Department of Defense in 1953 and 1954, practically all of official Washington agreed that the St. Lawrence Seaway should be built to provide an almost secure access to the iron ore of Labrador as well as to other not yet discovered or developed Canadian minerals. Furthermore, Americans wanted the Seaway to be jointly built, not by Canada alone as the Canadian government had anticipated. The assistant secretary of defence told the House Public Works Committee in June 1953 that though the interests of the two countries were close, they might not always coincide. Canada might even choose to remain neutral if the US went to war. Canada might also have different economic priorities from the United States. For example, Canada might set tolls to favour grains rather than minerals. For all of these reasons, as well as those of cost – it would be less expensive to transport ores by water than by rail – the American Congress might have been expected to vote the 1941 Seaway agreement into law, but it did not finally do so until early 1954 when the Canadian government was on the point of beginning construction of an all Canadian route.[47]

The Energy Crisis: Petroleum

Energy supply is an aspect of foreign relations about which Americans can and do become emotional. The use of the private automobile became common in the United States earlier than in any other country, and Americans continue to make more use of this type of transport than do any other people.[48] Add to this fact the many other civilian and military uses of petroleum, the American fondness for bright lights and electrical gadgets, and the awe and fear in which most people hold atomic power, the emotive impact of energy issues then becomes comprehensible.

This chapter does not attempt to deal with all kinds of energy. We will begin with trade in petroleum products, concentrating on the effects of the various Middle Eastern crises of 1973 to 1988. After a brief discussion of oil's counterpart, natural gas, we turn to the question of uranium supplies.

The United States was the first country in which mineral oil was found and exploited. By the 1920s, the US was a net exporter of oil. Petroleum products were rationed during the Second World War, but the rationing was removed almost as soon as the war was over. By 1946, Americans were again filling their cars as if petroleum were in unlimited supply. The illusion did not last long. In 1948, the United States became a net importer of petroleum and has remained so to this day.[49] American production of crude oil increased until the late 1960s, but it has been declining since 1970, in spite of the 1968 discovery of oil in Alaska. Since the 1970s, the United States has been importing more than 40 percent of the oil it uses.[50]

Canada's Northwest Territories produced oil during the Second World War, but such remote sites were not economical in peace time. Oil, however, was found in Alberta in 1947, and oil from that province (and to a limited extent the two adjoining provinces of British Columbia and Saskatchewan) could be and was economically sold in the northwestern United States. With the exception of a few years in the late 1970s and early 1980s, Canada has been a major supplier of oil to the United States since 1968.[51]

The defence mobilization effort of the early Cold War did not emphasize oil. Once the fear that the United States might soon be at war again (with its accompanying paranoia about shortages of raw material) began to wear off, Americans comforted themselves with the thought that enough oil was available within easy reach of the United States to last well into the twenty-first century.[52] This feeling of security (with a brief interruption for the Suez Crisis of 1956 and the Middle East War of 1967) lasted until 1969-70, by which time increasing imports as well as growing nationalism among Middle East oil producers (with the resulting higher oil prices) led to fears that the United States might not be able to obtain the oil it needed or would have to pay many times the usual price. These fears were intensified by the briefly successful OPEC embargo of 1973 and 1974. But the panic did not last long. By 1975-6, Americans were again comfortable in the belief that enough oil was available to meet their needs; polls showed that Americans thought the shortage had been engineered by the major oil companies. By 1978 the Carter administration was trying to hide an oil surplus to be able to plan a long-range energy policy. The 1979-80 Iranian revolution and crisis in Iranian-American relations followed by a lengthy (1980-8) war between Iran and Iraq caused renewed fears of petroleum shortages. But OPEC's cartel soon started to crumble, and after 1980, President Reagan was able to convince a majority of Americans that free enterprise could resolve any oil shortage.[53]

Every president since 1945 has at one time or another suggested that he might like to adopt a national energy policy, but until 1973 American policy did not reflect a fear of oil shortages. Indeed, before 1976, oil was not included in the stockpiling program, though since the 1920s there had been a so-called Naval Petroleum Reserve, which consisted of oil fields in the ground, which were to be left unused, so that they would be available for an emergency.[54] In 1948, the Department of Defense recommended that the rest of the world should get its oil from the Middle East, leaving Western Hemisphere resources for the US, with some of that left in the ground for emergencies. A National Security Council meeting of 16 November 1953 discussed contingencies during an all-out war and the degree to which the US might be able to supply itself and its allies with Western Hemisphere and Middle Eastern oil.[55]

When Americans perceived a shortage of oil, they did not at first think of Canada as a possible saviour. One of the State Department's first reactions to the discovery of major oil fields in Canada had been, What will this do to our friends the Venezuelans? In the words of one State Department memorandum, "The discovery and development of petroleum in the Near East and western Canada provides an increasing long-range threat to Venezuela's markets ... It is US policy to safeguard the nearby Venezuelan resources."[56] Before long, however, US policy makers came to see the advantages of a Canadian oil supply. In 1951, the National Security Council considered options for developing the Alberta tar sands. In 1954, the State Department wrote the Office of Defense Mobilization a glowing report about Canada's growing oil reserves and production. In 1959, a study for the Office of Civil and Defense Mobilization considered the possibility of using "nuclear bombs" to develop the Alberta tar sands.[57]

However, by 1959, some Americans began to worry that, now that Venezuela and Cuba had left-wing governments, if Canadians adopted similar policies Canadian oil might also not be entirely secure. In 1960, the Defense Department wrote of "a deterioration of Western control over world oil supplies." From 1968 to 1970, the State Department, the oil industry, and a cabinet task force on oil imports gave favourable accounts of the contribution Canada could make to future American oil supplies.[58] By 1972, experts were reducing their estimates of Canadian oil reserves, and as Canada began to cut back on exports to the United States, in 1973-4, Americans came to believe that Canada could and would not again be a major source of American oil supplies.[59] Yet, by the 1980s, Canada resumed its position as one of America's major suppliers.

For most of the 1950s and 1960s, the problem appeared to be one of too much oil, or at least of too much imported oil. There was constant pressure from American producers for restrictions on imports of crude oil. The American government responded in 1955 with an informal, and in 1957 with a more formal, agreement with importers to limit imports, and in March 1959 with "mandatory import controls" or quotas. The cabinet realized that these restrictions "would raise hell in Canada, Mexico and Venezuela – our friends – but it had to be."[60] But even the mandatory controls were ineffective. Various companies, foreign governments, and refineries negotiated exemptions. By 1971, the United States was more dependent on imports than it had been before controls were imposed.

All involved insisted that national security required the US to protect its petroleum industry and to limit imports; the 1957 import restrictions, for example, had been the result of a "finding" by the Office of Defense Mobilization "that crude oil is being imported into the United States in such quantities as to threaten to impair the national security." [61] But agreement ended there. Debates raged within Congress and the administration about whether all Western Hemisphere oil was almost as secure as American oil, whether Canadian and/or Mexican oil fell into a separate category, and whether it was better to import in peace time and leave some proportion of domestic oil in the ground for emergencies.[62] The case of Venezuela was especially difficult. Venezuela did and still does supply most of the oil used by Eastern Canada. The State Department argued that if the US limited imports of Canadian oil, Canadians might be tempted to build a pipeline that could bring Alberta oil as far as Montreal (instead of the Ottawa Valley which was the western terminus of the pipeline), and that such a pipeline could reduce Venezuelan exports and destabilize the Venezuelan government or cause it to retaliate against American oil companies.[63] (Some Canadian authors claim that this argument was a Canadian threat rather than an American fear, but we have found no evidence of such a threat.[64])

Generally, the Department of Defense, the Office of Defense Mobilization, and the Department of the Interior wanted to protect American producers, whereas the State Department and the presidents and their immediate advisors were inclined to favour a more liberal import policy. In 1955, the American ambassador to the United Nations threatened Canada with lower oil import quotas if it did not stop efforts to have more members admitted to the UN; in short, the imports were a bargaining chip, not a threat to national security.[65] In 1962, when the State Department prepared guidelines for policy and operations with respect to Canada, it included as the eleventh of sixteen aims "a gradual, continued growth in mutual US-Canadian trade in electric energy, coal, natural gas and related oilfield products ... and coordinated policies between the two countries which foster and promote the orderly development of the resources of both nations."[66] The use of the word "orderly" is interesting, because in this context it usually refers to the protection of American industries; that is, orderly marketing as compared with free competition. Here, the State Department was taking the defence of domestic industries as well as national defence into account:

The President's Cabinet Task Force on oil import reported in February 1970 that imports really did not represent that much of a threat to the national security, but that a totally unrestrained import policy might carry such a threat: Liberalization of import controls over a suitable period of time would not seriously weaken the national economy ... Total abandonment of all import controls *might* [italics added] on present evidence be deemed to threaten security of supply ... Relaxation of import control over time, coupled with appropriate Western Hemisphere preferences and a "security adjustment" to prevent undue Eastern Hemisphere imports would ... satisfactorily protect security of supply.[67]

In terms of policy, this approach meant that Venezuelan, Canadian, and later Mexican oil were exempted from most import restrictions. When the first import restrictions were implemented, District V (that is, the American West Coast, which until the 1980s purchased most of its oil from Canada) was exempted. When the mandatory controls were imposed, the president soon added an "overland exemption" (that is, oil coming in by rail, tanker truck, or pipeline would be exempt). While a provision was meant to favour Canada, it soon led to cheating at the Mexican border, where oil from other countries was loaded onto tank trucks and driven into the United States.[68]

Because oil had been plentiful until 1970, a specific American policy about Canadian energy resources was not required. The policy had changed from year to year without any serious consequences for the US. In 1957, the assistant secretary of state thought that Canada should not receive treatment more favourable than that accorded Venezuela, but the Office of International Trade and Resources preferred Canada to Venezuela. In 1958, the National Security Council stated that the US should encourage the development of "Western Hemisphere" petroleum resources, whereas the Defense Department thought Canadian oil should be given special treatment "because Canadian oil is more important to the US than Venezuelan oil and because Canada is more important than Venezuela in the defence of the US." In 1970, the cabinet task force on oil imports, found that "Canadian and Mexican oil is nearly as secure politically as our own" and recommended "common energy accords ... with those governments."[69]

Imports across the Canadian border continued to increase. In 1962, the American government changed the means of calculating the Canadian quota to ensure that less Canadian oil would get in. In 1965, President Johnson's advisors told him and then the Canadian ambassador that there had to be further cuts in imports. In 1967, in return for permission to build a spur to Chicago from the Canadian pipeline that already passed through Minnesota and Michigan, the Canadian government agreed to try to limit exports to the United States. But the Canadian attempt to limit exports was no more successful than the American effort to limit imports had been. In March 1970, the American government imposed specific controls on imports of Canadian petroleum.[70] This new tough policy was implemented at a time when senior American policy makers were already beginning to realize that the situation was changing and that the United States would soon need more, not less, Canadian oil. The policy was ineffective. Imports of Canadian oil doubled from 1965 to 1970, and doubled again from 1970 to 1973.[71]

In 1969, Henry Kissinger, with his geopolitical view of international relations, became President Nixon's national security advisor. The idea of a common Canadian-American energy policy was not new. The 1965 Merchant-Heeney report was only one of several official documents recommending such a policy. Kissinger, however, actually tried to implement it. Americans officially made such a proposal at a December 1969 meeting with the Canadian minister responsible for energy, Joe Greene. The Canadians seemed interested at first, but soon replied with their own proposal for more specific agreements (February 1970). Then came the March 1970 imposition of import quotas. David Dewitt and John Kirton claim that the quotas formed part of a hard-line negotiating tactic by the US, but though that possibility cannot be ruled out, the quotas could also just be a case where one part of the American government did not know what another part was doing.[72]

By September 1970, New York governor Nelson Rockefeller was pleading for more Canadian oil for Buffalo refineries. In December, OPEC called for new negotiations on oil prices, and in 1971, Libya and the Gulf states raised prices. From 1971 to 1973, the American government increased and then removed the quotas on Canadian oil. In February and March 1971, Peter Flanigan, an advisor to President Nixon, discussed a "common energy policy" and/or "common oil policy" (the terminology varies) with the Canadian ambassador, but found little interest. By April, Flanigan wrote to Kissinger, asking him to call the Canadian ambassador to "settle this outstanding problem." Flanigan said that the president would prefer to postpone his visit to Canada if this issue could not "be settled immediately."[73]

Secretary of Labor George Shultz wanted Americans to trade American access to Canadian oil in times of shortage for Canadian access to the American market in times of surplus, but the Canadians were not interested. On October 4, Flanigan wrote Kissinger to say "the Canadians have decided not to go forward with these talks at this time supposedly because their economic people are too busy with more important matters and 'because the climate does not seem an appropriate one.'" On 3 December, a telephone conversation between Flanigan and External Affairs in Ottawa still mentioned "an oil agreement" in the communique of the by then imminent presidential visit. Later that day, Flanigan wrote General Haig to say "sufficient progress has not been made to warrant any reference to this matter in the December 6 talks" (that is, during the presidential visit).[74] At the same time, the *Manhattan* was travelling through the Canadian Arctic (see Chapter 4). Though this was not an issue of bilateral energy policy, it must have caused Canadians to realize that their oil might be more needed in the future than in the past. It was also the year when discussion began of how to ship Alaskan oil to the United States. Should it go by pipeline through Canada or by pipeline to the Alaska coast and from there by tanker to the continental US? The Canadian government favoured the former route, the American government the latter option. This discussion also focused attention on the American need for oil.[75]

World oil prices continued to rise. In 1971 and 1972, Libya and then Iraq nationalized their oil industries. A world economic boom increased the demand for oil. By November 1972, as American refiners in the Mid-west were pleading for more Canadian oil, a White House energy expert wrote that the White House that arrangements for controlling Canadian imports "were breaking down completely." The Office of Emergency Preparedness claimed that the program for limiting Canadian oil imports had in fact become a rationing system for available Canadian oil. During summer 1973, gasoline shortages developed in parts of the US, and by September, the spot, or free market, price of oil exceeded the controlled price for the first time in more than a decade.[76]

American and Canadian government policies soon reflected these developments. In March 1973, Canadian and American negotiators abandoned their effort to negotiate a common oil policy. The Canadian minister for energy, mines and resources claimed that this outcome resulted from the Americans refusing to commit to help Eastern Canada with oil if the need arose. The documents tell a different story. The final sticking point was the fact that Canada would not commit to a precise amount of future exports to the US.[77] It was also in March that Canada imposed export controls on oil, one month before the Nixon administration abandoned its import quotas. By September, Canada was taxing exported oil (raising the tax in November) and using the proceeds to equalize prices throughout Canada. The Canadian government was also exploring possibilities for shipping Canadian oil to the East Coast. The pipeline to Montreal would take too long to build. The government therefore tried to ship some oil through the Great Lakes and the Panama Canal.[78] That was the situation when the OPEC governments imposed their embargo in October 1973.

The partial embargo (Israel, the United States, and the Netherlands were the main targets), followed by several concerted price increases and production cutbacks, was only one additional factor in a deteriorating oil supply situation. The American government responded on an international level, with diplomatic efforts to organize the buyers of oil, and on the domestic level, with attempts to make the US more self-sufficient. There was also a war in the Middle East, one in which the Soviet Union appeared to be supporting some of the Arab governments against America's de facto ally, Israel, as well as the Watergate scandal, which preoccupied Washington for much of 1973 and 1974. The Canadian government had already made it clear that it intended to keep as much oil as it could for the use of Canadians. For all of these reasons, Canadian energy resources did not figure as a major factor in the American response to the 1973 energy crisis.

On the diplomatic level, the American government responded with an attempt to organize oil consumers, not in order to form a buyers' cartel, but to "reduce their collective dependence on imported oil." Negotiated under the auspices of the OECD, the resulting international agreement, at first called the International Energy Program (IEP), soon became an arm of the OECD and to this day exists as the International Energy Agency (IEA).

Negotiations began in February 1974, and the IEA was signed in August. The negotiations were quick, largely because the governments whose interests differed from those of most of the OECD members (Norway, France) chose not to participate. Canada and the United States appear to have been in substantial agreement on the IEA, though the first reaction of the Canadian minister of external affairs had been cool. "Most countries had got by fairly well" without "international sharing" during the worst of the crisis, Mitchell Sharp grumbled on 11 February 1974. But the Canadian government agreed that in a severe shortage, it would share its energy with the United States. By 1975, when the crisis was over, the Canadian and American governments disagreed over whether the IEA should set a "floor price" for oil. The Canadians wanted a fairly high price; the Americans, a lower one.[79]

At home, the United States responded with a number of programs, including a de facto rationing system, price and export controls, the development of alternative energy sources (nuclear, solar), and energy conservation efforts (not to mention the creation of several more bureaucratic agencies). The bulk of the government's program can be found in President Nixon's 7 November 1973 speech entitled "Project Independence." As the title suggests, the main thrust of the administration's efforts was to make the US more self-sufficient in energy. Canada was not specifically mentioned, though the initial speech and the first annual report on Project Independence, in November 1974, include some cryptic references to "secure sources" and the reduction of "vulnerability" rather than the reduction of imports.[80]

Canada had its own version of energy independence. By the end of 1974, the Canadian government had put into place a set of policies designed to make Canada more self-sufficient. There was a tax on Canadian oil (produced in the West), with the proceeds used to subsidize the price of imported oil (for the East). The pipeline from the West was to be continued to Montreal. Under the Energy Supplies Allocation Act of January 1974, the government had the right to ration and set the price of oil, and in March 1974, that price was raised from $3.80 to $6.50 per barrel. In November 1974, the energy minister announced a precise timetable for the phasing out of all energy exports to the United States by 1983 (a policy which the Canadian government found as difficult to implement as the Americans had found their import controls).[81]

What little American policy toward Canada there was during the 1973-4 oil crisis consisted of some public blustering, some attempts at policy making, and some understanding and cooperation. The public blustering occurred in the US Senate, where Senator Lawton Chiles of Florida accused the Canadians of "highjacking $6 million a day out of our pockets ... We need to let them know that we will strike back if this nonsense continues," and in Maine, where the governor threatened to shut off the pipeline to Montreal. Even the American ambassador, speaking in Canada, threatened retaliation. The attempted policy making occurred in the White House where Henry Kissinger wrote the president about a possible comprehensive pipeline agreement with Canada, energy expert G.A. Lincoln wrote economic advisor Flanigan that higher prices for Canadian oil might lead to more exploration and thus more oil from such "secure sources," and a briefing paper on relations with Canada suggested trading access to the US for Canadian manufactured goods for American access to Canadian energy resources. The understanding came from the American energy administrator William Simon and Assistant Secretary of State Julius Katz, both of whom said they understood Canada's policy, and that in any case, Canada did not have as much oil as had been thought. Cooperation occurred in the form of a number of swapping arrangements between the two governments and the oil companies, so that Canadian firms could deliver oil to refineries in the American Mid-west in return for American deliveries through the Maine pipeline to Eastern Canada. There was much discussion of a pipeline to bring Alaskan oil to the continental United States, but Nixon eventually chose an all-American route, which would bring oil to the Alaska coast and then by tanker to Washington State. The Canadian government had opposed this arrangement because it feared spills and leaks from tankers passing down its coast.[82]

In August 1974, President Ford replaced President Nixon, and with Watergate seemingly behind it, the new administration could turn its attention to the energy problem. In January 1975, Ford sent Congress a thirteen-part energy independence bill. He also imposed a tariff on imported oil, intending to encourage domestic production. Congress removed the tariff and changed large portions of the energy bill. In December 1975, the president signed the new Energy Policy and Conservation Act.[83] The new act gave the president the authority to impose tariffs (which Congress had just recently removed). It also authorized the creation of a new Strategic Petroleum Reserve (SPR); that is, a stockpile analogous to that which already existed for other raw materials and authorized the use of oil from the Naval Petroleum Reserves. Although the act did not specify how the stockpile was to be filled, this objective was in fact met by pumping oil out of the Naval Petroleum Reserves and storing it in empty salt caverns. This practice may have been meant to ensure American self-sufficiency, but it hardly enhanced security in times of crisis. When under President Carter the government began to purchase oil to fill the SPR, the government found that it was contributing to rising prices and soon stopped the purchases. The SPR exists to this day, but it has never reached its legal capacity of one billion barrels, and even that would not meet American needs for a year.[84] By 1976, the public had for the most part lost interest in energy issues, and the administration had to admit that imports would stay the same or increase, no matter what any government did short of draconian rationing. In fact, in June 1976, Frank Zarb, President Ford's energy administrator, told a Senate committee that American imports of Middle Eastern oil had increased from 22 percent before the "energy crisis" to 45 percent.[85]

What policy toward Canada there was under Ford consisted, as it had under Nixon, for the most part of reactions to Canadian actions. These Canadian policies continued much as they had been during the Nixon years. Canada again raised the export tax on oil and reduced exports to the United States (moving the date for the total phase-out of exports from 1983 to 1981), while negotiating "swap arrangements" that allowed existing American refineries dependent on Canadian crude to continue to buy from Canada. At the same time, "expert" predictions of Canadian petroleum reserves continued to decline; in 1975, Canada became a net importer of oil.[86]

Though the swap arrangements supplied the Northern Tier US refineries, the announcement of reduced Canadian exports caused the market to act. American refineries began to find their oil elsewhere, and imports from Canada declined during 1974.[87] The two governments also agreed that swapped oil would not count as part of any American import or Canadian export quotas.[88] When Frank Zarb, President Ford's energy administrator, addressed a Senate committee in June 1976, he listed Canada as just one of eight "major suppliers." In public and in private, American policy was the same: disappointment *and* understanding that Canada did not have more oil to share. Higher prices were "inevitable."[89]

Another American response consisted of domestic arrangements to ensure supplies of crude oil for all American refineries (quotas allocating scarce Canadian oil to the Northern Tier refineries went into effect on 1 April 1976) and a few wistful references to the possibility of a common American-Canadian energy policy, which, however, Zarb thought, Canadians could not accept for "political reasons." He suggested the alternative of "parallel approaches to common [energy] issues," a policy President Ford seems not to have pursued in spite of some interest on Prime Minister Trudeau's part.[90]

President Carter, who succeeded Ford in January 1977, approached energy policy with the same moral commitment he brought to most of his policies. He was determined to reduce America's dependence on foreign oil and to wean the American people from their energy-wasting ways. Within three months of taking office, he addressed the nation on this issue: "Our decision about energy will test the character of the American people and the ability of the President and the Congress to govern this nation. This difficult effort will be the 'moral equivalent of war.'" [91]

The president tried to persuade Congress to pass two major packages of energy legislation, the first introduced in 1977, when the oil crisis had become but a bad memory for most Americans, and the second in 1979, when the crisis in the Iranian government had again brought the energy issue to the forefront.

The two Carter energy packages consisted of a number of complementary measures, such as the deregulation of oil and natural gas pricing, various inducements to practise conservation, and encouragement to use less import-dependent sources of energy (such as coal or uranium), or so-called alternative energy sources (such as solar and windpower). None of these measures involved Canada directly, though some of the president's advisors pointed out that no matter how successful his measures, the United States would continue to depend on foreign oil. The best that could be done, according to Robert Ellsworth, author of several congressional energy studies, was to obtain a larger portion of such supplies from relatively secure sources, such as the Western Hemisphere. "If the prospect of increased hemispheric energy supplies is bright," Ellsworth wrote, "how might the United States secure a substantial portion of these supplies?" And what "political constraints" might there be "upon US access to such supplies?"[92] Given Canadian policy at the time, it is not surprising that Ellsworth did not distinguish among the various Western Hemisphere countries, considering them all to be equally secure or insecure.

There was concern in other parts of the American government about the country's continued reliance on imported oil, especially Middle Eastern oil. A series of studies of America's oil import dependence by the State, Defense, Treasury, and Commerce Departments appeared in the *Federal Register* of 29 March 1979. These studies, though they reveal considerable concern with protection of the domestic oil industry, concentrate on one particular foreign policy aspect of oil imports: If the US depended on foreign oil, it would look weak in comparison with its oil-exporting rivals, the Soviet Union and China. How could its allies see the United States as a reliable protector as long as it was so dependent on imported oil?[93]

President Carter realized that the US would continue to need substantial quantities of imported oil and that the best his administration could hope to do was to keep imports from rising. Addressing the nation in July 1979, he pledged that "this nation will never use more foreign oil than we did in 1977 – never." Seven months later, he formulated the so-called Carter Doctrine, which declared the security of the Persian Gulf, and thus its oil supplies, to be a vital interest of the United States. The Carter Doctrine was an admission of the importance of Middle Eastern oil.[94]

It did not, however, amount to a policy on Canadian oil. In their eagerness "to do something" about the energy problem, the Carter people had put domestic priorities at the top of their agenda. By 1979, they felt ready to talk to Canada about energy cooperation. In June 1979, the two governments set up a cabinet-level committee to discuss energy policy, and the background notes for Carter's planned November 1979 trip to Ottawa contain several references to American-Canadian energy cooperation. Someone with an illegible signature wrote to Zbigniew Brzezinski on 22 October 1979, "We are trying to cook up a fairly impressive energy deal with Canada, to be consummated when the President goes to Ottawa." And a draft of Carter's speech in Canada mentions energy cooperation as well as oil and electricity exchanges.[95] But it was not to be. The Iranian hostage crisis meant that Carter's visit did not happen. In the meanwhile, the Canadian Conservative government of Joe Clark was replaced by Pierre Trudeau's, which lost no time in implementing the nationalistic National Energy Programme.

What American policy about Canadian energy existed under Carter consisted of individual and uncoordinated items. Much discussion focused on pipelines. In January 1977, the two governments signed, and later that year they ratified, a thirty-five-year agreement to protect and regulate oil and gas pipelines running across each other's territory. This agreement was followed in 1980 by another agreement to regulate the purchase of supplies for such pipelines.[96]

There was also a proposal for Canada to participate in the filling of the US Strategic Petroleum Reserve, by storing oil in abandoned salt caverns in Cape Breton, Nova Scotia. It is not clear whether this oil was to be Canadian or American-owned, but in any case the plan was cancelled when rising oil prices caused the Carter administration to interrupt the filling of its own reserve.[97] Another bit of cooperation occurred at the June 1979 Tokyo summit of the G-7 most industrialized countries, where the European governments sought to change the formula for counting oil imports in time of emergency, in order not to have to count the recent North Sea finds. Carter believed that proposal to be unfair and was glad of the support he received from Prime Minister Clark. In the end, the American position prevailed.[98]

Then there was the implementation of the threatened Canadian petroleum export reductions to the US. This policy, while not officially abandoned by Trudeau or Clark, proved unworkable. As long as Canada had oil to sell, no Canadian government was prepared to say the oil could not be sold. So, for example, during the cold winter of 1976-7, Canada supplied extra oil and gas to the US; in June 1977, Canada's National Energy Board exempted heavy crude from export licensing because Canada had a surplus of that product; in December 1978, the Canadian minister of energy told the American secretary of energy that Canada would not reduce shipments of Alberta light crude on 1 January 1979, as had been planned. In talks leading up to the planned November 1979 presidential visits, the two governments agreed to continue the system of oil exchanges, which in fact represented additions to the Canadian export quotas.[99]

By the end of the Carter administration, most American experts agreed that, in spite of such measures, Canadian products would not play a major role in the solution of the American oil import problem. Canada, so the conventional wisdom went, just did not have enough oil to share.[100]

The Reagan administration agreed with Carter's that the United States should be less dependent on foreign oil, but it saw the solution not in conservation and alternative fuels, but in market forces and decreased environmental regulation, which were expected to lead to the discovery of more domestic oil. That policy was not as simplistic as it appeared. Market forces meant higher prices, and higher prices in themselves led to conservation measures (and, of course, protection of the domestic industry). The Reagan policy was also not totally non-interventionist. Reagan put increased emphasis on the Strategic Petroleum Reserve and proceeded to fill it at an accelerated pace.[101]

Reagan's policy of market forces was almost the opposite of that followed by the Trudeau government, which was elected in 1980. As mentioned, the Canadian National Energy Programme sought to regulate the oil and natural gas industries and to keep Canadian resources in Canada, for the use and benefit of Canadians. The no-more-oil-exports policy of the 1970s followed by the NEP led to American demands for assured access to Canadian resources. By the 1980s, the United States was importing increasing quantities of Mexican oil, and the idea of a North American energy accord began to appear in some government reports and in Congress. There had been a flurry of such proposals during the 1979-80 presidential campaign, with potential candidates and non-candidates, such as Democrat Edward Kennedy and Republicans Jerry Brown, Howard Baker, and John Connally falling over each other to claim to be the first to suggest the idea of a North American energy accord. Canadian press reports claimed that the Carter administration was also interested in the idea and that the General Accounting Office was studying a North American oil market during summer 1979. The 1985 National Energy Policy Plan that President Reagan submitted to Congress included a veiled reference to such a pact. "The international energy policy of the United States involves special considerations in respect to our two closest neighbors."[102]

The American government protested strongly against several provisions of the NEP, and the Canadians led by Trudeau made some concessions; for example, by agreeing to pay for the 25 percent share of oil from federal land it was reserving for itself, and by promising no similar programs for other sectors. In 1984, the newly elected Mulroney government cancelled the NEP. At the time, the oil market had come full circle – again. A surplus meant that by 1985 the Canadian government was authorizing lower prices for sales to the US, a far cry from the export taxes of the 1970s.[103]

The Reagan administration was able to carry out a part of its policy (on Canadian energy) by means of the energy chapter in the Canada-United States Free Trade Agreement. (On the FTA, see Chapter 7.) When the Canadian government committed itself to the negotiation of a free trade agreement with the United States, the Americans insisted on a separate chapter on energy to forbid future export taxes and obligate Canada not to reduce its energy exports in times of shortage. Though this last provision was similar to one both governments had already accepted under the International Energy Association (IEA), the energy chapter of the FTA added extra certainty with respect to Canadian energy. For fear of nationalist protests, the Canadians had not wanted a separate chapter on energy. However, the Americans insisted on it, as well as on another chapter on investment, which would make it difficult for future governments to limit American investments in the Canadian energy (and other) industries, as the NEP had done.[104] (On investment policy, see Chapter 6.) In 1987, an official of the US Department of Energy told a conference organized by the Brookings Institute that "The recently negotiated Canadian Free Trade Agreement ... is another example of an international initiative that will have strong payoffs in energy security."[105]

Thus, by the end of the Cold War, the United States was as dependent on oil imports as it had been when the first oil crisis struck in 1973, but the free trade agreement with Canada and the possibility of a similar agreement with Mexico gave Americans assured access to some oil supplies in the Western Hemisphere. Canadian sales of oil to the United States had decreased from 1973 to 1980, in accordance with the policies of Canadian governments. But when oil supplies increased, the policies changed, and the oil sales increased. When Canadian companies reentered the American market, the Americans were importing much more oil. Canada did not regain the position as America's pre-eminent supplier that it had held in 1970, but with 13 percent of American oil imports in 1988, it continued to be a significant supplier.[106]

The Energy Crisis: Natural Gas

Natural gas issues do not pack as much emotional or political impact as oil issues. Yet natural gas accounts for almost a quarter of the energy used in the United States and keeps an even higher proportion of Americans warm than does oil during the cold winters that occur in the north of the country.

Americans began to use natural gas in large quantities during the Second World War, but they did not buy any from Canada until the Korean War, when the Department of Defense arranged for the purchase of some

Canadian gas for military bases in Montana.[107] Canada is the only foreign country from which the United States imports significant quantities of natural gas, but the proportion of imports is lower than for oil, rising from about 5 percent of consumption in the 1970s to 10 percent by the 1980s.[108] Nevertheless, the gas market has been subject to protectionist pressures similar to those experienced in the oil market, with the result that this market was thoroughly regulated; President Carter's energy bill, for example, set twenty-eight different regulated prices for gas from different sources. The discovery of major reserves of gas in Alaska in the 1960s added another factor to the mix of natural gas policies. American policy on Canadian natural gas has dealt with two distinct but related issues: purchases of Canadian gas and the construction of pipelines from Canada and/or Alaska to the United States.

After 1968, Americans were finding less gas than they needed to meet domestic demand. In 1969, the president of Husky Oil estimated that in future the US would have to meet two-thirds of its additional requirements with Canadian gas.[109] Nevertheless, when an American firm wanted to import natural gas from Canada, the firm had to justify the imports; for example, by demonstrating that they were needed in the West or Northwest, where American gas was not available.[110] This policy continued, even when American importers needed gas to meet the needs of states in New England, the West, and Mid-west, which did not have easy access to other foreign or American gas. From 1970 to 1973, Canadians tried to limit exports. The Canadian policy of limiting gas exports was not much more successful than it had been for oil exports. In 1973-4 and again during the cold winter of 1976-7, the Canadian government gave in to the pressure of its exporters, and in the latter case, the appeals of the American government, and allowed gas exports to continue. In 1974, major new finds of gas were made in Canada; Canadians now had an ample supply of this fuel, enough to last them several decades.[111]

The Canadian government also sharply increased the price of exported gas, in 1974 and again in 1976 and 1978. The Ford administration objected privately, but it does not seem to have otherwise reacted. President Ford wrote Brent Scowcroft in May 1976, "Why should US ask Canada to RII if they act like this?" (We do not know what this question means, but we assume it was not meant to be complimentary.) The Carter administration protested publicly and extracted a Canadian promise of more notice for future price increases.[112]

The Carter administration also attempted to define the precise role Canadian gas should play in the American energy mix. The 1978 Natural Gas Policy Act (specifying twenty-eight prices, mentioned above) raised the price of natural gas in the US and led to significantly higher production of gas in the lower forty-eight states. The administration had hoped for this result, because it saw Canadian (and Mexican gas) as a supplement to American sources. In 1979, the secretary of energy announced a list of seven priority sources for natural gas supplies. The list read: gas from the lower forty-eight states, Alaskan gas, gas made from American coal, "overland supplies from neighbouring sovereign countries (Canada and Mexico)," gas made from American petroleum, Western Hemisphere imports, and gas from the rest of the world. This was not a mere wish list. At about the same time, the Department of Energy refused a firm permission to import Algerian liquefied natural gas on the ground that the firm had failed "to demonstrate an overriding national or regional need for the gas."[113]

For gas, as for oil, shortage became surplus by 1982; the American government began to pressure Canadians to lower the price of gas. The Canadian government responded by first lowering (1983) and then deregulating (1984) the export price. The lower price resulted in protectionist demands for a restriction on Canadian imports. In February 1984, a US Department of Energy report warned of "undue dependence on unreliable sources of supply," though commentators later hastened to add that Canada was a secure source. Both the administration and a congressional report resisted protectionist demands with respect to Canadian gas; they affirmed their belief that access to Canadian gas was important to future American energy security.[114] The 1988 Free Trade Agreement and the 1991 NAFTA gave the United States assured access to Canadian natural gas, and Canada a guaranteed market there.[115]

While some Americans were not sure if the United States should import Canadian gas or try to rely on its own resources, most of those involved in energy issues and relations with Canada wanted pipelines built to bring Canadian and/or Alaskan oil to the United States.[116] But by the 1960s, Canadians were experiencing their own wave of nationalism. They had created a National Energy Board (in 1957), which had to approve exports of natural gas as surplus to Canadian needs, and in 1966, the Canadian government at first refused to approve a pipeline from Manitoba to Ontario through the United States. The American ambassador wrote the State Department: "In taking a nationalistic stance, the Government only succeeded in outraging every other legitimate interest including ... the United States."[117] He did not define what he meant by a legitimate interest, but the Canadian government bowed to the pressure and in October granted the permission it had refused in July.

After the discovery of vast reserves of gas in Alaska and the Canadian Arctic (mostly from 1968 to 1974), several different pipeline proposals appeared in Canada and the United States. Americans wanted to bring Alaskan natural gas to the lower forty-eight states, either through Canada, or in liquefied form, down the West Coast. Some Canadian and American firms wanted to build a pipeline or pipelines to bring Canadian gas to the western United States. In the mid-1970s, the American government had some concerns that Canadian nationalism would make a Canadian route less secure than an all-American one. A 1974 briefing book prepared for President Ford mentioned "Canadian sovereignty" as a "complicating factor" in the pipeline issue, and a congressional committee wrote President Ford in April 1976 "that recent anti-US Canadian actions ... indicate that Canada cannot be relied upon to maintain their [sic] side of the bargain."[118]

Relations became much better under President Carter, and the two governments decided that a pipeline from Alaska carrying Alaskan, Canadian Arctic, and Albertan gas to the United States would be in both their interests. They signed an agreement for the construction of the pipeline, in January 1977, Carter's first month in office. Seven months of intense discussions about the route for the pipeline followed. That spring, major reports, commissioned much earlier (the Berger report in Canada and the Litt report in the United States), made differing recommendations for the best location of the pipeline. After lengthy intergovernmental negotiations, the president and the prime minister announced in September the choice of the so-called Alcan route (from Alaska to Alberta, and from there to the US), recommended by neither of the inquiries, but not (according to one American source) until after the Defense Department had found the Canadian route to be as secure as the all-American route of shipment down the coast. After this announcement, the January agreement was duly ratified by Congress (November 1977) and the Canadian Parliament (April 1978). But the pipeline was not built. With the discovery of more gas in the continental US, private investors were not interested in raising the large amounts of money needed for the pipeline, and in spite of the earlier agreement regulating procurement issues, some members of Congress were dissatisfied with the chances American suppliers would have to bid for supplies and work on the Canadian section of the line.[119]

In the end, the controversy about the route and the procurement of supplies mattered little. By 1978, there was talk of "prebuilding" part of the Canadian section of the line, so that more Alberta gas could reach the US. The Canadian government feared that such "prebuilding" would mean that the more accessible Canadian reserves would flow to the US before the money needed to tap the more remote Alaskan sources came on stream. The government held out for financing guarantees and later construction of the entire line. The draft communique for the Carter visit to Ottawa in November 1979 mentions such a trade-off. (Because of the Iranian hostage crisis, the visit did not take place.) By July 1980, talk became reality. After both houses of Congress had passed resolutions of good faith to build the entire line later, the Canadian government agreed to allow the "prebuilding" of only the more southerly portion of the Canadian part of the line, so that Alberta gas could be brought to the US.[120]

In 1981 and 1982, the newly installed Reagan administration made some effort to revive interest in building the rest of the line, but with a surplus of natural gas on world markets, the money could not be raised. By 1985, one commentator wrote that "the project appeared further from commencement than at any time during its history."[121]

Uranium

Like oil, but unlike natural gas, uranium is a mineral the mention of which evokes an emotional reaction, because uranium not only is a source of heat and electricity; it also produces deadly weapons and life-threatening radiation. From the late 1930s and early 1940s, when the potential of uranium first became known, the American demand for, and hence the American government's interest in, controlling the supply of this mineral has varied more widely and more sharply than it has for most other commodities. The United States had considerable reserves of uranium ore; Canada had more. Significant quantities also occur in the former Soviet Union, Australia, and western and southern Africa.

During the Second World War, uranium ore was in short supply. The American government bought all available supplies (from Canada and the Belgian Congo) and gave British and Canadian researchers small amounts for their research.[122] The two atomic bombs dropped on Japan in August 1945 did not interrupt the relentless American search for uranium. When the war was over, the American government hoped and believed that it would continue to be able to control most of the world's uranium. In November 1945, General Leslie Groves, head of the American nuclear program, wrote to his and the British government that the US, Canada, and Britain should "take measures as far as practicable to secure control and possession ... of all deposits of uranium and thorium" in their respective territories, and that the three governments should "endeavor ... to acquire all available supplies ... in the British Commonwealth and other countries." A month later, speaking at a meeting of the three governments, General Groves was even more direct. He added that it should be the policy of the three governments "to try and secure control of all deposits and supplies of raw materials wherever they might be situated."[123]

Any American policy to control available uranium supplies inevitably involved Canada. The three governments (US, UK, and Canada) had attempted in 1943 and again in 1944 to survey the world reserves of uranium and thorium. At that time, it appeared that the two principal sources would be the Belgian Congo and northern Canada, though the reports also noted the existence of "lower-grade" deposits in Portugal, South Africa, southern India, Sweden, Brazil, Argentina, and Russia. Of these sources, the Congo, with about nine times as much ore as Canada was then known to have, was considered the most important.[124]

Much as they would have liked to, the Americans realized that they alone could not control all the known deposits of uranium. In 1943, Prime Minister Churchill and President Roosevelt had created the Combined Policy Committee (CPC) to deal with the exchange of information on atomic energy. This committee consisted of two American, two British, and one Canadian representative, though the Canadians had not been consulted about the creation of the committee and were (perhaps inadvertently) not invited to the first several meetings. In 1944, the CPC created another committee, the Combined Development Trust, to control the known sources of raw materials needed for the production of atomic energy. The pattern was as it had been for the CPC: the Trust was to have five members, two American, two British, and a Canadian. It was to allocate all the available raw materials to the three governments. Though it conducted surveys of reserves, the Trust did not work as a multinational institution. The American office continued to function as part of the American government, and the American government decided how much uranium it would need. The Canadian government kept for itself whatever limited amounts it needed (and made no financial contributions to the Trust). The British, whose task was to obtain control of the Congo ores (presumably in cooperation with the Belgian government), had to make do with whatever they could get.[125]

In November 1945, when the two prime ministers and the president met in Washington, they agreed to continue this pattern of wartime cooperation. The emphasis, however, changed. American dominance of the Combined Development Trust was institutionalized by a change in membership: there were to be three American, two British, and one Canadian member. British-American disputes over allocations of raw materials continued, but the Canadians, who had sold most of their available supplies to the American government, were content to emphasize their control of what they owned, but otherwise to stay out of the controversy.

With the end of wartime collaboration, trinational cooperation was markedly reduced. In 1946, both the American and the Canadian governments passed their own atomic energy control acts. The American act limited the sharing of information with other governments. That year also saw the beginnings of an apparent American attempt to allow the international control of atomic energy through the United Nations. Even with most of the documentation now available, it is not clear how sincere Americans were in this effort and to what extent they used the Canadian representative, General Andrew McNaughton, to lend legitimacy to their cause. What is relevant here is that the American proposals were vague about the control of raw materials. They mentioned "dominion" rather than outright ownership or allocation, a word which suggests that the Americans sought continued national ownership of uranium.[126]

For the first five years after the war, uranium continued to be in short supply. The American government, and by 1947 also the Canadian, introduced incentive programs for the discovery of uranium ores. New discoveries, however, take time. The American government continued its policy of attempting to control uranium resources, wherever they might be found. In October 1949, George Kennan made several recommendations for "this country's unsatisfactory uranium position." He wanted the Combined Policy Committee to buy "all deposits of uranium and thorium" found in the United States, Britain, and Canada. He wanted the three governments to "use every endeavour ... to acquire all possible supplies of uranium and thorium" found in "the remaining territories of the British Commonwealth and other countries." He also recommended that "in the interests of the common security, all sources and fissionable material not required for ... current industrial projects in the United Kingdom and Canada and elsewhere, as defined by the CPC, will be allocated to the United States." As a consequence, the American government surprised the British and Canadian delegations by showing renewed interest in the CPC. At a December 1947 meeting of the CPC, the American delegates declared themselves willing to give more information to the Canadians and the British, if the latter would let them use more of the Belgian ores. It was a deal the British could not refuse. By the so-called modus vivendi of 6 January 1948, the three governments agreed to let the American government have most of the available uranium for the next two years. The British government also promised to encourage uranium production throughout the Commonwealth.[127]

While allowing the British and Canadians to live with the illusion that the cosy three-government club of the Second World War days continued to be the centre of its atomic energy policy, the American government began to make other arrangements to assure itself of uranium supplies. It negotiated secret supply agreements with other governments, notably that of Belgium. The Combined Development Trust, renamed the Combined Development Agency, continued to function until 1950, but by 1949 it had become obvious that there was more uranium ore in the world than anyone had imagined. In September 1949, the CPC admitted there was enough ore to meet British and American (and presumably Canadian) requirements. By 1950, the Americans were still insisting that they needed all Canadian ore for the next eight years, but South African production was by now so large that the South African government aspired to join the Combined Policy Committee. The Americans were not prepared to dilute the value of membership in the club by admitting more members. They pointed out that it was only because of Canada's "wartime participation in the allied project" that the Canadians were members. Informally, however, the club was already expanding, without American permission. In 1949, the Soviets exploded their first atomic device. Repeated spy scandals (notably the Karl Fuchs case) reduced American faith in British collaboration. Several other countries (France, Brazil, India) were expanding their production of uranium. Nineteen fifty was the last time the nuclear club of three met as such.[128]

By 1952, the situation had changed so that Canada in some respects had become more special to Americans than the United Kingdom. In January 1952, the National Security Council judged that "the common defense and security would be substantially promoted" if the American government gave to the Canadians "restricted information ... which will allow the Canadians to operate at the highest possible efficiency the uranium ... refineries which will be constructed by the Canadians." But when it came to exchange of information with the British, the United States was "more restrictive than the United Kingdom would like." The "inhibiting factor" was the Atomic Energy Act of 1946, a factor which proved less inhibiting in the case of the Canadians, because it was interpreted leniently with respect to Canada.[129]

The 1950s and 1960s were years of transition for atomic energy. By 1953, when President Eisenhower gave his Atoms for Peace speech, American scientists had demonstrated the feasibility of producing electricity from atomic energy. Within a few years, the first commercial nuclear reactors in the United States began operation; there were ten by January 1961.[130] Canada, France, and Britain (as well as the Soviet Union) were also working on nuclear reactors. But the construction of reactors did not expand as rapidly as the production of uranium, a mineral that was in ever more abundant supply.

By 1959, American production exceeded Canadian. With the availability of domestic supplies, the American Atomic Energy Commission (AEC) saw less need for Canadian supplies and began to curtail its purchases from Canada. A 1951 report to the National Security Council stated that the US was purchasing virtually all of Canada's uranium. In 1955, an American-Canadian agreement stated that "substantial uranium production in Canada" had been made available to the United States, and that "these arrangements and contracts shall remain in force and effect except as modified or revised by mutual agreement." In 1956, the AEC dropped the price it paid for uranium from US$11.51 to $8 per pound; it also announced that no new contracts would be made for the purchase of Canadian uranium. By the end of 1958, the extent of Canadian reserves became known just as the US military began to realize that it had enough uranium for several years. The AEC began to cancel options to purchase uranium and to negotiate contracts so as to lower both prices and amounts. In 1964, the AEC announced that by 1966, it would no longer buy foreign uranium for enrichment and later use by American utilities.[131]

The effect on the Canadian industry, which had been exporting more than 80 percent of its production to the US, was dramatic. Both prices and production fell rapidly. In spite of Ottawa's 1965 announcement of its own stockpiling program, Canadian production fell from over 12,000 tons in 1959 to 2,847 tons in 1968. By 1969, the world price had fallen to US$4 per pound. Though American production also fell, it did not decline as rapidly (from 20,000 tons in 1959 to 10,000 tons in 1966), and there was even a limited revival after 1966, when the AEC's decision to allow private ownership of enriched uranium seemed to indicate that atomic power was becoming an industry like any other.[132]

By the 1960s, the club of nuclear weapons states expanded from two to five (the US, the USSR, the UK, China, and France). The Americans and then the Canadians discovered the virtues of nuclear non-proliferation. In 1957, the US led the UN in the creation of the International Atomic Energy Agency, whose safeguards (allowing states to produce nuclear energy without making nuclear weapons) came into effect five years later. The Americans had limited the exports of nuclear materials since at least 1946. In 1955 and again in 1959, Canada and the United States agreed not to transfer to other countries nuclear know-how one acquired from the other. Canada instituted export controls in 1958 (and tightened and refined them in 1965 and 1969). The 1968 Nuclear Non-Proliferation Treaty obligated both states to follow similar safeguards. Though close collaboration between the nuclear industries of the two nations continued throughout the 1950s and 1960s – the Americans reprocessed or "enriched" the plutonium produced by Canada's nuclear reactors – there is no indication that Canada discovered nuclear virtue because of American pressure. To the contrary, in 1965, the American embassy in Ottawa warned the State Department not to attempt to pressure Canada on such a sensitive subject as nuclear non-proliferation.[133] Non-proliferation became a subject of great concern after India's 1974 nuclear explosion. In September 1974, the United States and Canada combined with other states to tighten export controls on nuclear materials.[134]

Export controls at first depressed further an already depressed uranium market. In 1971, prices reached a new low of US$3.55 per pound. Though the AEC pleaded with the White House (in 1970 and 1971) at least to announce a future exemption for Canada, so that Canadian uranium could be enriched in the US, the Nixon White House ignored these pleas. In October 1971, the AEC reiterated its policy of not enriching foreign uranium for use in the US. When in 1972 the AEC announced that it would begin to dispose of its stockpile, that was yet another blow to the struggling Canadian uranium industry. In hindsight, some signs of a recovery in the demand for uranium are discernible, even as the market hit bottom. By 1970, a number of other governments had announced plans for the construction of nuclear-generating plants.[135]

The market revived well before the Arab oil embargo of November 1973. In 1972, the AEC had implemented a policy of allowing larger concentrations of uranium to remain in the "tails" or leftovers of the enrichment plants, a move that increased the demand for natural uranium. In January 1973, the AEC then demanded that utilities using its enrichment facilities have in hand contracts for at least eight years of uranium. This move caused an immediate increase in demand. Finally, in October 1973, the AEC announced that, beginning in 1974, it would phase out the embargo on the use of foreign uranium, though it warned that it would take "appropriate measures" to protect "the viability of the domestic uranium producing industry." Within three years, foreign uranium's share increased from 4 percent to 14 percent of the American market.[136]

When the uranium market was at its most depressed (that is, in 1971), the governments of Canada, France, South Africa, and Australia, together with the uranium-producing firms located in those countries, decided to help themselves.[137] In February 1972, they met in Paris and created a cartel to control the supply and price of uranium for the next five years. As a cartel, this one was less effective than most. As a commentator said, the cartel "produced more paper than uranium and enriched more lawyers" than uranium producers or miners.[138]

Several factors increased the demand for uranium ore from 1973 to 1978. In January 1973, the newly elected Australian Labour government of Gough Whitlam banned further export of the mineral. Several European countries were planning to build nuclear reactors, even before the Arab oil embargo of November 1973 created panic on world energy markets. Uranium prices rose from US$6.50 per pound in October 1973, to $26 per pound in August 1975, and touched a high (for future contracts) of $55 per pound in 1976. By June 1974, world prices had outstripped the cartel's prices, rendering it meaningless. In September 1975, the American firm Westinghouse decided to stop supplying uranium with the sale of its nuclear reactors, as it had committed to do, a move which in turn led to the "discovery" of the cartel.

The cartel had in fact been no secret. Press reports of it had appeared as early as February 1972, and the Canadian government had told the American government what it was doing. The American authorities, having decided to protect the domestic industry, chose to ignore information about the cartel. It was only after Westinghouse defaulted on its contracts (an action affecting utility companies in several states) that judicial proceedings and congressional investigations began in 1976. The question, thereafter, was not one of American access or refusal to buy Canadian resources, but rather the extraterritorial application of American anti-trust laws. Various American courts and congressional committees demanded that Gulf Canada, a subsidiary of an American firm, produce documents relating to the cartel. A New Mexico judge thundered, "Deference to the sovereignty and national interest of Canada ... cannot be accomplished through sacrifice of the sovereignty of New Mexico."[139] Gulf, with the support of the Canadian government and ultimately the Supreme Court of Canada, refused to do so. Insofar as there was an American policy on this issue, it came from the State Department, which was sensitive to the Canadian concern about the extraterritorial application of American laws. In the end, the court cases were settled out of court or by the imposition of ridiculously low fines. The congressional investigation led to no legislation nor to any administrative action. The "great uranium cartel," swept away by a sea of higher prices, lasted barely two years, had little or no effect on the world or the American market, and it became but a wrinkle in the history of resource policy. By 1980, when the last court case was settled, the uranium market had taken another turn for the worse.

The aftermath of the 1970s oil crisis was the nuclear industry's finest hour. In June 1976, the Federal Energy Resources Council wrote President Ford that it considered coal and "nuclear-power generation" to be "vital elements of our effort to avoid greater reliance on imported oil"; it also recommended reliance on domestic uranium.[140] President Carter's decision (in 1977) not to proceed with the construction of the so-called fast-breeder reactor and to stop reprocessing plutonium was expected to lead to an increase in demand for uranium. But 1979 saw the Three Mile Island accident in an American nuclear-power-generating facility. That, plus a greatly enhanced concern about nuclear proliferation – Israel, South Africa, Pakistan, Iraq, and other governments were rumoured to be making bombs – dampened enthusiasm for the nuclear generation of electricity. During the next oil crisis, uranium prices did not follow oil prices. Uranium prices continued to fall throughout the 1980s, to US$11 per pound in 1988, then $7.16 in 1991.[141] The end of the Cold War brought uranium and plutonium from dismantled nuclear weapons onto the market, and thus reduced the demand for natural uranium.

Under these conditions, American policies toward Canadian uranium supplies have dealt with two main issues. One issue is non-proliferation. By a 1977 agreement, confirmed in 1980, the two governments agreed to impose similar non-proliferation conditions on purchasers of nuclear materials from either Canada or the US. For example, if Japan buys Canadian uranium and has it enriched in the United States, it will not be subjected to two different non-proliferation regimes. This practice amounts to a common policy, which facilitates exports from both countries.[142]

The other issue is how little Canadian uranium the United States will buy. Canada has large uranium reserves. The US has few reserves left to profitably mine at the prices of the 1990s. The maintenance of a "viable" domestic uranium industry has been American government policy since the adoption of the 1954 Atomic Energy Act. From 1983 to 1992, the Secretary of Energy was required to make an annual "viability assessment" of the domestic industry. In 1984, the Secretary found the industry to be in difficulty, but because its problems were caused by the low quality of the remaining reserves, no government action followed. By the terms of the 1988 Free Trade Agreement, the United States agreed not to place an embargo on Canadian uranium; Canada in turn will not require the further processing of uranium for export. By 1992, many American and many Canadian uranium mines had closed, and others were operating below capacity; by 1994, the markets began to show signs of recovery.

The end of the Cold War also produced an interesting example of the way Canada can be neglected or forgotten when the American government has geopolitical as well as domestic interests. In 1991, the American government agreed to buy Soviet raw materials, including uranium, in return for dismantling some weapons and weapons systems. This led to an anti-dumping action from American uranium producers, an action which was settled by an American agreement with the states of the former Soviet Union (October 1992) aimed at maintaining a price of US$13 per pound. In February 1993, Russia and the United States signed an agreement by which the United States would buy enriched uranium from dismantled Soviet weapons. Protests from American producers then led to a further agreement which required Soviet sales to be matched with sales of American-produced uranium (with the Soviet uranium being sold below, and the American above, the world price). This agreement in turn led to complaints from Canada, which threatened legal action under NAFTA, because, by that agreement, the United States had promised not to bar sales of Canadian uranium. To forestall such an action, in a February 1995 exchange of letters with Canada, the American government agreed that it would not buy Russian uranium in such quantities as to squeeze out Canadian sales. Canada, with 24 percent of the American market, continues to be the Americans' major supplier.[143]

Conclusions

The mix of American policies toward Canada was somewhat different in the economic than in the political area. From Washington, Canada sometimes appeared to be not much more than a great storehouse of resources, but that perception did not necessarily mean that Canada should not process its own resources or that these resources should be owned or controlled by the United States. The uranium issue is a case in point. After the Second World War, the US asserted control over all "free world" sources of the mineral. In the Free Trade Agreement, the American government agreed to not embargo Canadian uranium if Canada would agree to not require uranium to be processed before it left the country; in other words, if Canada agreed to be a supplier of an unprocessed raw material. One could also interpret the American insistence on the construction of the St. Lawrence Seaway as further evidence; Americans wanted access to Canadian resources as if they were their own. But such an interpretation is not entirely fair. The Seaway provided mutual benefits, and the Canadian government was more insistent than the American that it be built.

On the issue of mineral policy during the early Cold War, two contradictory policy patterns predominated. For the most part, American policy makers assumed that they would have access to Canadian resources as if they were their own. They were concerned about the fact that so much of American nickel was produced by one firm, INCO, not that so much nickel came from Canada. At other times, Canada was just a foreign country like any other; for example, when some American military planners thought they might have to use military force to secure Canadian nickel supplies, or when Canada was ranked with Mexico as a relatively secure source of minerals. There were also the occasional flashes of *exemptionalism,* for example, when Canada was exempted from American import controls on lead and zinc.

On petroleum policy, Canada was at first a foreign country like any other. The first official American reaction to the discovery of oil in Canada was fear that Canadian oil might damage American-Venezuelan relations. Within ten years, the American government was trying to limit Canadian oil imports. In principle, Canadian and Mexican oil had an overland exemption. In fact, the American government tried to limit Canadian oil imports because of pressure from the domestic oil industry. In this case, policy was clearly driven by a domestic agenda. Canada was just a foreign country like any other, at least according to policy. Practice was something else, because American-owned firms and American importers did not cooperate with voluntary restraints.

When oil became expensive after 1970, the Nixon administration demanded a North American oil policy. But the Canadians refused and soon started to reduce exports to the US. The Americans resolved their problem by finding oil domestically and elsewhere. Canada was therefore again just a foreign country like any other. However, through "swap" arrangements (providing Canadian oil for refineries in the northern US) Canada became exceptional. Similarly, some of President Ford's advisors thought that it might be advantageous to the United States to have a common North American raw materials policy, one which included supplies other than oil, so that Canadian restrictions would not in future apply to other raw materials.[144] But the advisors seem not to have pursued this idea. President Carter treated Canada as a foreign country; that is, he had *no specific Canada policy*. Toward the end of his administration, Carter suggested a common North American oil and electricity policy, but other matters preoccupied him for the remainder of his term.

The Reagan administration pursued the idea of a common North American energy policy with some vigour, but in spite of a receptive Canadian government (after 1984), no such policy was implemented. The Free Trade Agreement gives the United States access to scarce Canadian energy resources in a shortage, but it does so in terms not much different from those stipulated by the International Energy Agency. Neither policy has been put to the test. Once again, Americans see access to Canadian resources as their right, but in legal terms, Canadian energy is not treated much differently from that of other members of the OECD (though Mexico gained more favourable terms under NAFTA).

On natural gas, Canada has shown much less firmness in resisting American demands. Canadian gas is now sold freely in the US and routed there by pipelines approved by the Canadian government. Canada is part of the American energy mix. This practice is a clear demonstration of the "Canada is to be treated like part of the US" policy. In the days of energy crisis, however, when Canada agreed to share its gas with the US, one sees hints of Canada as a friend and ally.

On uranium, the early postwar policies were mostly cases of *exceptionalism*. Canada was an ally which, because of its uranium supply, merited a special role with respect to US policy on nuclear issues (although at times the Americans were inclined to treat all of the world's uranium ore supplies as theirs to control). As uranium was discovered in the United States, American policy came to be driven by domestic concerns. Canada was a country like others, which produced something American producers wanted to be protected from. As the two governments developed common non-proliferation standards, they cooperated. Canada, like the US, was an opponent of the proliferation of nuclear weapons. The United States and Canada developed a common set of standards for dealing with third countries wishing to buy nuclear technology or supplies.

With respect to the uranium cartel, the American administration treated Canada as one foreign country among others; Congress and the courts thundered on about the observance of American laws, but the administration did not. It had known about the cartel and apparently let the Canadians do what any other foreign government might do. Indeed, the American reaction to OPEC was much stronger than to the uranium cartel. Yet those subsidiary institutions, such as the courts, that did deal with the uranium cartel practised the kind of policy Canadians profess to detest, the extraterritorial application of American laws (in this case, anti-trust laws).

When uranium became scarce during the 1970s, no special American attempt was made to obtain the Canadian mineral at lower prices. Unlike the oil situation, Canadians made few attempts to restrict Canadian resources to Canadians. Since then, the American government has agreed to give Canadians some access to the American market, even given the need to absorb surplus uranium from the former Soviet Union. Canada is exceptional, but not quite so exceptional as the former superpower, which has first call on the American market.

American policies toward Canadian resources during the Cold War did not for the most part fall into the pattern Canadian nationalists might have expected. Few deliberate attempts limited Canada to the production of unprocessed materials. Far from coveting Canadian resources, American interests often sought protection from Canadian imports. Where Canada was included in US policy, its role was no more special than that of Mexico. While Canada did not always succeed in having the policy it chose adopted (on pipelines, for example), the US insisted that Canada adopt American policies in only a few cases. And the Trudeau government did, albeit briefly, succeed in gaining greater control of the Canadian oil industry. The one example of the extraterritorial application of American laws described in this chapter – that of the anti-trust laws and the uranium cartel – was of little significance. When the Canadian government removed the controls on exports of oil and gas, a change the American government had sought for more than ten years, this outcome was not the result of American pressure but rather the initiative of a willing Canadian government, which wanted to show the American administration how friendly and pro-American it was. In short, we found little evidence of resource imperialism, but plenty on the importance of domestic pressure groups.

6
Policies on American Investment in Canada

Of the areas of American government policy discussed in this book, investment policy is the most difficult to describe and analyze, mainly because most Americans do not see policies on this issue as a normal or suitable subject for government intervention. A second problem is delimiting the topic. There are two kinds of foreign investment: direct (meaning the ownership of firms or their subsidiaries for the purposes of "controlling the use of these assets") and indirect (meaning just about any other type of ownership from stocks to bonds to loans).[1] Indirect investment can be either private or public; that is, government as well as private individuals might buy and sell bonds in another country. A third problem is that investment issues relate closely to and are thus difficult to separate from other aspects of economic policy. Investment relates to the more general issue of international monetary policy and to the balance of payments, but investment is also closely connected with trade in goods and is often indistinguishable from trade in services. (If an American bank does business in Canada, is the bank exporting a service or making a foreign investment?) A fourth problem, which makes the conduct of public policy particularly difficult, concerns the timing of cause and effect. Money the government of the United States borrows in one year may help to balance the current account in that year, but the interest that needs to be paid could cause a problem in future years. A fifth problem is the difference between perception and reality. Common sense suggests, and politicians thus are likely to act as if, a trade deficit translates automatically into a balance of payments problem. The fact is, however, that the movement of money (tourist spending and capital investments, to name just two examples) into an economy for other purposes will allow it to live with a trade deficit for an indefinite period.

Complex as the issues may be, a study of American policies toward Canada would be incomplete without the inclusion of investment policies. We have extracted three specific issues from the general category labelled investment policies to try to find an American policy toward Canada: balance of payments and monetary policy, direct investment by American firms in Canada, and attempts by the American government to apply export control laws to the subsidiaries of American firms operating in Canada. As in the last chapter on raw materials policy, we begin each section with a brief introduction on American policies on the issue in question and then continue with specific policies as they applied to Canada.

Balance of Payments and Monetary Policy
At the end of the Second World War, the American dollar was the currency everyone in the world needed to import anything. The US controlled more than two-thirds of the world's monetary reserves and enjoyed a huge balance of payments and trade surplus. Most American economists could not imagine that this situation would ever change. They led the world in the creation of a monetary system based on the American dollar[2] and its relationship to gold.[3]

But this system carried the seeds of its own destruction. As Americans helped other economies buy the goods those economies needed to recover, as American capital flowed to other countries to take advantage of the money to be made in that recovery, and as American money flowed over the non-Communist world (to Western Europe, Korea, and Vietnam, among other locations), the positive American balance of payments began to shrink. On 1 January 1968, Lyndon Johnson told the American people that the United States had had a deficit in its "international accounts [for] 17 of the last 18 years." But there are many ways of calculating the balance of payments, even accounting tricks to make a surplus or deficit look smaller. Regardless of the accounting method, economists began to perceive a problem with the American balance of payments by the late 1950s and early 1960s.

As early as 1955, the American secretary of the Treasury said that "the world dollar shortage which was so evident two years ago has changed." Four years later an internal State Department document expressed concern "over the implications of a continuing adverse trend in the United States balance of payments." The international dollar shortage had become a dollar glut, and American policy makers from the time of John Kennedy believed there to be a balance of payments deficit and acted accordingly.[4]

The American government's first reaction consisted of an attempt to reduce the amounts of money private citizens and multinational firms were sending out of the country. Voluntary guidelines in 1965 were followed by mandatory controls in 1968. As in the case of oil, governments find it difficult to control movements of goods, money, or people across their borders. In spite of the monetary crisis of 1971, the American government terminated its attempt at controls of capital movements in 1974. That attempt had become so "weighted down with escape clauses" that it had become meaningless.[5]

In 1968, the American government had to admit that the value of the dollar had fallen when it allowed a two-price system for gold: monetary gold, which was to be fixed at US$38 an ounce, and all other gold, which was allowed to increase in price according to market forces (and it did so, sharply). By 1971, the American government could no longer afford to support the dollar's link to gold. In August 1971, it severed the fixed link between the dollar and gold, in effect leaving every other government to control (or not to control) its currency's relationship to the dollar. Despite a brief attempt to re-establish fixed exchange rates (the Smithsonian Agreement of December 1971), the dollar had fallen to a still lower value by February 1973, forcing the governments of the world's major economies to give up the attempt to control the value of their currencies in relation to the dollar. In 1985, Secretary of the Treasury James Baker tried to improve the worsening American balance of trade by pushing down the value of the dollar. He persuaded the monetary authorities of the major industrialized countries to intervene in international monetary markets to reduce the value of the dollar and raise that of their currencies (the Plaza Accord). The effort succeeded partially with respect to the value of the dollar, but it did not bring the desired improvement in the balance of trade.[6]

Since then, bilateral and regional arrangements have linked some currencies to each other (for example, the European Monetary System) or bilateral arrangements have supported specific currencies (American attempts to shore up the Mexican peso in 1981 and 1994), but the dollar's value has been the responsibility of only the United States. In other words, the US needed a monetary policy to protect the dollar, a policy it did not need as long as the entire international monetary system revolved around American currency.[7]

As luck would have it, however, the American need for a monetary policy arose when it had become difficult for any government to protect the value of its currency. Since the 1960s, the international flow of money has increased so dramatically that on only rare occasions and with great effort have governments been able to resist a market-imposed change in the value of their currencies. The near collapse of the European Monetary System in fall 1993 and the similar collapse of the Mexican peso in 1994 are two recent and dramatic examples of this fact.

The Canadian dollar has not, however, been just another currency. Since the creation of the postwar international monetary system, it has had a special relationship to the American dollar, in that Canadians judge the value of the Canadian dollar in relation to the American dollar. All other Canadian monetary relationships flow from that one. An imbalance in the flow of funds between the two countries, therefore, has an effect on the

Canadian dollar and cannot usually be offset by a surplus elsewhere. From the end of the Second World War until 1962, the Canadian dollar "floated" in relation to the American dollar; that is, the Canadian government intervened only to prevent large deviations from the value of the American currency. The Canadian dollar was "pegged" at US92.5 cents from 1962 to 1970, but its value has been floating ever since. (See Figure 1, which shows the value of the dollar from 1947 to 1993.)

The first postwar imbalance in the flow of money between Canada and the US occurred in 1947. Europeans had experienced a cold winter, and that meant they needed more food and fuel imports than anticipated. As a result, Europeans were unable to pay for the raw materials they needed from Canada. At the same time, Europeans, and particularly the British, could not produce most of the manufactured goods Canadians had bought from them before the war. Canadians therefore bought from Americans. By September 1947, Canadian reserves of gold and American dollars were at the minimum level Canadian authorities considered necessary. They

Figure 1

Relationship of Canadian and American dollars, 1947-93

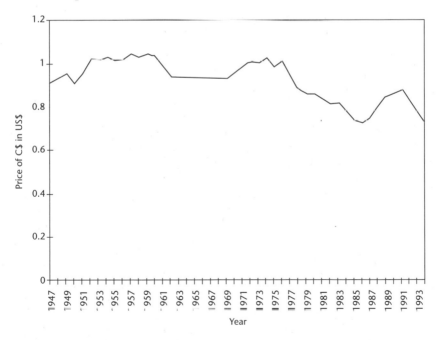

Sources: Canadian Economic Observer, Historical Statistical Supplement, annual data up to 1994; United States Federal Reserve Data Base (FRED):
<http://www.stls.frb.org/fred/data/exchange/excaus>.

asked the American government for trade concessions and a loan of $750 million; they later added a request to allow so-called offshore purchases under the Marshall Plan; that is, Canadians wanted Europeans to be allowed to spend their Marshall Plan dollars in Canada as well as in the US.

The American response, while described as generous by Canadians, was not automatic. Andrew Foster of the State Department's Division of British Commonwealth Affairs wrote to the American ambassador in Canada: "Top side in Washington is so preoccupied with the crisis in the UK and Western Europe that I fear it is going to be difficult to get much of a hearing for Canada's problems ... Canadians ... will be up against the difficulty that $750,000,000 is not to be had for the asking in Washington these days." In the end, the Canadians *did* manage to get some attention in Washington. They negotiated an agreement that included a $300 million loan and some trade concessions. (Discussions that – almost – resulted in a Canada-US free trade area also flowed from this crisis; see Chapter 7.)

At the same time, the Canadian government on 15 November 1947 announced a series of import and exchange controls. In April 1948, Congress adopted the Marshall Plan with the provision for offshore purchases. By then, Canadian reserves were already recovering. By 1949, when the British were forced to devalue the pound by 30 percent, Canada's reserves were in good shape, and Canada allowed its dollar to fall by only about 10 percent to stay competitive in Britain.[8] What is significant about these events in terms of American policies toward Canada is that Canada was one foreign country among others, whose problems had to be ranked accordingly.

By 1962, during the next Canadian monetary crisis, one aspect of the situation had changed. Britain was no longer a major player in terms of Canada's problems. In May 1962, the Diefenbaker government tried to peg the value of the Canadian dollar at US92.5 cents to prevent it from falling further. In June 1962, when the government could no longer support even that value, it turned to the United States for assistance, as the Mackenzie King government had done in 1947. The Canadian government also sought the support of the International Monetary Fund (IMF). The American government and the IMF agreed to loans and credits of $300 million, while the Canadian government cut spending, raised interest rates, and increased tariffs in an effort to salvage its falling currency. The American assistance was granted as a routine measure, with no more than a stern warning to pursue long-term reform of Canadian problems, such as the budget deficit. Behind the scenes, however, American policy makers resented the Canadian import surcharges, which Under-Secretary of State George Ball described as "pure protectionism." He added, "We had to run a fast rescue operation in view of the urgency of the crisis," but thought that "it would be a great mistake for us to let the Canadians get away, for any length of time, with such a cheap and easy solution as increased import restrictions."[9]

As mentioned, the Kennedy administration was the first postwar American administration to be concerned about the American balance of payments problems. In October 1962, Secretary of the Treasury Douglas Dillon wrote President Kennedy to point out that unusually large transactions with Canada had caused an increase in the American balance of payments deficit. By April 1963, President Kennedy's Balance of Payments Committee was discussing means of restricting foreigners' access to American capital markets. By that time, Canada had a balance of payments surplus with the US. In May, when President Kennedy met Prime Minister Pearson at Hyannisport, he asked Canada to follow "appropriate policies" to help the Americans! In the discussions leading up to that meeting, Secretary Ball thought that the American administration "would have to find some way of dealing with genuine Japanese and Canadian need"; that is, exempting those two countries from restrictions imposed on foreign investors. Secretary Dillon added that Canadians ought to receive special consideration, because they "held their dollar balances cheerfully" and "did not demand gold" (unlike the French).[10]

In July 1963, the President announced a so-called Interest Equalization Tax of up to 15 percent on indirect investments outside the United States, a tax which would make it more expensive for American investors to buy stocks and bonds outside the United States and for foreigners to borrow money in the US. Within four days, Canada had dispatched a high-level delegation to Washington. The delegation obtained a partial exemption for Canada. Later, as the complex financial measures wound their way through the committee system of the American Congress, Canadians managed to obtain further exemptions, presumably because American firms did not want restrictions on their freedom to buy, sell, and invest in Canada.

Nevertheless, the Canadian government continued to press for a total exemption. When President Johnson met Prime Minister Pearson in January 1964, Johnson's advisors told him to tell Pearson that other governments (such as the Japanese) would resent further exemptions for Canada and that such exemptions would hinder the balance of payments relief the tax was meant to bring. Canada's position was weakened by the fact that even as its government pleaded for exemptions from the American tax on indirect investment, the Canadian government was introducing measures to discourage direct American investment in Canada. The inconsistency did not escape the American ambassador in Ottawa, who on 8 February 1964 cabled the State Department, advising it to tell the Canadian minister of finance that "we can administer the Canadian exemption either rigorously or leniently." The records do not show whether the State Department accepted the advice.[11]

With the Interest Equalization Tax, a public Canadian commitment not to allow foreign exchange reserves to rise above set limits, and a secret Canadian commitment not to raise interest rates above the American level, Canadian borrowing in the United States dropped dramatically for 1963. During 1964 and 1965, however, such borrowing increased, and American threats to review the Canadian exemption or even to cut defence spending in Canada made no difference to the Canadian government, which pleaded *its* balance of payments deficit with the United States. In November 1965, the American government nevertheless renewed the Canadian exemption.[12]

Mostly because of the cost of the Vietnam War, the American balance of payments continued to deteriorate. In 1965 and 1966, the Johnson administration announced voluntary guidelines on spending by major US-based multinationals outside the US, guidelines from which Canada was exempted to various degrees, partly because of the needs of the Canadian economy, but also because the American government did not want to discriminate "against the American companies with affiliates operating in Canada."[13]

The guidelines, however, did not achieve their purpose. By 1967, both the American and the Canadian balance of payments were worse. On 1 January 1968, when President Johnson announced mandatory exchange controls to protect the American balance of payments, an assistant secretary of state and an assistant secretary of commerce flew to Florida, where Prime Minister Pearson was vacationing, to warn him of the measures. Negotiations to exempt Canada began almost immediately, but because the Americans feared that Canada could become a "pass-through" for funds flowing to other countries, the two governments needed to negotiate stringent administrative controls. This delay coupled with some political uncertainty in Canada – an upcoming Liberal leadership convention meant that Prime Minister Pearson would soon be replaced by another, as yet unknown person – caused an exchange crisis for the Canadian dollar at the beginning of March. Americans feared a Canadian devaluation even more than they feared the Canadian exemption. An advisor wrote President Johnson that a "Canadian devaluation would shake the whole system. Other countries would follow and the run on gold could not be stopped." Intensified negotiations led to a bilateral agreement (the Benson-Fowler Agreement, named for Canada's Minister of Finance Edgar Benson and Secretary of the Treasury Henry Fowler) so that Canada would be exempt from most of the new American measures in return for carefully monitored controls to ensure that Canada would not become a "pass-through" for American funds flowing to third countries. The Canadian government made this commitment as well as a commitment to invest in American government securities. It would not, however, for "political reasons," agree to impose foreign exchange restrictions similar to those imposed by President Johnson. When the Canadian government, in September 1968, came up with its own voluntary guidelines for capital outflows, the US Department of Commerce found them insufficient and did not recommend further exemptions for Canada. By December 1968, however, the Canadian balance of payments had improved so dramatically that in another exchange of letters, Minister of Finance Benson and Secretary of the Treasury Fowler agreed that Canada's foreign exchange reserves need not to be "limited to any particular figure."[14]

During 1969 and 1970, the Canadian reserves of foreign exchange continued to improve as those of the US deteriorated. By 31 May 1970, the upward pressure on the Canadian dollar was such that the Canadian government decided to return to a floating exchange rate rather than trying to hold the value of the dollar down, an effort that could only have harmed the American balance of payments. Official Washington, however, seems to have paid little attention to this new Canadian problem (although the IMF objected, and that may be a reflection of American policy, expressed indirectly). Washington was – understandably – preoccupied with the Vietnam War and the American balance of payments problem.[15]

In August 1971, the American government cut the link between gold and the American dollar, in effect devaluing that currency. At the same time, the US government imposed a 15 percent surcharge on many imports (most raw materials were exempt), subsidized investments in the capital goods industry, and introduced a type of export subsidy (usually known by its acronym, DISC). Canada no longer rated an exemption from these trade and investment measures. The usual coterie of Canadian ministers flew to Washington, but this time without success.[16]

Canadians feared that the import surcharge would have dire consequences for their economy. Prime Minister Trudeau's foreign policy advisor, Ivan Head, considered the issue important enough to arrange a summit meeting between the prime minister and president. By the date of the meeting, 6 December 1971, it was clear that the surcharge would not do as much damage as had been predicted. By the end of December, the American government had in any case cancelled the surcharge.

In December 1971, the governments of the world's ten largest economies (including Canada's) met in France and then in Washington to try to restore order to the international monetary system. Though the other governments agreed to a new set of parities for their currencies (the Smithsonian Agreement of December 1971), the Canadian dollar continued to float; that is, it was exempted from the newly agreed rules. A Mrs. Junz of the American Federal Reserve System wrote to a Mr. Bryant to say that if the Canadian dollar remained at its December 1971 level, the effective depreciation of the American dollar (that is, the advantage for American exporters) would be cut from 12 percent to 9 percent. The Canadian dollar, however, continued to float. Exemptionalism, it seems, "was not quite dead, just undergoing analysis in Dr. Kissinger's global clinic."[17]

Even the governments of the ten largest economies working together no longer had the will, or as the international flow of money in private hands increased perhaps the means, to defend their currencies against overwhelming market pressures. In June 1972, Britain and Ireland adopted a floating exchange rate.[18] By March 1973, the remaining ten governments had followed suit, so that most governments had a Canadian-type floating, but managed, exchange rate. With some exceptions, that has been the situation to this day.[19]

With the end of fixed exchange rates among currencies, the relationship of the American to the Canadian dollar became a bilateral rather than a multilateral issue. However, it is not an issue that, barring the revelation of other factors, seems to have been the subject of policy discussions between the two governments. The two dollars have floated, and they have traded at a wide variety of levels, from C$0.64 to C$1.03, and when the fluctuations have become sharp, central banks have intervened to stabilize the rate. But overall, the "market" rather than governments has set the pace.

There was one possible exception to this laissez-faire approach. Shortly after the Canada-US Free Trade Agreement came into force on 1 January 1989, the Canadian dollar started to rise and continued to do so for about two years. Stories in the press, supported by at least one press interview with a former minister, Sinclair Stevens (who resigned before the FTA was negotiated), claimed that the Mulroney government had made a deal with the Reagan administration. In return for American acceptance of the FTA, Canada would raise the value of its dollar (to make Canadian exports less competitive in the American market). This story, strongly denied by American ambassador Edward Ney, cannot be refuted or accepted on present evidence. It only raises the possibility that the American and Canadian dollars do not float as independently of government influence as governments would have us believe.[20]

Direct American Investment in Canada
While even the most free enterprise of governments will admit a responsibility for monetary policy, direct investment is another issue. A government, such as that of the United States, committed to a high degree of economic liberalism, has usually eschewed responsibility for the control of inward or outward direct investment.[21] But exceptions always arise, and the exceptions in postwar America have arisen in two main ways. One type of exception occurred when the need to use or protect outward foreign direct investment (the type of investment discussed in this section) impinged on other national objectives. Thus, the Johnson administration

perceived an outflow of investment so large as to affect the value of the American currency. The other exception occurred when the policies of other governments toward direct American investment were seen as attacks on the rights of American citizens to invest and make money as they pleased. This was the case with the expropriations following the 1959 Cuban Revolution as well as with various Mexican and Canadian laws. A third exception, considered less significant by most observers, occurred when the American government called on American companies operating outside the United States to help it fulfil an objective of American foreign policy.[22]

American policies about US direct investment abroad (USDIA) thus consist of exceptions to a more general policy of non-intervention. When did the American government consider what kind of exceptions necessary so as to promote national objectives?

For the first ten years after the Second World War, the American government encouraged the outward flow of USDIA. They believed that USDIA would aid in the reconstruction of Europe, the economic development of the underdeveloped countries, the expansion of American trade, and access to raw materials. Beginning in 1948, a number of American government programs have insured private firms against the risks inherent in foreign investments. Some programs even gave direct financial assistance to firms that wanted to invest in mining or processing outside the US. In 1950, the State Department unsuccessfully attempted to persuade the Treasury to change American tax laws to favour USDIA. As late as 1959, the deputy assistant secretary of state for economic affairs listed "the promotion of private investment" as one of the three principal economic objectives of American foreign policy.[23]

As the economies of Europe recovered and the American current account began to slip into the red, the government reversed its official encouragement of USDIA. In his message of 1 January 1968 (see page 142), President Johnson announced mandatory controls on American investment in "continental Western Europe and other developed countries."

Such controls and restrictions, however, proved impossible to enforce. American investment outside the United States continued to grow, but it was accompanied by even more rapidly growing foreign investment from other countries in the United States. In 1985, for the first time since 1914, foreign investment within the United States was greater than American investment outside the country (see Figure 2). This development presented the American administration with a new problem: growing demands from Congress for controls of foreign investment in the US. With some exceptions, supposedly for national security reasons, American administrations maintained their ideological free enterprise stand and refused to impose controls on foreign investment within the US. Since the

1960s, if not earlier, official American policy has been that of "national treatment" – meaning that host governments should treat foreign (that is, American) investment the same as they treat their own investors – though the American government itself did not always adhere to this policy.[24] A 1988 survey by the Department of Commerce showed that the United States had placed "national security" restrictions on investment in nuclear energy, defence industries, offshore oil and gas, communications, public utilities, and transportation; individual states also had regulations on investment in farmland and railroads. President Ford's administration began a policy of monitoring foreign investment and of asking foreign governments contemplating major investments in the US to consult with the American government, although it did not impose any additional controls on investment in the US. However, subsequent administrations did not continue these policies.[25]

By the mid-1970s, the policy agenda was moving toward another concern with USDIA. At that time, host governments[26] were especially sensitive to the actions of the often US-based multinational corporations (MNCs). The focus of the American government shifted toward preventing interference with the operations of such firms. American administrations led the OECD in the drafting of the 1976 Declaration on International

Figure 2

Ratio of American direct investment stock abroad to foreign direct investment stock in the United States, 1972-92

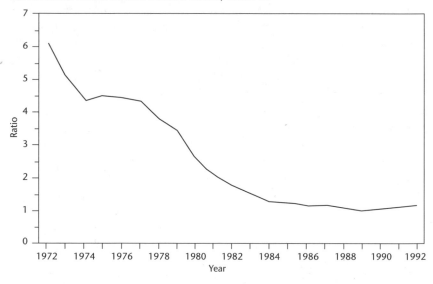

Source: Edward M. Graham and Paul R. Krugman, *Foreign Direct Investment in the United States* (Washington, DC: Institute for International Economics, 1995), 41.

Investment and Multinational Enterprises and in establishing a monitoring committee with the same name. According to Marc Leland, assistant secretary for international affairs in the US Treasury, the "United States Government has been pressuring other governments to focus on restrictive investment policies and how they distort trade flows" and "has taken the lead in pressing" the OECD "to analyze performance requirements and investment incentives." Later multilateral measures included the 1986 OECD Code of Liberalization of Capital Movements and the Trade Related Investment Measures section of the 1993 Uruguay Round World Trade Agreement. In fall 1981, the Subcommittee on International Economic Policy of the US Senate Committee on Foreign Relations held hearings on "US Policy toward International Investment." Speaker after speaker, from the Departments of State and Commerce, from the Treasury, and the Office of the United States Trade Representative, denounced "incentives" and "performance requirements," which they claimed foreign governments were imposing on American firms. They counselled retaliation, bilateral agreements, and international codes to counter such measures.[27] On 29 September 1983, President Reagan issued a "Statement on International Investment Policy," in which he reiterated the American position on national treatment and indicated that the United States would use both multilateral and bilateral means to achieve that end. This concern persisted to the end of the Reagan administration and beyond, and appears to have been one of the prime American motivators for the FTA and the NAFTA.[28]

American policies toward investments in Canada were largely a reflection of the more general American policies explained here. From the Depression until the election of the Diefenbaker government in 1957, there scarcely seemed to be a need for any American policy about direct investment in Canada. The American government had a policy of encouraging outward investment, and the Canadian government encouraged inward investment. It was a marriage made in heaven. In 1956, B.S. Keirstead, a professor of economics at the University of Toronto, wrote in an annual summary of Canada's foreign relations: "The matter of American investments in Canada ought not to require any considerable examination in a book of this sort. They were made, however, the subject of some controversy by a minority of Canadians who seemed to believe that they created some kind of threat to Canadian independence, and Radio Moscow also took up the matter." So, in other words, concerns about American investment in Canada were not to be taken more seriously than Radio Moscow broadcasts. Not surprisingly, American direct investment in Canada increased rapidly during the early postwar years, from C$2,428 million in 1946 to C$10,549 million in 1960, which in turn equalled 82 percent of all foreign direct investment in Canada.[29]

At about the time Americans began to perceive a problem with their reserves of foreign currency, a number of Canadians began to worry about the effects of so much foreign direct investment in the Canadian economy. In a rational world, this policy would appear to be a good match: some Canadians wanted less American investment and the American government did not want so much money to leave their country. But matters were neither that simple nor that rational. On the one hand, the Diefenbaker government was ambivalent about American investment; some cabinet members favoured, and others disapproved of it, a fact of which American policy makers were well aware.[30] Americans also were divided. While the government tried to pursue the overall national objective of protecting its foreign reserve position, American firms did not want to be deprived of the right to invest as they pleased.

These trends intensified after Kennedy replaced Eisenhower, and Pearson, Diefenbaker. In June 1963, Pearson's finance minister, the nationalist Walter Gordon, presented a budget that proposed to tax foreign takeovers of Canadian firms and to increase taxes on dividends paid to foreigners. This proposal arose after the prime minister had promised the president that the budget might encourage investment by Canadians but would not penalize foreigners. The reaction of the Canadian investment community was faster and more vigorous than that of the American government. In Canada, the president of the Montreal stock exchange led the public outcry. In the US, the Treasury saw certain elements of discrimination in the budget. When Prime Minister Pearson visited President Johnson in January 1964, one of the briefing papers urged the president to "reiterate strong US view that new Canadian tax is openly discriminatory." In February 1964, the American embassy in Ottawa cabled the State Department, "we must make it clear to Gordon that we intend to protect the interests of Americans who have some twenty billions invested in Canada by all the legitimate means at our disposal." By then, several measures had already been withdrawn or watered down, largely because of Canadian objections. Indeed, what the ambassador had written a month earlier (that "it was in our interest for the Liberal government to burn its fingers on this issue") seemed more appropriate than the later ringing declaration in defence of American interests.[31]

But the irony did not end there. In July 1963, President Kennedy introduced an Interest Equalization Tax (IET) of up to 15 percent on indirect American investment abroad. As mentioned in the previous section, the Canadian government immediately sent a delegation to Washington to seek an exemption. Why should it do that? If the American government wanted less American money to leave the United States and the Canadian government wanted less American investment, the two policies would appear to be complementary. That, however, was not the case, and hence the request for the Canadian exemption. The Gordon budget specifically sought to shift American investment in Canada from direct to indirect instruments, whereas President Kennedy's IET specifically exempted direct investment. The policies were therefore not complementary but in almost direct contradiction: the Canadians wanted less *direct* American investment, while the American policy favoured the flow of capital into direct rather than indirect investment outside the US.[32]

In the end, the Canadians and Americans compromised. The Canadian government diluted or removed several of its fiscal measures, and the Kennedy administration, as mentioned, exempted Canada from the IET on new issues of bonds and stocks. Along the way, the American government applied some pressure by "dragging [its] feet" on negotiations on a double-tax treaty the Canadians were anxious to conclude. It did so not because it intended to apply direct pressure on the Canadian government, but because, in the words of a presidential briefing note, "internal opposition" in Canada to the Gordon budget was considerable, and "failure to achieve early renegotiation of the double-tax treaty will strengthen opposition and increase the possibility of modification." When Gordon backed down on his withholding tax, Ambassador Butterworth credited his advice with respect to the double-taxation treaty. He cabled Washington that the "real reason was unquestionably US resistance to renegotiation of US Canadian tax treaty," and that "on balance, a battle has been won against those Canadians seeking to 'buy back Canada' and/or Canadianize foreign subsidiaries by utilizing discriminatory tax penalties. However, we cannot assume that Gordon or his supporters have left the field."[33]

With or without the unneighbourly gesture of retaliation via the tax treaty, the two sides would likely have worked out some accommodation. Their economies had become too tightly related for one to retaliate against the other to any great extent (unless, of course, citizens were prepared to accept major economic hardship).

In 1965 and 1966, some strong American protests arose when the Canadian government passed legislation to prevent the closing of the sale of the Mercantile Bank of Montreal to Citibank of New York. An eventual compromise postponed the takeover, but it reiterated the foreign investment restrictions on Canadian banks.

In the late 1960s and early 1970s, Canadian public concern over the extent of American investment in Canada continued to grow, as did that investment. Interestingly, for public opinion is not usually considered so rational, foreign ownership in Canadian industry peaked in 1972, whereas public opinion directed against that ownership peaked in 1973.[34] The titles of some of the books published in Canada during those years are revealing: Andrew Lamorie's *How They Sold our Canada to the U.S.A.* (Gravenhurst: Northern Books, 1964); former finance minister Walter

Gordon's *A Choice for Canada: Independence or Colonial Status* (Toronto: McClelland and Stewart,1966); and Ian Lumsden's *Close the 49th Parallel: The Americanization of Canada* (Toronto: University of Toronto Press, 1970). What is interesting for the study of American policy is that Canada seemed to have become just one more country complaining about American investment and the behaviour of American multinationals.[35]

Another factor worth keeping in mind is the great difference between the proportion of American investment in Canada and the proportion of Canadian investment in the United States. During the 1970s, Canadian investment in the US amounted to less than a quarter of all direct foreign investment in the US. American investment in Canada amounted to over three-quarters of foreign investment in Canada, and in some industries (such as publishing and transportation equipment), foreign ownership amounted to over 80 percent of all assets.[36]

In spite of the strong public feeling in Canada, the Canadian government, having burned its fingers on the Gordon budget, took few measures on foreign investment for the next eleven years. The American government seems to have concentrated its attention on other issues and not worried too much about the investment policies of the Canadian government. After the 1971 Canadian federal budget was introduced, Robert M. Dunn of the Board of Governors of the Federal Reserve System wrote a Mr. Ghiardi that the budget did "not include the widely feared signs of Canadian nationalism." Canadians clearly would continue to want American money, no matter what the opinion polls said.[37]

It is ironic, or perhaps a comment on how slow governments can be, that the Canadian government introduced legislation to deal with the perceived problem of foreign investment in 1974, after public concern on the issue had peaked. During that and the following year, the Canadian government implemented the Foreign Investment Review Act (FIRA), which provided for screening major takeovers of Canadian firms and of new investments by foreign firms. As a condition of investing in Canada, foreign firms could be required, for example, to export a proportion of their production or to buy a proportion of their equipment in Canada.

Although the FIRA contradicted the American policy of "national treatment," the American government at first reacted cautiously and primarily on the multilateral level. Several American government sources mention the OECD code on multinational firms as a possible means of dealing with this Canadian problem. This approach, however, was not likely to succeed. C. Fred Bergsten, who had been an official in the Treasury and State Departments during the Johnson and Carter administrations, told the Senate Subcommittee on International Economic Policy that Canada and Australia had "resisted even [the] limited degree of agreement" that the OECD had been able to achieve.[38]

A number of specific examples of what Americans considered to be unjustified government incentives (ironically, intended to attract American investment to Canada) caused a stir in the American government. The two issues that seem to have received the most attention were the 1978 decision of the Ford Motor Company to build an engine plant in southern Ontario, rather than in Ohio, supposedly because of an Ontario government subsidy, and the 1975 nationalization of the potash industry by the government of the Saskatchewan. In both cases, the American government expressed strong concern and threatened retaliation, but it did not actually retaliate. A third case concerned the decision of the Michelin Tire Company to build a plant in Nova Scotia, supposedly because of Canadian federal government's regional development grants (which had nothing to do with FIRA). In this case, the American government imposed sanctions by penalizing the importation of the tires.[39]

Official American concern over FIRA intensified in the early 1980s for two reasons. One factor emanated from Canada and was called the National Energy Programme. Adopted by the newly re-elected Trudeau government in 1980, this policy, among several other features, included a target of 50 percent Canadian ownership for the Canadian energy industry and an automatic 25 percent share of all new oil and gas discoveries for the newly created and nationally owned energy company, Petrocan.

The other factor was worldwide and concerned the obstacles American firms complained they were encountering as they invested in other countries. A survey by the US Department of Commerce, published in October 1981, showed that only a small proportion of American firms was complaining about other governments giving incentives or imposing performance requirements. Canada was by no means the country most frequently complained about. Complaints about government incentives varied from a high of 38 percent of firms citing Luxembourg to a low of 5 percent for Hong Kong, with Canada, at 19 percent, occupying an intermediate position; complaints about performance requirements varied from 15 percent for Panama and Liberia to 2 percent for Hong Kong and Luxembourg, with Canada at 4 percent.[40] The American firms' complaints nevertheless led to a series of congressional hearings. The first set of hearings in 1981 and 1982 concerned USDIA in general, although even in these hearings Canada was a frequently mentioned example. The second set of hearings, in March 1982, dealt exclusively with Canada. Speakers for the State Department, the Treasury, the Department of Commerce, and the Office of the US Trade Representative carefully explained American policy toward Canadian restrictions on direct investment to a small group of senators.

That policy had three aspects. The first was bilateral. The American administration, according to Harvey E. Bale of the Office of the US Trade

Representative, had "responded to the FIRA and the NEP by holding a number of high-level consultations with the Government of Canada. The president himself has raised our concerns on several occasions." Robert E. Hormats of the State Department gave the subcommittee a list of senior American officials who had met with Canadian government representatives "to enumerate our concerns ... with the frankness characteristic of our countries' relationship" (that is, bluntly). Hormats continued by advocating that "we continue and intensify bilateral pressure."[41]

The second aspect, retaliation, was also bilateral. In the diplomatic words of Marc Leland, assistant secretary for international affairs in the US Treasury, "We have conducted ... an intense review and analysis of our economic relations with Canada." In the slightly less diplomatic words of Raymond Waldmann of the Department of Commerce, "We can also take action unilaterally. However, such actions will require extreme political and economic sensitivity since they may invite retaliation." He continued by mentioning the possibility of retaliation under the notorious Section 301 of the 1974 Trade Act. (Section 301 allows the president to retaliate not just against foreign companies deemed to be exporting goods to the US at unfairly low prices; "Super 301" allows retaliation against entire countries.[42])

A third aspect was multilateral and included expressing concern through the OECD, where, as mentioned, the United States had led that organization in drawing up standards for the treatment of international investment. According to Raymond Waldmann, "during discussions in OECD's XCSS and Investment Committees we have challenged Canadian policies as a derogation from the 1976 OECD declaration on national treatment of investment."[43]

The OECD, however, has no power to make binding decisions. Another multilateral institution, the GATT, does have that power. The US launched a complaint against Canada in January 1982, alleging that the performance aspects of FIRA (and some aspects of the National Energy Programme) interfered with the freedom of international trade; for example, if a firm was required to export part of its production or to buy equipment in Canada as a condition of investing there, that requirement would interfere with the freedom of international trade. The GATT panel's decision, announced in July 1983, gave the United States some cause for satisfaction. The panel found that FIRA's power to require investors to buy supplies and equipment in Canada contravened the GATT, but the requirement to export from Canada was allowed under GATT rules.[44]

Besides responding to Canada directly by complaining to the GATT, the American government also sought to harness the GATT to its agenda of opposing trade-related investment requirements. It asked the GATT to make an inventory of all such measures, including, of course, the Canadian measures.[45] Resorting to the GATT and the OECD represented a departure from the normal procedure of America's Canada policy, which was to deal with Canadian issues on a bilateral level. The resort to multilateral forums could be seen as a further development of Nixon's Canada policy; that is, to treat Canada as a country like any other.

If FIRA and NEP had temporarily made Canada the bad boy of American foreign economic policy, the investment provisions of the 1988 Free Trade Agreement and the 1992 NAFTA restored Canada to its role as almost a shining example of the economic policies the US expected from its allies. The two governments first talked about the possibility of a free trade agreement at the Mulroney-Reagan summit in March 1985. In July 1985, senior Canadian officials first travelled to Washington to discuss a free trade agreement with their counterparts from the office of the US Trade Representative. Since those meetings, it was clear that investment was a high priority, perhaps at the top of the list of issues the American government wanted included in any such negotiations. When Clayton Yeutter, the United States trade representative, formally recommended free trade negotiations with Canada to President Reagan on 17 September 1985, he mentioned four "significant barriers" to American access to the Canadian market. Two of these were the "obstacles to US investment" and the closely related subject of "regulations which impede US exports of services."[46]

The American delegation maintained this emphasis on investment throughout the negotiations that followed (from 1986-8). At first, it seemed that the American objective would encounter no obstacle, because the Mulroney government had unilaterally abolished or liberalized most of the provisions of FIRA and NEP. The American government, however, sought full national treatment for American investment in Canada, which was more than even the Mulroney government was willing to concede. In the end, the Americans settled for a substantial liberalization for American investment in Canada: after a transition period of four years, the Canadian government would no longer be able to scrutinize direct investments by US-based firms (that is, takeovers) worth C$150 million or less (that amount inflation indexed at its 1992 value). New, or so-called greenfield investment, would not be screened. The Canadian government, however, retained the right to screen and control (subject to some limitations) takeovers of cultural and energy industries and financial services, and to maintain existing investment controls not specifically abolished or altered by the FTA.[47]

These provisions were perhaps not as much as the Americans sought, but probably as much, or more, than they expected to get. According to Robert A. Cornell, the American negotiator for the investment chapter, "Our investment objectives in the FTA therefore were *first,* to prevent any backsliding by the Canadians and *second,* to build upon the liberalization already affected by the Mulroney Administration. We wanted to push the

Canadians as far as we could to liberalize their standards, policies and laws ... We obviously did not achieve as much as we would have liked ... But we achieved a substantial and important – even critical measure of success." The Americans chose to forego the right to impose similar restrictions, even when the Canadians invited them to include a similar protection for themselves in the agreement. According to Cornell, "It simply does not make sense to abandon an open investment climate – which has helped to stimulate economic growth in the US – because a treaty partner has chosen, for nationalistic reasons, to sacrifice some of the benefits of foreign investment flows."[48]

Such holier-than-thou attitudes often bring forth their own nemesis. As mentioned at the beginning of this section, foreign direct investment into the United States has grown rapidly, so that by some measures the US became a "debtor" nation by 1985. Americans were beginning to show more concern about the consequences of foreign investment in *their* country. Even as the FTA was working its way through the American legislative process, the Exon-Florion amendment to the 1988 US Omnibus Trade and Competitive Act gave the president the authority "to review and block foreign acquisitions of US firms on the basis of 'national security' considerations." The president consequently created the Committee on Foreign Investment in the United States (CFIUS). As a result, half of foreign acquisitions in the US now require review on national security grounds, and some have been refused. As early as 1983, the US Defense Department successfully persuaded Spedel Metals Corporation not to sell one of its subsidiaries to Nippon Steel; in 1990, President Bush ordered a branch of the government of China to sell a Seattle-based airlines parts manufacturer, and a few years later, a congressional committee persuaded Thomson (of France) not to buy the LTV missile manufacturing firm. In 1992, Congress extended the authority of CFIUS to include the need for "US technological leadership in sectors related to defence."[49]

Accordingly, when the negotiations began in 1991 for a trilateral North American Free Trade Agreement (NAFTA), the American position was somewhat more nuanced than it had been in 1986. The Mexican government was even more sensitive on the issue of foreign investment than that of Canada. As a consequence, American negotiators were not as successful in achieving their aims for investment as they had been during the FTA negotiations. With respect to Canada, the American NAFTA negotiators had three principal aims: to eliminate the remaining authority of Investment Canada (which had replaced FIRA in 1985) to screen foreign investment; to gain acceptance of the principle of "national treatment" of foreign investment; and to impose a compulsory arbitration procedure for disputes between investors and governments. This last goal is particularly ironic, because during the FTA negotiations, Canada had insisted on compulsory dispute resolution for trade in goods, a concession the Americans did not make until the last days of the talks, and then only in return for Canadian concessions on foreign investment.[50]

The American administration did not achieve the first aim. It achieved the other two in principle but not in substance. National treatment as a principle is included in NAFTA, but it is in fact contradicted by the "reservations." These reservations are exceptions that the Mexican and Canadian governments made for sectors such as culture (in the case of Canada) and energy (in the case of Mexico). In addition, all three governments reserved the right to screen investments on the grounds of national security. The principle of compulsory arbitration by the International Centre for the Settlement of Investment Disputes (ICSID) is included in NAFTA, but this procedure cannot be used to review the decision of Investment Canada or the CFIUS and their Mexican equivalents. Because the principle does not apply to the one agency of the Canadian government that screens foreign investment, it is in fact almost meaningless for Canada. Also, during the course of the NAFTA negotiations, the Canadian government unilaterally removed most of the NEP restrictions on foreign investment in the energy sector, even though the Canadian negotiators pleaded with their government not to undermine their position by such a unilateral concession. Another American achievement during the NAFTA negotiations was to broaden the definition of investment to include most types of indirect investment, whereas the FTA rules had applied only to takeovers of firms, that is, to direct investment.[51]

American Export Controls on American Firms in Canada

The political culture of American foreign policy relies more heavily than that of most other nations on the use of economic sanctions for foreign policy ends. This trend, which some have traced back to pre-Revolutionary days, has intensified during the twentieth century. From the Trading with the Enemy Act of 1917 through the Neutrality Acts of the 1930s to the Export Control Act of 1949 (superseded by the Export Administration Acts of 1969 and 1979), the American government has built up a complex network of legislation and administrative controls designed to ensure that American exports contribute to the supreme objective of national security.[52]

This goal of national security in turn divides into three principal and several secondary objectives. The "short supply" scenario limits exports to conserve vital supplies for American use. This subject is dealt with in the previous chapter. The trading with the enemy scenario seeks to limit the export of goods and technologies that may further the military and economic potential of enemies and potential enemies of the United States. Non-proliferation controls also fall into this category. The third and residual scenario is sometimes called foreign policy objectives, and it usually involves punishing governments and peoples considered hostile to the United States, or its ideals or aims. Using this justification, the American government has imposed various export controls on Cuba, China, North Korea, Vietnam, Cambodia, Iraq, Iran, Libya, and South Africa, among others, over the last forty years. Additional objectives, such as preventing crime or combating transnational terrorism, are sometimes added to the three basic objectives.

Although the targets and intensity of such export controls have varied over the years, the controls have stayed in place, and allies such as Canada have been pressured to adopt them. American controls were particularly onerous during the early Cold War, the Vietnam War, and the first Reagan administration. The chief targets were the Soviet Union and its allies, to which China, North Korea, and later Cuba were added.[53]

The imposition of export controls relates to the topic of American policy toward investments in Canada, because at various times during the Cold War, the American government has tried to impose such controls on the subsidiaries of American firms that are incorporated in and located in Canada. Another related issue, not dealt with in this chapter, concerned the more general American effort to coordinate export controls of all the Western allies with respect to Warsaw Pact and other Communist countries. This effort finds its institutional expression through Coco, the Coordinating Committee for Multilateral Export Controls. Formerly linked to NATO, this intergovernmental committee has taken on an institutional life of its own.

During the Second World War, the American and Canadian economies operated almost as one, and during the early Cold War and Korean War years, the international situation seemed so threatening that Canadians accepted many American security measures, such as control over exports from Western bloc countries, without hesitation. The two governments exchanged export control lists, and in some cases Canada retained controls the US had already lifted.[54] However, the situation changed after 1955 as the first signs of detente appeared. Since then, the issue of American export controls as applied to American subsidiaries in Canada has been a frequent irritant in American-Canadian relations. Officials close to the situation, the ambassador in Canada, and officials in the State and Commerce Departments, frequently recommended that such controls be lifted or relaxed, because they were a cause of resentment in Canada and a cause of economic loss for the US. When this issue arrived at a decision-making level, however, the policy changed only little.[55]

Thus, from June 1956 to June 1957, the Eisenhower administration embarked on a major effort to persuade its allies to tighten controls on trade with the People's Republic of China. The allied governments resisted, and the American government had to retreat from one position to another. In May 1957, the State Department tried to influence Canada, in advance of a multilateral meeting, presumably to get a favourable response it could use to convince the other countries in attendance. The effort did not succeed. At the multilateral meetings, Canada maintained a neutral position between the Benelux, German, Italian, Turkish, and Greek governments who supported the latest American compromise, and the French, British, Norwegian, Portuguese, Japanese, and Danish governments, who refused the American proposals. By June, the State Department still could not discern the Canadian position. By December 1957, the American effort seems to have petered out.[56]

In 1958, the Department of Commerce reviewed regulations relating to foreign subsidiaries of American firms. Of the nine examples cited, six concerned American firms operating in Canada, including Ford of Canada's tentative sale of passengers cars to China, and American Cyanamid of Canada's sale of fertilizer, again to China. The department concluded: "1. US foreign transaction controls as applied to foreign firms controlled by US interests are becoming an irritant in our government-to-government commercial relations with a number of countries. 2. These controls, except as applied to strategic goods, are difficult to justify on economic defence grounds." Yet when the National Security Council took up the recommendation on 15 January 1959, Secretary of State John Foster Dulles thought that the Chinese government placed orders only to spread dissension among the allies and that these orders were often withdrawn after the permission for the sale was given. He did not offer any evidence for this opinion. Secretary of Commerce Lewis L. Strauss added that any exemption for Canadian firms would only encourage American firms to establish facilities in other countries for the purpose of selling to China. In the end, the decision was to postpone any decision and to name a committee to study whether another commission should be appointed to study the issue![57]

The issue of American control over American-owned firms continued to be a problem in the 1960s, when Cuba was added to the list of countries with which Canadian subsidiaries were not to trade. In February 1961, when Prime Minister Diefenbaker complained to President Kennedy that Imperial Oil was being prevented from selling oil to China, the president replied that Canada should find a Canadian-owned firm to do the sale. (Imperial eventually did sell the oil.) Senator Kenneth Keating (Republican-New York) commented that "it was impossible to understand why a country 'willing to supply troops for the defence of freedom should not be willing to make economic sacrifices for this same objective.'" In April 1962, Kennedy told the Canadian ambassador that he did not think "the West derived any benefit" from Canadian wheat sales to China, and in 1963, the *New York Daily News* wrote that Canadian wheat sales "constituted 'aid and comfort to our Soviet enemies and to our Red Chinese enemies.'" In January 1964, when Prime Minister Pearson visited President Johnson, one of the president's briefing papers encouraged him to stress the positive aspects of Canadian trade policy toward Cuba (that is, the enforcement of the American re-export prohibitions) but to ask for the termination of shipments of "critical commodities" and of air cargo service.[58]

In 1966, the Joint United States-Canadian Committee on Trade and Economic Affairs issued a communique on control over foreign assets and exports of technical data and promised that "further consideration will be given to the possibilities of additional modifications of the regulations." In September 1967, a briefing paper on Canadian issues written for National Security Adviser Walt Rostow claimed that "procedures have been established to deal with problems of this nature on an individual basis." However, if there were such procedures, they seem not to have been applied. In his year-end report in January 1968, Ambassador Walton Butterworth reminded the State Department of "the need for doing away with this needless irritant to US-Canadian relations by the establishment of a general license arrangement for exports by US subsidiaries in Canada." When the State Department wrote a summary of its activities for the incoming Nixon administration in 1968, the department pointed out that American regulations "designed to curb trade" with China and Cuba had become a "major irritant in US-Canadian relations," but that "the issue remained unresolved, although the United States remained ready on an *ad hoc* basis" to make exemptions as cases arose.[59]

The issue flared up again in the last days of the Ford administration, when an official wrote Secretary of the Treasury William Simon, suggesting that Unitours of Canada be prevented from selling Americans tours to Cuba. The recommended strategy was to harass the American banks that would forward the funds for such trips, in spite of the fact that Unitours was a wholly Canadian-owned firm.[60] The Carter administration did not carry out this threat, but after a few months, Unitours gave up its attempt to sell Cuban holidays to Americans. The issue of trade with Cuba has continued to plague America's Canada policy beyond the Cold War. In 1993, the Canadian media reported that Eli Lilly of Canada, a pharmaceutical manufacturer, and H.J. Heinz of Canada, both Canadian subsidiaries of American firms, had refused possible sales to Cuba on orders from their head office, although Canadian legislation prohibited Canadian-incorporated firms from following such orders.[61]

The issue of trade with Cuba or Libya or any other country the American administration may consider hostile is not necessarily related to American investment in Canada. In 1961, the US Treasury blocked the sale to Canada of vacuum pumps manufactured in the US, but needed in Canada to load wheat for China from freight trains onto ships. In this case, the American government (which in any case backed off after representations from the Diefenbaker government) was preventing an American firm from exporting to Canada. The 1996 Helms-Burton Act differs in seeking to punish Canadian firms operating in Canada and Cuba, not the subsidiaries of American firms in Canada. The act is thus not an issue related to American investment in Canada.

Conclusions

Investment policy is cited repeatedly by those who think that American governments try to orchestrate Canada policies. This chapter, however, found no convincing evidence of a deliberate policy of American governments using American capital to expand American influence in Canada. American policy makers may have found some of Canada's policies puzzling, but before the time of President Reagan and the Free Trade Agreement (discussed further in the next chapter), they were not prepared to do more than oppose specific Canadian government measures. Thus, Secretary of State Dean Rusk wrote President Johnson in December 1963 that Canadians "could undoubtedly improve their standard of living if they ... permitted a gradual integration of the Canadian market with our own. But because they are so conscious of the overwhelming size and power of the United States, they tend to pursue highly nationalistic policies."[62]

To deal first with monetary policies, the Canadian and American dollars had a special relationship throughout the postwar years. Even before 1971, when the relative value of the world's major currencies was fixed, the Canadian dollar "floated." And when its value was briefly fixed (from 1962 to 1970), it was fixed only in terms of American dollars. Yet, there is no evidence that the American government used this special relationship to dominate the Canadian economy or to manipulate the Canadian currency in its favour (the Sinclair Stevens' story excepted). It is true that when Americans began to perceive a need to protect the outflow of money *from* the US, they pressured Canadians to harmonize interest rates and keep them not too far above the American, but this harmonization was in return for exemption from the American measures. Accordingly, Canada was exempt from most of the American foreign exchange controls.

Nevertheless, a fine distinction exists between a special policy for other countries and that same policy adapted to suit Canada. Offshore purchases with Marshall Plan funds, provide an example. The Europeans received aid, but Canada, which had resources the Europeans needed, received offshore purchases. On the other hand, the August 1971 measures were a clear attempt to treat Canada as a *foreign country* like any other, an attempt that lasted only until December when the reassertion of a special link between the Canadian and the American dollars led to renewed acceptance of a special policy.

As for direct investment, the model that best applies is that of Canada as a country like most others. While American government speakers objected strongly to some aspects of Canadian investment policy (such as the 25 percent share for Petrocan on all newly found oil lands), the fact that emerges most consistently from the statements and congressional hearings is that Americans saw Canada as a model for other countries. In that sense, it is possible to speak of a borderline case – between a special policy and a policy that considered Canada as a country like others. Canada was expected to be exceptional, responding to American investment as Americans desired (that is, allowing investment liberally and with few controls). When Canada departed from this exceptional model and began to impose some controls – even if in comparison with those of many other industrialized, let alone developing nations, these controls were not onerous – Americans reacted with outrage. How could Canadians do this to them? According to the testimony of Robert Hormats of the State Department, "Canada is not alone in this respect. There are other countries who are doing things of a similar nature. But Canada is a country that we look to set a higher standard." Fifteen years earlier, another American diplomat, Ivan White, told a Canadian-American study group, "If a mature country like Canada deviates substantially from this principle [of non-discrimination] ... investments in less sophisticated parts of the world ... stand to suffer from the precedent." Also in 1966, Secretary of the Treasury Fowler told Finance Minister Mitchell Sharp that his department and the State Department feared that Canada's Bank Act "would provide a precedent for other countries."[63]

Once again, much depends on point of view. In foreign investment, Americans said that they expected Canada to set a precedent or a "higher standard." That approach does treat Canada as one foreign country among others, but the so-called higher standard could also be seen as a means of giving Canada a special role. Or it could be seen as an example of the idea that Canada is expected to toe the American line more closely than other governments.

In foreign investment, there is also one example of linkage among policies toward Canada: the Kennedy administration's successful attempt to link conclusion of the double-taxation treaty and exemptions from the interest equalization measures.

Thus, with respect to foreign investment, Canada for a time seemed to be becoming like any other country, but for the most part, the US wanted Canada to remain *exceptional*. Indeed, for the same reason, administration speakers presented the investment provisions of the free trade agreement as a model, which, once achieved, should be followed in other international negotiations.[64]

Export controls resulting from the presence of American direct invest-ment in Canada do tend to support the idea that the US might direct Canadian policy. The American government attempted to use the Cana-dian subsidiaries of American firms for general foreign policy purposes. Canadians were more willing than Americans to trade with countries the United States had put on an enemy list. But from the American point of view, and that is the topic here, the case was one of extending control over American subsidiaries outside the US. Here, we do find some evidence for what Canadian nationalists fear: American firms in Canada as an object and an instrument of American foreign policy.

Yet again, much depends on point of view. Canadians rightly complain that they appear to be an especially frequent target of American export controls, but that fact may be a reflection of the amount of American investment in Canada. Many other governments, including those of France, Germany, and even Margaret Thatcher's Britain have objected to the attempted imposition of similar controls. Canada was therefore to some extent a country like the others. The American government had no policy on American investment directed exclusively toward Canada.

7
Canada in American Trade Policy

In trade policy, perhaps more than in any other policy field, the broad over-all policy behind the minutiae of everyday disputes is difficult to discern. American and Canadian trade relations are typical. A look at the products at issue during the free trade (then called "Reciprocity") negotiations of 1854 shows that disputes over lumber, fish, and wheat are not new. A history of American-Canadian trade disputes would fill many volumes, but it would not add much to our knowledge of either country's policies.

This chapter looks at the way Canada fit into American trade policy from 1945 to 1993. It begins with a brief review of American trade policy and then examines two topics in detail. The largest part of the chapter analyzes the various attempts to "free" American-Canadian trade; that is, to arrive at some general agreement to govern and to a large extent liber-alize trade in goods between the two countries. This part of the chapter proceeds chronologically, from the abortive free trade agreement of 1948 to the North American Free Trade Agreement (NAFTA) of 1992. The chap-ter also presents one of several examples of "managed trade" between the two countries, the regime governing the trade in automobiles and parts.

A delimitation of subject matter is in order. Chapters 5 and 6 show that economic policies are not easily compartmentalized. Problems in foreign exchange are related to imbalances between exports and imports, and monetary policy and the value of a currency can have major effects on the competitiveness of a country's exporters. In recent years, international trade negotiators have added to their agendas many subjects, such as trade in services, intellectual property, and trade-related investment measures. Because investment was covered in Chapter 6, this chapter will deal primar-ily with trade in goods, but it also includes such agreements as the Canada-US Free Trade Agreement (FTA), which dealt with a number of other topics.

American Trade Policy since 1945
Throughout its history, the United States has protected its industries. The young republic used tariffs to help its infant industries; later in the

nineteenth century, governments used tariffs to raise money, and during the 1930s, the American government raised tariffs to unprecedented heights (the 1930 Smoot-Hawley Act) in a vain attempt to fight off the Depression. By the mid-1930s, a reaction set in as the United States began to negotiate bilateral trade agreements that lowered some of the prohibitively high Smoot-Hawley rates.[1]

Many of President Franklin Roosevelt's advisors, most notably Cordell Hull, his long-serving secretary of state, believed that trade restrictions not only harmed the American economy but also led to conflict and even war among states. They wanted to inaugurate a postwar economic order based on free trade. Americans were fortunate. Economists believed that the strongest economies with the most competitive industries would be the earliest and biggest winners in a free trading system, and in 1945 the United States was the world's major exporter and largest economy. From 1944 to 1945, the American government led the victorious allies in the negotiation of a three-headed postwar international economic system, the heads consisting of the International Monetary Fund (IMF), the International Bank for Reconstruction and Development (the World Bank), and the International Trade Organization (ITO). However, the regulation of world trade to prevent the kind of protectionism that had bedeviled the 1930s was considered so important that in 1947 eighteen governments negotiated a temporary arrangement to provide for common trading rules – the General Agreement on Tariffs and Trade (GATT). American leaders believed that the liberalization, if not total freeing, of international trade, among the non-Communist countries at least, would not only help to promote prosperity but would also strengthen the western alliance.[2]

Protectionism, however, was a deeply ingrained habit in the US Congress and the American business community. Although the American administration had negotiated provisions for the protection of agriculture and for various "escape clauses" in the event that specific industries or the balances of payments were threatened, the ITO obviously could not survive a vote in Congress. By the 1948 American elections, the ITO was attacked both by free traders, who objected to the many exceptions and escape clauses, and by protectionists, who believed that the ITO did not adequately protect American industry. The Truman administration turned its attention to more immediate Cold War problems (see Chapter 2) and in 1950, it abandoned the effort to push the ITO through Congress. The GATT was left in place, and for the next forty-five years, it would bear the overall responsibility for the regulation of trade among free enterprise, industrialized countries.[3]

Congressional opposition notwithstanding, American presidents continued efforts to liberalize trade, and for the most part, they managed to win congressional approval for specific packages of tariff reductions. Thus, the Truman administration used the 1951 Trade Act to lead the Torquay Round of trade liberalization negotiations, the Eisenhower administration continued with the Dillon Round, and John Kennedy initiated the Kennedy Round (completed in 1967, four years after his death).

By the late 1960s, as it became clear that the American economy would not maintain its dominant postwar position, protectionist sentiment revived in the United States. In 1971, the US recorded its first annual trade deficit since 1894. Many trade restricting measures were being introduced in Congress; members of Congress proposed quotas on everything from textiles and steel to dairy products and electronic goods. When the Nixon administration in 1972 introduced a new trade act (adopted in 1974), members of Congress, labour leaders, and business groups loaded it down with protectionist clauses, such as Section 301 which allowed foreign firms to be penalized with "countervailing duties" for "dumping" goods in the American market or for accepting government subsidies. The 1974 Trade Act, however, included two provisions that changed American trade policy. It allowed for the negotiation of a bilateral free trade arrangement with Canada, and it provided for the so-called "fast-track" procedure, for Congress to accept – or reject – an international trade agreement in its entirety, without changing the details of its provisions (as long as the administration presented such an agreement within a time period specifically determined by Congress). This procedure was important, because in the increasingly protectionist climate of the 1970s, representatives and senators could otherwise have added dozens of provisions protecting local industries to a trade bill and thus nullifying any agreement the administration had negotiated.[4]

The 1974 act was the first of several trade acts that followed in fairly regular intervals in 1979, 1984, and 1988. Each act included a more detailed and imaginative list of measures by which the administration – or American industry – could protect American producers. Yet each act also included measures to allow the president to negotiate various international agreements to liberalize trade at a multilateral or bilateral level. Because each act built on the preceding one, they are best described together.[5]

American trade policy since 1974 can be compared to a three-ring circus. On one stage was the ever more protectionist legislation adopted by Congress. The 1988 act, for example, included Super 301, which allowed the president to retaliate not only against firms judged by American authorities to have traded unfairly, but to place entire countries on a list of unfair traders. Allowed to lapse in 1990, Super 301 was re-introduced by President Clinton in 1994. In the background of this stage were hundreds of protectionist bills that representatives and senators introduced every year (300 in 1985-6 alone). Most of these bills had no chance of being adopted, but they served the purpose of intimidating foreign suppliers.[6]

A second ring consisted of the increasing number of "trade actions" American firms filed against foreign importers. American legislation and GATT rules allowed for several types of such actions, including anti-dumping complaints alleging that goods were being sold below cost, and countervailing duty claims, alleging that imports were subsidized by the exporting country.

On the third stage was a series of international, multilateral negotiations, authorized by the same American trade acts that included the above-mentioned protective measures, but which also attempted to liberalize world trade. There was the Tokyo Round of further GATT liberalization measures, initiated in 1974 and completed in 1979; followed by the Uruguay Round, begun in 1986 but not adopted until 1994. These trade negotiations are notable for the fact that they dealt with more than the trade in goods, which was the subject of traditional international trade negotiations. These negotiations included intellectual property, investment, environmental regulations, and labour standards. The 1994 Uruguay Round agreement also created a new international organization, the World Trade Organization, which has taken over most of the functions of the GATT and added some new ones.

On another part of this third stage of American trade policy, one can see a trend toward regional, multilateral, and bilateral agreements. In the 1930s and 1940s, American policy makers objected to the British Common-wealth system of trade preferences as discriminatory. Yet their successors in the 1950s and 1960s encouraged freer trade arrangements in Western Europe as contributions to economic reconstruction and western solidarity. As mentioned, the 1974 Trade Act advocated that the United States participate in such arrangements. In 1982, the Reagan administration initiated a program of tariff reduction for the Caribbean, dubbed the "Caribbean Basin Initiative." The 1984 Trade Act specifically authorized the president to negotiate free trade agreements with Canada and Israel, and the US signed an agreement with Israel within a year. Negotiations with Canada began in 1985. In 1991, President Bush's administration began negotiations for a North American (that is, trilateral) free trade agreement.[7] Economic policy experts disagree about whether such regional agreements constitute a further manifestation of protectionism and thus a rejection of multilateral free trade, or whether such agreements are stepping stones toward wider free trade agreements, islands of virtue in a protectionist world. But even those American economists who believed in multilateral free trade were willing to make an exception for a bilateral free trade agreement with Canada, whose economy they argued was so closely tied to the US that a bilateral agreement would not really consti tute a derogation from multilateralism.[8]

Many economists believed that the American trade deficit resulted from the overvaluation of the American dollar. Therefore, they sought to improve American trade performance (that is, the deficit between exports and imports) by reducing the value of the American dollar in relation to other currencies. This belief was one of the motivations behind the 1971 delinking of the value of the dollar and gold, and it was the primary reason for the 1985 Plaza Accord, in which the governments of the world's major economies promised to raise the value of their currencies in relation to the American dollar. Although the dollar fell temporarily, this drop did not have the desired effect on the balance of trade, and a number of factors, unrelated to trade, caused the dollar to rise again. The perceived overvaluation of the dollar, however, forms an important background factor to American trade policy.[9] (On US-Canada monetary relations, see Chapter 6.)

American Canadian Free Trade Discussions during the Postwar Years

Most Americans involved with economic policy making have considered trade with Canada as a special case, different from American trade policy overall. Since the Reciprocity Agreement of 1854, freer trade with Canada is an issue that has appeared on the American policy agenda from time to time. The initiative, however, has usually come from Canada, because trade with the United States is more important to Canada than the reverse. By the 1980s, about 14 percent of Canada's GDP depended directly on trade with the United States (more, if the indirect effects were counted), while only about 2 percent to 3 percent of the American GDP depended on trade with Canada.[10]

During the Second World War, the Canadian and American economies had to a large extent worked as a single economy. After the war, the American government hoped to lead the world in the creation of a liberal, multilateral trading system, in which Canada would be an important member, but still only one important member among many. In December 1945, the American government invited fifteen other governments to a preliminary conference to discuss "trade and employment." All except one government (the Soviet Union) accepted the invitation, Canada, being the second to do so (after the United Kingdom). In February 1946, the State Department Division of Commercial Policy suggested that the negotiations for an international trade charter should run parallel to but separate from discussion about tariffs. The latter, though multilateral in scope, would in fact consist of a series of bilateral discussions, with each government making its own offer on tariffs, quotas, export restrictions, and related issues. Although the United Nations Economic and Social Council officially called the trade conference into being by a resolution adopted in April 1946, the Americans pushed ahead with the trade negotiations, which had little connection with the UN after the preparatory conference began its sessions in London in October 1946.[11] The conference itself began in Geneva in April 1947. As planned, negotiations for a general charter to govern international trade and negotiations on tariff reductions took place simultaneously.[12]

As the tariff negotiators began to work, the Americans made it one of their main purposes to break "the Empire bloc" and to substitute general multilateral rules for special, preferential trading arrangements. American negotiators saw no need to push Canada on the issue of Commonwealth preferences, because they sensed that Canada was already distancing itself from the Commonwealth connection. American-Canadian negotiations at the conference seem to have been no different from most other bilateral tariff negotiations there. Thus, the American negotiations mentioned Canada as helpful, but each time in conjunction with others. For example, in July 1947, the American delegation reported good support on charter negotiations from Belgium, the Netherlands, and Canada, in that order.[13] During the various bilateral tariff sessions, Canadian-American sessions also took place, but these sessions were no different from those with other delegations, though the Canadians were not above pointing out that the Americans should not be too hard in their tariff demands, because "Canada had been the strongest supporter of the United States in this whole program."[14]

By August 1947, the tariff negotiations were going badly, at least from an American point of view, and the American delegation proposed separate agreements with governments judged to be willing to make satisfactory agreements (Norway, Benelux, Lebanon, and Syria) or at least "fair" ones (Canada and China). Once again, Canada was one among others. By October, however, the tariff negotiations had reached a stage considered satisfactory, and the American delegation was prepared to recommend that the president implement the tariff agreements, even before congressional approval, with the ITO charter to be left for later adoption. At the same time, the American delegation insisted that the British and Canadian delegations make a commitment to substitute GATT rates for the former Commonwealth tariffs; this commitment appears not to have been made. The GATT agreement did, however, specifically supersede the separate trade agreements Canada, the UK, and the US had negotiated in the 1930s.[15]

While the governments were negotiating freer trade in Geneva, Canada was experiencing a serious foreign exchange problem, as explained in Chapter 6, a problem which was to a large extent caused by the failure of the British economy to recover. In June 1947, Norman Robertson, the Canadian high commissioner to London, wrote to Lester Pearson, then the under-secretary of external affairs in Ottawa. Robertson suggested that when the United States was asking the Europeans to practise economic cooperation on a "continental basis" (in the context of the Marshall Plan),

Canadians might consider a similar policy. He preferred "continental integration" with the American economy rather than ties to "an impoverished sterling area." Perhaps Canadians should "be thinking of a real reciprocity agreement with the United States."[16]

Robertson's idea was not taken up in Ottawa until September, when the exchange crisis had begun to bite, and when the GATT negotiations were almost over. Now it may seem strange that Canadians were pursuing free trade with the Americans, even as they were imposing foreign exchange controls against American imports, but what Canadians sought was assured access to the American market, which they hoped would help to resolve their exchange crisis. In October, the Canadian embassy in Washington once again spoke with the State Department about a possible bilateral trade agreement. The State Department in turn consulted the American ambassador in Ottawa, who on 29 October reported "that Canada today more than ever before appears ready to accept virtual economic union with the United States as a necessary substitute for the multilateralism of the Atlantic triangle now believed to have disappeared." State Department officials had no objections to a trade agreement with Canada. Indeed, George Kennan, the policy guru of the postwar State Department, had already suggested "a sharing of certain of the powers of sovereignty" among the US, Canada, and Britain, as a possible solution to Britain's economic problems – but the State Department did not want Congress to find out about further liberalization measures before the GATT and the ITO were adopted. Secret negotiations continued throughout the winter of 1947-8.[17]

The Canadian negotiators faced another problem. They feared that the large segment of Canadian public opinion that still clung to the British connection might object to a customs union with the United Sates, with all that implied in terms of common rules. A helpful American official, Paul Nitze, thought of a solution. He suggested a kind of partial customs union in which the two partners would dismantle all tariffs against each other but maintain their previous tariffs against third parties.[18] In this way Canada could have free trade with the United States *and* Empire preferences. Subsequently, the customs unions, which have common external tariffs, and free trade areas, which dismantle internal tariffs only, were specifically mentioned in Article XXIV of GATT as permissible exceptions to the multilateral free trade regime.

Negotiations for a Canadian-American free trade area began in January 1948, and by the beginning of March 1948, the two sides had agreed on the outline of an agreement. It was simple. All tariffs were to be removed. There were to be exceptions to protect vulnerable industries, a transition period of five years, and special provisions to exempt most agricultural products.

As State Department officials began thinking of how to put the plan to

Congress, the aging Canadian prime minister, Mackenzie King, was changing his mind. King had been kept fully informed of the negotiations, but the exchange crisis was over by 1948 and attendance at the wedding of the future Queen Elizabeth II and Prince Philip in November 1947 had aroused his royalist sentiments. Somehow, it seems by coincidence, *Life* magazine ran an article about possible economic union between Canada and the United States just as the two governments were getting ready for detailed negotiations. Public reaction in Canada was strongly negative. Although King credited divine intervention with his change of mind, his good political instincts were a more likely factor. In office for thirteen years, King was not to be opposed. At the end of March, he said "No" to free trade with the United States. When the most powerful of his ministers, C.D. Howe, told some American officials just to wait for the old man's retirement, King heard about the conversation and threatened to postpone his planned resignation. The Canadian ambassador in Washington tried to put a good spin on Canada's refusal: the Canadian government would now be able to concentrate on the proposed "security pact" (that is, NATO).[19] There was a brief attempt to revive the idea of a Canadian-American free trade agreement in February and March 1949, apparently at Canadian initiative. But the Canadians were worried lest the electorate find out before the Canadian elections, and the Americans were worried that Congress might find out. Nothing happened.[20]

Security concerns dominated these early Cold War years. The records of the Policy Planning Staff for January 1948 include a strange document that envisages a situation in which the United States might be cut off from the rest of the world and would be able to trade only with the Western Hemisphere. Of the countries in that hemisphere, the author – Wilfred Malenbaum – considered only Argentina and Canada as important American trade partners. He therefore tried to calculate the changes in commercial policy the American government would need to make if it could trade with only these two countries. Eighteen months later, George Kennan envisaged another situation, one where the British economy was so weakened that a joint British-American-Canadian economic zone would become necessary.[21] The following year, when Secretary of State Dean Acheson advised President Truman on the way to present the failure of the ITO, he pointed out that "the expansion of trade is an indispensable part of our total effort to create strength and unity in the free world."[22] Also in 1950, there were American suggestions for a new economic organization of the Marshall Plan Aid recipients, the US, and Canada, a kind of economic equivalent of NATO. But the European governments, with their war-torn economies, did not feel ready for such an association of sovereign equals with the United States. In spite of Canadian support, the suggestions did not reach the level of intergovernmental negotiations.[23]

Judith Goldstein, an American political scientist, has pointed out that trade negotiations, like other international negotiations, are driven by ideology and *Weltanschauung* as much as by self-interest. In principle, the Americans continued their efforts to liberalize trade to consolidate the interests of the free world, but the 1951 GATT negotiations in Torquay soon sank into the trenches of international trade negotiations: wool versus cheddar cheese, plywood, and canned salmon. This time, Canada was to be the stalking horse that broke the Commonwealth preferences, which the declining importance of Britain was in any case rendering irrelevant. "Good Canadian agreement may break through on preferences and force good agreements all around," the head of the American delegation wrote to the secretary of state. Canada's chief negotiator, Dana Wilgress, even agreed to report to the Americans on his talks with the British. But apart from this topic, Canada was again only one American negotiating partner among others. There was no talk of free trade or a special relationship.[24]

In 1953, the Americans suggested Canadian-American free trade. In May 1953, Prime Minister St. Laurent visited the recently inaugurated President Eisenhower in Washington. When the Canadian prime minister expressed concern about increasing American protectionism, the American defence secretary, Charles Wilson, suggested free trade or a special tariff relationship between the two countries. The State Department began a feasibility study, but when the Canadian ambassador learned of this study, he pointed out that there was no chance of the Canadian government accepting such a proposal. Indeed the St. Laurent government, which was facing an election, also worried that the proposal might become public and would damage its chances of re-election. In 1957, another Eisenhower advisor, Clarence Randall, suggested Canadian-American economic integration, "in parallel with the establishment of the Common Market ... in Europe." Secretary of State John Foster Dulles thought that the Canadians were bound to oppose such a proposal, that any common market should include "other American Republics," and that any such proposal was unwise: "We try to work together as good neighbours and not to embarrass each other."[25] That put an end to Canadian-American free trade discussions for the next quarter of a century.

Twenty-Five Years of Normality
During the Kennedy Round (1962-7) of GATT negotiations, Americans still occasionally expected Canadians to set a good example. As in many multilateral forums, Canadians and Americans consulted frequently. But for the most part, Canadian-American trade relations did not rise above the softwood lumber and fish fillets, which have been at issue for over a century. Surprisingly, a 1964 public opinion survey found 65 percent of Canadians in favour of "economic union with the United States," but governments

shied away from the issue.[26] The 1965 Merchant-Heeney report, a hall-mark of the "special relationship," went no further than to suggest a study "for the longer range future ... of the practicability of further progressive reductions in tariffs and other barriers to trade." (Longer than what was not specified, but perhaps the comparative form was just meant to refer to a very long period of time.[27])

Canadian-American free trade was an issue that would not disappear. In 1962, when the State Department reviewed policies toward Canada, it wrote: "We should seek to promote our liberal trade policy in our relations with Canada and work with the Canadians in bringing about further reductions in trade barriers to promote a favorable market situation in Canada and elsewhere ... We should also look with favor on the idea of a closer economic integration over a period of time in the field of power and energy."[28] Even during the years of Canadian economic nationalism, two Canadian economists published a study of the effects free trade might have on the Canadian economy. Perhaps Ambassador Butterworth had seen this study. In his 1967 year-end report, he wrote to Washington predicting that if Canadians became frustrated with multilateral efforts toward free trade "new pressures will develop for reducing trade barriers with the US ... but this is all in the future." A few months later, Butterworth concluded that free trade between Canada and the US might not be needed after all, because the Kennedy Round had achieved "virtual free trade in industrial raw materials."[29]

The 1971 devaluation of the American dollar (discussed in Chapter 6) included a temporary surcharge on imports into the US and subsidies to American exports. Canadians tried to negotiate exemptions from these measures. Not only did they not succeed, they were faced with threats of cancelling the Autopact. The surcharges were dropped after the currency settlement of December 1971 and seem to have had no major effect on Canada. The bilateral negotiations the Canadians had demanded to compensate for the surcharge were quietly suspended during summer 1972. Such problems led to a few calls for Canadian-American free trade. *US News and World Report* (25 October 1971) claimed that some Canadians were calling for a "North American Common Market," and in February 1973, a Canadian senator, Maurice Lamontagne, did make such a suggestion. But in Canadian politics, senators are not usually considered important policy makers. And the Nixon administration showed no interest in such a proposal.[30]

Congress, however, did. By the mid-1970s, three streams converged in Washington. One led from the disillusionment with multilateral freer trade to the idea of bilateral or regional accords, in the European mode. Another sprang from the 1973-4 energy crisis and pointed to Canada's importance as a possible future source of energy. A third, more specifically

Canadian factor was disappointment with the Autopact (discussed in the next section). Some senators from auto-producing states felt that general negotiations on freer trade could lead to a revision of the Autopact. Accordingly, the 1974 Trade Act included two provisions in two separate sections. Section 105 authorized the president to enter into negotiations leading to "bilateral trade agreements," subject, of course, to the later approval of Congress. Section 612 stated the "sense of Congress [to be] that the United States should enter into a trade agreement with Canada which will guarantee continental stability ... In order to promote such economic stability, the President may initiate negotiations ... to establish a free trade area covering the United States and Canada."[31] The 1979 Trade Act included a similar clause, but instead of referring to Canada, it referred to the "northern portion of the Western hemisphere." The legislative history published with the act explained that this quaint wording was meant to include Mexico and the Central American and Caribbean countries "to promote mutual economic stability."[32] Also in 1979, in the speech announcing his candidacy for the Republican nomination, Ronald Reagan called for closer economic relations, though not free trade, among the US, Canada, and Mexico. He does not seem to have returned to this theme during the remainder of the campaign.[33]

Nor did the fading Carter administration take up the theme. In June 1980, Reubin Askew, Carter's trade representative, gave a congressional committee a vague answer when asked about the bilateral trade provisions of the 1979 Trade Act. "We are looking ahead and moving on that." The incoming Reagan administration showed no more enthusiasm. In October 1981, spokespersons for the Treasury, State, and Commerce Departments told a Senate committee that closer economic ties among the three North American nations would need to be considered "in an evolutionary way," "over a period of time." In everyday language that means: We are not going to do anything about it. Another official used stronger language. Obstacles, he said, ruled out "the giant leap into a free trade area."[34] There is no evidence that during the Tokyo Round GATT negotiations American and Canadian negotiators did anything other than consult on issues of obvious bilateral interest (such as wheat). To the contrary, Canada seems often to have been forgotten. Steve Dryden's detailed account of how the Carter and Reagan administrations bumbled their way toward an import restraining agreement on Japanese cars makes no mention of Canada and the Autopact. A 1974 background paper on the grain trade, prepared by the State Department for the Ford administration, does not mention nor even include Canada as a separate line in the accompanying tables.[35]

A few Canadians were, however, continuing to speak of freer trade or free trade with the US. In 1975, the Economic Council of Canada published a study of the possible political effects of free trade with the US. This study may have been prompted by the 1974 Trade Act, but nothing in the study indicates that. In 1979, a political science professor claimed, "Free trade with the US is currently becoming a political issue in Canada." And in 1981, a retired Canadian diplomat published an essay on Canadian-American relations in which he predicted that if the Reagan administration found the Europeans, the Japanese, and the Third World cold to its advances of Cold War alignments, "last-ditch isolationism" might persuade it to turn to "Fortress America."[36] In that region, several bilateral sectoral agreements were already in effect. They included American-Canadian agreements on some agricultural equipment and automobiles. The next section describes the agreement on automobiles.

The Autopact: Part 1

From 1927 until the arrival of the Japanese firms, practically all automobile manufacturing plants in Canada were American-owned. This American-owned, "Canadian" industry was protected by tariffs and by a special protective regulation that required cars sold in Canada to be at least 60 percent Canadian in manufactured content. As a result, the industry was not efficient. It produced many models at a relatively high cost, yet paid lower wages than its American counterpart. This issue was a Canadian problem that did not require an American policy.

In 1963, the Canadian government tried to improve the efficiency of the automobile industry by introducing a complex export rebate scheme for automobiles and parts, to encourage exports and thus create longer, more efficient production runs. At the same time, it maintained the Canadian content requirement. Export rebates are not allowed under the GATT and were and are countervailable under American law. As a result, some American parts manufacturers began the legal process which, if successful, would have required the American government to impose extra duties on Canadian-made automotive parts. And, of course, senators and representatives from the affected states supported their constituents. Such countervailing duty actions have become common since the 1980s, but they were a rare occurrence in the 1960s.[37]

The possibility of countervailing duties against a major employer in Canada set off alarms in the Johnson administration. Opposition came from two principal sources. The first was the American automobile firms that owned the Canadian plants. On 16 September 1964, Henry Ford wrote to President Johnson to tell him that Canada would retaliate and that the consequent dislocation to the American economy would be worse than if no action were taken. The other was the State Department, which feared an anti-American backlash in Canada, where a minority government might face an election at any time. Senator Vance Hartke of Indiana (which has an auto-parts industry) was later to make repeated claims that the American government gave the Canadians a generous deal on the automobile industry to gain Canadian support for the Vietnam War. As mentioned in Chapter 3, some argue that the Autopact was a reward for Canadian cooperation on Cyprus. In any event, Senator Hartke was wrong. By the time the automobile agreement was negotiated, there was little chance of any significant Canadian support for American policy in Vietnam. Documents now available including letters from the secretary of state to President Johnson show that the State Department's main concerns were to maintain reasonably good relations with Canada and to ensure that John Diefenbaker and his Conservatives were not re-elected.[38]

Accordingly, when Prime Minister Pearson visited President Johnson in January 1964, the president's advisors instructed the president to suggest a joint task force to study the rationalization of the North American auto industry, while maintaining the threat of countervailing duties to persuade the prime minister. Although the task force was not appointed until after a cabinet-level meeting of both governments in April, negotiations after that date proceeded quickly, especially because the American side maintained the possibility of imposing the countervailing duties if the negotiations did not succeed. The American negotiators, led by Julius Katz and Philip Trezise, both from the State Department, suggested a kind of free trade in cars and parts, but with many protective measures to assure the Canadian-based sector of the industry a share of the work.[39] This suggestion became the basis for a solution both governments accepted.

In January 1965, the president and the prime minister signed an agreement which provided for the production in Canada of at least 75 percent as many cars as were sold there and for the maintenance of Canadian value-added in Canadian-made vehicles at least at the 1964 level. The Canadian government also signed letters of understanding with the major car manufacturers, by which the manufacturers agreed to raise the level of Canadian value-added in Canadian-made cars. These letters of understanding later became controversial because some American Senators claimed that they constituted an underhanded Canadian tactic. But correspondence from the Johnson White House shows that the American negotiators knew about these "side deals."[40] From then on, all went well, and after parliamentary and congressional approval, the president signed the American implementing legislation on 21 October 1965.

The 1965 Autopact does appear generous to Canada. At the time, the postwar warm glow that allowed Americans to feel generous toward its allies and friends had not faded. But more important was the fact that the Canadians had a domestic American constituency on their side – the American auto companies, who preferred an integrated, regulated market to a free one. When presidential advisor McGeorge Bundy was preparing the Autopact for submission to Congress, he wrote the president, "The big companies are all in line (Ford and Chrysler with gusto)."[41] This agreement is not an example of free trade, but of carefully managed government-circumscribed trade.

For ten years or perhaps longer, the Autopact succeeded in bringing peace and prosperity to the auto industries of the two nations. Trade and employment expanded rapidly. During the Autopact's first three years, trade in automotive products between the two countries increased almost fivefold. Trade in automotive products became an ever more important component in Canadian-American trade, rising from 5 percent of bilateral trade in 1965 to 34 percent in 1971, a level maintained since that time. The problem that caused many complaints on both sides of the border was that, given changes in production plans by the major firms and changes in consumer taste for different models, the "trade balance" in automotive products fluctuated rapidly. Seen from the Canadian side, this was the picture in Canadian dollars: 1965, −$600 million; 1971, +$200 million; 1975, −$1,400 million; 1985, +$5,100 million. This situation naturally caused complaints and calls for government action addressed to the government of the temporarily disadvantaged country.[42]

The State Department remained attached to the Autopact as one of its contributions to harmonious Canadian-American relations. In August 1971, President Nixon announced the series of measures intended to show that the United States, currently suffering from a trade deficit and an overvalued dollar, must demand that its allies stand on their own feet and no longer rely on American generosity. (See Chapter 6.) According to one source, one of the many measures the administration intended to announce was the unilateral cancellation of the Autopact. Julius Katz, still with the State Department, saw the announcement in the pile of documents about to be released to the press. He foresaw the disruption to the North American economy such a measure could cause, not to mention that he perhaps valued his own handiwork. He pulled the announcement from the pile and asked Secretary of State William Rogers to intervene with John Connally, the Treasury secretary, on the Autopact's behalf. Rogers obliged, successfully.[43]

The Autopact was saved, for the time being. By the end of the 1970s, a new situation led to renewed calls for change from American parts manufacturers and the Congress. The Autopact had been based on the assumption that the North American auto industry would continue to be dominated by the three major US-based firms. But by the late 1970s, first Volkswagen and Volvo, and then on a much larger scale Japanese and other Asian firms, became important suppliers to the American and Canadian markets. As with several other industries, one of the first American reactions was to try to protect the American industry by limiting imports. The Canadian reaction was different. The Canadian government tried to persuade the

Japanese manufacturers to locate some of their production facilities in Canada. To this end, they reinterpreted the terms of the Autopact to allow financial incentives to third-country firms. This approach caused strong opposition in the United States, especially when the Japanese-owned Canadian-based firms began to export some of their production to the United States under the terms of the Autopact. It was to become a topic in the next round of American-Canadian trade negotiations.

The Road toward American-Canadian "Free Trade"

In hard times, Canadians have frequently looked for freer trade with the US. That was the case in 1854, in the 1890s, in 1935, and again in 1983. Conversely, when Canadians turned down the American offer of free trade in 1911, Canada was prosperous. When the 1982 recession hit Canada, the business community and even the Liberal-dominated Senate responded with demands for "free trade" with the US. With the Reagan administration in Washington, such demands fell on fertile soil. President Reagan himself had long favoured the idea of freer trade, both in his previous incarnation as a New Deal Democrat and in his current one as a pro-business Republican. His first trade representative, William Brock, had similar pro-free trade ideas. And when a major American effort to start another GATT round of trade liberalization failed in November 1982, regional and bilateral trade liberalization agreements formed a natural alternative, as well as a useful bargaining chip to use against the recalcitrant Europeans and Japanese.[44]

But as long as the suggestions for freer trade did not come from the Canadian government, any American initiative would have rendered the Reagan administration vulnerable to charges of interference in Canada's internal affairs.[45] The Trudeau government in Ottawa faced an election, in 1984 if not sooner, and it could not be deaf to the pleas of its business community. A government, elected in 1980 on a platform of nationalist economic measures, could hardly advocate free trade with the US, but in August 1983, its minister for trade, coincidentally called Gerald Regan, suggested sectoral free trade, on the model of the Autopact. He named steel, computers, mass transit equipment, and agricultural equipment as possible sectors.[46]

The Reagan administration would have preferred a general free trade agreement, but it did not want to rebuff the Canadian initiative and agreed to negotiate. The negotiators, however, had barely begun their talks before election campaigns in both countries forced their suspension. In the US Ronald Reagan was re-elected, but in Canada the change of government had a major effect on American-Canadian trade relations.

Elected prime minister in 1984, Brian Mulroney had campaigned on a platform of better relations with the United States, though he had not mentioned free trade during the campaign. Within two weeks of taking office, in September 1984, the new prime minister travelled to Washington to call on President Reagan. None of the press reports or communiques of that meeting mentioned free trade, but it may well have been discussed. A month later, Mulroney's minister of external affairs, Joe Clark, addressed a group of businessmen in Ottawa. He made the ritual pledge to multilateralism and continued, "But what better place to look first than our own backyard with our predominant trading partner."[47] Three months later, in January 1985, the Canadian government issued a hesitant "discussion paper" which suggested that free trade with the United States might be good for the Canadian economy.

Equally significant developments occurred in Washington. The 1984 Omnibus Trade Act specifically authorized the president to negotiate free trade agreements with Canada and Israel (the agreement with Israel was signed a year later). The president was also instructed to study the effects of such free trade agreements. In March 1985, the International Trade Commission reported that thirty-three of thirty-five major industrial sectors studied would benefit, or at least not lose, from free trade with Canada.

With support from much of their business community assured, the two conservative leaders were now ready to adopt the policy they both favoured. In March 1985, President Reagan made his first official visit to Canada. Among the communiques issued after the meeting, a short one dealt with "trade in goods and services." It called for the following:

- the reduction or elimination of "existing barriers to trade ... through a reduction in *tariff barriers*"
- "national treatment ... with respect to *government procurement and funding programs*"
- a "market approach" to "*energy trade*"
- "facilitation of *travel* for business ... purposes"
- "cooperation to protect *intellectual property rights*"
- "elimination or reduction of tariff and non-tariff barriers to trade in *high-technology goods and related services*." [italics in the original]

Not coincidentally these were some of the principal aims of the Reagan administration as it sought to launch a new series of GATT liberalization talks.[48] At the bilateral level, the Canadian minister for international trade and the United States trade representative were to report within six months on the way these aims could be achieved.

Neither government had yet formally adopted a policy of free trade with the other. That changed in September when, after a long-awaited study of the Canadian economy recommended free trade with the US, the Canadian government formally requested negotiations with the US. It was exactly six months after the Reagan-Mulroney summit. The report the two leaders had asked for was ready and also recommended bilateral free trade. So, too, did an internal report prepared for the new United States Trade Representative Clayton Yeutter, but that report did so in much more hesitant terms than the equivalent Canadian or the bilateral studies: "We are committed to pursue negotiations aimed at a further liberalization of trade, be they on a bilateral, plurilateral, or multilateral basis ... From preliminary informal discussion ... I believe that a number of US industries have an interest in expanding their access to a prosperous and expanding proximate Canadian market."[49] Nevertheless, the two governments were now committed. Under the Canadian system of government, Prime Minister Mulroney could now begin to put his negotiating team in place. But the American president needed first to obtain congressional approval. Given the procedure in force under the various trade acts, the best way for the president to enter into international trade negotiations was for him to ask for "fast-track" authority. This approach meant that once the agreement was negotiated, Congress would have to adopt or reject it in its entirety, without changing the contents.

To obtain such authority, the president had to notify both houses of Congress of his intention and then to wait ninety working days. If neither house did anything, the president would have his authority. The president wrote Congress on 10 December 1985. The House of Representatives chose to let him have his negotiating authority by default, but the Senate Finance Committee began discussions of Reagan's request on 11 April 1986, two weeks before the president would have had his authority without a vote. The Senate discussions were long and dull; the senators talked about fish, uranium, asbestos, and lumber, not the principles of bilateral or multilateral free trade. The Reagan White House tried to persuade the senators to support the President's initiative. The Canadian press gave the American Senate hearings coverage normally reserved for the World Series; the American press carried a few paragraphs on the inside pages. On 26 April, the last possible day, and after President Reagan had called at least one key senator one last time, the committee voted ¬ ten to ten – which by the rules of the American Senate meant that the president had his negotiating authority.

Negotiations officially began on 21 May 1986, and continued until 5 October 1987, the very day on which, under the fast-track authority, President Reagan had to submit the agreement to Congress. In fact, the president did not actually meet the deadline. What he sent to Congress in October 1987 was an outline and description of what the agreement would contain. It took lawyers two more months to produce the text of the agreement.

The negotiations succeeded largely because the two heads of government, Brian Mulroney and Ronald Reagan, were personally determined to have them succeed. At the same time, the trade agreement with Canada conformed to a number of general and more specific American foreign and trade policy aims. Apart from the general aim of strengthening its trade relationship with Canada, at a time when its relationship with other allies presented problems, the American administration sought to use the Canadian negotiations as an example of what could be done to further American aims in international trade negotiations. As early as February 1985, the President's annual economic report to Congress had stated: "Perhaps, most importantly, ... the possibility of FTA or, more broadly, plurilateral negotiations offers the United States and others the option of using a free-trade instrument, rather than protectionism, as a lever against protectionist countries that are recalcitrant in multilateral negotiations." Or, in the more trenchant words of American foreign trade guru, Jeffrey Schott, "In essence, the United States has been using bilateralism as both a carrot and a stick to further the process of trade liberalization."[50]

The Uruguay Round of GATT talks began in 1986, while the Canadian-American talks were in progress. Much of what was on the agenda during the bilateral talks reappeared on the American agenda for the multilateral ones: freer trade in services, better protection of "intellectual property" (patents, copyrights, and trademarks), limitations on the rights of governments to subsidize industries and regions, and access to government procurement contracts in other countries. The American delegation wanted not only to show what could be done if trade partners were cooperative. It also wanted to demonstrate that it had alternatives and could form its own regional trade bloc if governments in other parts of the world did not cooperate.

In addition, the American delegation had specific aims relating to relations with Canada. Four predominated. The United States wanted assured access to Canadian energy resources, so that the National Energy Programme could not happen again. It also wanted American firms to have the right to invest in Canada without government reviews of such investments, to have access to Canadian government contracts (government procurement), and to be allowed to compete for business in the Canadian market for cultural goods (television, sound recordings, books, magazines, and films).[51]

A review of the course of the negotiations shows that in spite of President Reagan's commitment, the American administration did not at first, indeed for many months, attach much importance to them. It left the negotiations in the hands of one chief negotiator (a rather junior personality named Peter Murphy who had recently returned from sick leave), two full-time staffers, and a small number of officials, no more than forty in number, many of them part-timers seconded from other agencies. In contrast, the Canadians had a full-time staff of more than 100, headed by three senior negotiators, who could rely on help from various government departments in Ottawa. (In fairness, it should be mentioned that the American team was able to use the existing American system for the consultation of industry during international trade negotiations, whereas the Canadians had to devise their own procedure.) The Canadian office also had a semi-independent status equivalent to that of an American executive agency, whereas the Americans worked out of the Office of the US Trade Representative.[52]

To date, there have been only two detailed studies of the 1986-7 United States-Canada free trade negotiations, both written by Canadians; one is based largely on Canadian newspaper sources and personal interviews, the other on personal interviews.[53] Doern and Tomlin claim that the American negotiators had a deliberate strategy of stonewalling and leaving all major decisions to the end, in the hope that the Canadians, who had invested so much political capital in these negotiations, would give in on most issues. If that indeed was the American strategy, it did not succeed. Though the American Treasury and the Canadian Department of Finance had done their work and produced an agreement on banking and financial services, many of the major issues of interest to the Americans were still unresolved, when, two weeks before the congressional deadline of 3 October 1987, the Canadian chief negotiator staged a walkout (and no one has seriously disputed that the walkout was a tactic), saying that progress was impossible. By this means, the Canadians achieved what they had requested and been refused two weeks earlier:[54] a bumping up of the negotiations from the technical to the political level.

Both Doern and Tomlin and Michael Hart give graphic, though somewhat different, accounts of these last frantic negotiations. In the end, the Canadians accepted an American proposal for binational panels to rule on Canadian interpretations of Canadian trade law and American interpretations of American trade law. Canadians had sought common rules to define subsidies and dumping, so that Americans could not arbitrarily interpret what Canadians had done with respect to Canadian industries. A 1986 case had strengthened Canadian resolve in this respect. American administrative tribunals had found that the fees (called "stumpage fees") Canadian provincial governments charge companies before they can cut trees on publicly owned land were so low as to constitute a subsidy. American state governments, the tribunals found, were levying much higher fees. As a result, the American government had the right to levy additional duties on imports of Canadian lumber, duties the Canadian government was able to avert only by taxing its own lumber industries an additional 15 percent on exports of softwood lumber to the US. In short, the Americans had forced – or persuaded – Canadians to change the tax laws applying to Canadian industries in Canada.

This pressure was only one example. Other pressures arose from other industries. The Canadians did not like this kind of interference in their affairs. They hoped that a common, agreed-upon definition of what constituted a subsidy would protect them from such actions in the future. However, the definition of an allowable subsidy was a problem international trade negotiators had been trying to resolve for years. It was not to be done during the last frantic days of the American-Canadian negotiations. Nor were the American negotiators able to curtail the privileges of tribunals Congress had created. The two sides agreed to a substitute solution, suggested by Sam Gibbons, chair of the trade subcommittee of the House of Representatives. There would be a binational procedure for reviewing administrative trade decisions made by tribunals of either government. If one of the two governments made a decision to impose punitive duties or other charges on imports from the other, the firm(s) concerned would have the right to appeal the decision to a "panel" consisting of two Americans, two Canadians, and a fifth person chosen by the other four. Such a procedure would meet the Canadian objective of not being subject to the vagaries of the decisions of American tribunals (whose members were usually political appointees).

In return for this concession, Canadians agreed to flexible rules on foreign investment, allowing all but the most major American investments in Canada to proceed without review by the Canadian government. The Canadians had already agreed not to limit future energy exports to a degree no greater than that allowed by the guidelines of the International Energy Association. (See Chapter 5.) The Canadians also made some concessions on the Autopact (discussed later in this chapter), but they were allowed to retain their cultural policies, though if the American government found that Canadian cultural policies were detrimental to American commercial interests, the Americans would have the right to retaliate. On government procurement and intellectual property, little that was new went into the agreement itself, but the Canadians agreed to a "side-deal" by which they promised to improve patent protection for pharmaceuticals. This protection would help American as well as European-based multinationals.[55] Agriculture, as usual in international trade negotiations, was subject to special rules.

The conclusions of the negotiations thus revealed that investment and energy had probably been the Americans' main concern, because in those two fields they insisted on concessions. As far as the negotiators were concerned, free trade itself (that is, the removal of tariffs on industrial goods) proved to be almost uncontroversial, because the two sides had agreed to the removal of tariffs when they entered into the negotiations.

In the United States, congressional approval of the FTA was almost a formality. After hearings and debates, first the House of Representatives and then the Senate approved the FTA by overwhelming majorities. In general, American opponents of the FTA (unions and independent petroleum producers) did not have much political clout and were geographically scattered. In Canada, the FTA was more controversial, and the Canadian government had to call an election before it could get parliamentary approval of the agreement. But the government won the election – though a majority of the electorate voted for political parties that did not support the FTA. The parliamentary type of electoral system used by Canadians makes such results possible. By the end of 1988, both governments had passed the legislation needed to implement the FTA,[56] which came into force on 1 January 1989.

The FTA negotiations with Canada demonstrated that the United States had moved some distance from the multilateral trade liberalization it had espoused in 1947. Though Canada was and is the most important trading partner of the United States, American policy did not identify Canada as the object of this new policy. Instead, Canada presented itself and became the test case. What is unclear was whether the FTA constituted a refreshment stop, a long detour, or a turn down a different road. Before the FTA had come into force, Americans had begun consideration of a bilateral free trade area with Mexico. Perhaps that new process would reveal the road taken.

The North American Free Trade Agreement (NAFTA)
Since at least the 1890s, various American presidents have advocated closer economic relations with Latin America. The idea of a North American free trade or economic area appeared in the 1970s, after the energy crisis and when it had become clear that Canada was as much an American as it was a "British" state.

Donald Barry's careful research reveals that discussion of a North American economic union, or cooperation agreement – the terminology varies – appeared in various American forums beginning in 1979. That year, the National Governors Association commissioned a study on North American cooperation; a year later, the association consulted the Canadian premiers and Mexican state governors about their proposal. Also in 1979, Senator Max Baucus of Montana (a border state) added a provision requiring the president to study North American "economic interdependence" to the US Trade Act. During the 1980 election campaign, Senator Edward Kennedy spoke of a "continental energy market," and Governor Jerry Brown of California advocated a "North American Community." As mentioned, Ronald Reagan had made a similar proposal when he launched his campaign for the presidency.[57]

Ironically, given later developments, the Canadian and Mexican governments not only showed no interest in such proposals, they rebuffed and opposed advances from the American presidential candidates, who sought to bolster their stature by displaying their creativity in foreign policy. When Canada's Prime Minister Pierre Trudeau met Mexico's President José López Portillo in May 1980, the two leaders issued a statement to say that "tripartite schemes 'would not serve the best interests of their countries.'"[58]

We have already seen how Canada changed its policy, a policy it was then able to implement because of the American interest in bilateral trade agreements. While Canadian policy was changing, Mexican policies were also evolving, but in Mexico the changes were greater than in Canada. In Mexico, the government had for decades played a major role in the economy. It owned the oil industry, regulated agriculture, and used protection and incentives to try to develop secondary industries. These policies meant that foreign investment played a limited and carefully circumscribed role in the Mexican economy.

In the mid-1980s, the Mexican government began to change its economic policies. It liberalized the rules for foreign investment and liberalized foreign trade, to such an extent that in 1986 Mexico was allowed to join the GATT. For Mexico as for Canada, the United States represents the major export market, and the signs of protectionism that worried the Canadian governments of the 1980s made a similar impression in Mexico. Mexicans noted the Canadian solution: an agreement for free trade with the United States. But from the Mexican point of view, there was worse ahead. The FTA had the potential of favouring Canada over Mexico in access to the American market. With the Autopact, Canada already had favourable access for automobiles and parts. It would now be able to compete with Mexico in other goods, including textiles.

President Bush, elected in 1988, had a long-standing interest in Latin America. On 27 June 1990, he proposed an "Enterprise for the Americas," a program of freer trade, debt relief, economic liberalization, and better access for American investment. The president was careful to specify that a free trade zone for the Americas was a "long term goal," which reassured Latin Americans that "our government will not be doing much about this."[59]

American government had long been preaching to Latin Americans about the virtues of free enterprise. President Reagan, concerned about socialism in Cuba and Nicaragua, was pleased by Mexican changes in policy. In November 1987, the American and Mexican governments signed a "framework agreement" that promised further bilateral talks on trade and investment. When in June 1990 the Mexican government requested free trade negotiations with the United States, the Bush administration could not but respond favourably, and not only to appear consistent. Bush and his advisors believed that encouraging the Mexican reforms by giving Mexico access to the American market would strengthen Mexico's economy and stabilize its political system. A pro-NAFTA economist, Paul Krugman, summarized the political case for NAFTA in an article which bears the sub-title "It's Foreign Policy, Stupid." He wrote: "Carlos Salinas de Gortari's government [1988-94] is not a model of democratic virtue ... Salinas has overseen a radical liberalization of the Mexican economy ... For the United States, this agreement ... is about what we can do to help a friendly government succeed." The American ambassador, speaking to a group of Canadian business people was just as explicit: "The Mexican economy, which was not long ago one of the world's most protected, is now one of the most open. The United States government feels strongly that these measures deserve our support." Nearly two years later, when he presented the complete NAFTA to Congress, President Bush made a similar point: "In the last 5 years, President Salinas has dismantled many longstanding Mexican trade and investment restrictions, our exports to Mexico have nearly tripled ... This agreement helps us lock in these gains and build on them."[60]

Nevertheless, the American government was surprised by the nature and extent of the Mexican request. In September 1988, a former USTR staffer told a congressional committee that a "full-blown FTA" with Mexico was "not possible, economically or politically." And even in April 1990, Carla Hills, by then the US trade representative, told the *Washington Post* that a "sweeping free trade pact" with Mexico was "years away."[61]

Yet on 10 June 1990, when President Bush met President Salinas (who had replaced López Portillo in 1988), the two presidents announced that they had asked their trade ministers to begin preparatory work on a "comprehensive free trade agreement."[62] The Mexican request reached Washington a year and a half after the Canada-United States agreement had come into force, and six years after the United States had granted preferential access to several Caribbean nations.[63] Any agreement the Mexicans negotiated would need to allow for the privileges gained by the other two entities.

While the American government must have welcomed the Mexican initiative, Canada and its FTA at first appeared to be no more than a complication, a technicality to be kept in mind. When Presidents Bush and Salinas announced that the negotiations would begin, a White House spokesperson told reporters that a "trilateral FTA ... would have to wait until the achievement of a Mexico-US agreement." Such statements must have caused some alarm in Ottawa, where the Conservative government had presented the FTA as a great achievement in gaining access to the American market. The Canadian minister for international trade, John Crosbie, met his Mexican counterpart, Jaime Serra Puche, three days after the American-Mexican announcement to begin discussions on Canada's role in the American-Mexican discussions. However, on 25 September

1990, when President Bush notified Congress of his intention to negotiate free trade with Mexico, he merely added that "Canada had expressed a desire to participate."[64]

It was not until 5 February 1991 that Canada was formally accepted into the talks. On that day, President Bush began a press conference by announcing that the three governments "intend to pursue a trilateral free trade agreement." The transcript of the rest of the conference shows no questions or comments on this subject. Reporters were more interested in the Gulf War. A Canadian newspaper claimed that Canada had gained acceptance by supporting the United States during that war, and other newspaper reports claimed that the Mexican government had been cautious about accepting Canada into the negotiations. Government reports released to another newspaper showed that the Canadian government's own economists doubted the economic advantages of a trade agreement with Mexico. But Canada had little choice. The fact that the bilateral FTA existed made some kind of Canadian-American negotiations, be they trilateral or sequential, essential.[65]

The American Congress voted fast-track authority on 23 and 24 May 1991. Negotiations for the NAFTA began in Toronto on 12 June 1991. The three governments published a detailed draft of the agreement on 12 August 1992, but as in the case of the FTA, the final legal text took another month and a half to complete, and further negotiations took place on issues such as tariff classifications and government procurement during that process.[66]

Elections first in the US and then in Canada delayed the ratification procedure. The Clinton administration, which took office in January 1993, negotiated side agreements on environmental and labour standards. These agreements, completed in August 1993, set up panels to hear complaints that any of the governments involved is not enforcing its own environmental or labour standards. If a government is found guilty, it could be fined, with the fines to be paid into a special fund that will work to improve the environmental and labour conditions. The Canadian government will allow its courts to enforce such fines; the United States and Mexico reserved the right to impose trade sanctions if fines are not paid. For example, if the Mexican government does not pay a fine levied on it by the NAFTA Environmental Commission, the American government can impose trade sanctions against it, whereas the Canadian government insisted that court decisions and fines would suffice because it suspected that sanctions might become yet another excuse to protect American industry.

In Canada, the Liberal government of Jean Chrétien, elected in October 1993, sought further assurances on national controls over energy, water supplies, and the definition of subsidies, even though both houses of

Parliament had adopted the NAFTA agreements in June 1993. It received some assurances on the last two topics, but the American government was not prepared to concede anything on energy, having already conceded more to Mexico than it had allowed Canada in 1987. Mexico, unlike Canada, retains the right to control its energy resources and investment in those resources, though the NAFTA does include some IEA type of provisions for sharing in emergencies. (Mexico was not a member of the IEA; Canada was.) The House of Representatives adopted the NAFTA agreement on 17 November 1993; the Senate followed a few days later. In the end, both the American and the Canadian governments ratified the NAFTA, in spite of the doubts Clinton and Chrétien had expressed during their respective election campaigns.[67] Mexico had cautiously waited until the American and Canadian constitutional requirements were in place before it initiated its own ratification procedure. The NAFTA came into force on 1 January 1994.

The American administration made it clear that the primary aim of the NAFTA negotiations was to gain access to Mexican trade and investment. Canada had not been a major topic for Americans (though NAFTA was an important issue for Canadians). President Bush repeated American goals with respect to the NAFTA several times: elimination of tariffs and non-tariff barriers to trade, "establishment of an open investment climate," and enforcement of intellectual property rights. Canada was not specifically mentioned. The twenty-six-page overview of the agreement published by the United States trade representative on 12 August 1992, includes only three or four scattered references to Canada. The two main points with respect to Canada are that the FTA will remain in effect with some changes and that American exporters will gain better access to the Canadian market for services under NAFTA than under the FTA.[68]

In short, NAFTA is not nearly as relevant to American policies toward Canada as is the FTA. Perhaps some of the changes sought by the United States as it negotiated the NAFTA revealed what the United States had failed to gain during the FTA negotiations. These included further measures on intellectual property rights, revisions of the Autopact, wider access to government procurement in Canada, and better access to the Canadian market for services. Many American firms will now be able to provide services in Canada without opening an office there, and the patent provisions, not officially linked to the FTA, became a binding part of NAFTA.[69]

NAFTA adopted and adapted the panel system of dispute resolution which had been one of the most innovative, and in the United States the most controversial, features of the bilateral FTA. Several other aspects of the FTA were expanded or amended by the NAFTA. There are, for example, more detailed provisions on financial services. To the extent that the NAFTA used and adapted provisions of the FTA, the demonstration effect, as motive for the FTA, was confirmed.[70]

For the record, the NAFTA frees trade in most industrial products, except automobiles and parts and textiles. Apart from trade, the agreement deals with investment, government procurement, intellectual property, competition policy, land transportation, and travel for business purposes. The labour and environmental side agreements need to be added to that list. The NAFTA is thus much more than a trade agreement. It deals with economic integration in many sectors, and it sets rules and limits on some of the domestic legislation the three-member governments can adopt. The NAFTA also includes an accession clause to allow other governments to join. However, the failure of the Clinton administration to obtain fast-track authority for further negotiations rules out other accessions for now. The collapse of the Mexican peso and the reappearance of the Mexican debt problems within one year of the adoption of the NAFTA have also dampened some of the optimistic predictions of NAFTA's proponents.[71]

To return to the topic of Canada in American policy, Canada was a minor concern of the American administration throughout the NAFTA negotiations. Canada played a role on several specific issues, such as the environmental agreement, in which it refused to accept the possibility of trade sanctions. But otherwise Canada played a role mainly as a precursor, a demonstration model. This role had been one of the American justifications for the FTA, and it was borne out by the NAFTA.

The Autopact: Part 2

When Canadians and Americans sat down to negotiate the Free Trade Agreement, revisions to the Autopact were high on the list of American objectives. The FTA would probably have had much greater difficulty in Congress had it not been for these revisions.

This issue is very technical, but briefly the FTA changed the rules of the Autopact. Canada would no longer be allowed to give Japanese or European firms financial incentives in the form of export rebates for exports to the United States. Japanese firms already established in Canada were still allowed to qualify for other Autopact privileges, but only if what they exported was at least 50 percent Canadian/American in content.[72]

The FTA also provided for the appointment of a special panel to study future rules for the auto industry. When that panel recommended that the Canadian/American minimum content for Autopact-tradable goods be raised to 60 percent, the Canadian government refused to accept the recommendation. Shortly thereafter, a complaint by American parts manufacturers led to an investigation of Honda Canada. On March 1992, this American investigation found that the cars Honda was selling to the United States from its Canadian plants were not 50 percent Canadian/American in content, if the production costs were calculated in a manner different from that used by Honda. Such problems meant that by the time the

NAFTA negotiations were under way, the American negotiators faced considerable pressure to demand further changes in the Autopact.[73]

In addition, NAFTA had to deal with the Mexican version of regulation of the auto industry. In Mexico, as in Canada before 1965, the auto industry was protected and governed by national rules, which required a fixed proportion of national contents in cars sold in Mexico and assigned exports targets to firms that wanted to import into Mexico. And as in Canada, the major American firms had invested in Mexico and acquired a vested interest in the protection of that market.[74]

NAFTA requires Mexico to phase out most of its auto industry regulations and in effect creates a kind of trilateral but asymmetrical Autopact. The old 1965 Autopact stays in effect for Canada and the US, but its rules are changed. North American content for example will rise to 62.5 percent, and the means of calculating the percentage are to be defined more precisely. However, not all existing plants will have to meet that target immediately. As Mexico phases out its protective system for its automotive industry, it will adopt the 62.5 percent North American content rule, bringing it in effect into this part of the Autopact. Other and detailed provisions relate to trade in used cars.

This brief summary of the NAFTA provisions of the Autopact (the annex and text dealing with the auto industry cover more than ten pages of fine-print text) is meant to make one point: the automobile industry is part of a managed trade system, in which the governments in negotiations with the major firms set the rules. This approach has little to do with the classical model of free trade. The Autopact also demonstrates that when the economic, and thus the political stakes, are large enough, the American-Canadian special relationship can still function quite well.

Conclusions

The conclusions on trade policy are short and surprising. The abortive 1947-8 free trade negotiations constitute a case of *exceptionalism*. The American government was willing to help Canada with its balance of trade problem. As for the rest of American-Canadian trade relations, it was for the most part business as usual from 1957 (when an Eisenhower administration official last suggested Canadian-American free trade) until about 1983 (when the issue of free trade reappeared on the public agenda in Canada). Canadians and Americans sometimes cooperated and sometimes opposed each other in international trade negotiations, but Americans saw no need for a particular policy on trade with Canada.

That changed in 1985, when Canada was the second country (after Israel) to begin negotiations for a free trade agreement with the United States. Now this case would appear to be fairly clear-cut *exceptionalism*, but it is more than that because the FTA and the NAFTA, like the energy policy and investment provisions they include, were meant to be demonstration projects, to show other governments what should be done. So, as in the case of the energy, trade, and investment provisions of the FTA, this case offers a specific Canadian expression of a more general policy which at the same time borders on *exceptionalism*, because Israel, Canada, and Mexico were chosen as demonstration models. (They also happened to be available.) On the other hand, the idea of a demonstration model can also be interpreted as a policy of Canada, a foreign country like any other. Canada, and later Mexico, was expected to show the way for what the American government hoped to achieve during the Uruguay Round.

It is also possible to find some elements of *peripheral dependence* in the free trade agreement, notably the provision that Canada would not enact laws to require the processing of uranium ores before they were exported. The rigidity of the provisions guaranteeing American firms the right to invest in Canada (and limiting the precise dollar amounts of investment Canada could still control) may also be interpreted as peripheral dependence, as could the provisions that give Americans somewhat easier access to Canadian energy than they have under the terms of the International Energy Agency.

The story is somewhat different for the Autopact. That agreement represents an almost perfect example of *exceptionalism*. American-based firms had controlled practically all of the Canadian auto industry from the 1920s to the 1970s. This situation, and not the ineluctable facts of geography, led to the need for the Autopact, a Canadian-American arrangement which the NAFTA extends to Mexico. Although the Autopact cannot be classified as anything but exceptionalism, it is part of a general trend, perhaps not specific enough to be called a policy, in international trade relations. Though the American government is one of many to pay lip service to the concept of free trade, it in fact participates in a large number of informal and not so informal industry-by-industry arrangements to limit and control trade in many goods, from steel to textiles to computer chips. Such arrangements, some of them bilateral, others global, may undermine the need for American-Canadian free trade. If the American government seeks to control trade industry by industry, the advantage of a free trade arrangement with one's largest trading partner disappears.

What was true of the FTA is doubly true for NAFTA, in which Canada was a relatively minor player, and just one country whose special position, like that of the Caribbean nations, was being eroded. In negotiating the NAFTA, the Bush administration sought to achieve general foreign policy objectives with respect to Mexico and possibly other Latin American countries. Canada entered into the picture mostly as a complication; that is, as a country on which only a bit of a particular policy was required.

8
Conclusions

We began by asking if the United States could be said to have had a Canada policy in the years since 1945. We continued by presuming an answer to our question and by posing further questions about America's Canada policy. Was its emphasis on "high" or on "low" politics? Were there consistent policies across issues and over time? What kind of judgments can we make about America's Canada policy? Was Canada treated as an ally or a satellite?

To determine the existence of an American Canada policy, we needed first of all to determine whether at least some of the Canada-directed policy actions taken by the various American administrations *originated* in Washington. This step is important because if official Washington reacted only when someone from Ottawa did something to elicit an American response, it is hardly possible to speak of America's Canada policy.

We found that much of America's Canada policy began with American initiatives. The overwhelming difference in the amount of attention Canadians give to their relations with the United States – they in fact sometimes seem obsessed with the subject – and the little attention Canada receives in American official circles, in American academic writing, and in the American media, may give the impression that there is little American policy toward Canada. Lawrence Aronsen writes of a "diplomatic action reaction pattern established on trade issues ... [with] the Canadians taking the initiative and the Americans responding" and continuing on other issues, such as the St. Lawrence Seaway.[1] But this pattern is not typical of all or most of America's Canada policy. There were many American initiatives in the period covered in this book, even if those initiatives seldom added up to a coherent policy. The defence agreements of the early Cold War, Canada's service on the International Commission of Control and Supervision in Vietnam, participation in the first Cyprus peacekeeping force, inclusion in the stockpiling program, and the postwar allocation of uranium ores were all clearly American initiatives. Of course, there also were Canadian initiatives, such as Pearson's actions during the Suez Crisis or the Canadian restrictions on oil and gas exports during the 1970s energy crisis, the Canadian request with respect to British Guiana, and the Canadian policies with respect to the auto industry, which led to the negotiations that produced the Autopact. There were yet other cases of reciprocal action in which it is impossible to identify the originating point of a policy. This was the case in both the 1947 and the 1985 negotiations on bilateral free trade. In short, it is not possible to speak of a typical pattern of initiative or reaction.

During the early part of the Cold War, as the US put its defence strategies in place, Canada was clearly an ally that fit into those strategies, and received requests from the United States. But Canada was not treated any differently from any other ally, except insofar as geography might dictate special considerations. The story is not much different for the 1960s and 1970s. On Vietnam, China, and Cuba, the American government requested Canadian support and assistance, which it sometimes received, and at other times did not. In those instances when the Canadian government tried to take the initiative, such as the recognition of the People's Republic of China or the Vietnam War, the attempt produced anger and resentment in Washington. On the Quebec issue, one would have expected the existence of such a serious problem on the border of the United States to elicit an American policy, but such was not the case. The situation was similar for North-South issues. In several cases, such as the invasion of the Dominican Republic, Canada had no role in American policy. In other cases, such as southern Africa and the Commonwealth, the situation was similar to other major strategic security issues: the US had a policy, in which Canada was asked to play a role.

Whoever coined the term "high" and "low" politics (General de Gaulle was fond of the terminology and may be its author) obviously had a hierarchical view of foreign policy. It follows that actions in low politics should, if need be, flow from high politics; that is, for example, if the overriding purpose of American foreign policy were the defence of Western Europe and the Western Hemisphere against the perceived possibility of Soviet aggression, then American policies on minerals or oil would ensure that the necessary supplies to make possible that defence were available. Our study, however, did not reveal such a hierarchical pattern.

It is true that from the late 1940s to the end of the Korean War, some American military planners tried to control supplies of uranium and other minerals almost as if a total war were still raging. These efforts did not have the support of other parts of the American government and, therefore, failed. On other economic issues, such as oil, natural gas, investment, and trade, American policy was driven by either domestic interests or a combination of domestic interests and the overall perception of the nation's economic interests as expressed by the policy makers currently in office (Jimmy Carter on energy or George Bush on NAFTA, for example). Aronsen has discovered some interesting examples of the ways American policy makers used the national security argument to convince Congress and the public to support policies which might help Canada. Canada was an important ally, from which both the State Department and the White House frequently wanted help or support, especially because American and Canadian economic interests sometimes coincide. But to get support on issues such as the St. Lawrence Seaway and "offshore" purchases under the Marshall Plan, America's leaders consciously used the national security argument.[2] This approach was low politics masquerading as high politics. Export controls provide the one clear-cut exception to this pattern. Here, considerable American pressure was exerted on Canada to adopt American policies that Americans believed to be strategically important. This pressure seldom succeeded, even when the companies in question were Canadian subsidiaries of American firms.

Over the years a clear shift in emphasis from high to low politics has taken place. But this shift says next to nothing about American-Canadian relations. It is a general trend in world politics, which nearly every foreign office in the world has experienced, and which has become especially pronounced since the last of the Cold War's hot wars, that in Afghanistan.

The rational model of foreign policy making assumes that governments have foreign policy goals from which they derive specific policies to apply to various countries and issues. There is little evidence that American policy toward Canada was made in this fashion, except perhaps during the earliest Cold War years. If such a rational policy framework had been developed, linkages among various issues in American policy which applied to Canada could be identified. In fact, however, we found few examples of such linkages.

The Autopact illustrates several of these aspects of America's Canada policy. The pact, it is generally agreed, has been beneficial to Canada's economy. Was it a reward for a Canadian concession in another area? Senator Hartke claimed it was meant to buy Canadian support for America's Vietnam policy, but that is a chronological impossibility. Others claim that it was meant to reward Canada for sending troops to Cyprus when President Johnson had great difficulty in getting any government to agree to do so. That may help to explain why the president gave the Autopact his final seal of approval when he was not involved in any of the earlier negotiations that delineated the important details of the pact, when most of the concessions were made. Yet almost a year elapsed between the Cyprus phone call and the initial Autopact agreement, and it was a year and a half before President Johnson signed the implementing legislation, a year and a half that included the Temple University affair. Another more likely explanation for the American acceptance of the Autopact can be found in the strong advocacy of the three largest American car manufacturers which have a tradition of influence in Washington. Similarly, when the Nixon administration in 1971 threatened cancellation of the Autopact if Canada did not cooperate with the new American policy on foreign investment, it was American interests, within and without the government, not Canadian pleas, that saved the pact.

All the other examples of linkage that we found were either in closely related technical subfields (policies on direct versus indirect investment, a double-taxation treaty for relaxation of Canadian investment controls) or consisted of crude threats that were not carried out. Thus, in 1955, America's ambassador to the United Nations threatened Canada with import controls on its oil unless Canada abandoned efforts to have more countries admitted to the UN. Canada did not give up, and no import controls were imposed until 1968, by which time UN memberships had expanded widely. Similarly, the Nixon administration threatened Canada first with the cancellation of a presidential visit if – ironically – Canada did not increase its exports of oil to the US. Canada pursued its policy (though implementation was another matter), and Nixon visited Ottawa anyway.

That linkage was seldom tried, and when tried did not succeed at the implementation level, does not mean that linkage did not exist at the policy-making level. It is possible that the American administration made a Canada policy, in either the White House or the State Department, and that instructions then went out to apply this policy to all the various issues, from resources to trade to security. However, there is no evidence of such a process. During the time covered by this book, at least four general reviews of American-Canadian relations took place, three of which were American, and one of which was bilateral. The three American reviews of relations with Canada – one conducted by the State Department policy planning staff in 1951 which concentrated on Canada as a strategic factor in American foreign policy,[3] a second undertaken by the Kennedy administration after the dust-up with Diefenbaker, and a third initiated by the Nixon administration in 1971 as part of a general effort to rationalize American foreign policy, as well as the 1965 bilateral Merchant-Heeney report (also an attempt to put the Diefenbaker problems to rest) – seem not to have led to policy measures of any consequence.

To the contrary, every indication points to next to no coordination on the many issues affecting Canada. While President Johnson was grateful to his friend Mike Pearson for sending peacekeeping troops to Cyprus, the American decision to reduce purchases of Canadian uranium was putting entire Canadian towns out of work. Shortly after the Nixon administration threatened Canada for its failure to cooperate with American policies on investment and trade, Henry Kissinger was pleading with the Canadian government to serve on the International Commission on Control and Supervision in Vietnam. Soon after the Canadian government agreed to do so, and served even longer than it initially promised to do, the Americans were threatening retaliation because of the Canadian policy of restricting oil exports to the United States. These examples are from a time when Henry Kissinger, known for his rational classical diplomacy, supposedly controlled American foreign policy.

If there was little coordination across issues, there was also little coordination over time. This situation resulted in part from the nature of the American political system, where all except the most basic foreign policy guidelines change from one administration to the next. But it also resulted from another often-neglected factor in the study of American-Canadian relations: the importance of American domestic interests, which can influence foreign policy on all but the most basic strategic security issues. The protectionist demands of American producers of minerals, oil, and uranium overrode the advocacy of administrations which thought it wise to maintain access to Canadian resources. The Autopact was a response to a Canadian stimulus, but its content was heavily influenced by the large American auto firms. The so-called Free Trade Agreement with Canada became possible only when American and Canadian industries worked, each with their own government, to produce an agreement acceptable to the major corporations and to a large number (if not a majority) of the people in both countries. These domestic interests include Congress, which often prevented the president and his advisors from following a policy which the latter considered to be in the national interest. It was Congress, for example, that prevented a trade agreement with Canada in advance of the GATT (in 1945 or 1946), and Congress that delayed the St. Lawrence Seaway for thirteen years.[4]

If America's Canada policy was largely an ad hoc affair, the tone of the relationship varied greatly from one administration to the next, sometimes because of the personality of the leaders or because of the style in which that administration conducted foreign policy. Prime Minister Diefenbaker's erratic and provocative behaviour, and President Johnson's rage over the Temple University speech, clouded relations briefly. But such personal factors should not be exaggerated. President Johnson signed the Autopact into law only a few months after the Temple University affair, and cooperation on investment issues continued even as Diefenbaker and his ministers were causing anger in Washington over the nuclear weapons issue. Nor did the excellent personal relations between Prime Minister Mulroney and President Reagan lead to American concessions in the Free Trade Agreement or on acid rain. They did, however, push the Reagan administration to a point where a solution to the Canadian objections to American trade remedy law almost *had* to be found, because the Reagan administration was so heavily committed to the agreement, a factor that strengthened the hands of the Canadian negotiators.

All of this said, it is still possible to identify some patterns in America's Canada policy. One pattern, sometimes called liberal internationalism, sees Canada as a strong and independent ally, helping the United States as need be, but differing from and moderating American policy when American enthusiasm leads to a policy that is too militant. This image has some validity when applied to American-Canadian relations in the first ten years after the Second World War. The joint North American defence effort of the early postwar years, Canada's role as a supplier of uranium ore and as a pioneer in nuclear technologies, and its role in the founding of NATO provide classic examples of the liberal-internationalist pattern. During the negotiations leading to the creation of NATO, for example, Americans consulted Canadians and Canadians insisted on the inclusion of Article II, which purported to make NATO more than just a military alliance. Canada was also an important founding member of the United Nations and provided the Americans with assistance and advice during the early years of that organization. In Korea, before the outbreak of war, liberal internationalism took an ironic twist, when Canada, after much American pressure, agreed to serve on UNTCOK, presumably because the Americans expected Canada to behave as a compliant ally. When the Canadian observers and their government turned out to have opinions different from those of the Americans about the policies that should be followed in Korea, the Americans criticized them sharply. UNTCOK and the Korean War provide examples of another frequent phenomenon in American-Canadian relations: the Canadians think that they can give advice and moderate American policy, but the Americans will have none of it.

Liberal internationalism reached its zenith during the 1956 Middle East crisis, in which Canada's Lester Pearson's mediatory efforts won him the Nobel Peace Prize. Americans did find Canadian efforts helpful in that case. But relatively few examples of American acceptance, much less advocacy of, a liberal internationalist role for Canada have occurred since that time. The two most significant examples are peacekeeping in Cyprus in 1964, where Canada's role was considered so important that Lyndon Johnson used his persuasive powers over the telephone, and southern Africa toward the end of the Cold War, where the United States needed an intermediary that was not closely identified with any of the factions in Angola or with the apartheid government of South Africa. The Vietnam War is a more complex case, which includes a number of American policies toward Canada. Briefly, when Canadians carried messages to China and North Vietnam (the Seaborn mission), or when, in the early years, Americans were still willing to listen to Canadian advice, Canada can be seen as an independent and helpful ally. Perhaps this was also the role

Canada played in the case of the International Commission of Control and Supervision Commission of 1973, which was to help supervise the American withdrawal from Vietnam (not to be confused with the ICC which in the 1950s supervised the French withdrawal from Indochina). Canadians participated on the ICCS reluctantly after much American pressure, partly because they hoped to be able to assist in the ending of that unfortunate war. The 1980 rescue by Canadians of some Americans held hostage in Iran can perhaps also be put into this category. After all, in this case, Canadians seem to have used the trust the Iranian government still had for them to help their American friends.

A question raised in Chapter 1 relates to the liberal internationalist pattern in American-Canadian relations. Did Canada make a difference? That is, did Canada change any of the policies enunciated or planned by the US? There are few examples. None except Article II of NATO is identified in this book. (Canada did make a difference in the sense that Lester Pearson helped to resolve the problem in Suez, but the difference was not one that involved changing American policy.) President Franklin Delano Roosevelt may have valued Prime Minister Mackenzie King's advice, but postwar presidents had little use for Canadian advice. Presidents Johnson and Nixon did not want Prime Minister Pearson's counsel on Vietnam, Prime Minister Trudeau's peace initiative only annoyed the Reagan White House and Prime Minister Mulroney could not persuade his friend Reagan to take a stronger stand against South Africa's *apartheid* policies. Canada did sometimes make a difference at the implementation stage of American foreign policy; for example, its stand on Cuba prevented the flawless execution of the American policy of isolating that island state. More frequently, however, Canada made a difference by adding to, not subtracting from, American policy. As Aronsen points out, in several cases, especially during the early postwar years, Canadian leaders supported American policy because they believed that Canadian and American interests were similar, or at least complementary.[5] Canada gladly opened mines to feed the American stockpile, supported a liberal international trading and investment regime, relied on the US to protect its northern territories from Soviet incursions, valued American advice on British Guiana, and gained prestige by helping to resolve the South West Africa (Namibia) problem.

Canadian scholars have identified another pattern in American-Canadian relations, which they have labelled exceptionalism and exemptionalism.[6] Exceptionalism means that Canada is treated differently from any other ally, exemptionalism that Canada is exempted from measures applied to other countries. Except in cases where geography obviously imposed a common solution (the DEW line, NORAD), we found only a few examples of this policy pattern. Two major areas where exceptionalism occurred are monetary policy – the Canadian dollar has had a special relationship with the American dollar over the last fifty years – and trade, where the United States and Canada tried to negotiate a free trade agreement in 1948, and where the United States did adopt a policy of free trade with Canada after 1985. The 1991 addition of Mexico, however, made Canada somewhat less special. (The United States also has a free trade agreement with Israel.) The Autopact provides another clear-cut example of exceptionalism. Though the study of the Autopact may seem technical and irrelevant to the larger issue of world affairs, it is of great importance to the economies of the two countries. As mentioned in Chapter 7, about one-third of Canadian trade with the United States consists of automobiles and automotive products. The importance of this trade for Ontario and Michigan is even greater. Since 1965 and through the FTA and the NAFTA, the two (later three) governments have decided to impose a managed trade regime on this industrial sector.

Exemptionalism usually applies to a specific economic or administrative issue. Thus Canada was exempted from many of the American controls and taxes on outward-flowing foreign investment (until 1971), and from most oil import quotas. Canadians were and still are exempt from many border formalities, such as the need to hold a current passport.

The flip side of exceptionalism and exemptionalism is a policy that treats Canada as one ally among others. This pattern became more common after 1960, by the time Western Europe had recovered from the war and Canada was less important to the United States. Furthermore, this pattern applies with equal frequency to policies in the political and the economic fields. In politics, the first appearance of Canada as an ally like any other (among our cases at least) occurred during the latter stages of the Korean War, when Canada was one of several allies advocating solutions and offering advice. A year or two later, there was the ICC in Indochina, where the American administration sought a government, any Western government, that was willing to serve there. The situation was similar during the Vietnam War, where Canada became just one of many of the allies of the United States, criticizing and offering solutions. On the Law of the Sea, Canada also was just one of many participants which advocated international rules different from those sought by the United States. Canada claimed sovereignty over passages of water surrounded by Canadian territory on three sides (the Gulf of St. Lawrence) or flowing between two pieces of Canadian territory (the Northwest Passage). The Americans disagreed with Canada, as they did with several other governments, including those of Iceland, Indonesia, and Ecuador.

Yet a fourth pattern identified by Canadian and some American scholars is that of peripheral dependence; that is, Canada is treated as a satellite expected to comply with American policy, whether or not that policy is in the interest of Canada or Canadians. A voluminous Canadian literature, academic and otherwise, denounces American policy in many areas. The three issues of American policy on Vietnam, American investment in Canada and the 1988 Canada-US Free Trade Agreement have each been the subject of literally hundreds of books and articles denouncing American policy on things Canadian. Though some Canadians, usually of a left-wing persuasion, try to identify this pattern as typical of America's Canada policies, the number of cases in which it occurred is limited. Two of these cases are from the height of the Cold War, in the early 1950s. American insistence that Canada adopt its policy toward the recognition of China and the Americans use of Canada to sell weapons to Israel that they preferred not to sell themselves constitute clear-cut examples of peripheral dependence. Three other examples occurred during the 1960s. The Canadian government decided for the most part to accept American guidance for its policy toward Cheddi Jagan's government in British Guiana. As a member of the International Control Commission in Vietnam, Canada, which at first had been a relatively independent observer and reporter on events, by the mid-1960s became a lackey of American policy, at times using its position on the ICC to transmit information to the Americans about conditions in North Vietnam. In Yemen, Canada agreed to follow American policy and to act on behalf of the United States. Dean Rusk also asked Prime Minister Pearson to speak for the American point of view at the 1964 Commonwealth summit, but there is no indication that he did so. One last case straddles the entire period covered in this book. As mentioned, the American insistence that American subsidiaries of Canadian firms accept the same politically motivated export controls as those imposed on American firms in the US has often been cited as an example of American imperialism, or at least a determination to impose American policies on Canada. And while this point is true and irrefutable, Canada has by no means been the only target of such American policies, which American governments have at various times tried to impose on American-owned subsidiaries in Britain, France, and Germany, to name only the major countries involved. It is worth noting that Canada and Canadian companies often refused to comply with such requests.

One other policy pattern does not fit into any of the established categories Canadian and American scholars have used to characterize American-Canadian relations: Canada as the good boy of American policy who is expected to set an example for America's other allies and friends. Part exceptionalism, part peripheral dependence, this policy enrages many Canadian nationalists: Why should Canada be expected to accept American investment with fewer conditions than most other countries in the world? Why should Canada accept free trade with the United States when no countries other than Israel had done so? While it is easy enough to denounce such American policies as attempts to gain more control over

Canadian affairs than the US has over the affairs of, say, Mexico or the United Kingdom, to treat Canada as if it were a part of the US (witness the statements on mineral policy in Chapter 5 or those of Dean Acheson on military bases cited in Chapter 2), this negative view does not provide the whole explanation for such policies. Some American leaders have believed that Canadians are just like them and thus ought to be happy to accept American policies. President Truman liked Canada because he could speak English there. Other Americans have seen Canada as kind of a guinea pig, a place that ought to set an example to try or accept American policies other governments were not yet ready to accept. This expectation was the case for the investment provisions and intellectual property chapters of the Free Trade Agreement and the ready access to Canadian energy resources that the Mulroney government gave the United States. In its most extreme form, this policy sees Canada as a place that can be treated just like the United States.

One last policy pattern is that of Canada as the forgotten ally. According to John Holmes, for a long time the outstanding Canadian expert on relations with the United States, "one persistent problem is that the US forgets about us."[7] During the Cuban Missile Crisis, Canada was all but forgotten by the top echelons in Washington. Only those military commanders whose task it was to think about Canadian territory did so. Similarly with the Dominican Republic after the American invasion in 1965, with Panama after President Carter negotiated a new settlement of the Canal Zone problem, and with Afghanistan after the Soviet invasion, Canada mattered only peripherally, and when it made itself known, if at all. On Afghanistan, there was later a need for a Canadian policy when President Carter decided not to increase wheat sales to the Soviet Union in retaliation for the invasion. On NAFTA, President Bush and his advisors forgot about the complications that a bilateral deal with Mexico would cause for the already existing Canada-US Free Trade Agreement. The threat of Quebec separation appears also to fall into this no policy category, but here appearances may be deceiving; the continuing political sensitivity of the issue has led to the declassification of relatively few documents.

Where so many policy patterns apply, none predominates. There is no single American Canada policy, only a number of different policies, which applied at different times, and on different issues. What patterns do exist may be the result of habits, attitudes, or geographical facts, but not of a consistently thought-out or implemented policy. For this fact, Canadians should perhaps be thankful.

Suggestions for Further Research

There is always more to do. This book has uncovered the need for at least three kinds of further work. First, on the *historical level,* many stories remain to be told. This is especially true for more recent years. There is much to learn about the 1971 monetary and trade crisis. Just what plans did the Nixon administration have for Canada with respect to that change in American policies? Later, it will be possible to learn who was most influential in driving Reagan's free trade policy through the Washington policy jungle and perhaps to learn the reasons these promoters gave for their policy. Much remains to be learned even for the earlier period. Why, for example, did several proposals for freer trade come out of the Eisenhower administration? What did the Carter people, and later the Bush administration, ask Canada to accomplish in southern Africa? The release of documents over the next several years will help answer some of these questions.

On a *political* and a *policy* level, there is much to learn about policy coordination among the various American government departments. Because the documentation does not seem to tell much of a story on this point, distinct policy studies focusing on the *making* of America's Canada policy are needed before we can conclude that Americans really do not coordinate their Canada policies. Such studies do exist for other aspects of American foreign policy (for example, on Vietnam, Cuba, and Korea).[8] Although these studies may not provide an ideal model for studies of America's Canada policy, because they deal with very different issues, their methodology could be adapted. A more thorough understanding of how America's Canada policies are made should be useful to both Canadian and American policy makers – so that, in terms of their own policy goals, they can do better in the future.

On a *theoretical* level, there has been little work in recent years. During the late 1960s and early 1970s, there was an explosion of theoretical work on foreign policy. Political scientists devoted much time and effort to devising models and paradigms for the comparative study of foreign policy.[9] Little has happened in this field over the past twenty years. A glance at recent journals and books in the field reveals an abundance of studies of specific foreign policies – that of the new Russia, or Egypt, or the new Germany, or Botswana, or just about any of the 180 countries that now cover our globe. There are also some interesting case studies, and studies of some more general, but yet topically specific issues, such as diversionary foreign policies practised by democratic systems, but there is a dearth of studies of the concept of foreign policy.[10]

Now it is, of course, healthy for a discipline to have time to consolidate, to allow for testing of the many theories that flow from an explosion of theoretical work. Nevertheless, the world of the foreign policy maker has changed so much that the conventional models should at least be assessed to determine if they are still as useful as they could be. The globalization of many economic forces, the explosion of communication technologies alongside the persistence of the nation-state, the end of the Cold War –

these factors might lead us to expect researchers to fall over one another to develop new models for the study of foreign policy. While the field of international relations generally has benefited from much theorizing since the advent of globalization and the end of the Cold War, foreign policy appears to have been neglected. Is it possible to devise paradigms for the study of asymmetric foreign policy dyads, such as the United States and Canada, or Botswana and South Africa? How does the control by non-governmental agents of many important economic factors affect the making, and the study, of foreign policy? How can foreign policy makers allow for the increasing importance of transnationally active groups (multi-national corporations included) in the process of making foreign policy? These are just a few of the many questions that arise. Historians can begin to work as the material becomes available. Political scientists should get to work now.

Notes

Chapter 1: Canada As Seen from the United States

1 Douglas LePan, "The Outlook for the Relationship: A Canadian View," in *The United States and Canada,* ed. John Sloan Dickey (Englewood Cliffs: Prentice-Hall, 1964), 164.

2 Gordon T. Stewart, *The American Response to Canada since 1776* (East Lansing: Michigan State University Press, 1992).

3 Lawrence Robert Aronsen, *American National Security and Economic Relations with Canada, 1945-1954* (Westport: Praeger, 1997).

4 Charles Doran, *Forgotten Partnership: US-Canada Relations Today* (Baltimore: Johns Hopkins University Press, 1984), 189.

5 White House Central File, box CO9, folder CO 1-9, Carter Archives, Atlanta, GA.

6 John Redekop, in "A Re-interpretation of Canadian-American Relations," *Canadian Journal of Political Science* 9, 2 (1976): 227-43, develops the idea of continental political, economic, and social systems of which the American and Canadian constitute major and minor subsystems, respectively.

7 Louis S. St. Laurent, "The Foundations of Canadian Policy in World Affairs," *Canadian Foreign Policy, 1945-1954: Selected Speeches and Documents,* ed. R.A. Mackay (Toronto: McClelland and Stewart, 1971), 394.

8 Livingston Merchant to the President, letter, 28 June 1965, National Security File (NSF), Country File: Canada, box 167, Canada and the United States: Principles for Partnership; Lyndon Baines Johnson Archives, Austin, TX; K. Curtis and J. Carroll, *Canadian-American Relations* (Toronto: Lexington Books, 1983), 94.

9 *Life with Uncle: The Canadian-American Relationship* (Toronto: University of Toronto Press, 1981), 45, 73.

10 Burns Papers, Box 62, Gerald Ford Presidential Archives, Ann Arbor, MI.

11 Examples of historians who ignore Canada include Norman A. Graebner, *America As a World Power: A Realist Appraisal from Wilson to Reagan* (Wilmington, DE: Scholarly Resources, 1984); Robert H. Ferrell, *American Diplomacy, The Twentieth Century* (New York: Norton, 1988); Melvyn P. Leffler, *A Preponderance of Power: National Security, the Truman Administration, and the Cold War* (Stanford: Stanford University Press, 1992). Henry Kissinger makes only a passing reference to Canada (in a quotation); Henry Kissinger, *Diplomacy* (New York: Simon and Schuster, 1994), 801. James T. Patterson, whose book deals with the twentieth century, does likewise in *America in the Twentieth Century: A History* (San Diego: Harcourt, Brace, Jovanovich, 1989). The following books, which specialize in the period since 1945, also ignore Canada: William H. Chafe, *The Unfinished Journey: America since World War II* (New York: Oxford University Press, 1986 and 1991); John Patrick Diggins, *The Proud Decades: America in War and Peace, 1941-1960* (New York: Norton, 1988); Melvyn P. Leffler, *A Preponderance of Power: National Security, the Truman Administration, and the Cold War* (Stanford: Stanford University Press, 1992). John Morton Blum's *Years of Discord: American Policy and Society, 1961-1974* (New York: W.W. Norton, 1991), has but one passing reference to Canada (p. 233). Arthur Schlesinger, Jr.'s

five-volume series, *Dynamics of World Power: Documentary History of US Foreign Policy, 1945-1973* (New York: Chelsea House, 1973) mentions Canada only five times – four in vol. II (224, 226, 499, 736) and always in a multilateral context, and once in vol. IV (28), where the under-secretary of state for political affairs tells an audience interested in Japan-America relations that Japanese trade with the United States was second only to Canada's. There are three passing references in the otherwise comprehensive book by Edward H. Judge and John W. Langdon, *A Hard and Bitter Peace: A Global History of the Cold War* (Upper Saddle River, NJ: Prentice Hall, 1996), 73, 227, 264. See also Dean Acheson, *Present at the Creation: My Years in the State Department* (New York: Norton, 1969), 513.

12 Walter LaFeber, *The American Age: United States Foreign Policy at Home and Abroad since 1750* (New York: Norton, 1989); Walter LaFeber, Richard Polenberg, and Nancy Woloch, *The American Century: A History of the United States since the 1790s* (New York: McGraw-Hill, 1992).

13 Thomas G. Paterson, J. Garry Clifford, and Kenneth J. Hagan, *American Foreign Policy: A History since 1900* (Lexington, MA: D.C. Heath, 1991).

14 Regarding nuclear technology, see Allan M. Winkler, *Modern America: The United States from World War II to the Present* (New York: Harper and Row, 1985), 41-2; John M. Carroll and George C. Herring, eds., *Modern American Diplomacy* (Wilmington: Scholarly Resources, 1986), 160-1; Arthur Schlesinger, Jr., *Dynamics of World Power: Documentary History of US Foreign Policy, 1945-1973* (New York: Chelsea, 1973), II, 224, 226. Regarding the Soviet spy ring, see Melvyn Dubofsky and Athan Theoharis, *Imperial Democracy: The United States since 1945* (Englewood Cliffs: Prentice Hall, 1988), 27; Carroll and Herring, 123; Paterson et al., 444; LaFeber et al., 286 and 318. Regarding NATO, see George Moss, *America in the Twentieth Century* (Englewood Cliffs: Prentice Hall, 1989), 250; Paterson et al., 456; LaFeber et al., 346; Forrest C. Pogue, *George C. Marshall, Statesman* (New York: Penguin, 1987), 316-35.

15 George Bush and Brent Scowcroft, *A World Transformed* (New York: Random House, 1998), 62-3.

16 Robert Keohane and Joseph Nye, Jr., "Introduction: The Complex Politics of Canadian-American Interdependence," *International Organization* 28, 4 (1974): 601.

17 George Ball, *The Discipline of Power* (Boston: Little Brown, 1968), 113.

18 Laura McKinsey and Kim Nossal, eds., *America's Alliances and Canadian American Relations* (Toronto: Summerhill, 1988), 26.

19 On the problem of whether the study of policy begins with general principles or the analysis of specific actions, see Stephen Brooks, *Public Policy in Canada: An Introduction* (Toronto: McClelland and Stewart, 1989), 16.

20 Stephen Krasner, *Defending the National Interest* (Princeton: Princeton University Press, 1978), 11.

21 Christopher Andrew, *For the President's Eyes Only* (New York: Harper Collins, 1995), 471.

22 Cited in Stewart, *The American Response to Canada*, 105.

23 Annette Baker Fox, *The Politics of Attraction: Four Middle Powers and the United States* (New York: Columbia University Press, 1977).

Chapter 2: The Cold War, Part I

1 The Ambassador in Norway (Bay), Oslo, to the Secretary of State, Washington, 9 April 1948, *Foreign Relations of the United States, 1948,* III, 81. Cited hereafter as *FRUS.*

2 James F. Byrnes, *Speaking Frankly* (New York: Harper and Brothers, 1947), 265-8. One Canadian commentator agrees that Canada accommodated readily to American nuclear policies; see Joseph Levitt, *Pearson and Canada's Role in Nuclear Disarmament and Arms Control Negotiations, 1945-1947* (Montreal and Kingston: McGill-Queen's University Press, 1993).

3 United States Assistance to Other Countries from the Standpoint of National Security: Report by the Joint Strategic Survey Committee, Washington, 29 April 1947, *FRUS, 1947,* I, 736-8.

4 Ibid., 739.

5 Report by the Policy Planning Staff, Washington, 6 November 1947, *FRUS, 1947,* I, 770.

6 See, for example, "Instructions for the United States Representatives attending the

London Western Union Talks," enclosed in a letter from the secretary of state to the embassy in the United Kingdom, Washington, 16 July 1948, *FRUS, 1948*, III, 191. Interestingly, however, in his memoirs, former secretary of state Dean Rusk – head of the State Department's Office of Special Political Affairs from 1947 to 1949 – mentions the "special relationship" between the United States and Great Britain during the postwar period, but he does not mention a special relationship between the United States and Canada. Indeed, his memoirs all but ignore Canada; see Dean Rusk, *As I Saw It* (New York: Norton, 1990), 267.

7   US State Department, Records of the Policy Planning Staff, 1947-53, George Kennan to the Secretary of State, 7 May 1948, RG 59, box 13, folder Canada, 1952-3, National Archives and Record Center, College Park, Maryland. Cited hereafter as NARA.

8   US State Department, Policy and Planning Staff, 1947-53, United States Position or Considerations under which the US Will Accept War and/or Atomic Warfare, RG 59, box 5, folder 5, NARA.

9   Acting Secretary of State to President Truman, memorandum, 1 October 1946, *FRUS, 1946*, V, 56.

10 Ibid., 56. The Canadian counterpart to *Foreign Relations of the United States, Documents on Canadian External Relations (DCER)* makes clear that standardization of military equipment was a long, slow process; see *DCER*, XIII (1947), 1495-6.

11 President Truman to the Canadian Prime Minister (Mackenzie King), n.d. (but written late September or early October 1946), letter, *FRUS, 1946*, V, 59.

12 Ibid., 61. See also Assistant Chief of the Division of British Commonwealth Affairs (Parsons), memorandum, *FRUS, 1946*, V, 62; Canadian-United States defence conversations held in Ottawa in Suite "E," Chateau Laurier Hotel, memorandum, 16 and 17 December 1946, *FRUS, 1946*, V, 73. The Secretary of War (Patterson) to the Acting Secretary of State, Washington, letter, 27 March 1947, *FRUS, 1947*, VIII, 108.

13 Secretary of War (Patterson) to the Acting Secretary of State, Washington, letter, 17 April 1947, *FRUS, 1947*, VIII, 110. For more information on US-Canada defence cooperation, see public release issued by the State Department, 12 February 1947, *FRUS, 1947*, III, 104-6.

14 Joint Chiefs of Staff to the Secretary of Defence (Forrestal), Washington, memorandum, 19 June 1948, *FRUS, 1948*, IX, 217.

15 Ibid., 740.

16 Minutes of the Thirty-Seventh Meeting of the Policy Committee on Arms and Armaments, Washington, 7 March 1947, *FRUS, 1947*, I, 725.

17 Ibid., 727.

18 Margaret Truman, *Harry S. Truman* (New York: William Morrow and Company, 1973), 373-4.

19 Roy Jenkins, *Truman* (New York: Harper and Row, 1986), 80-8.

20 Robert J. Lamphere and Tom Schachtman, *The FBI-KGB War: A Special Agent's Story* (New York: Random House, 1986), 32-6, 80-4. Lamphere was an FBI agent.

21 John Bryden, *Best-Kept Secret: Canadian Secret Intelligence in the Second World War* (Toronto: Lester, 1993), 264-326. See also Christopher Andrew, *For the President's Eyes Only: Secret Intelligence and the American Presidency from Washington to Bush* (New York: HarperCollins, 1995), 127, 136-7, 162-3, 167, 217; James Bamford, *The Puzzle Palace: A Report on America's Most Secret Agency* (Boston: Houghton Mifflin, 1992), 129, 315, 317; Jeffrey T. Richelson and Desmond Ball, *The Ties that Bind: Intelligence Cooperation between the UKUSA Countries – the United Kingdom, the United States of America, Canada, Australia, and New Zealand* (Boston: Allen and Unwin, 1980); Bill Robinson, "The Fall and Rise of Cryptanalysis in Canada," *Cryptologia* 16, 1 (1991): 23-38; Scott Anderson, "The Evolution of the Canadian Intelligence Establishment, 1945-1950," *Intelligence and National Security* 9, 3 (1994): 448-71.

22 For a summary of North American air defence during the early years of the Cold War, see Joseph T. Jockel, *No Boundaries Upstairs: Canada, the United States, and the Origins of North American Air Defence, 1945-1958* (Vancouver: UBC Press, 1987). For a summary of Canadian policy as seen through the eyes of the minister of national defence, Brooke Claxton, see David Jay Bercuson, *True Patriot: The Life of Brooke Claxton, 1888-1960* (Toronto: University of Toronto Press, 1993), 170-2, 186-90, 261, 263.

23 Chairman of the National Security Resources Board (Symington) to the President, Washington, memorandum, n.d., *FRUS, 1951*, I, 27.

24 Carleton Savage, Member of the Policy Planning Staff, Washington, memorandum, 23 May 1951, *FRUS, 1951,* I, 834.

25 David J. Bercuson, "SAC vs. Sovereignty: The Origins of the Goose Bay Lease, 1946-52," *Canadian Historical Review* 70, 2 (1989): 206-22; Raymond B. Blake, "An Old Problem in a New Province: Canadian Sovereignty and the American Bases in Newfoundland 1948-1952," *American Review of Canadian Studies* 23, 2 (1993): 183-201.

26 Secretary of State to the President, Washington, memorandum, 31 July 1950, *FRUS, 1950,* II, 584.

27 Special Assistant to the Secretary of State (Arneson), Washington, memorandum of conversation, 7 April 1951, *FRUS, 1951,* I, 809-11. R. Gordon Arneson was summarizing a conversation of that same date he had with Canadian ambassador Hume Wrong and with George Ignatieff, first secretary at the Canadian embassy in Washington. See also Special Assistant to the Secretary of State (Arneson), Washington, memorandum of conversation, 12 April 1951, *FRUS, 1951,* I, 811-4; Special Assistant to the Secretary of State (Arneson), Washington, memorandum of conversation, 7 May 1951, *FRUS, 1951,* I, 827-9. For further information about non-nuclear complexities of the American bases at Goose Bay and Harmon, see *FRUS, 1951,* II, 870-901.

28 US State Department, Records of the Policy Planning Staff, Use of Atomic Weapons, memorandum submitted by Paul Nitze to M. Matthews, 25 May 1951, RG 59, box 5, folder 5, NARA.

29 The Canadian note is quoted by the Special Assistant to the Secretary of State (Arneson), Washington, memorandum of conversation, 7 May 1951, *FRUS, 1951,* I, 828. As on 7 and 12 April, this note resulted from a meeting of Arneson with Wrong and Ignatieff.

30 US State Department, Executive Secretary of the Atomic Energy Committee to National Security Council, 10 September 1948, NSC/30, attached to office memorandum, 23 June 1950, RG 59, folder Canada, NARA.

31 Special Assistant to the Secretary of State (Arneson), Ottawa, memorandum of conversation, 12 May 1951, *FRUS, 1951,* I, 829-33.

32 Secretary of State, Washington, to the Secretary of Defense (Marshall), Washington, 14 June 1951, *FRUS, 1951,* I, 843-4.

33 Special Assistant to the Secretary of State (Arneson), Washington, memorandum of conversation, 25 May 1951, *FRUS, 1951,* I, 841-2; Special Assistant to the Secretary of State (Arneson), Washington, memorandum of conversation, 14 June 1951, *FRUS, 1951,* I, 845-53. Note prepared by the Canadian embassy, Washington, 14 June 1951, *FRUS, 1951,* I, 853-4. The quotation comes from the note.

34 Special Assistant to the Secretary of State (Arneson), Washington, memorandum of conversation, 13 July 1951, *FRUS, 1951,* I, 855-9; Joseph Chase of the Office of the Special Assistant to the Secretary of State (Arneson), Washington, memorandum of conversation, 27 July 1951, *FRUS, 1951,* I, 859-64. See also the Secretary of Defense (Robert A. Lovett) to the Secretary of State, Washington, 5 November 1951, *FRUS, 1951,* I, 894-7. Deputy Director of the Policy Planning Staff (Ferguson), memorandum of conversation, 6 August 1951, *FRUS, 1951,* I, 875-80. The quotation is from p. 876, but the emphasis is added.

35 Assistant Secretary of State for European affairs (Perkins) to the Deputy Under-Secretary of State (Matthews), Washington, memorandum, 17 October 1951, *FRUS, 1951,* II, 898-900.

36 Carlton Savage of the Policy Planning Staff, Washington, memorandum of conversation, 11 February 1952, *FRUS, 1952-1954,* I, 234-5.

37 Paul H. Nitze and Carlton Savage of the Policy Planning Staff, Washington, memorandum, 6 May 1953, *FRUS, 1952-1954,* I, 318-9.

38 US State Department, Records of the Policy Planning Staff, 1947-53, RG 59, box 13, folder Canada, NARA. See also US State Department, Records of the Policy Planning Staff, 1947-53, memorandum of conversation, Canadian Position on Southern Canadian Early Warning Line, 6 November 1953, RG 59, box 13, folder Canada, NARA.

39 Cole to Wilson, 7 May 1954, *FRUS, 1952-1954,* VI, 2123-4.

40 George Lindsey, "Canada-US Defense Relations in the Cold War," in *Fifty Years of Canada-United States Defense Cooperation: The Road from Ogdensburg,* eds. Joel J. Sokolsky and Joseph T. Jockel (Lewiston: Edwin Mellen Press, 1992), 67.

41 "National Security Council: Canadian Access to Nuclear Weapons in Peacetime," Annex to NSC 5822, 12 December 1958, Jeffrey T. Richelson, ed., *Presidential Directives on National Security from Truman to Clinton* (NSC: Washington, 1993), item 575.

42 Jon B. McLin, *Canada's Changing Defense Policy, 1957-1963: The Problems of a Middle Power in Alliance* (Toronto: Copp Clark, 1967), 37-167.

43 Palmiro Campagna, *Storms of Controversy: The Secret Avro Arrow Files Revealed* (Toronto: Stoddart, 1992).

44 Denis Smith, *Rogue Tory: The Life and Legend of John G. Diefenbaker* (Toronto: Macfarlane Walter and Ross, 1995), 324-5.

45 Robert Bothwell, *Eldorado: Canada's National Uranium Company* (Toronto: University of Toronto Press, 1984). See the summary in Edelgard E. Mahant and Graeme S. Mount, *An Introduction to Canadian-American Relations* (Toronto: Nelson, 1989), 177-82.

46 Chairman of the Joint Congressional Committee on Atomic Energy (Hickenlooper) to the Secretary of State, Washington, 29 August 1947, *FRUS, 1947*, I, 833.

47 Statement by the Under-Secretary of State (Acheson) to an Executive Session of the Joint Congressional Committee on Atomic Energy, Washington, 12 May 1947, *FRUS, 1947*, I, 810.

48 For example, General United States Policy With Respect to International Control of Atomic Energy, *FRUS, 1947*, I, 603, 611-8; also Under-Secretary of State (Acheson), 1 February 1947, memorandum of conversation, ibid., 785-9; Chairman of the United States Atomic Energy Commission (Lilienthal) to the Commissioners, Washington, memorandum, 23 April 1947, ibid., 804-5; Minutes of a Meeting of the American Members of the Combined Policy Committee, Washington, 3 November 1947, ibid., 854; Counsellor (Bohlen) to the Under-Secretary of State (Lovett), Washington, memorandum, 17 September 1948, *FRUS, 1948*, I, 631-2.

49 McGeorge Bundy, *Danger and Survival: Choices about the Bomb in the First Fifty Years* (New York: Random House, 1988), 112, 149-50.

50 Peter C. Newman, *Renegade in Power: The Diefenbaker Years* (Toronto: McClelland and Stewart, 1964), 366.

51 For example, Secretary of Defense (Forrestal), memorandum of conversation, *FRUS, 1947*, I, 864-6; Minutes of the Meeting of the American Members of the Combined Policy Committee with the Chairman of the Joint Committee on Atomic Energy and the Chairman of the Senate Foreign Relations Committee, Washington, 26 November 1947, ibid., 873; Edmund A. Gullion, Special Assistant to the Under-Secretary of State (Lovett), Washington, memorandum of conversation, 20 December 1947, ibid., 907; Minutes of the Meeting of the American Members of the Combined Policy Committee, Washington, 6 July 1948, *FRUS, 1948*, I, 721-3.

52 Minutes of a Meeting of the American Members of the Combined Policy Committee, Washington, 5 November 1947, *FRUS, 1947*, I, 856.

53 Ibid., p. 855; also Secretary of Defense (Forrestal), Washington, memorandum of conversation, 16 November 1947, *FRUS, 1947*, I, 864-5.

54 Edmund A. Gullion, Special Assistant to the Under-Secretary of State (Lovett), memorandum of conversation, 20 December 1947, *FRUS, 1947*, I, 907.

55 Christopher Andrew and Oleg Gordievsky, *KGB: The Inside Story* (New York: HarperCollins, 1990), 318-20, 334, 369, 377, 391-401. See also Oleg Kalugin, *The First Directorate: My 32 Years in Intelligence and Espionage against the West* (New York: St. Martin's, 1994), 143-5.

56 Edmund A. Gullion, Special Assistant to the Under-Secretary of State (Acheson), memorandum of conversation, 5 June 1947, *FRUS, 1947*, I, 817.

57 Assistant Chief of the Division of British Commonwealth Affairs (Foster), Washington, memorandum of conversation, 26 February 1947, *FRUS, 1947*, I, 797-9; also Deputy United States Representative on the United Nations Atomic Energy Commission (Osborn), New York, to the Director of the Office of Special Political Affairs (Rush), Washington, 29 October 1947, ibid., 848-9.

58 Rusk, *As I Saw It*, 265.

59 General United States Policy with Respect to International Control of Atomic Energy, *FRUS, 1947*, I, 611; United States Assistance to Other Countries from the Standpoint of

National Security: Report by the Joint Strategic Services Committee, Washington, 29 April 1947, ibid., 742.

60 For example, Minutes of a Meeting of the American Members of the Combined Policy Committee, Washington, 20 November 1947, *FRUS, 1947*, I, 866-70; Minutes of the Meeting of the American Members of the Combined Policy Committee with the Chairman of the Joint Committee on Atomic Energy and the Chairman of the Senate Foreign Relations Committee, Washington, 26 November 1947, ibid., 870-9; Acting Secretary of State to the Ambassador to the United Kingdom (Douglas), Washington, 24 December 1947, ibid., 879-82.

61 Adrian S. Fisher and R. Gordon Arneson to the Secretary of State, Washington, memorandum, 18 June 1950, *FRUS, 1950*, I, 499-503; for the comments on Fuchs, see the editorial note in ibid., 524.

62 Secretary of State, Washington, to the Embassy in Belgium, 22 February 1950, *FRUS, 1950*, I, 537. See also, Secretary of State, Washington, to the Secretary of Defense (Johnson), Washington, 3 April 1950, *FRUS, 1950*, I, 546-7.

63 US State Department, Records of the Policy Planning Staff, 1947-53, US Position on Considerations under which the US Will Accept War and Atomic Warfare, RG 59, box 5, NARA.

64 Minutes of the Meeting of the American Members of the Combined Policy Committee, Washington, 25 April 1950, *FRUS, 1950*, I, 549-50.

65 Ibid., 547-8, 551. See also Secretary of State, Washington, to the South African Ambassador (Jooste), Washington, 24 August 1950, *FRUS, 1950*, I, 571. See also American Members of the Combined Policy Committee, memorandum prepared for, 18 April 1950, *FRUS, 1950*, I, 552. Also, Interim Uranium Allocation Agreement for 1950, 18 April 1950, ibid., 553.

66 F.W. Marten, First Secretary, British Embassy, Washington, to R. Gordon Arneson, Special Assistant to the Under-Secretary of State (Webb), 18 October 1950, *FRUS, 1950*, I, 589; Arneson to Marten, 4 December 1950, ibid., 592.

67 Summary Log of Atomic Energy Work in the Office of the Under-Secretary of State, Washington, n.d., *FRUS, 1950*, I, 580-1.

68 Expressed opinions of Alger Hiss, director of the State Department's Division of International Security Affairs, later known as United Nations Affairs, and of Secretary of State James Byrnes; United States Policy Regarding Elections to Certain Organs, Commissions, and Committees of the United Nations, *FRUS, 1946*, I, 121-2; Minutes by the United States Delegation of the Five-Power Informal Meeting Held at London, Claridge's Hotel, 20 January 1946, *FRUS, 1946*, I, 162. See also United States Policy Regarding Elections to Certain Organs, Commissions, and Committees of the United Nations, *FRUS, 1946*, I, 122. For opinions on the possibility of Soviet influence in Norway, see Minutes of the United States Delegation (Executive Session), Held at London, Claridge's Hotel, 26 January 1946, 3:00 PM, *FRUS, 1946*, I, 172-80. See also Lester B. Pearson, *Mike: The Memoirs of the Right Honourable Lester B. Pearson* (Toronto: University of Toronto Press, 1972), I, 192-3; Minutes by the United States Delegation of the Five-Power Information Meeting Held at London, Claridge's Hotel, 20 January 1946, *FRUS, 1946*, I, 162.

69 Ibid., 168.

70 Minutes of the Meeting of the United States Delegation (Executive Session), Held at London, Claridge's Hotel, 26 January 1946, 3:00 PM, *FRUS, 1946*, I, 176-7.

71 United States Policy Regarding Elections to Certain Organs, Commissions, and Committees of the United Nations, *FRUS, 1946*, I, 119.

72 Acting Secretary of State, Washington, to the Ambassador in Belgium (Kirk), 25 March 1947, *FRUS, 1947*, VII, 810-1; Deputy Director of the Office of Far Eastern Affairs (Penfield), Washington, memorandum of telephone conversation, 16 April 1947, *FRUS, 1947*, VII, 820-1; Chief of the Division of Chinese Affairs (Ringwalt), Washington, memorandum, 28 May 1947, *FRUS, 1947*, VII, 834-5.

73 Endnote 16, *FRUS, 1948*, VIII, 4.

74 Ambassador to China (Stuart), Nanking, to the Secretary of State, Washington, 19 May 1948, *FRUS, 1948*, VIII, 245.

75 United States Representative at the United Nations (Austin) to the Secretary of State, Washington, 8 May 1948, *FRUS, 1948*, V, 939. This observation is totally compatible with the findings of David J. Bercuson, *Canada and the Birth of Israel: A Study in Canadian Foreign Policy* (Toronto: University of Toronto Press, 1985).

76 For example, the United States Representative at the United Nations (Austin) to the Secretary of State, Washington, 9 May 1948, *FRUS, 1948*, V, 949-53.

77 Rusk, *As I Saw It*, 150-1; The United States Representative at the United Nations (Austin), to the Secretary of State, Washington, 19 May 1948, *FRUS, 1948*, V, 1014.

78 Secretary of State to the Acting Secretary of State, Washington, 19 September 1950, *FRUS, 1950*, II, 301.

79 US Representative at the UN (Austin), New York, to the Secretary of State, Washington, 12 September 1950, *FRUS, 1950*, II, 331-3.

80 Minutes of the Seventh Meeting of the US Delegation to the General Assembly, New York, 26 September 1950, *FRUS, 1950*, II, 343-4.

81 US Delegation Working Paper, New York, 10 October 1950, *FRUS, 1950*, II, 403.

82 US Representative at the UN (Austin), New York, to the Secretary of State, Washington, 20 October 1950, *FRUS, 1950*, II, 411-3.

83 US Representative at the UN (Austin), New York, to the Secretary of State, Washington, 21 October 1950, *FRUS, 1950*, II, 413-4; US Representative at the UN (Austin), to the Secretary of State, Washington, 23 October 1950, *FRUS, 1950*, II, 419-20.

84 *FRUS, 1950*, II, 303-581; Deputy Director of the Office of United Nations Economic and Social Affairs (Green) to David H. Popper, Principal Executive Officer of the United States Delegation to the General Assembly, memorandum, *FRUS, 1950*, II, 580.

85 Gordon S. Reid of the Division of Central America and Panama Affairs, memorandum of telephone conversation, *FRUS, 1947*, VII, 23. See also *DCER*, XIII (1947), 1023-50.

86 Robert H. Ferrell, "George C. Marshall," in Robert H. Ferrell and Samuel Flagg Bemis, eds., *American Secretaries of State and Their Diplomacy* (New York: Cooper Square, 1966), 179. A memorandum to the Canadian cabinet dated 14 October 1947 suggested that avoidance of the word "republics" might facilitate Canada's eventual entry into any inter-American organization; see *DCER*, XIII (1947), 1042.

87 R. Gordon Arneson, Washington, Special Assistant to the Under-Secretary of State (Webb), Washington, memorandum, 29 December 1949, *FRUS, 1950*, I, 4.

88 Deputy Under-Secretary of State (Rusk), Washington, to the Counsellor (Kennan), Washington, memorandum, 6 January 1950, *FRUS, 1950*, I, 8.

89 Assistant Secretary of State for United Nations Affairs (Hickerson), Washington, memorandum, 11 January 1950, *FRUS, 1950*, I, 12.

90 Howard Meyers, Office of UN Political and Security Affairs, Washington, memorandum of conversation, 12 September 1951, *FRUS, 1951*, I, 521. At a 1951 discussion, Hickerson was recalling the 1949 talks.

91 Charles H. Russell, Advisor, US Mission at the UN, New York, memorandum of conversation, 17 January 1950, *FRUS, 1950*, I, 17-9.

92 Assistant Secretary of State for UN Affairs (Hickerson), Washington, to the Secretary of State, Washington, memorandum, 5 April 1950, *FRUS, 1950*, I, 216.

93 Howard Meyers at the Office of UN Political and Security Affairs, Washington, memorandum of conversation, 16 October 1951, *FRUS, 1951*, I, 543.

94 Bernard G. Bechhoefer of the Office of UN Political and Security Affairs, Washington, memorandum of conversation, 24 October 1951, *FRUS, 1951*, I, 562-4.

95 James N. Hyde, Advisor, US Mission at the UN, memorandum of conversation, 20 February 1951, *FRUS, 1951*, I, 621-3.

96 Philip C. Jessup, Ambassador at Large, Washington, memorandum of conversation, 3 April 1950, *FRUS, 1950*, I, 60-1.

97 David H. Popper of the Office of UN Political and Security Affairs, memorandum of conversation, 21 July 1950, *FRUS, 1950*, I, 80-1.

98 Philip C. Jessup, Ambassador at Large, New York, memorandum of conversation, 21 September 1950, *FRUS, 1950*, I, 100-1.

99 Ward P. Allen, Advisor, US Delegation to the General Assembly, New York, memorandum

of conversation, 6 December 1950, *FRUS, 1950,* I, 117-9; Minutes of the Fifty-First Meeting of the United States Delegation to the General Assembly, New York, 12 December 1950, ibid., 119-20.

100 Resolution Adopted by the General Assembly at its 323rd Plenary Meeting, New York, 13 December 1950, *FRUS, 1950,* I, 125.

101 Report to the National Security Council by the Secretary of Defense, 20 July 1948, in Richelson, item 23.

102 Deputy Director of the Office of British Commonwealth and Northern European Affairs (Satterthwaite) to the Deputy Assistant Secretary of State for European Affairs (Thompson), memorandum, 8 February 1950, *FRUS, 1950,* I, 144.

103 Report to the President Pursuant to the President's Directive of 31 January 1950, *FRUS, 1950,* I, 249.

104 Report by the National Security Council, 25 August 1950, *FRUS, 1950,* I, 377.

105 Policy Record Guide Statement Prepared in the State Department, 22 September 1950, *FRUS, 1950,* I, 399; memorandum prepared by the Policy Planning Staff; 9 December 1950, *FRUS, 1950,* I, 465.

106 Paper presented by the Policy Planning Staff, 20 September 1949, *FRUS, 1950,* I, 616.

107 Acting Secretary of State (Webb), Washington, to the Embassy in Liberia, 28 November 1951, *FRUS, 1951,* V, 1310.

108 Acting Secretary of State (Webb), Washington, to the US delegation at the UN, 22 September 1950, *FRUS, 1950,* IV, 57.

109 Secretary of State, Washington, to the Executive Secretary of the National Security Council (Lay), memorandum, 16 October 1950, *FRUS, 1950,* IV, 1473; Secretary of State, Washington, to the Embassy in France, 27 October 1950, ibid., 1487.

110 Acting Deputy Director of the Office of Eastern European Affairs (Higgs), Washington, memorandum of conversation, 31 October 1950, ibid., 1489-90; Record of the Under-Secretary's Meeting, State Department, Washington, 22 June 1951, *FRUS, 1951,* I, 327.

111 Secretary of State to the Chairman of the House Committee on Foreign Affairs (Richards), Washington, 7 August 1951, *FRUS, 1951,* I, 359.

112 Note by the Secretaries of the State-Army-Navy-Air Force Coordinating Committee, Washington, 15 March 1949, *FRUS, 1949,* I, 258; also Report by the SANACC Subcommittee for Rearmament, 18 August 1948, ibid., 262.

113 Report by the SANACC Subcommittee for Rearmament, 18 August 1948, ibid., 264; Staff Paper Prepared for the National Security Resources Board and the National Security Council by an Independent Working Group, Washington, 1 June 1949, ibid., 339.

114 Don Cook, *Forging the Alliance: The Birth of the NATO Treaty and the Dramatic Transformation of US Foreign Policy Between 1945 and 1950* (New York: Arbor House/William Morrow, 1989), esp. 192-3, 205, 221. See also Alex K. Henrikson, "Ottawa, Washington, and the Founding of NATO," in Sokolsky and Jockel, 83-125.

115 Minutes of the Second Meeting of the United States-United Kingdom-Canada Security Conversations, Held at Washington, 23 March 1948, *FRUS, 1948,* III, 65.

116 Minutes of the Third Meeting of the United States-United Kingdom-Canada Security Conversations, Held at Washington, 24 March 1948, *FRUS, 1948,* III, 66.

117 Director of the Office of European Affairs (John D. Hickerson), memorandum of conversation, 3 January 1949, *FRUS, 1949,* IV, 1-3.

118 *FRUS, 1949,* IV, 281-5.

119 Minutes of the 11th Meeting of the Washington Exploratory Talks on Security, 14 January 1949, *FRUS, 1949,* IV, 30; memorandum by the Secretary of State, Washington, 2 March 1949, ibid., 141.

120 *FRUS, 1949,* IV, 292.

121 Minutes of the 12th Meeting of the Washington Exploratory Talks on Security, 8 February 1949, ibid., 85-6; Dean Acheson, *Present at the Creation: My Years in the State Department* (New York: W.W. Norton, 1969), 276-84; Lester B. Pearson, *Mike: The Memoirs of the Rt. Hon. Lester B. Pearson* (Toronto: University of Toronto Press, 1973), II, 56-8.

122 Counsellor of the State Department (Charles Bohlen), Washington, memorandum of conversation, 8 April 1949, *FRUS, 1949,* IV, 291; Assistant Secretary of State of European

Affairs (Perkins), Washington, memorandum of conversation, 3 August 1949, ibid., 315-7. The Secretary of State, Washington, to Certain Diplomatic Officers (Brussels, Copenhagen, Lisbon, London, Oslo, Ottawa, Paris, Reykjavik, and Rome), 28 July 1950, *FRUS, 1950*, III, 151; Ambassador in the UK (Douglas), London, to the Secretary of State, Washington, 8 August 1950, *FRUS, 1950*, III, 191.

123 Ambassador in France (Bruce), Paris, to the Secretary of State, Washington, *FRUS, 1950*, III, 9 August 1950, 194.

124 Secretary of State, New York, to the Acting Secretary of State, Washington, 16 September 1950, *FRUS, 1950*, III, 309.

125 Douglas to Acheson, 30 August 1950, *FRUS, 1950*, III, 251-5.

126 US Deputy Representative on the North Atlantic Council (Spofford), London, to the Secretary of State, 7 January 1951; Spofford to Acheson, 12 January 1951, 26; Spofford to Acheson, 22 March 1951, 102; Chairman of the National Atlantic Council Deputies (Spofford), London, communique, 5 May 1951, 156-9; all in *FRUS, 1951*, III. See also Chargé in Canada (Bliss) to the Ambassador at Large (Jessup), memorandum, 14 September 1951, *FRUS, 1951*, III, 651.

127 Livingston Merchant, US Ambassador in Canada, in Northern European Chiefs of Mission Conference, London, statement,19-21 September 1957: Summary of Proceedings, *FRUS, 1955-1957*, IV, 618.

128 Officer in Charge of Commonwealth Affairs (Peterson), memorandum, *FRUS, 1952-1954*, VI, 2054; attached to memo of 19 November 1952.

129 Chargé in Canada (Bliss) to the Director of the Office of British Commonwealth and Northern European Affairs (Raynor), 24 April 1953, *FRUS, 1952-1954*, VI, 2079.

130 United States Delegation at the North Atlantic Council Ministerial Meeting to the State Department, Paris, telegram, 11 March 1955, *FRUS, 1955-1957*, IV, 19.

131 Professor Robert Bothwell agrees that Korea was a serious obstacle to US-Canada harmony; Robert Bothwell, *Canada and the United States: The Politics of Partnership* (Toronto: University of Toronto Press, 1992), 46-52.

132 Ambassador in Canada (Atherton), Ottawa, 27 December 1947, memorandum of conversation, *FRUS, 1947*, VI, 880-3. See also Bercuson, *True Patriot*, 190, 210.

133 Acting Secretary of State (Robert Lovett), Washington, to the Canadian Prime Minister, Ottawa, telephoned via Ambassador Atherton, 30 December 1947, *FRUS, 1947*, VI, 883-6. See also *DCER*, XIII (1947), 950-1007.

134 Acting Secretary of State (Robert Lovett), Washington, memorandum of conversation, 3 January 1948, *FRUS, 1948*, VI, 1078-81.

135 Harry S. Truman, Washington, to the Canadian Prime Minister, Ottawa, 5 January 1948, *FRUS, 1948*, VI, 1081-3; Harry S. Truman, Washington, to the Canadian Prime Minister, Ottawa, 24 February 1948, *FRUS, 1948*, VI, 1086-7.

136 Chief of the Division of British Commonwealth Affairs (Wailes) to the Under-Secretary of State (Lovett), Washington, memorandum, 9 January 1948, *FRUS, 1948*, VI, 1084; the Political Advisor in Korea (Jacobs), Seoul, to the Secretary of State, Washington, 2 February 1948, *FRUS, 1948*, VI, 1090; the Political Advisor in Korea (Jacobs), Seoul, to the Secretary of State, Washington, 5 February 1948, *FRUS, 1948*, VI, 1094.

137 Political Advisor in Korea (Jacobs), Seoul, to the Secretary of State, Washington, 12 February 1948, *FRUS, 1948*, VI, 1107; Deputy Director of the Office of European Affairs (Reber), Washington, memorandum of telephone conversation, 30 December 1947, *FRUS, 1947*, VI, 887.

138 Lieutenant General John R. Hodge, Seoul, to the Secretary of State, Washington, 22 February 1948, *FRUS, 1948*, VI, 1126.

139 Lieutenant General John R. Hodge, Seoul, to the Secretary of State, Washington, 26 February 1948, *FRUS, 1948*, VI, 1133.

140 Political Advisor in Korea (Jacobs), Seoul, to the Secretary of State, 22 April 1948, *FRUS, 1948*, VI, 1180; Under-Secretary of the Army (Draper), Washington, to the Under-Secretary of State (Lovett), 3 May 1948, *FRUS, 1948*, VI, 1187.

141 Robert A. Spencer, *Canada in World Affairs: From UN to NATO, 1946-1949* (Toronto: Oxford University Press, 1967), 106.

142 Chief of the Division of Northeast Asian Affairs (Allison), Washington, memorandum of conversation, March 1948, *FRUS, 1948,* VI, 1145.
143 The Secretary of State, Washington, to the United States Representative at the United Nations (Austin), 11 March 1948, *FRUS, 1948,* VI, 1149-50.
144 Lester B. Pearson, *Mike: The Memoirs of the Right Honourable Lester B. Pearson* (Toronto: University of Toronto Press, 1973), 144.
145 Lieutenant General John R. Hodge, Seoul, to the Secretary of State, Washington, 20 June 1948, *FRUS, 1948,* VI, 1219-20.
146 Canadian Under-Secretary of State for External Affairs (Pearson) to the American Counsellor of Embassy (Harrington), Ottawa, 13 August 1948, *FRUS, 1948,* VI, 1274-5.
147 US Representative at the United Nations (Austin) to the Secretary of State, 26 June 1950, *FRUS, 1950,* VII, 190.
148 Harry S. Truman, *Memoirs: Years of Trial and Hope* (New York: Signet,1956), 389.
149 Secretary of State to All Diplomatic Missions and Certain Consular Offices, 29 June 1950, *FRUS, 1950,* VII, 232.
150 Deputy Assistant Secretary of State for Far Eastern Affairs (Livingston Merchant) to the Assistant Secretary of State for Far Eastern Affairs (Dean Rusk), memorandum, 19 July 1950, *FRUS, 1950,* VII, 432-4.
151 Secretary of State to Certain Diplomats and Consular Offices, 21 July 1950, *FRUS, 1950,* VII, 441. For an interpretation of Canada's naval role in Korea, see Marc Milner, "A Canadian Perspective on Canadian and American Naval Relations since 1945," in Sokolsky and Jockel, 159.
152 Substance of statements made at Wake Island Conference (between President Truman and General Douglas MacArthur), 15 October 1950, *FRUS, 1950,* VII, 959. Pearson is quoted as saying that he would prefer to send ground forces to Europe. *FRUS* contains several communications about the desirability of additional Canadian combat forces; *FRUS, 1950,* VII, 434, 473-4, 482, 541, 542, 1163, 1412; *FRUS, 1951,* VII, 194, 284, 381-2, 827.
153 William Manchester, biographer of General Douglas MacArthur, makes no mention of Canadian involvement in the Korean War, although the Koreans did serve under MacArthur's command for a few weeks before his dismissal; *American Caesar: Douglas MacArthur, 1880-1964* (Boston: Little, Brown, 1978).
154 The information on Canada's Korean War effort appears in J.L. Granatstein and David J. Bercuson, *War and Peacekeeping: From South Africa to the Gulf – Canada's Limited Wars* (Toronto: Key Porter, 1991), 103-13. See also John Melady, *Korea: Canada's Forgotten War* (Toronto: Macmillan of Canada, 1983).
155 David McCullough, *Truman* (New York: Simon and Schuster, 1992), 935.
156 John English, *The Worldly Years: The Life of Lester Pearson, 1949-1972* (Toronto: Knopf Canada, 1992), 62-3.
157 In his memoirs, Eisenhower made no mention of Canada in connection with Korea; Dwight David Eisenhower, *The White House Years: Mandate for Change, 1953-1956* (New York: Doubleday, 1963). Stephen E. Ambrose, Eisenhower's biographer, omits Canada from his index and has only one reference for Lester Pearson – in connection with the Suez Crisis; Stephen E. Ambrose, *Eisenhower, the President* (New York: Simon and Schuster, 1984), 365. Dean Rusk, then the assistant secretary of state for Far Eastern affairs also failed to mention Canada in his memoirs; Dean Rusk, *As I Saw It* (New York: W.W. Norton, 1990), 154-77. For the Canadian attempts see, Canada, Department of External Affairs, *Documents on Canadian External Relations (DCER),* XIX, 56-280.
158 Deputy Director of the Office of Chinese Affairs (Perkins), Washington, memorandum of conversation, 3 November 1950, including summary of telegram, 25 October 1950, from Ronning in Nanking to the Department of External Affairs, Ottawa, *FRUS, 1950,* VII, 1031-2; The Counsellor of the Canadian Embassy (Ignatieff) to the Assistant Secretary of State for European Affairs (Perkins), plus enclosure: "Canadian Government Memorandum on Korea, 2 December 1950," ibid., 1339-40.
159 Acting Officer in Charge of Korean Affairs (Arthur B. Emmons III), Washington, memorandum of conversation, 6 November 1950, *FRUS, 1950,* VII, 1065-6. Present at the talks were Hume Wrong, the Canadian ambassador; Charles Ritchie, first secretary of the Canadian embassy; Dean Rusk; Arthur B. Emmons III.

160   Acheson, *Present at the Creation*, 513. See also Burton I. Kaufman, *The Korean War: Challenges in Crisis, Credibility, and Command* (New York: Knopf, 1986), 296.
161   Pearson, *Mike*, Appendix II, 325-33.
162   Acheson, *Present at the Creation*, 578-9.
163   The Ambassador in Canada (Woodward) to the Secretary of State, 14 November 1950, *FRUS, 1950*, VII, 1155-6; Woodward had been speaking to Canada's under-secretary of state for external affairs, Arnold Heeney. See also Woodward to the Secretary of State, 15 November 1950, ibid., 1159-60.
164   Officer in Charge of Korean Affairs (Emmons), Washington, memorandum of conversation, 1 October 1951; in attendance to discuss a possible course of action in the event "that no cease fire is reached" were Wrong, Rusk, and Emmons.
165   For example, Acting Officer in Charge of Korean Affairs (Emmons), Washington, memorandum of conversation, 14 December 1950: Subject – Exchange of Correspondence between Pearson and Indian Prime Minister Nehru; participants Peter R.G. Campbell, Second Secretary of the Canadian Embassy, and Emmons, 14 December 1950; *FRUS, 1950*, VII, 1543-4. See also The Secretary of State (Acheson), New York, to the State Department, 17 November 1952, *FRUS, 1952-1954*, XV, 646.
166   Truman, *Memoirs*, 583-4.
167   Ibid., 506.
168   Ibid., 423-48, 490-510, esp. 435.
169   Acting Secretary of State to the Embassy in Japan, 19 May 1953, *FRUS, 1952-1954*, XV, 1058.
170   Granatstein and Bercuson, *War and Peacekeeping* (p. 72), indicate that shortly after the arrival of the Canadians at the front, 700,000 enemy troops faced 245,000 Americans, 152,000 South Koreans, 11,500 from the Commonwealth, and 10,000 from other members of the United Nations.
171   Deputy Director, Office of Northeast Asian Affairs (McClurkin), Washington, memorandum of conversation, 21 July 1953, *FRUS, 1952-1954*, XV, 1408-10.
172   Joseph C. Goulden, *Korea: The Untold Story of the War* (New York: Quadrangle, 1982); Pearson, *Mike*, 165-90; Ambrose, *Eisenhower, the President*.
173   US Representative at the UN (Austin) to the Secretary of State, 18 November 1950, *FRUS, 1950*, VII, 1569; Acting Secretary of State (Walter Bedell Smith), Washington, to the US Mission at the UN, 17 August 1953, *FRUS, 1952-1954*, XV, 1496-7.
174   For a summary of Canadian thoughts on Quemoy and Matsu, see Donald C. Masters, *Canada in World Affairs, 1953-1955* (Toronto: Canadian Institute of International Affairs, 1959), 102-10. See also Robert Reford, *Canada and Three Crises* (Toronto: Canadian Institute of International Affairs, 1968), 9-72.
175   Editorial note, *FRUS, 1955-1957*, II, 384-5.
176   Message from British Foreign Secretary Anthony Eden to the Secretary of State, 28 March 1955, *FRUS, 1955-1957*, II, 416-7.
177   Eisenhower, *The White House Years: Mandate for Change, 1953-1956* (New York: Doubleday, 1963), 478.
178   John G. Diefenbaker, *One Canada: Memoirs of the Right Honourable John G. Diefenbaker – The Years of Achievement, 1956-1962* (Toronto: Macmillan, 1976), 101, 113, 152-5.
179   See Donald C. Masters, *Canada in World Affairs, 1953-1955* (Toronto: Canadian Institute of International Affairs, 1965), 79-96; also James Eayrs, *In Defence of Canada* (Toronto: University of Toronto Press, 1983).
180   There are shelves of books on the United States and its involvement in Vietnam. Two of the most significant are *The Pentagon Papers* (New York: New York Times, 1971) and Stephen Ambrose, *Eisenhower, the President* (New York: Simon and Schuster, 1986).
181   Special Representative in Vietnam (Collins), Saigon, to the State Department, telegram, 10 March 1955, *FRUS, 1955-1957*, I, 117.
182   Secretary of State, Washington, to the Embassy in Vietnam, Saigon, telegram, 19 March 1955, *FRUS, 1955-1957*, I, 134.
183   Secretary of State Dulles and Foreign Minister Pearson, Ottawa, memorandum of conversation, 26 September 1955, *FRUS, 1955-1957*, XXI, 685-6; Embassy in Laos to the Embassy in Burma, telegram, 7 October 1955, *FRUS, 1955-1957*, XXI, 687; Director of the Office of

Philippine and Southeast Asian Affairs (Young) to the Deputy Assistant Secretary of State for Far Eastern Affairs (Sebald), memorandum, 20 February 1956, ibid., 744.

184 Under-Secretary of State for Economic Affairs (Dillon) to the Assistant Secretary of Defense for International Affairs (Sprague), letter, 20 August 1958, *FRUS, 1958-1960*, XVI, 475; Director of Southeast Asian Affairs (Kocher) to the Assistant Secretary of State for Far Eastern Affairs (Robertson), memorandum, 29 December 1958, ibid., 493; State Department (signed by Dulles) to the Commander in Chief, Pacific's Policy Advisor (Steeves), memorandum, 20 January 1959, ibid., 503; Embassy in Laos to the State Department, memorandum, 21 November 1958, ibid., 543.

Chapter 3: The Cold War, Part II

1 That Canada was less important to the United States as a Cold War ally after 1960 than it had been is also the opinion of Tom Keating, *Canada and World Order: The Multilateralist Tradition in Canadian Foreign Policy* (Toronto: McClelland and Stewart, 1993), 97. As evidence of Canada's reduced importance, note the paucity of commentary on Canada in the principal diplomatic memoirs of the era as compared with the attention devoted to the other allies (France, Germany, Italy, Japan, the United Kingdom) of what would become in 1976 the G-7 nations: Henry Kissinger, *White House Years* (Boston: Little, Brown, 1979); Henry Kissinger, *Years of Upheaval* (Boston: Little, Brown, 1982); Jimmy Carter, *Keeping Faith: Memoirs of a President* (Toronto: Bantam, 1982). George Shultz, secretary of state for most of the Reagan presidency, felt obliged to explain his interest in Canadian affairs, but he dealt at length with "the special relationship" between the United States and the United Kingdom; George P. Shultz, *Turmoil and Triumph: My Years As Secretary of State* (New York: Charles Scribner's, 1993), 128-30, 151-4.

2 J.L. Gawf, First Secretary, for Ambassador Walton Butterworth, US Embassy, Ottawa, to the State Department, Washington, 30 March 1966, National Security File (NSF), Country File: Canada, IV, box 166, item 71, Lyndon Baines Johnson Archives, Austin, Texas. Cited hereafter as LBJ. This was also the message of a State Department Policy Planning Council paper of April 1967, The Future of US-Canadian Defense Relationships, ibid., vol. 5, box 16, item 125, LBJ. See also a letter from Rusk to the US Embassy, Ottawa, 19 August 1967, ibid., V, box 166, item 93.

3 George Lindsey, "Canada-US Defense Relations in the Cold War," in Joel J. Sokolsky and Joseph T. Jockel, *Fifty Years of Canada-United States Defense Cooperation: The Road from Ogdensburg* (Lewiston: Edwin Mellen Press, 1992), 63.

4 John Bryden, *Best-Kept Secret: Canadian Intelligence in the Second World War* (Toronto: Lester, 1993), 323-30. For further information on Herbert Norman, see the hostile biography of James Barros, *No Sense of Evil: Espionage, the Case of Herbert Norman* (Toronto: Deneau, 1986). For a more friendly biography, see Roger Bowen, *Innocence Is Not Enough: The Life and Death of Herbert Norman* (Vancouver and Toronto: Douglas and McIntyre, 1986). For further information about Kim Philby, see Christopher Andrew, *Secret Service: The Making of the British Intelligence Community* (London: Heinemann, 1987), 490, 574, 646, 658, 682, 687, 691.

5 Henry Kissinger, *Diplomacy* (New York: Simon and Schuster, 1994), 223, 354, 534, 548, 573, 596-7, 602, 611, 614.

6 Calculated from the *World Almanac, 1993,* 698.

7 Rusk to Canadian Ambassador, Washington, 8 December 1964, NSF, Country File: Canada, II, box 165, item 48-f, LBJ. For a brief review of Canadian defence policy until 1987, see Joel J. Sokolsky, *Defending Canada: US-Canadian Defense Policies* (New York: Priority Press, 1989), esp. 3-10.

8 US Joint Chiefs of Staff, "Canadian-United States Communications Instructions for Reporting Vital Intelligence Sightings," March 1966, National Security Archives, *The US Intelligence Community, 1947-1989* (Washington: NSA, 1990), item 613.

9 NSF, Country File: Canada, V, box 166, item 125, ix, LBJ.

10 US State Department, General Records of the Policy Planning Staff, RG 59, box 213, folder Canada, National Archives and Record Center, College Park, Maryland. Cited hereafter as NARA.

11   Interview with the author (Mount), Austin, Texas, 11 May 1993. Cited hereafter as Rostow interview.

12   Telephone interview with the author (Mount), 13 July 1993. Mount was in Atlanta, Georgia, Rusk at his home in Athens, Georgia. Cited hereafter as Rusk interview.

13   Memorandum of conversation, 8 March 1961, *FRUS, 1961-1963*, XIII, 1150.

14   Rusk, Geneva, to the State Department, Washington, 14 May 1961, *FRUS, 1961-1963*, XIII, 1152.

15   Memorandum of conversation, 17 May 1961, *FRUS, 1961-1963*, XIII, 1154.

16   Another memorandum of conversation, 17 May 1961, *FRUS, 1961-1963*, XIII, 1161.

17   *FRUS, 1961-1963*, VIII, 1165-7.

18   Merchant, Ottawa, to Rusk, Washington, 26 February 1962, *FRUS, 1961-1963*, XIII, 1165-6.

19   Merchant to Rusk, 27 February 1962, *FRUS, 1961-1963*, XIII, 1167.

20   US State Department, General Records of the Policy and Planning Staff 1962, RG 59, box 213, folder Canada, NARA.

21   Ball, Washington, to Merchant, Ottawa, 8 May 1961, *FRUS, 1961-1963*, XIII, 1177.

22   State Department Press Release No. 59, Washington, 30 January 1963, *FRUS, 1961-1963*, 1195-6.

23   Rusk interview. However, in his memoirs, the CIA's Chester Cooper – who had responsibility for both Canada and Asia – was more complimentary; Chester Cooper, *The Lost Crusade: America in Vietnam* (New York: Dodd, Mead, and Company, 1970), 186.

24   Rostow interview.

25   Butterworth, Ottawa, to the State Department, 3 January 1964, NSF, Country File: Canada, I, box 165, item 30, p. 11, LBJ.

26   Chester L. Cooper, *The Lost Crusade: America in Vietnam* (New York: Dodd, Mead and Company, 1970), 186, 372.

27   Arthur Andrew, *The Rise and Fall of a Middle Power* (Toronto: Lorimer, 1993), 111-2.

28   "Documents Pertaining to the Settlement of the Indochina War," cited in Robert F. Randle, *Geneva 1954: the Settlement of the Indochina War* (Princeton: Princeton University Press, n.d.), 577.

29   Larry Berman, *Planning a Tragedy: The Americanization of the War in Vietnam* (New York: Norton, 1982), 16-23. See also David Halberstam, *The Making of a Quagmire: America and Vietnam during the Kennedy Era* (New York: A.A. Knopf, 1988); and John M. Newman, *JFK and Vietnam: Deception, Intrigue and the Struggle for Power* (New York: Warner Brothers, 1992).

30   The actual figures indicate roughly 900 at the end of December 1960 and 16,300 at the end of 1963; Ramesh Thakur, *Canada, India, Poland, and the International Commission* (Edmonton: University of Alberta Press, 1984), 192. In 1962 alone, the numbers rose from 2,600 to 11,000; Peter Poole, *The United States and Indochina from FDR to Nixon* (Hinsdale, Illinois: Dryden Press, 1973), 81.

31   Poole, *The US and Indochina*, 73.

32   For details of the Kennedy-Diefenbaker relationship, see Arthur Schlesinger, Jr., *A Thousand Days: JFK in the White House* (Greenwich, CT: Fawcett, 1967, 320; Theodore Sorensen, *Kennedy* (New York: Bantam, 1966), 348-9. Their findings are compatible with those of Canadian writers Peter C. Newman, *Renegade in Power: The Diefenbaker Years* (Toronto: McClelland and Stewart, 1964); H. Basil Robinson, *Diefenbaker's World: A Populist in Foreign Affairs* (Toronto: University of Toronto Press, 1989); Robert Smith Thompson, *The Missiles of October: The Declassified Story of John F. Kennedy and the Cuban Missile Crisis* (New York: Simon and Schuster, 1991), 123-8, 244, 253-4, 351-2. Diefenbaker himself expressed a similar opinion; John George Diefenbaker, *One Canada: Memoirs of the Right Honourable John George Diefenbaker* (Toronto: Macmillan, 1976), passim.

33   At an ICC meeting of 31 January 1961, Polish and Canadian members opposed an Indian plan to deal with an alleged Soviet-North Vietnamese violation of the Geneva Accords; according to an official of the American embassy in Saigon, this was the "first time in [the] history of [the] ICC [the] Indians found themselves in [a] minority"; US Embassy, Saigon, to the Secretary of State, 4 February 1961, RG 59, box 1746, 751g.00/2-461, NARA. For an overview of the ICC's voting record in Vietnam, see J.L. Granatstein and

David J. Bercuson, *War and Peacekeeping: From South Africa to the Gulf – Canada's Limited Wars* (Toronto: Key Porter, 1991), 205.

34 The most shrill of these critics is the late Claire Culhane, who accused Canadian members of the ICC of serving as "'hired help' to the Pentagon"; Claire Culhane, *Why is Canada in Vietnam?: The Truth about Our Foreign Aid* (Toronto: NC Press, 1972), 21. More serious is Charles Taylor who wrote that Canada's Department of External Affairs intimidated Canadians on the ICC. Anyone who was ambitious and career-oriented, according to Taylor, was wise to ignore American and South Vietnamese violations of the Geneva Accord whenever possible; Charles Taylor, *Snow Job: Canada, the United States, and Vietnam, 1954-1973* (Toronto: Anansi, 1974), 14-26.

35 US Embassy, Saigon, to the Secretary of State, 24 May 1961, RG 59, box 1746, 751g/005-2461, NARA.

36 US Embassy to Secretary of State, 4 February 1961, RG 59, box 1746, 751g.00/2-461, NARA.

37 US Embassy, Saigon, to the Secretary of State, 6 January 1961, RG 59, box 1746, 751g.00/1-661, NARA.

38 US Embassy, Saigon, to Secretary of State, 11 January 1961, RG 59, box 1746, 751g.00/1-1161; 26 February 1961, 751g.00/2-2661; 23 March 1961, 751g.00/3-2261, NARA.

39 US Embassy, Saigon, to Secretary of State, 27 January 1961, RG 59, box 1746, 751g.00/1-2761, NARA.

40 US Embassy, Saigon, to the Secretary of State, 3 October 1961; RG 59, box 1746, 751k00/10-361; 10 October 1961, 751g.00/10-961, NARA. Also, Telegram from the Embassy in Vietnam, Saigon, to the State Department, Washington, 18 October 1961, *FRUS, 1961-1963*, I, 393.

41 Rusk to the US Embassies, Saigon, London, Ottawa, Paris, New Delhi, 26 May 1961, RG 59, box 1746, 751g.00/5-2261, NARA.

42 H. Basil Robinson, 202.

43 Deputy Director of the Vietnam Task Force (Wood) to the Deputy Under Secretary of State for Political Affairs (Johnson), Washington, memorandum, 25 October 1961, *FRUS, 1961-1963*, I, 438.

44 Ibid.

45 Embassy in Vietnam, Saigon, to the State Department, Washington, telegram, 21 November 1961, *FRUS, 1961-1963*, I, 646.

46 State Department to the US Embassy, Saigon, 31 October 1961, RG 59, box 1746, 751g.00/10-2961, NARA.

47 State Department (signed by Rusk), Washington, to the Embassy in Vietnam, Saigon, telegram, 9 February 1962, *FRUS, 1961-1963*, II, 117-9.

48 Embassy in India, New Delhi, to the State Department, Washington, telegram, 14 February 1962, *FRUS, 1961-1963*, II, 127.

49 Memorandum of conversation: Viet-Nam and the ICC, 15 March 1961, RG 59, box 1746, 751g.00, NARA.

50 Memorandum of conversation, 2 March 1962, RG 59, box 1746, 751k.00, NARA.

51 State Department to US Embassies in Saigon, Ottawa, New Delhi, 24 March 1962, RG 59, box 1746, 751g.00/3-2462, NARA.

52 State Department to US Embassies in Saigon, Ottawa, New Delhi, 16 March 1962, RG 59, box 1746, 751g.00/3-162.

53 Memorandum of conversation, 2 March 1962, RG 59, box 1746, 751k.00, NARA.

54 State Department to Embassies in Saigon, Ottawa, New Delhi, 16 March 1962, RG 59, box 1746, 751g.00/3-162, NARA.

55 State Department to US Embassies in Saigon, Ottawa, New Delhi, 24 March 1962, RG 59, box 1746, 751g.00/3-2462, NARA.

56 State Department to US Embassy, Ottawa, 27 March 1962, RG 59, box 1746, 751g.00/3, NARA.

57 State Department, Washington, to the Embassy in Vietnam, Saigon, telegram (signed by Ball), 24 March 1962, *FRUS, 1961-1963*, II, 275.

58 Embassy in Vietnam, Saigon, to the State Department, Washington, telegram, 23 May 1963, *FRUS, 1961-1963*, II, 419-20.

59   Editorial note, *FRUS, 1961-1963,* II, 434.
60   Embassy in Vietnam, Saigon, to the State Department, Washington, telegram, 4 June 1962, *FRUS, 1961-1963,* II, 436.
61   Prime Minister of Canada, Lester Pearson, to the President, 8 November 1964, telephone conversation notes, NSF, Country File: Canada, II, box 165, item 30a, LBJ.
62   Lester B. Pearson, *Mike: The Memoirs of the Rt. Hon. Lester B. Pearson* (Toronto: University of Toronto Press, 1975), III, 125-8; Lawrence Martin, *The Presidents and the Prime Ministers* (Toronto: Doubleday, 1982), 219-22.
63   "Lists of Visits of Foreign Chiefs of State and Heads of Government to the US, 1789-1967," NSF, Subject File, box 39, folder: Presidential Contacts with Foreign Leaders, 1963-1967, item 1b, LBJ.
64   Charles Taylor, *Snow Job: Canada, the United States and Vietnam, 1954 to 1973* (Toronto: Anansi, 1974); James Eayrs, *In Defence of Canada* (Toronto: University of Toronto Press, 1983); Victor Levant, *Quiet Complicity: Canadian Involvement in the Vietnam War* (Toronto: Between the Lines, 1986).
65   Douglas Ross, *In the Interests of Peace: Canada and Vietnam, 1954-1973* (Toronto: University of Toronto Press, 1984), 382-4.
66   Robert Bothwell, *Canada and the United States* (Toronto: University of Toronto Press, 1992), 96-7.
67   Acting Secretary of State George Ball to the President, 14 December 1964, NSF, Country File: Vietnam, XXIII, box 11, LBJ. For further information on the purpose of the Seaborn missions, see Rusk to Assistant Secretary of State William P. Bundy, 27 February 1965, NSF, Country File: Vietnam, XXIX, box 14, LBJ.
68   White House Staff Member Sullivan to US Embassy, Ottawa, 25 June 1964, NSF, Country File: Vietnam, III, box 54, LBJ; also Tab H, NSF, Country File: Vietnam, box 197, LBJ.
69   Robert S. McNamara, *Retrospect: The Tragedy and Lessons of Vietnam* (New York: Random House, 1995), 196.
70   Rusk (from William P. Bundy) to the President, 5 June 1965, NSF, Country File: Vietnam, XXXV, box 18, LBJ.
71   William P. Bundy, memorandum, 24 July 1965, NSF, Country File: Vietnam, XXVII, box 20, LBJ.
72   Pearson, *Mike,* 124-5. However, Pearson's biographer thought the meeting significant; John English, *The Worldly Years: The Life of Lester Pearson, 1949-1952* (Toronto: A.A. Knopf, 1992), 358-9. The quotation is from a memorandum of conversation between President Johnson and Prime Minister Pearson, Hilton Hotel, New York, 28 May 1964, *FRUS, 1964-1968,* I, 394-6.
73   Sullivan to William Bundy, 24 June 1964, *FRUS, 1964-1968,* I, 526-7.
74   Embassy in Laos, Vientiane, to the State Department, telegram, 27 July 1964, *FRUS, 1964-1968,* I, 581.
75   Assistant Secretary of State for Far Eastern Affairs (William Bundy), Washington, memorandum, 13 August 1964, *FRUS, 1964-1968,* I, 675.
76   Paper presented by the Executive Committee, Washington, 2 December 1964, *FRUS, 1964-1968,* I, 971-2.
77   Johnson to Taylor, 3 December 1964, *FRUS, 1964-1968,* I, 977. See also *The Pentagon Papers* (New York: New York Times, 1971), 344.
78   *The Pentagon Papers,* 441.
79   Johnson to Pearson, 30 March 1965, NSF, Head of State Correspondence File, box 1, item 15. Also, in White House Central Files, Countries (WHCF, CO), CO 43, box 19, folder 1/1/65-5/31/65, LBJ.
80   English, *The Worldly Years,* 359.
81   Martin, *The Presidents and the Prime Ministers,* 1-5; Knowlton Nash, *History on the Run: The Trenchcoat Memoirs of a Foreign Correspondent* (Toronto: McClelland and Stewart, 1984), 256-61; Pearson, *Mike,* 137-48.
82   The draft letter (item 94) and the letters from Johnson to Pearson, 11 April 1965 (item 93) and November 1966 are available in the NSF, Head of State Correspondence File, box 1, folder: P.M. Pearson, I, 3 December 1963 to 11 November 1966, LBJ.

83 Butterworth to Rusk, 17 August 1965, NSF, Country File: Canada, box 166, folder: Canada, Cables, III, part 1, item 45d. Jack Valenti to Johnson, 14 August 1964, WHCF, CO, box 19, CO 43, folder 6/1/65-7/19/66, LBJ.
84 Memorandum, 24 June 1965, NSF, Country File: Vietnam, XXXVII, box 20, LBJ.
85 Walt Rostow to Johnson, 7, 13, and 20 February 1967, NSF, Country File: Canada, boxes 167-8, items 169, 170, 171; also Rostow to Johnson, 13 March 1967, NSF, Country File: Canada, box 166, folder: Canada, Cables, V, part 1, item 21, LBJ. President Johnson indicated his concurrence with the Pearson luncheon by ticking the box marked "Yes."
86 A.E. Ritchie, Canadian Ambassador in the US, to W.W. Rostow, 6 March 1967, WHCF, CO, box 19, CO 43, folder 7/20/66-6/19/67, LBJ.
87 Butterworth's 2 January 1968 report (on 1967), 3-4; the quotation comes from p. 3. The report is available in NSF, Country File: Canada, boxes 167-8, item 116a, LBJ.
88 Rostow to Johnson, 15 July 1966, NSF, Country File: Canada, memos, IV, part 2, item 123, LBJ.
89 Katzenbach, Washington, to Rusk, Punta del Este, 13 April 1967, NSF, Country File, "Canada," V, box 166, item 160a, LBJ.
90 Rostow to Johnson, 20 June 1966, NSF, Country File: Canada, boxes 167-8, folder: Ronning Mission, item 5a, LBJ.
91 McNamara, *Retrospect,* 247-8.
92 Rusk to the US embassies in Ottawa, New Delhi, Warsaw, London, Saigon, Moscow, Vientiane, Bangkok, Paris, 22 July 1966, NSF, Country File: Canada, IV, box 166, item 89, LBJ.
93 Rusk to the US Embassy, Ottawa, 21 July 1966, NSF, Country File: Canada, IV, box 166, item 90, LBJ.
94 Martin, *The Presidents and the Prime Ministers,* 238; J.L. Granatstein and Robert Bothwell, *Pirouette: Pierre Trudeau and Canadian Foreign Policy* (Toronto: University of Toronto Press, 1990), 46.
95 L.T. [Temple] to Johnson, 29 August 1968, NSF, Country File: Canada, box 166, folder: Canada, Cables, V, part 1, item 16g, LBJ. See also Rostow to Johnson, 29 August 1968, NSF, Country File: Canada, box 166, V, item 16i, LBJ.
96 Granatstein and Bothwell, *Pirouette,* 50.
97 For an explanation of the working of the International Commission of Control and Supervision, see Henry Kissinger, *White House Years* (Boston: Little, Brown, 1979), 1442. For a cynical assessment of Nixon's Vietnam policy in 1973, see Tad Szulc, *The Illusion of Peace: Foreign Policy in the Nixon Years* (New York: Viking, 1978), 653-754, esp. 657, 677, 715-6.
98 Trudeau to Nixon, 30 March 1973, Country File 28 (Canada), box 15, Nixon Project, National Archives of the USA, College Park, MA. Also, interview with Mitchell Sharp, October 1987.
99 NSC Convenience Files: Copies of material from the US embassy, Saigon, box 4, folder: Washington to Saigon 6/11/73-7/12/73 012700142, Gerald Ford Presidential Archives, Ann Arbor, Michigan. Cited hereafter as GFA.
100 *New York Times,* 11 July 1993, I3.
101 The 450th Meeting of the National Security Council, Washington, memorandum of discussion, 7 July 1960, *Foreign Relations of the United States, 1958-1960,* VI, 988, 991. Cited hereafter as *FRUS.*
102 Embassy in Canada to the State Department, telegram, 24 July 1960, *FRUS,* 1024-5.
103 Assistant Secretary of State for Inter-American Affairs (Rubottom) to the Secretary of State, memorandum, 25 July 1960, *FRUS,* 1027. Secretary of State Herter agreed; 453rd Meeting of the National Security Council, Newport, Rhode Island, memorandum of discussion, 25 July 1960, ibid., 1029-30. See also 451st Meeting of the National Security Council, Washington, memorandum of discussion, 15 July 1960, *FRUS,* 1018-19.
104 Secretary of State and the Secretary of the Treasury (Anderson), Washington, memorandum of telephone conversation, 14 July 1960, 10:50 AM; *FRUS,* 1013.
105 The 464th Meeting of the National Security Council, Washington, memorandum of discussion, 20 October 1960, *FRUS,* 1098.
106 The 450th Meeting of the National Security Council, Washington, memorandum of discussion, 7 July 1960, *FRUS,* 988-91.

107 The 451st Meeting of the National Security Council, Washington, memorandum of discussion, 15 July 1960, *FRUS*, 1018.

108 John G. Diefenbaker, *One Canada: Memoirs of the Right Honourable John G. Diefenbaker* (Toronto: Macmillan, 1976), I, 175-6.

109 State Department, memorandum of conversation, 1 August 1960, 2:00 PM, *FRUS*, 963.

110 The 450th Meeting of the National Security Council, Washington, memorandum of discussion, 7 July 1960, *FRUS*, 985-6.

111 Secretary of State's Staff Meeting, State Department, Washington, notes, 18 July 1960, *FRUS*, 1019.

112 The 464th Meeting of the National Security Council, Washington, memorandum of discussion, 20 October 1960, *FRUS*, 1095-6.

113 A letter of 1 December 1959 from Eisenhower to Diefenbaker begins "Dear John" and is signed "Ike"; Diefenbaker, *One Canada*, 157-8.

114 John C. Pool of the Office of Caribbean and Mexican Affairs to the Assistant Secretary of State for Inter-American Affairs (Thomas Mann), Washington, memorandum, 26 October 1960, *FRUS*, 1100-2.

115 Diefenbaker, *One Canada*, 177.

116 The 464th Meeting of the National Security Council, Washington, memorandum of discussion, 20 October 1960, *FRUS*, 1095-6.

117 NATO Ministerial Meeting, Oslo, 8-10 May 1961, *FRUS, 1961-1963*, X, 514-5.

118 Peter T. Haydon, *The 1962 Cuban Missile Crisis: Canadian Involvement Reconsidered* (Toronto: Institute of Strategic Studies, 1993), 9, 25-6, 78-84, 155-75). See also Marc Milner, "A Canadian Perspective on Canadian and American Naval Relations since 1945," in Sokolsky and Jockel, *Fifty Years*, 159.

119 Jocelyn Maynard Ghent, "Canada, the United States, and the Cuban Missile Crisis," *Pacific Historical Review* 48, 2 (1979): 159-84. See also Haydon, 19, 21, 183.

120 Rusk interview, 13 July 1993. For a Canadian insider's opinion, see that of Basil Robinson, the under-secretary of state for external affairs: Basil Robinson, *Diefenbaker's World: A Populist in Foreign Affairs* (Toronto: University of Toronto Press, 1989), 283-95.

121 Pearson Visit Briefing Book, 5/10-11/63, NSF, Country File: Canada, box 167, item 18, LBJ.

122 Pearson Visit Briefing Book, 1/211-22/64, NSF, Country File: Canada, box 167, items 16, 54, 56, LBJ.

123 LBJ/Pearson Meeting, Briefing Book, 9/16/64, NSF, Country File: Canada, box 167, item 14, LBJ.

124 For an account of Trudeau's 1976 trip to Latin America, see James John Guy, "Trudeau's Foreign Policy and Latin America," *Revista/Review Interamericana* VII, 1 (1977): 99-108.

125 Mike Hornblow, White House, to George Springsteen, State Department, 22 January 1976, WHCF, CO, box 11, folder: CO 28: Canada 1/1/76-4/30/76, GFA. The actual letter remained classified at the time of the author's visit (October 1993), but the withdrawal slip provided information.

126 A summary of American interests and actions in Cyprus appears in NSF: NSC History, box 16, Cyprus Crisis, December 1963-December 1967, folder: I, background. See other correspondence in box 16, LBJ.

127 Pearson, *Mike*, 134.

128 Paul Martin, *A Very Public Life* (Toronto: Deneau, 1985), II, 547-8.

129 LBJ/Pearson Meeting, Briefing Book, 9/16/64, box 167, NSF, Country File: Canada, items 13 and 16, LBJ.

130 Granatstein and Bercuson, *War and Peacekeeping*, 222-6.

131 *CBC Prime Time News*, 15 June 1993.

132 Stephen J. Randall and John H. Thompson, *Canada and the United States: Ambivalent Allies* (Athens: University of Georgia Press, 1994), 232.

133 Chester Bowles, memorandum for the president, 6 February 1962, and W.W. Rostow to George Ball, Sale of Grain to Communist China, 16 March 1961, both in US State Department, General Records of the Policy Planning Staff 1962, RG 59, box 214, folder: China, NARA.

134 Rusk, *As I Saw It*, 283.
135 Pearson Visit Briefing Book, 1/21-22/64, NSF, Country File: Canada, box 167, items 1g, 14, LBJ; Charles A. Ritchie, Ambassador for Canada in the United States, and William R. Tyler, Assistant Secretary of State for European Affairs, memorandum of conversation, 18 January 1964, NSF, Country File, Canada, I, box 165, item 94a, LBJ.
136 Butterworth's 1965 report, 11; Butterworth's 1967 report, 4.
137 Visit of Prime Minister Pearson, 15 January 1965: Chinese Representation in the United Nations, NSF, Country File: Canada, boxes 167-8, folder: Pearson Visit Briefing Book, item 23.
138 Martin, *A Very Public Life*, 507-28.
139 Butterworth's 1967 report, 4.
140 Granatstein and Bothwell, *Pirouette*, 186-7.
141 Pierre Elliott Trudeau, *Memoirs* (Toronto: McClelland and Stewart, 1993), 211.
142 Documentation on the Ford administration's concerns about Taiwan and the Montreal Olympics appears in box 7 of the David Gergen Papers, folder: Olympics, GFA. All documents are undated and unsigned. For an interpretation of events, see Donald MacIntosh, Donna Greenhorn, Michael Hawes, "Trudeau, Taiwan, and the 1976 Montreal Olympics," *American Review of Canadian Studies* 21, 4 (1991): 423-48.
143 *Public Papers of the Presidents, 1980*, I, 107-8.
144 *International Canada*, January 1980, 2.
145 Documentary evidence of American pressure or even bilateral communication on the issue is minimal, if it exists at all.
146 *International Canada*, January 1980, 1. See also Granatstein and Bothwell, *Pirouette*, 199-200; Carter, 474-7.
147 From Jacques Parizeau's memoirs, *Pour un Québec souverain* (Montreal: VLB, 1997).
148 Butterworth to the State Department, 1 April 1964, NSF, Country File: Canada, I, box 165, item 7, LBJ.
149 The findings in this chapter are compatible with those of Roger Frank Swanson, "The Ford Interlude and the US-Canadian Relationship," *American Review of Canadian Studies* VIII, 1 (1978): 3-17. Pierre Elliott Trudeau, *Memoirs* (Toronto: McClelland and Stewart, 1993), 197.
150 Robert Hunter, NSC, to Denis Clift, 28 March 1977, WHCF, CO, box 14, folder CO 28, 3/1/77-5/31/77, Carter Presidential Archives, Atlanta, Georgia. Cited hereafter as CPA.
151 White House memo, 5 January 1978, WHCF, CO, box 14, folder CO 28, 10/1/77-4/30/78, CPA.
152 Head to Brzezinski, 1 May 1978, WHCF, CO, box 14, folder CO 28, 5/1/78-12/31/78, CPA.
153 CTV transcript, Staff Offices Press (Advance), Edwards, box 2, folder: Brzezinski, Zbigniew – Canadian TV (CTV), CPA.
154 NSC note for file, 17 or 18 October 1979, WHCF, Foreign Affairs, box FO-6, folder CO 28, CPA.
155 Miller Centre Oral History Interviews – Brzezinski, Zbigniew, 18 February 1982, CA.
156 Brzezinski to Mondale, 29 December 1977, WHCF, CO, box 14, folder CO 28, 10/1/77-4/30/78, CPA.
157 Campbell wrote a guest article on the *Globe and Mail*'s op-ed page on 24 September 1996.
158 Jean François Lisée, *In the Eye of the Eagle* (Toronto: HarperCollins, 1990), 149-63.
159 Robert Hunter, NSC, to Denis Clift, 28 March 1977, WHCF, CO, box 14, folder CO 28, 3/1/77-5/31/77, CPA.
160 Granatstein and Bothwell, *Pirouette*, 346-50, esp. 348.
161 Jimmy Carter, *Keeping Faith: Memoirs of a President* (Toronto: Bantam, 1982), 112-4, 474-7, 486, 538.
162 Granatstein and Bothwell, *Pirouette*, 260.
163 *International Canada*, May 1980, 90, and March 1981, 49, 55-6. See also David Cox, "Canada and Ballistic Missile Defense," in Sokolsky and Jockel, *Fifty Years*, 239-62.
164 Andrew Richter, "North American Aerospace Defence Cooperation in the 1990s: Issues and Prospects," Optional Research and Analysis Establishment, ORAE Extra-Mural Paper No. 57, The Canadian Institute of Strategic Studies, July 1991, 10.
165 James J. Blanchard, *Behind the Embassy Door: Canada, Clinton, and Quebec* (Toronto: McClelland and Stewart, 1998), esp. 224-61.

Chapter 4: North-South Issues

1 "Economic Importance of Canada," memorandum, n.d., Arthur Burns Papers, box 62, GFA.

2 Stephen J. Randall and Graeme S. Mount, *The Caribbean Basin: An Illustrated History* (London: Routledge, 1998), 100-1.

3 State Department to the Embassy in Canada, telegram (signed by Dulles), 12 April and 18 July 1956, *FRUS, 1955-1957*, XV, 527-8, 858-9.

4 Memorandum of conversation [Dulles, Pearson, Arnold Heeney (Canada's ambassador in Washington), and Livingston Merchant (American ambassador in Ottawa)], Secretary Dulles's Residence, Washington, 28 March 1956, *FRUS, 1955-1957*, XV, 426.

5 Delegation at the North Atlantic Council Ministerial Meeting, Paris, to the State Department, telegram, 6 May 1956, *FRUS, 1955-1957*, XV, 618; British Ambassador (Makins) and the Counsellor of the State Department (MacArthur), State Department, Washington, memorandum of conversation, 23 May 1956, ibid., 655.

6 *Mike: Memoirs of the Rt. Hon. Lester B. Pearson* (Toronto: University of Toronto Press, 1973), 224.

7 Livingston Merchant, Ottawa, to the State Department, 29 June 1956, *FRUS, 1955-1957*, XV, 764.

8 State Department, memorandum of conversation, 30 May 1956, *FRUS, 1955-1957*, XV, 693.

9 Editorial note, *FRUS, 1955-1957*, XVI, 23-4.

10 For a Canadian account of the F-86 episode, see Parson, 223-5, 236. For an Israeli account, see Michael B. Oren, "Canada, the Great Powers, and the Middle Eastern Arms Race, 1950-1956," *International History Review* 12, 2 (1990): 280-300.

11 See editorial note, *FRUS, 1955-1957*, XVI, 933; State Department, Washington, memorandum of conversation, 2 November 1956, ibid., 940-1; State Department, memorandum of conversation, 3 November 1956, ibid., 953.

12 Rostow interview, 11 May 1993.

13 Ambassador Walton Butterworth, notes, 26 May 1967, NSF, Country File: Canada, box 166, item 122a, LBJ.

14 Summaries of two telephone calls of 24 May 1967 to Pearson, NSF, International Meetings and Travel File, box 20, item 13, LBJ archives.

15 Interview with the author, Austin, Texas, 11 May 1993. For evidence that those at the luncheon did discuss the Middle East, see the report written by Ambassador Butterworth, 25 May 1967, NSF, Country File: Canada, V, box 166, item 73, LBJ.

16 Telephone conversation with the author (Mount), 13 July 1993.

17 Rusk to David Ormsby Gore (British Ambassador in Washington), 19 October 1963, *FRUS, 1961-1963*, XVIII, 746.

18 The voluminous correspondence concerning Yemen is interspersed among other Middle Eastern matters throughout *FRUS, 1961-1963*, XVIII.

19 Acting Chief of Staff of the Defense Intelligence Agency (Glass) to the Deputy Assistant Secretary of Defense for International Security Affairs (William P. Bundy), Washington, memorandum, 21 June 1963, 599-600.

20 UN Secretary-General U Thant, as relayed from the Canadian delegation to the United Nations to the Department of External Affairs, statement, 25 April 1963, RG 25, box 5438, file 11282-40, part 6, National Archives of Canada, Ottawa. Cited hereafter as NAC.

21 Howard Green Infogram to Canadian diplomats at the United Nations, London, Washington, Paris, Cairo, Bonn, Rome, Beirut, Ankara, Tehran, Tel-Aviv, and Karachi, 18 October 1962, RG 25, box 5437, file 11282-40, part 4, NAC.

22 Department of External Affairs to Canadian Embassies in Washington and Cairo, telegram, 11 December 1962, RG 25, box 5437, file 11282-40, part 5, NAC.

23 Norman A. Robertson, Under-Secretary of State for External Affairs, Ottawa, to Green, 31 May 1963, RG 25, box 5438, file 11281-40, part 7.

24 Komer to Bundy, *FRUS, 1961-1963*, XVIII, 747.

25 Robertson to Green, 21 January 1963, RG 25, box 5438, file 11282-40, part 6, NAC.

26 Charlotte Girard, *Canada in World Affairs* (Toronto: Canadian Institute of International Affairs, n.d.), 284-5.

27 Walter LaFeber, *The Panama Canal: The Crisis in Historical Perspective* (Oxford: Oxford University Press, 1979), 138-40.

28 Johnson Archives, Austin, Texas, NSF, Country File: Canada, boxes 167-8, folder: Canada, Pearson Visit, document 22c (State Department, memorandum of conversation, 22 January 1964).

29 George W. Ball, *The Past Has Another Pattern* (New York: W.W. Norton, 1982).

30 Jimmy Carter, *Keeping Faith: Memoirs of a President* (Toronto: Bantam, 1982), 161.

31 Carter Archives, Atlanta, White House Central File, Country, box CO 9, folder CO 1-9 (Briefing Paper for Canada).

32 National Security Council Report, 16 February 1959, Appendix B, *FRUS, 1958-1960*, V, 114-5; also, "Address before the Canadian Parliament," 17 May 1961, *Public Papers of the Presidents (Kennedy)*, 384-5.

33 L.J. McGowan, president of The Foundation Company of Canada, Limited, Montreal, to A.W. Thomas, Assistant General Manager, Export Credits Insurance Corporation, Ottawa, 26 January 1960, RG 25, box 68455, file 3493-40, part 2, Political Reports, 1959-60, NAC. Cited hereafter as Political Reports. McGowan identified W.D. Pawley, "one of the directors of our Dominican company" and said that Pawley was "quite close to the Vice-President of the United States." It was Pawley who had summarized Nixon's thoughts.

34 W.W. McVittie, British Embassy, Ciudad Trujillo, to Selwyn Lloyd, Foreign Secretary, London, Dominican Republic: Annual Review for 1959, Political Reports.

35 C. Hardy, American Division, Department of External Affairs, to A.E. Ritchie, 19 November 1959, Political Reports.

36 W.B. McCullough, Canadian Chargé d'Affaires, Ciudad Trujillo, to Secretary of State for External Affairs (SSEA), Ottawa, "Political Situation in the Dominican Republic," 6 February 1959, Political Reports.

37 Confidential Briefing Paper on the Dominican Republic, Ottawa, 19 June 1962 (stamped "seen by John Diefenbaker"), RG 25, box 2522, file 22-10-DOM-1, NAC.

38 Norman Robertson to Green, 9 June 1960 (stamped "seen by the Minister") onto which an official had written: "SSEA said that there was to be no change in Can. representation in Dominican R. with whom we have no quarrel." Political Reports.

39 Piero Gleijeses, *The Dominican Crisis: The Constitutionalist Revolt and American Intervention* (Baltimore: Johns Hopkins, 1978); Abraham F. Lowenthal, *The Dominican Intervention* (Cambridge, MA: Harvard University Press, 1921); Jerome Slater, *La Intervención Dominicana* (Santo Domingo: Editorial de Santo Domingo, 1976); Tad Szulc, *Dominican Diary* (New York: New York Times, 1965).

40 Paul Martin, *A Very Public Life* (Toronto: Deneau, 1985), 664; Butterworth's 1965 report, 17, NSF, Country File: Canada, box 166, LBJ. See also Joseph W. Scott, US Embassy, Ottawa, to the State Department, 7 May 1965, NSF, Country File: Canada, box 166, folder: Canada, Cables, III, part 2, item 74. US Embassy, Ottawa, to State Department, July 1968, NSF, Country File: Canada, box 166, folder: Canada, Cables, V, part 1, item 49.

41 Graeme Mount, "Aspects of Canadian Economic Activity in the Caribbean," *Laurentian University Review* V, 1 (1972), 93-6.

42 Randall and Mount, *The Caribbean Basin*, 104-7, 134-7.

43 Pearson Visit Briefing Book, 1/21-22/64, NSF, Country File: Canada, box 167, items 18z and 58; memorandum of conversation, 22 January 1964, NSF, Country File, Canada, box 167-8, folder: Canada-Pearson Visit, item 22a, LBJ.

44 For a summary of developments before 1945, see Edelgard E. Mahant and Graeme S. Mount, *An Introduction to Canadian-American Relations* (Toronto: Nelson, 1989), 137-8.

45 Dr. Wilbert M. Chapman, of the Office of the Special Assistant to the Under-Secretary for Wildlife and Fisheries, to the Under-Secretary of State (Webb), memorandum, 29 May 1950, *FRUS, 1950*, I, 800.

46 Paper prepared in the Office of the British Commonwealth and Northern European Affairs, Washington, 17 July 1950, *FRUS, 1951*, I, 1690.

47 State Department Statement, 1 July 1951, *FRUS, 1951*, I, 1723-4.

48 Repeated throughout *FRUS, 1958-1960*, II, 643 to 827. See, for example, Delegation to the

Conference on the LOS, Geneva, to the State Department, telegram, 1 April 1958, 676-8; State Department to the Delegation to the Conference on the LOS, telegram, 3 April 1958, 680-1; State Department, memorandum of conversation, 16 June 1960, 818-22. See also Senator Warren G. Magnuson and Senator Henry M. Jackson to the Under-Secretary of State (Herter), letter, 15 April 1958, ibid., 681; Magnuson and Jackson to the Secretary of State (Herter), 11 February 1960; ibid., 750-1; Secretary of State to Magnuson, letter, 10 March 1960, ibid., 755-7.

49   State Department Policy Statement, 1 July 1951, *FRUS, 1951,* I, 1723.

50   Embassy in Iceland to the State Department, telegram, 17 April 1958, ibid., 699.

51   For example, State Department, memorandum of conversation, 16 June 1960, ibid., 819.

52   Chief of Naval Operations (Arleigh Burke) to the Secretary of State, letter, 16 April 1958, ibid., 696-7.

53   For example, Delegation to the Conference on the LOS to the State Department, telegram, 1 April 1958, ibid., 676-8; State Department, memorandum of conversation, 16 June 1960, ibid., 818-22.

54   John H. Pender of the Office of the Legal Adviser for Special Functional Problems and the Counselor of the Portuguese Embassy (Abreu), memorandum of conversation, State Department, 26 March 1958, ibid., 669-70.

55   Conference on the LOS to the State Department, telegram, 16 April 1958, ibid., 693-6.

56   Delegation to the Conference on the LOS, Geneva, to the State Department, telegram, 21 April 1958, ibid., 703.

57   State Department to Certain European Missions, circular airgram, 29 October 1959, ibid., 732-3; Special Assistant for LOS Matters (Richards) and the British Minister (Hood), memorandum of conversation, State Department, 10 May 1960, ibid., 814-5.

58   Editorial comment on the Second LOS Conference, 26 April 1960, ibid., 807.

59   Marcel Cadieux, Canada's Under-Secretary of State for External Affairs, and William R. Tyler, Assistant Secretary of State for European Affairs, memorandum of conversation, 6 July 1964, NSF, Country File: Canada, I, box 165, item 43; Cadieux and U. Alexis Johnson, Deputy Under-Secretary of State, memorandum of conversation, 25 March 1964, NSF, Country File, I, box 165, item 64a, LBJ.

60   Benjamin H. Read to McGeorge Bundy, 12 February 1964, folder: Canada Cables, I, part 2, 12/63-7/64, item 69. Pearson Visit Briefing Book, 1/21-22/64, NSF, Country File: Canada, box 167, items 40, 80, LBJ. Canada, Pearson Visit Briefing Book, 9/16/64, NSF, Country File: Canada, box 167, items 11, 14, LBJ.

61   Rusk to Johnson, 14 January 1964, NSF, Country File: Canada, box 167, folder: Pearson Visit Briefing Book, 1/65, item 7, LBJ.

62   Briefing Paper on Canadian Territorial Seas Proposal, Visit of Prime Minister Pearson, 15 January 1966, NSF, Country File: Canada, boxes 167-8, folder: Canada, memos, V, part 1, item 25; Rostow to Johnson, 26 October 1967, ibid., item 135, LBJ.

63   Butterworth's 1967 report, 5-6, NSF, Country File: Canada, box 166, LBJ.

64   State Department, statement, 26 October 1967, 5:30 PM, NSF, Country File: Canada, boxes 167-8, folder, memoranda, V, part 1, item 137a.

65   Flanagan to Henry A. Kissinger, 4 October 1971, File CO 28 (Canada), box 15, Nixon Project, NARA.

66   Cocke to Nixon; anonymous White House official to Cocke; n.d., Nixon Project, NARA.

67   *Globe and Mail,* 7, 8, and 12 December 1987 and 12 January 1988. For a scholarly account of the 1988 accord, see Christopher Kirkey, "Canadian-American Bargaining in the North: The January 1988 Arctic Cooperation Agreement," paper presented to the Canadian Political Science Association, 8 June 1993, Carleton University, Ottawa.

68   *Globe and Mail,* 24 February 1993, A7.

69   Rusk to US Embassy, Ottawa, 1 July 1964, NSF, Country File: Canada, I, box 165, document 3, LBJ.

70   A.J. Wills, *An Introduction to the History of Central Africa: Zambia, Malawi, and Zimbabwe* (Oxford: Oxford University Press, 1987), 495-6.

71   Cyrus Vance, *Hard Choices: Critical Years in America's Foreign Policy* (New York: Simon and Schuster, 1983), 259, 273.

72 Vance, *Hard Choices*, 271.
73 Ibid., 259.
74 A. Glenn Mower, Jr., *Human Rights and American Foreign Policy: The Carter and Reagan Experiences* (New York: Greenwood, 1987), esp. 124-7, 134-5.
75 Vance, *Hard Choices*, 256-71. Not only Vance, but his colleagues in the State Department evidently found Canada irrelevant to the Rhodesian situation; Diane B. Bendahmane and John W. McDonald, Jr., eds., *Perspectives on Negotiation: Our Case Studies and Interpretations (The Panama Canal Treaties, The Falkland/Malvinas Islands, The Cyprus Dispute, Negotiating Zimbabwe's Independence* (Washington: State Department, 1986), 153-187.
76 White House Central File (WHCF), CO, box 9, folder CO 1-9, CPA. Also, briefing paper, n.d., ibid.
77 A copy of the draft speech, never delivered because of the Iranian hostage crisis, is available in The Speechwriters, chronological file, folder 11/9/79, CPA.
78 Vance, *Hard Choices*, 302-3.
79 Ibid., 276.
80 Department of Foreign Affairs, *South West Africa: Basic Documents* (Pretoria: Department of Foreign Affairs, 1980). The documents show that Jamieson personally attended the meeting of 29 September 1978.
81 *International Canada*, February 1980, 23. See also Jean Pelletier and Claude Adams, *The Canadian Caper: The Inside Story of the Daring Rescue of Six American Diplomats Trapped in Iran* (Toronto: Macmillan, 1981), 59-60; Stansfield Turner, *Terrorism and Democracy* (Boston: Houghton-Mifflin, 1991), 47-8, 63-4, 90-4.
82 Vance to Carter, Staff Offices, Office of Staff Secretary, Handwriting File, box 183, folder 4/28/30, CPA. Trudeau to Carter, n.d. January 1979 (definitely before 8 January), Staff Offices Counsel, Cutler, box 113, folder: Trudeau, Pierre Elliott, CPA.
83 State Department, *Foreign Travels of the Secretary of State, 1866-1990* (Washington: Department of State Publications, 1990), 63-4.

Chapter 5: Canada As a Source of Natural Resources

1 For the early history of American mineral policy, see Alfred E. Eckes, *The United States and the Global Struggle for Minerals* (Austin: University of Texas Press, 1979), 1-118.
2 On the interwar discussions of these issues, see also, David Haglund, "The New Geopolitics of Minerals," in *The New Geopolitics of Minerals: Canada and International Resource Trade*, ed. David Haglund (Vancouver: UBC Press, 1989), 17-8 and I.O. Lesser, *Resources and Strategy* (New York: St. Martin's Press, 1989), 61; on metals, see G. Kolko, *Century of War* (New York: New Press, 1994), 418.
3 Cited in Major John M. Dunn, "American Dependence on Materials Imports the World-Wide Resource Base," *Journal of Conflict Resolution* 4 (1960): 119.
4 William L. Thorp, "The New International Economic Challenge," *Department of State Bulletin*, 13 August 1951, 250.
5 Genesis of a Foreign Commodity Policy for the United States, Editorial Note, *FRUS, 1946*, 1372-3.
6 Alfred E. Eckes, *A Search for Solvency* (Austin: University of Texas Press, 1975), xi.
7 For a detailed history of the American stockpiling program from 1946 to 1964, see Glenn H. Snyder, *Stockpiling Strategic Materials* (San Francisco: Chandler, 1966).
8 Ian O. Lesser, *Resources and Strategy* (New York: St. Martin's Press, 1989), 102-3.
9 *United States Treaties and Other International Agreements* (1950): I, 716-8.
10 Cited in Eckes, *The United States and the Global Struggle*, 176.
11 Snyder, *Stockpiling Strategic Materials*, 35 and 39.
12 On the International Materials Conference, see *Keesing's Contemporary Archives*, 3-10 February 1951, 11255-6; 24 February to 3 March 1951, 11481; 7-14 July 1951, 11578; 27 October to 3 November 1951, 11803; 8-15 March 1952, 12079; 13-20 September 1952, 12456; 29 November to 6 December 1952, 12600; 21-28 November 1953, 13268; and Willis C. Armstrong, "The International Materials Conference," *Department of State Bulletin*, 2 July 1951, 23-29.
13 Hans H. Landsberg, Leonard L. Fischman, and Joseph L. Fisher, *Resources in America's*

Future: Patterns of Requirements and Availabilities, 1960-2000 (Washington: John Hopkins Press, 1963), 11.

14 United States, National Commission on Materials Policy, *Final Report*, Washington, June 1973, section 9.

15 W.D. Eberle to L. William Seidman and Paul A. McCracken, 4 October 1974, Council of Economic Advisors, box 7; Frederick B. Dent to Trade Policy Committee, 10 April 1975, Seidman Papers, box 176; undated, unsigned study, "International Commodities." Seidman Papers, box 135, all in the Gerald R. Ford Archives (hereafter GFA).

16 Lawrence S. Eagleburger, "U.S. Policy towards Western Europe and Canada," *Department of State Bulletin*, August 1981, 67; Uri Ra'anan and Charles M. Perry, eds., *Strategic Minerals and International Security* (Washington: Pergamon-Brassey's, 1985); Lesser, *Resources*, 148, 158-9.

17 Stephen Krasner, *Defending the National Interest* (Princeton: Princeton University Press, 1978), 14-7, 39.

18 Lesser, *Resources*, 160.

19 *Keesing's Contemporary Archives*, 13 January 1946, 7874; John Hutcheson, *Dominance and Dependency* (Toronto: McClelland and Stewart, 1978), 85; Assistant Secretary of State for Congressional Relations (McFalls) to the Chairman of the Senate Foreign Relations Committee, 22 September 1950, *FRUS, 1950*, II, 585; "Canada. Industrial Mobilization," in *United States Treaties and Other International Agreements* (Washington: Department of State, 1950), I, 716-7; C. Fred Bergsten, *The International Economic Policy of the United States* (Lexington: D.C. Heath, 1980), 294.

20 F.H. Soward, *Canada in World Affairs: From Normandy to Paris, 1944-1946* (Toronto: Oxford University Press, 1940), 58.

21 Eckes, *The United States and the Global Struggle*, 123-9.

22 Cited in Snyder, *Stockpiling Strategic Materials*, 33.

23 *Resources for Freedom: A Report to the President by the President's Materials Policy Commission* (Washington: US Government Printing Office, 1952), I, 11, 20-1. See also, David G. Haglund, "Conclusion," in *The New Geopolitics of Minerals*, 253.

24 The best account of the stockpiling program is the administrative history written by Glenn H. Snyder, referred to in note 7 above. Snider makes many references to the slippage in the purposes of the stockpiling program, from one of national security to one of aiding domestic industry. See, for example, 3-5, 49, 53, 77.

25 "National Stockpiling Program," Department of Defence report, 12 October 1951, in *FRUS, 1951*, I, 220-1.

26 Snyder, *Stockpiling Strategic Materials*, 147-9, 158, 168, 189-90; "Committee of Mineral Policy reports to President," *Department of State Bulletin*, 27 December 1954, 988-90; *Government and the Nation's Resources*, 140-1.

27 Raymond Mikesell, *Nonfuel Minerals. Foreign Dependence and National Security* (Ann Arbor: University of Michigan Press, 1987), 225. Summary of Findings of CIEP, *Special Report Critical Imported Materials;* Seidman Papers, 15 February 1975, box 53, Council of International Economic Policy Reports, GFA.

28 United States National Commission on Supplies and Shortages, *Government and the Nation's Resources* (Washington: Government Printing Office, 1976), x, xvi; Krasner, *Defending the National Interest*, 52; United States Council on International Economic Policy, galley proofs of 1974 International Economic Report, Seidman Papers, box 53, GFA.

29 David Leo Weimer, *The Strategic Petroleum Reserve* (Westport: Greenwood Press, 1982), 6; *A Congressional Handbook*, 232-4.

30 Leonard L. Fischman, *World Mineral Trends and Supply Problems* (Washington: Resources for the Future, 1980), xxxiii, 3-4, and 454-5; on American minerals policies during the 1970s, see Eckes, *The United States and the Global Struggle*, 244-53.

31 US House of Representatives, 97th Congress, *A Congressional Handbook on US Materials Import Dependency-Vulnerability*, A Report to the Subcommittee on Economic Stabilization of the Committee on Banking, Finance and Urban Affairs (Washington: Government Printing Office), 35-79.

32 J. Kaplan, "US Resource Policy: Canadian Connections," in *Natural Resources in US-Canadian Relations,* eds. C. Beigie and Alfred Hero (Boulder, CO: Westview, 1980), 105-11; *A Congressional Handbook,* 68, 70-3, 245, 398-9.

33 Lawrence Robert Aronsen, *American National Security and Economic Relations with Canada, 1945-1954* (Westport: Praeger, 1997), 119.

34 Eckes, *The United States and the Global Struggle,* 212; the 167th Meeting of the National Security Council, memorandum of discussion, 22 October 1953, *FRUS, 1952-1954,* I, 1032-3.

35 Memorandum of conversation, 24 May 1957, *FRUS,* IX, 237-9; Eckes, *The United States and the Global Struggle,* 222; Snyder, *Stockpiling Strategic Materials,* 195, 210

36 Gordon T. Stewart, *The American Response to Canada since 1776* (East Lansing: Michigan State University Press, 1992), 177-8.

37 Aronsen, *American National Security,* 115.

38 Snyder, *Stockpiling Strategic Materials,* 112-9, 129-32.

39 *Resources for Freedom,* I, 60, 63, 91-2; Chargé in Canada (Bliss) to the Director of the British Commonwealth and North European Affairs (Rayner), memorandum, Ottawa, 24 April 1953, *FRUS,* II, 2079.

40 National Security Council, statement, 24 October 1993, *FRUS, 1952-54,* I, 1034-7.

41 Dunn, "American Dependence," 118.

42 On nickel, see Aronsen, *American National Security,* 127-8; David G. Haglund, "The New Geopolitics of Minerals: An Inquiry into the Changing International Significance of Strategic Minerals," 12-3; and David G. Haglund, "Canadian Strategic Minerals and US Military Potential," 164-5; both in *The New Geopolitics of Minerals.* See also, David Haglund, "Canadian Strategic Minerals and United States Military Potential," *Journal of Canadian Studies* 19 (1984): 13-5, and J.I. Cameron, "Nickel," in *Natural Resources in US Canadian Relations,* 68 70.

43 Gordon T. Stewart, *The American Response,* 177-8.

44 On Senator Malone's report, see Eckes, *The United States and the Global Struggle,* 206-8; Malone asked the Canadian ambassador to give him and later received a detailed account of resources available from Canada; see Melissa Clark-Jones, *A Staple State: Canadian Industrial Resources in Cold War* (Toronto: University of Toronto Press, 1987), 108.

45 Kaplan, "US Resource Policy," 111; James B. Reston, Jr., to Douglas Cater, memorandum, 26 June 1964, White House Central Files, SP Speeches 11/22/63-8131/64, box 1.

46 Council on International Economic Policy, *Special Report on Critical Imported Materials,* December 1974, GFA; State Department Briefing Paper, November 1974, Seidman Papers, box 130; *A Congressional Handbook,* 304, 321, and 326.

47 On the history of the Seaway, see E. Mahant and G.S. Mount, *An Introduction to Canadian-American Relations* (Toronto: Nelson, 1989), 205-8. The Paley Commission included a short section on the Seaway in its report; see *Resources for Freedom,* I, 166-7. A most useful compilation of documents is that presented by Senator Wiley on 15 November 1954; see *St. Lawrence Seaway Manual: A Compilation of Documents* (Washington: United States Government Printing Office, 1955), 83rd Congress, 2nd session, Senate Document 165.

48 P.E. Jones, *Oil: A Practical Guide to the Economics of World Petroleum* (Cambridge: Woodhead-Faulkner, 1988), 270.

49 D. Airgun, *The Prize: The Epic Quest for Oil, Money and Power* (New York: Simon and Schuster, 1991), 409-10.

50 *Statistical Abstract of the United States 1994* (Washington: US Department of Commerce, 1994), 594; "Appendix," in *Energy Policy in Perspective: Today's Problems, Yesterday's Solutions,* ed. C.D. Goodwin (Washington: Brookings Institution 1981), 694; W. Mead et al., *Oil in the Seventies: Essays on Energy Policy* (Vancouver: Fraser Institute, 1977), 260-1; "Message to Congress" and "Fact Sheet" in US Senate, Committee on Energy and Natural Resources, *Executive Energy Documents* (Washington: General Printing Office, 1978), 18 April 1973, 35; D.C. Williams, "United States Energy Policy and Federalism," in *Politique de l'énergie et fédéralisme,* ed. L.M. Thur (Toronto: Institute of Public Administration of Canada, 1981), 99.

51 *Statistical Abstract,* 594; Mead et al., *Oil in the Seventies,* 249.

52 H.H. Landsberg, L.L. Fischman, and J.L. Fisher, *Resources in America's Future: Patterns of Requirements and Availabilities, 1960-2000* (Baltimore: John Hopkins Press, 1963), 402.

53 On the Carter period, see, J.L. Cochrane, "Carter Energy Policy and the Ninety-Fifth Congress," in *Energy Policy,* 489, 511-2, and 593.

54 D.L. Weimer, *The Strategic Petroleum Reserve: Planning, Implementation and Analysis* (Westport: Greenwood Press, 1982), 7.

55 Goodwin, *Energy Policy,* 105-6; Statement of Policy by the National Security Council, *FRUS, 1952-1954,* I, 1054-9.

56 State Department Policy Statement, 30 June 1950, *FRUS, 1950,* II, 1027.

57 Goodwin, *Energy Policy,* 112n; Assistant Secretary of State for Economic Affairs (Waugh), to the Director of the Office of Defense Mobilization (Fleming), *FRUS, 1952-1954,* I, 1140; Study Prepared by an Interagency Group Chaired by the Office of Civil and Defense Mobilization, *FRUS, 1958-1960,* IV, 605.

58 Administrative History of the State Department, Lyndon B. Johnson Library, I, ch. 3, section i; D.G. Haglund, "Canadian Strategic Minerals and US Military Potential," in *The New Geopolitics of Minerals,* 170; H. Frank and J. Schanz, *US-Canadian Energy Trade: A Study of Changing Relationships* (Boulder, CO: Westview, 1978), 4-5, 21-2.

59 P.E. Jones, *Oil: A Practical Guide to the Economics of World Petroleum* (Cambridge: Woodhead-Faulkner, 1988), 271; Chief of Naval Operations (Burke) to the President's Special Assistant for National Security Affairs, letter, 19 November, *FRUS, 1958-1960,* IV, 655; Haglund, "Canadian Strategic Minerals," 171; P. Daniel and R. Shaffner, "Lessons from Bilateral Trade in Energy Resources," in *Natural Resources in US Canadian Relations,* 323; Mead et al., *Oil in the Seventies,* 183, 261; John E. Gray, *US Energy Policy and Policy Committee* (Cambridge: Ballinger, 1981), 167.

60 Cabinet Task Force on Oil Import Control, *The Oil Import Question. A Report on the Relationship of Oil Imports to the National Security* (Washington: Government Printing Office, 1970), 3-4; memorandum of conversation, 22 March 1959, *FRUS,* IV, 42-3; Goodwin, *Energy Policy,* 225-52.

61 Director of the Office of Defense Mobilization (Gray) to the President, memorandum, 23 April 1957, *FRUS, 1955-57,* X, 673-4.

62 For a flavour of some of these debates, see the various documents in *FRUS, 1955-1957,* X, 659-81, 695-9, 717-30.

63 President's Special Assistant (Paarlberg) to the President's Personal Secretary (Whitman), memorandum, 27 April 1959, *FRUS, 1958-1960,* 608-9.

64 J.S. Nye, "Transnational Relations and Interstate Conflicts: An Empirical Analysis," *International Organization* 28 (1974): 987.

65 J. Kirton and Dave Dewitt, *Canada As a Principal Power* (Toronto: John Wiley, 1983), 279; J. Granatstein and N. Hillmer, *For Better or For Worse. Canada and the United States in the 1990s* (Toronto: Copp Clark, 1991), 187.

66 RG 59, General Records of the Department of State, Records of the Policy Planning Staff 1962, box 213, folder: Canada.

67 *The Oil Import Question,* 129.

68 On District V, see *The Oil Import Question,* 15-7; Fourth Meeting of the Special Committee to Investigate Crude Oil Imports, memorandum, *FRUS, 1955-1957,* X, 729; on the overland exemption, see Goodwin, *Energy Policy,* 253-4; on cheating on the overland exemption, see ibid., 379 and Yergin, *The Prize,* 539.

69 M. Robert Rutherford of the Fuels Division, Office of International Trade and Resources, memorandum for files, 11 April and 3 May 1957, *FRUS, 1955-1957,* X, 668, 679; Assistant Secretary of State for Inter-American Affairs (Rubottom) to the Secretary of State, memorndum, 6 July 1957, *FRUS, 1955-57,* VII, 1157; National Security Council, Canadian Access to Nuclear Weapons in Peacetime, Annex to NSC 5822, 12 December 1958, National Archives, Section A; National Security Council, memorandum of discussion, 23 December 1958, *FRUS, 1958-1960,* IV, 588; *The Oil Import Question,* 135.

70 Visit of Prime Minister Pearson, 10-11 May 1963, folder, Visit of Prime Minister Pearson, Vice-Presidential Security Files, LBJ Library; Secretary of State, memorandum for the president, 12 December 1963, NSF, Country File: Canada, 1, box 165, LBJ Library; memorandum

to the president [signed Marvin], 26 August 1965, White House Central Files, Country file Canada, box 19, folder 61, 6/65-7/19/66, LBJ Library; State Department, memorandum of conversation, 12 November 1965, NSF, Country File: Canada, box 166, LBJ Library; Francis Bator, White House memorandum, 15 February 1967, White House Central files, Country 43, Canada, 1967-8, LBJ Library; Francis Bator, White House memorandum (addressed to the president and containing the handwritten notation "Call me about this."), papers of Francis M. Bator, box 6, folder, chronological file 8/16/67-9/14/67; Administrative History of the Department of State, I, Ch. 3, Europe, Sections D(c) and (i), 1968, LBJ Johnson Library; Peter Flanigan, memorandum to the files, 5 January 1970, and Peter Flanigan, memorandum to the president, 21 March 1970, both in TA4/Oil, Country 28, Nixon Project, 7/1/69-10/31/69, box 14.

71 P. Daniel and R. Shaffner, "Lessons from Bilateral Trade in Energy Resources," in *Natural Resources in US-Canadian Relations*, 308-9; C.T. Tuohy, *Policy and Politics in Canada* (Philadelphia: Temple University Press, 1992), 264.

72 L.T. Merchant and A.D.P. Heeney, "Canada and the United States-Principles for Partnership," *Atlantic Community Quarterly* 3 (1965): 386-7; Nelson Rockefeller to President Nixon, letter, 23 September 1970, Nixon Project, Country 28, Canada, 6/1/69-11/30/69, box 16; Dewitt and Kirton, *Canada as a Principal*, 294-8.

73 Memorandum for the files, 24 February 1971, memorandum for the files, 3 March 1971, and memorandum for Henry Kissinger, 23 April 1971, all three in Nixon Project, Country 28, Canada, 1/1/71, box 15; H. Frank and J. Schanz, *US-Canadian Energy Trade: A Study of Changing Relationships* (Boulder, CO: Westview, 1978), 26. On developments in the Middle East, see J.P.D. Dunbabin, *The Post-Imperial Age; the Great Powers and the Wider World* (London: Longman, 1994), II, 349.

74 Peter Flanigan to Henry Kissinger, Philip Trezise, and G.A. Lincoln, memorandum, 4 October 1971; memorandum of telephone conversation, 3 December 1971; and Peter Flanigan to General Haig, memorandum, 3 December 1971, all in Nixon Project, Country 28, Canada 1/1/71, box 15. On George Shultz, see Robert Bothwell, *The Politics of Partnership* (Toronto: University of Toronto Press, 1992), 218.

75 On the pipeline issue, see E.E. Mahant and G .Mount, *An Introduction to Canadian-American Relations* (Toronto: Nelson, 1989), 258; and meeting with Secretary of State Rogers Morton, notes, 20 March 1972, Nixon Project, Country 28, Canada, 1/1/71- 30647, box 15.

76 J.L. Granatstein and R. Bothwell, *Pirouette: Pierre Trudeau and Canadian Foreign Policy* (Toronto: University of Toronto Press, 1990), 84; Dunbabin, *Post-Imperial Age*, 349-51; Executive Office of the President, Office of Emergency Preparedness, G.A. Lincoln to Peter Flanigan, 17 November 1972, Nixon Project, Country File, Canada 1/1/71, 4 of 4), and File EXTA4/CM Tariff-Imports, Country 28, November 1972, WHCF, Subject Files, TA (Trade), box 35, Nixon Project.

77 *Canadian Annual Review of Politics and Public Affairs, 1973*, 230; Peter Flanigan to Bill Simon, Jules Katz, and Jim Atkins, memorandum, 22 March 1973, Nixon Project, Country 28, Canada, 11/1/71-6/30/73, box 15.

78 On the Canadian controls and taxes, see "Canada: A Fair-Weather Friend?" *Economist* 17 (1974): 50-2 and *Canadian Annual Review of Politics and Public Affairs, 1973*, 231. On the other Canadian policies, see J.N. McDougall, "Canada and the World Petroleum Market," in *A Foremost Nation*, eds. N. Hillmer and G. Stevenson (Toronto: McClelland and Stewart, 1977), 89; on American policy, Federal Energy Administration, Revision of the Mandatory Oil Import Program, 10 July 1976, Seidman Papers, GFA, box 131; on the Great Lakes and the Panama Canal, see H. Frank and J. Schanz, *US-Canadian Energy Trade: A Study of Changing Relationships* (Boulder, CO: Westview, 1978), 27.

79 On the International Energy Agency, see D. Blair, "Canadian Participation in the International Energy Agency," in *The New Geopolitics of Minerals*, ed. D. Haglund (Vancouver: UBC Press, 1989), 126-9; R. Rosencrance, *The Rise of the Trading State* (New York: Basic Books, 1986), 9-12. Also see State Department Briefing Paper, November 1974, box 130; International Economic Issues Briefing Book, 12/06/74, box 135; and Council on International Economic Policy, International Economic Report of the President, 9 September 1976 (1976 is clearly a typo for 1975 because the document refers to March 1976 as in the

future), box 137 – all three in the Seidman Papers, GFA. On the Canadian position, see *Canadian News Facts,* 1-15 February 1974, 1155; *Canadian Annual Review of Politics and Public Affairs, 1974,* 286, and *1975,* 245-6.

80 On Project Independence, see "Address on the Energy Emergency," 7 November 1973, in *Executive Energy Documents,* 81-93; Goodwin, *Energy Policy,* 464-73; Mead et al., *Oil in the Seventies,* 264; and United States, Federal Energy Administration, *Project Independence: A Summary* (Washington: Government Printing Office, 1974), esp. 19. On the other domestic responses, see the Nineteenth Annual Report on the Trade Agreements Program – 1974, an otherwise undated document from the GFA and Statement by the President, 4 December 1973, Savage Papers, Subject File CIA, GFA.

81 Frank and Schanz, *US-Canadian Energy,* 122-3; *Canadian Annual Review 1974,* 299.

82 J. McDougall, "Canada and the World Petroleum Market," in *A Foremost Nation: Canadian Foreign Policy in a Changing World,* eds. N. Hillmer and G. Stevenson (Toronto: McClelland and Stewart, 1977), 92; *Canadian Annual Review 1974,* 300-1; J. Katz, *Current Foreign Policy: United States and Canada, Facing the Energy Crisis* (Washington: Department of State Bureau of Public Affairs, 1973), Publication 8747, 2; Special Trade Arrangements with Canada in International Economic Issues Briefing Book, 10/5/74, Seidman Papers, box 135, GFA; Henry Kissinger, memorandum to the president, 7 June 1974, Nixon Project, Country 28, 4/1/74-6/30174, box 15; Kenneth Rush letter to Robert Yancey, 5 July 1974, Nixon Project, Country 28, Canada, 1/1/73, box 14; G.A. Lincoln to Peter Flanigan (as in note 70 above). On the declining estimates of Canadian oil reserves, see, B.F. Wilson, *The Energy Squeeze* (Ottawa: Canadian Institute for Economic Policy, 1980), 29-33.

83 *Executive Energy Documents,* 15 January 1975, 253; *Canadian Annual Review of Politics and Public Affairs, 1975,* 250; Goodwin, *Energy Policy,* 487-8, 511, 526, 530-1.

84 D.L. Weimer, *The Strategic Petroleum Reserve* (Westport: Greenwood, 1982), 7, 12-5, 64-5; H. Geller et al., "U.S. Oil Import Dependence," *Energy Policy* 22, 6 (1994): 476. *The Economist* reported on 4 May 1996, 29, that the Clinton administration was selling oil from the SPR to hold prices down.

85 Testimony of Frank Zarb before the Senate Foreign Relations Committee, Subcommittee on Near East and South Asian Affairs, 30 June 1976, GFA photocopy; *Project Independence,* 7.

86 Eric Mallin, *Washington Post,* 23 November 1974; *Canadian Annual Review of Politics and Public Affairs, 1974,* 399, and *1976,* 394; J.E. Gray, H.H. Fowler, and J.W. Harned, *US Energy Policy and US Foreign Policy in the 1980s* (Cambridge: Ballinger, 1981), 151; Frank and Schanz, *US-Canadian Energy,* 125, 128.

87 Nessen for White House Press Room, 5 December 1974, Savage Papers, Subject File CA, GFA.

88 Statement of Frank Zarb before the Joint Economic Committee, Congress of the United States, 15 September 1976, GFA photocopy.

89 Ron Nessen, News Conference, 4 December 1974, Ron H. Nessen Files, box 4, GFA; State Department Briefing Paper for Economic Policy Board, Executive Committee Meeting, 2 December 1974, Council of Economic Advisors, Alan Greenspan Files, box 57, GFA; "Canadians Feel US Has Played Too Big a Role in Their Affairs: Interview with Thomas Enders," *US News and World Report,* 21 June 1976, 67-8; Arthur Hartman Press Conference, 4 December 1974, Savage Papers, Subject File CA, GFA; US Canadian Relations, 14 June 1976, Nessen Papers, box 122, GFA.

90 Frank Zarb to Melvin A. Conant, Assistant Administrator, International Energy Affairs,17 January 1975, and A. Denis Clift, memorandum for Secretary Kissinger, 21 February 1975, both in WCF, Country 28, box 11, GFA; Frank Zarb, memorandum for the Executive Committee, Energy Resources Council, Northern Tier Report, 2 August 1976, Seidman Papers, box 131, GFA; W.D. Eberle, memorandum for Executive Committee of the Economic Policy Board, 17 October 1974, Seidman Papers, box 181, GFA.

91 Jimmy Carter, *Keeping Faith: Memoirs of a President* (Toronto: Bantam, 1982), 91.

92 "Introduction," signed by Robert Ellsworth, to a report prepared by Melvin Conant, United States Senate Committee on Energy and Natural Resources, *The Western Hemisphere Energy System* (Washington: US Government Printing Office, 1979), Publication 96-45, 2, 24.

93 *Federal Register,* 29 March 1979, 18818-28, 18841-2.
94 Jimmy Carter, "Energy and National Goals," *Presidential Documents: Administration of Jimmy Carter,* 20 July 1979, 1239. On the Carter Doctrine, see Carter, *Keeping Faith,* 483, and J.J. Romm, *Defining National Security: The Nonmilitary Aspects* (New York: Council on Foreign Relations Press, 1993), 39.
95 A note simply headed "Zbig" in WCF, box TR[ips] 31, and Canadian Parliament Speech GS [1], folder 11/9/79, Speechwriters Chron File, WHF, both in Carter Library.
96 On the pipeline agreement and controversy, see *Canadian Annual Review 1977,* 244-5, *1979,* 188-91, and *1980,* 164-5; J.H. Ashworth, "Continuity and Change in the US Decision-Making Process in Raw Materials," in *Natural Resources in US-Canadian Relations,* 92-3; Frank and Schanz, *US-Canadian Energy,* 128-30.
97 On this incident see, *Canadian Annual Review 1978,* 254, and *1979,* 191.
98 Carter, *Keeping the Faith,* 112-4.
99 *Canadian Annual Review 1977,* 246, and *1978,* 254; draft of joint Canada-American communique, 6 November 1979, WHCF, Country 28, box 14, 6/1/79-1/20/81, Carter Library.
100 Melvin A. Conant, in *Western Hemisphere Energy System,* 153; E.F. Wonder, "US-Canadian Energy Relations," in *US Energy Policy and US Foreign Policy in the 1980s,* ed. John E. Gray (Cambridge: Ballinger, 1981), 138, 151, 167; D.H. Haglund, "Canadian Strategic Minerals and US Military Potential," in *The New Geopolitics of Minerals,* 171-2.
101 *Securing America's Energy Future: The National Energy Policy Plan.* A Report to the Congress Required by Title VIII of the Department of Energy Organization Act (Washington: US Department of Energy, 1981), 1, 5, 22; *The National Energy Policy Plan* (Washington: US Department of Energy, 1985), 3-4; E.R. Fried, "Overview," in *Oil and America's Security,* eds. E.R. Fried and N.M. Blandin (Washington: The Brookings Institute, 1988), 2-6; Weimer, *Strategic Petroleum Reserve,* 5, 63.
102 *Globe and Mail,* 20, 24, 31 July, 17 August 1979; *The National Energy Policy Plan,* 1985, 30.
103 *Canadian Annual Review 1981,* 237, 239, 243, 281, *1982,* 153, and *1985,* 168; J.L. Granatstein and N. Hillmer, *For Better of For Worse: Canada and the United States in the 1990s* (Toronto: Copp Clark, 1991), 276; P.E. Jones, *Oil. A Practical Guide to the Economics of World Petroleum* (Cambridge: Woodhead Faulkner, 1988), 276-7.
104 G.B. Doern and B.W. Tomlin, *Faith and Fear: The Free Trade Story* (Toronto: Stoddart, 1991), 82, 122-4, 157.
105 W.F. Martin, "Energy Policy and US National Priorities," in *Oil,* 74-5.
106 *Statistical Abstract of the United States,* 1994, 593-4.
107 J.N. McDougall, "North American Interdependence and Canadian Fuel Policies," in *Canada's Foreign Policy: Analysis and Trends,* ed. B. Tomlin (Toronto: Methuen, 1978), 76-7.
108 Goodwin, *Energy Policy,* 697; *Statistical Abstract of the United States,* 1994, 584.
109 G.E. Nielsen, *The Line that Joins,* Waterton-Glacier International Peace Conference, 14 June 1969, pamphlet in GFA, 7.
110 T. Lloyd, *Canada in World Affairs, 1957-1959* (Toronto: Oxford University Press, 1968), 88-9, J. Eayrs, *Canada in World Affairs: October 1955 to June 1957* (Toronto: Oxford University Press, 1959), 131.
111 "Canada: A Fair-Weather Friend?" *Economist* 17 (1974): 50-1; Mead et al., *Oil in the Seventies,* 264; Daniel and Shaffner, "Lessons from Bilateral Trade in Energy Resources," in *Natural Resources in US-Canadian Relations,* 323; Conant, *World Gas Trade,* 213-4; Philip E. Ruppe, untitled congressional study on US-Canadian relations, 29 April 1976, WHCF, Country 28, box 11, GFA.
112 *Canadian News Facts,* 16-31 December 1974, 1314; *Canadian Annual Review 1976,* 304; Increase in Price of Canadian Natural Gas Exports to the US, 6 May 1976, unsigned paper, in Nessen Papers, box 122, GFA; Frank Zarb to the President, memoranda, 24 May 1976 and 10 June 1976. Zarb Files, box 2, GFA; Jimmy Carter to Joe Clark, undated letter, Staff Offices, Office of Staff, Secretary's Handwriting File, box 169, folder 2/8/80, Carter Library; Dewitt and Kirton, *Canada as a Principal,* 308; *Canadian Annual Review 1980,* 167-8.
113 On the act, see J.P. Stern, *Natural Gas Trade in North America and Asia* (Aldershot: Gower, 1985), 8; the priorities are cited in Stern, *Natural Gas Trade,* 118 and 120, and summarized in *National Energy Plan II,* 93-4.

114 *Canadian Annual Review 1983,* 158-9, and *1985,* 168-9; Stern, *Natural Gas Trade,* 124-7 and 131.
115 *Improving US Energy Security,* 149-50; *National Energy Policy Plan, 1985,* 30-1.
116 W.W. Rostow, memorandum for Joseph Califano and Eugene Rostow, 23 December 1966, NSF, Country File: Canada, box 166, Canadian Cables, IV, 1/66-12/66, LBJ Library; D.E. Gibson and M. Willrich, "Canadian Natural Gas Trade with the United States," in *The World Gas Trade,* ed. M.A. Conant (Boulder, CO: Westview, 1985), 209-11.
117 W. Butterworth to the State Department, 6 January 1967, WHCF, Country File: Canada, 5, box 166, LBJ Library.
118 International Energy Issue – Alaska Natural Gas Pipeline, International Economic Issues Briefing Book 3, Nessen Papers, box 40, 1974, and Ruppe report, 29 April 1976, both in GFA.
119 *Canadian Annual Review 1978,* 251-3; on the route controversy, see Frank and Schanz, *US-Canadian Energy Trade,* 48, 52, 129, and J.H. Ashworth, "Continuity and Change in the US Decision-Making Processing Raw Materials," in *Natural Resources in US-Canadian Relations,* 92-3; on the procurement problems, see *Canadian Annual Review 1979,* 186-8, and John Dingell to Stuart Eizenstat, memorandum, 8 November 1979, Carter Library.
120 J. Kirton, "Canada and the United States," *Current History* (1980): 146-7; Canada Visit, 6 November 1979, WHCF, Co28, box 14, 6/1/79-1/2081, Carter Library; *Canadian Annual Review 1979,* 186-8, and (1980), 164-8.
121 Stern, *Natural Gas Trade,* 15; *Canadian Annual Review 1981,* 282, *1982,* 153, and *1984,* 150-1.
122 For the early history of uranium in Canadian-American relations, see E.E. Mahant and G. Mount, *An Introduction to Canadian-American Relations* (Toronto: Nelson, 1989), 177-82.
123 Commanding General, Manhattan Engineering District, memorandum, 16 November 1945, and Minutes of a Meeting of the Combined Policy Committee, 4 December 1945, both in *FRUS, 1945,* II, 75-6, 88-9.
124 For summaries of these reports, see the Chairman of the Combined Development Trust (Groves) to the Chairman of the Combined Policy Committee (Patterson), 3 December 1945, and Minutes of a Meeting of the Combined Policy Committee, 4 December 1945, both in *FRUS, 1945,* II, 84-8; see also, T. Greenwood and A. Streeter, "Uranium" in *Natural Resources in US-Canadian Relations,* 324; Margaret Gowing, *Britain and Atomic Energy, 1939-1945* (London: Macmillan, 1964), 312-9.
125 On the early history of the Combined Development Trust, see Gowing, *Britain and Atomic Energy,* 297-305.
126 On the Canadian position in the Combined Development Trust, see *Documents on Canadian External Relations, XII, 1946,* 413-33; on the two governments' atomic energy legislation, see Earle Gray, *The Great Uranium Cartel* (Toronto: McClelland and Stewart, 1982), 38-43; on the attempts to create a United Nations atomic energy agency, see Mahant and Mount, *An Introduction to Canadian-American Relations,* 181-2, and the minutes of meeting of the American delegation to the United Nations, 30 September 1948, *FRUS, 1948,* I, 440-2; on "dominion," see J. Holmes, *The Shaping of Peace: Canada and the Search for World Order, 1943-1957* (Toronto: University of Toronto Press, 1982), II, 51.
127 On exploration incentives, see Greenwood and Streeter, "Uranium," 345; the best account of the December 1947 meeting is that in James Eayrs, *In Defence of Canada* (Toronto: University of Toronto Press, 1972), 316-8; on the modus vivendi, see Eayrs, *In Defence of Canada,* 313-7, and Draft Agreement between the Governments of the United States, the United Kingdom and Canada, 6 January 1948, in *FRUS, 1948,* I, 683-7. On Kennan, see George Kennan to Mr. Lovett, untitled memorandum, 24 October 1947 and Appendix 1 to that memorandum in RG 59, General Records of the Department of State, General Records of the Policy Planning Staff 1947-53, box 6, folder Atomic Energy – Armaments 1947-8.
128 Policy Planning Staff, Atomic Energy Policy vis-à-vis UK and Canada, 7 February 1949, RG 59, General Records of the Department of State, Records of the Policy Planning Staff 1947-53, folder Atomic Energy – Armaments, 1949 Meeting of Combined Policy Committee, 30 September 1949, *FRUS, 1949,* I, 548-53; summary log of Atomic Energy Work

in the Office of the Under-Secretary of State, May-Sept. 1950, and F.W. Marten, First Secretary, British Embassy, to R. Gordon Arneson, 8 October 1950, both in *FRUS, 1950,* I, 580-7, 589-90.

129 R. Gordon Arneson, NSC Report 120/1: Communication of Data to Canadians Concerning New Ore Refinery, 11 January 1952 (and several attachments), RG 59, General Records of the Department of State, Records of the Policy Planning Staff Relating to the State Department participation in the NSC, 1955-62, box 7, folder Communication of Data to Canadians Concerning New Ore Refinery; R. Gordon Arneson to Mr. MacArthur, untitled memorandum, 3 December 1953 (and several attachments); RG 59, General Records of the Department of State, Records of the Policy Planning Staff 1947-53, box 6, folder Atomic Energy – Armaments 1952-3.

130 Goodwin et al., *Energy Policy,* 281-2.

131 A Report to the National Security Council on Communication of Data to Canadians Concerning New Ore Refinery, 21 December, Washington, NSC Registry (p. F); "Agreement signed at Washington, June 15, 1955," in *Canadian-American Relations, 1867-1967* (Ottawa: United States Information Service, 1994), 57-64; Greenwood and Streeter, "Uranium," 324-6, 345-6; E. Gray, *The Great Uranium Cartel,* 58-61.

132 Greenwood and Streeter, "Uranium," 324-7, 345-6; H. McIntyre, *Uranium, Nuclear Power and Canada-US Energy Relations* (Montreal: Canadian-American Committee, 1978), 14-5; M. Radetzki, *Uranium* (New York: St. Martin's Press, 1981), 37-9; M. Webb, "Canada as an Insecure Supplier," in *The New Geopolitics of Minerals,* ed. D. Haglund (Vancouver: UBC Press, 1989), 193-9.

133 Greenwood and Streeter, "Uranium," 347, 355; Webb, "Canada as an Insecure," 201; "Agreement signed at Washington, June 15, 1955" and "Agreement signed at Washington, May 22, 1959," both in *Canadian-American Relations,* 54-78; W. Eggleston, *Canada's Nuclear Story* (Toronto: Clarke Irwin, 1965), 205, 233; Benjamin Head in State Department, memorandum for McGeorge Bundy, 13 April 1965, NSF, Country File: Canada, III, box 166.

134 Webb, "Canada as an Insecure," 216; Greenwood and Streeter, "Uranium," 356, 368.

135 D.L. Spar, *The Cooperative Edge: The Internal Politics of International Cartels* (Ithaca: Cornell University Press, 1994), 91, 97-9; Will Kriegsman to Peter Flanigan, memorandum, January, 1970 and letter written for Chairman of United States Atomic Energy Commission (signature illegible) to Peter Flanigan, 10 December 1971, both in Nixon Project, Country File 28, Canada, box 14, 7/1/69-10/31/69 and box 15, 1/1/71.

136 Gray, *The Great Uranium Cartel,* 99, 157, 171; Greenwood and Streeter, "Uranium," 327-8.

137 The best two accounts of the uranium cartel are those found in D.L. Spar, *The Cooperative Edge,* and E. Gray, *The Great Uranium Cartel.* The following account is based on these two sources, unless otherwise acknowledged.

138 Spar, *The Cooperative Edge,* 121.

139 Gray, *The Great Uranium Cartel,* 235.

140 Federal Energy Resources Council, *Uranium Reserves, Resources, and Production* (Washington, 15 June 1976), 1-3.

141 Spar, *The Cooperative Edge,* 122; D. Haglund, S.N. MacFarlane, and V. Popov, *Change in the Former Soviet Union and Its Implication for the Canadian Minerals Sector* (Kingston: Centre for Resource Studies, 1994), 134.

142 Webb, "Canada as an Insecure," 212.

143 Ibid., 193, 219; D. Haglund, *US Trade Barriers and Canadian Minerals: Copper, Potash and Uranium* (Kingston: Queen's University Centre for Resource Studies, 1990), 147-76; Haglund, MacFarlane, and Popov, *Change,* 131-41; Robert T. Whillans, "Uranium," *Canadian Minerals Yearbook 1994* (Ottawa: Natural Resources Canada, 1995), 54.7-.9; *Globe and Mail,* 3 June 1994, B1, and *Montreal Gazette,* 24 February 1994, B6.

144 "We will, therefore, seek Canadian cooperation in developing supply access guidelines." State Department Briefing Paper, November 1974, Seidman Papers, box 134, GFA.

Chapter 6: Policies on American Investment in Canada

1 Edward M. Graham and Paul R. Krugman, *Foreign Direct Investment in the United States* (Washington: Institute for International Economics, 1995), 8.

2 Except when described otherwise, the word "dollar" in this chapter refers to the American dollar.

3 For a brief history of the international monetary system and the dollar's role within it, see Benjamin Cohen, "A Brief History of International Monetary Relations," in *International Political Economy: Perspectives on Global Power and Wealth*, eds. Jeffrey Frieden and David Lake (New York: St. Martin's Press, 1995), 209-29.

4 For a general review of American monetary policy and a brief statistical summary, see Raymond Vernon and Debora L. Spar, *Beyond Globalism: Remaking American Foreign Economic Policy* (New York: The Free Press, 1989), ch. 4; Cohen, "A Brief History," 222-8; and Robert M. Dunn, *Canada's Experience with Fixed and Flexible Exchange Rates in a North American Capital Market* (Washington: National Planning Association, 1971), 4-5. For the statement by Lyndon Johnson, see "Statement by the President Outlining a Program of Action to Deal with the Payments of Problem," in *Public Papers of the Presidents of the United States: Lyndon B. Johnson*, 1968-9, Book 1 (Washington: US Government Printing Office, 1970), 8-13; "Joint US-Canadian Committee on Trade and Economic Affairs," 11 October 1955, *FRUS, 1955-1957*, IX, 153; International Payments Position of the United States, paper prepared in the State Department, 24 July 1959, *FRUS, 1958-1960*, IV, 115-7.

5 Raymond Vernon and Debora Spar, *Beyond Globalism: Remaking American Foreign Economic Policy* (New York: The Free Press, 1989), 118-9.

6 Stephen Cohen, *The Making of United States International Economic Policy* (New York: Praeger, 1988), 214-6.

7 Michael Webb, "Canada and the International Monetary Regime," in *Canadian Foreign Policy and International Economic Regimes*, eds. A. Claire Cutler and Mark Zacher (Vancouver: UBC Press, 1992), 161-5; Vernon and Spar, *Beyond Globalism*, 79, 81-92, 101-5.

8 On the 1947 foreign exchange crisis, see *Keesing's Contemporary Archives*, 18-25 October 1947, 8885-6; Atherton (ambassador to Canada) and Andrew Foster (British Commonwealth Affairs), correspondence, in *FRUS, 1947*, III, 117-20, 123, 125, 130-3; Robert Spencer, *Canada in World Affairs: From UN to NATO 1946-1949* (Toronto: Oxford University Press, 1959), 218-21, 224-6, 231-9, 194-9. The 1949 British foreign exchange crisis is discussed in W.E.C. Harrison, *Canada in World Affairs: 1949 to 1950* (Toronto: Oxford University Press, 1957), 129-33, 135-9, 141-4.

9 Under-Secretary of State (Ball) to Secretary of the Treasury Dillon, letter, 5 July 1962, *FRUS*, XIII: 1185-7; *Canadian Annual Review 1962*, ed. John Saywell, 173-87; *New York Times*, 25 June 1962.

10 Memorandum for the Record, 24 April 1963, *FRUS*, IX, 51-3; Joint Communique Following Meetings between President John F. Kennedy and Prime Minister Lester Pearson, Hyannisport, Massachusetts, 10-11 May 1993, Record Group 25 (External Affairs), 5030, file 1415-10, part 12.

11 State Department, incoming untitled telegram (signed Butterworth), 8 February 1964, NSF, Country File: Canada, box 165, I, LBJ Library. See also, Visit of Canadian Prime Minister Pearson, 21-22 January 1964, Talking Points Paper, NSF, Country File: Canada, box 167-8, LBJ Library; Secretary of State, memorandum for the president, US-Canadian Problems, 12 December 1963, NSF, Country File: Canada, box 165, I, LBJ Library; *Canadian Annual Review 1963*, ed. John Saywell (Toronto: University of Toronto Press, 1964), 205-10.

12 Douglas Dillon, memorandum for the president, Balance of Payments Problems with Canada, 15 January 1965, NSF, Country Files: Europe and USSR, boxes 162-5; unsigned memorandum to the president, Your call to Prime Minister Pearson on Balance of Payments, 9 February 1965, WHCF, Co43, box 19; Office of the Secretary of Defense to Charles Drury [signature illegible], letter, 4 March 1965, Papers of Henry Fowler, box 54, folder: International Balance of Payment, Classified material, Canada-US, Fall 1965; Record of Meeting, US-Canadian Balance of Payments Committee, 19 November 1965, and untitled paper dated 24 November 1965, both in Papers of Henry Fowler, box 67, folder: International Classified Material, 1965-6. All of the above from LBJ Library.

13 Jacob Kaplan, "US Resource Policy: Canadian Connections," in *Natural Resources in US-Canadian Relations* (Boulder, CO: Westview, 1980), 116; Michael Barkway, "United States Investment in Canada," in *Neighbors Taken for Granted*, ed. Livingston Merchant (Toronto:

Burns and MacEachern, 1966), 68; John Kirton and Robert Bothwell, "A Proud and Powerful Country: American Attitudes towards Canada," *Queen's Quarterly* 92, 1 (1985): 112; The United States Department of Commerce during the Administration of President Lyndon B. Johnson, Administrative History – Department of Commerce, box 1, folder I, part 1, LBJ Library.

14 The History of the Mandatory Foreign Direct Investment Program 1968, in Administrative History of the Department of Commerce, box 1, I, part I, 26-7, 101-2, 160-77, 218, LBJ Library; Edward Fried and James Dusenberry, memorandum for the president, 7 March 1968, NSF, Country Files, box 166, V, 1/67-10/68, LBJ Library; Dunn, *Canada's Experience,* 28-43. See also Hillmer and Stevenson, *A Foremost,* 76, and *Canadian Annual Review 1968,* 307-15.

15 Dunn, *Canada's Experience,* 67-71; *Canadian Annual Review 1970,* 405-6.

16 Mahant and Mount, *An Introduction to Canadian-American Relations* (Toronto: Nelson, 1989), 244-5.

17 Mrs. Junz to Mr. Bryant, untitled office correspondence on letterhead of the Board of Governors of the Federal Reserve System, 3 February 1972, Arthur Burns Papers, box 4, Gerald Ford Library; for a somewhat different calculation, see *Canadian Annual Review 1971,* 327. On the Smithsonian Agreement and the floating Canadian dollar, see Clyde Farnsworth, *New York Times,* 5 December 1971, and Edwin Dale, *New York Times,* 19 December 1971. The quotation and the information on the summit meeting are from J.L. Granatstein and Robert Bothwell, *Pirouette: Pierre Trudeau and Canadian Foreign Policy* (Toronto: University of Toronto Press, 1990), 68-70.

18 "Floating" here does not mean free-floating, but rather a carefully monitored movement of most currencies, with the central banks or their equivalents (that is, the US Federal Reserve) using various types of intervention to keep the "float" within a relatively narrow limit on any given day. (Over the longer run, say, a year, significant changes in the relative value of currencies should be expected.)

19 On the collapse of the attempt to create a new system of fixed exchange rates, see Joan Edelman Spero, *The Politics of International Economic Relations* (New York: St. Martin's Press, 1990), 43-8.

20 G. Bruce Doern and Brian W. Tomlin, *Faith and Fear: The Free Trade Story* (Toronto: Stoddart, 1991), 292, claim there was no such deal. Mel Hurtig, *The Betrayal of Canada* (Toronto: Stoddart, 1991), 14, suggests that there was such a deal. Michael C. Webb, "Canada and the International Monetary Regime," in *Canadian Foreign Policy and International Economic Regimes,* eds. A. Claire Cutler and Mark Zacher (Vancouver: UBC Press, 1992), 180, points out that because the G-7 in any case set targets for their members' currencies, the Americans could have made such an arrangement with Canada without linking it to the FTA. The original interview is summarized in the *Globe and Mail,* 3 December 1990, and refuted in the *Toronto Star,* 3 December 1990.

21 C. Fred Bergsten, *The United States in the World Economy* (Lexington: D.C. Heath, 1983), 187-8.

22 Stephen Krasner, *Defending the National Interest* (Princeton: Princeton University Press, 1978), 39.

23 "Trade Policy and National Security. Report by the Deputy Assistant Secretary of State for Economic Affairs (Beale)," *FRUS, 1958-60,* IV, 214; Deputy Director of the Office of Financial Development (Spiegel) to the Assistant Secretary of State for Economic Affairs (Thorp), memorandum, 21 July 1950, *FRUS, 1950,* I, 689; Stephen Krasner, *Defending,* 94-5.

24 The first reference to national treatment we found is in a telegram from the State Department to the embassy in Canada, 28 June 1963, *FRUS, 1961-63,* XIII, 1209.

25 Barbara Jenkins, *The Paradox of Continental Production* (Ithaca: Cornell University Press, 1992), 85-97; US Department of Commerce, International Trade Administration, *International Direct Investment: Global Trends and the US Role* (Washington: US Government Printing Office, 1988), 51-2, 73. On "national treatment" as an American policy, see Sidney L. Jones, memorandum for members of executive committee, Economic Policy Board, Department of the Treasury, 23 September 1975, Seidman Papers, box 26, Gerald Ford Library. On the monitoring of foreign investment in the US, see a draft of the

International Economic Report of the President, 9 September 1976, Seidman Papers, box 137, 6-8, GFA.

26 In the terminology of international investment flows, a "host" government is the government of the country in which money coming from a country based in another country is invested; the "home" government is the government of the country in which the corporation making the investment is based (or the individual making the investment lives). When Chrysler has a plant in Canada, the United States is the home, Canada, the host government. In practice, these concepts are becoming difficult to apply. Increasingly, large firms, such as Dupont, INCO, or Shell are owned by shareholders who have their legal residence in several different states, so that the "home" government is difficult to determine. This is especially true between Canada and the United States for firms such as INCO or Alcan.

27 Hearings before the Subcommittee on International Economic Policy of the Committee on Foreign Relations, United States Senate, 97th Congress (Washington: US Government Printing Office, 1982), 30 July, 28 September, and 28 October 1981; the quotations by Marc Leland are from 28 September 1981, 221. On the OECD, see US Department of Commerce, *International Direct Investment*, 80; on the Uruguay Round, see Jeffrey Schott, *Uruguay Round* (Washington: Institute for International Economics, 1994), 112-5.

28 Reagan's statement: *Public Papers of the President: Administration of Ronald Reagan, 1983*, 1243-8. Studies disagree about the extent to which government regulations can encourage or discourage investment flows (although, in some cases, such as that of Cuba, they can be cut off almost totally). Jenkins, *The Paradox of Continental Production*, 51-61, claims that regulations make little difference to the amount of investment; Bergsten, on the other hand, claims that incentives and performance requirements can seriously "distort" the flow of investment; see Bergsten to the Hearings of the Subcommittee on International Economic Policy, 30 July 1981, 2-5, 13-4, and Bergsten, *The United States in the World Economy*, 11-2. For a recent example at further multilateral limits on investment controls, see two reports by the Organization for Economic Cooperation and Development, *A Multilateral Agreement on Investment* (Paris: 1995) and *Multilateral Agreement on Investment: Progress Report by the MAI Group* (Paris: 1996).

29 B.S. Keirstead, *Canada in World Affairs: September 1951 to October 1953* (Toronto: Oxford University Press, 1956), 219-20. On Canadian and American policies during this period, see Jenkins, *The Paradox of Continental Production*, 126-8 and State Department Briefing Paper, Foreign Investments, November 1974, Seidman Papers, box 134, Gerald Ford Library. The statistics are given in Edelgard Mahant and Graeme Mount, *An Introduction to Canadian-American Relations* (Toronto: Nelson, 1989), 312-4.

30 Report on Canadian Talks with US and Commonwealth, Washington, 15 October 1957, *FRUS*, IX, 267-70.

31 Visit of Canadian Prime Minister Pearson, 21-22 January 1964, NSF, Country File: Canada, box 167-8; Ottawa to the Secretary of State, two untitled telegrams, dated 8 February 1964, NSF, Country File: Canada, box 165, I; W. Walton Butterworth, A New Look at our Relations with Canada, telegram addressed to State Department, 4 January 1964, NSF, Country Files: Canada, box 165, I. All three from the LBJ Library. O.W. Dier, Hyannis Port Meetings – May 10-11, 1963, Record Group 25 (External Affairs), 5030, file 1415-40, part 12.

32 John Saywell, ed., *Canadian Annual Review 1963*, 204-5; Embassy in Ottawa to the State Department, untitled and unsigned telegram, 8 February 1964, NSF, Country File: Canada, box 165, I, LBJ.

33 Memorandum for the President, Your Meeting with Prime Minister Pearson, Pearson Visit Briefing Book 1/21-22/64, NSF, Country File: Canada, box 167; Embassy in Ottawa to the State Department, untitled and unsigned telegram, 8 February 1964, NSF, Country File: Canada, box 165, I; Visit of Canadian Prime Minister Pearson, 21-22 January 1964, Canadian Tax on Dividends to Non-Residents and Double Tax Treaty, NSF, Country File: Canada, 1/21/22/64, box 167; Ambassador Butterworth, two telegrams, 18 March 1964, in NSF, Country File: Europe and USSR, boxes 162-5, all in LBJ Library.

34 For public opinion on foreign investment, see "Public Attitudes towards Foreign Policy Issues," *International Perspectives* (May-June 1976): 38.

35 For a brief summary of Canadian reactions to American investment during these years,

see Mahant and Mount, *An Introduction to Canadian American-Relations*, 230-1. For a more detailed discussion, see Richard Gwyn, *The 49th Paradox: Canada in North America* (Toronto: McClelland and Stewart, 1985), chs. 4 and 5.

36 Gwyn, *The 49th Paradox*, 79-80; Jacob Kaplan, "US Resource Policy: Canadian Connections," in *Natural Resources in US-Canadian Relations*, 119; US Department of Commerce, *International Direct Investment*, 56.

37 Robert M. Dunn, The Canadian Budget and Tax Reform Proposals, memorandum written to Mr. Ghiardi, 28 June 1971, Arthur Burns Papers, box B12, GFA. On the Mercantile Bank affair and Canadian public opinion, see Mahant and Mount, *An Introduction to Canadian-American Relations*, 230-2.

38 On the US, Canada, and the OECD code, see Alan Greenspan and Brent Scowcroft, Puerto Rico Summit Overview. Memorandum for the President, 25 June 1976, in Council of Economic Advisors. Alan Greenspan Files, box 39, GFA; C. Fred Bergsten, *The International Economic Policy of the United States* (Lexington: D.C. Heath, 1980), 210-1; C. Fred Bergsten to the Hearings of the Subcommittee on International Economic Policy, 17; and Kirton and Bothwell, "A Proud and Powerful," 122-3. On the American reaction to FIRA, see also the statement by Harvey E. Bale of the Office of the US Trade Representative to the Hearings of the Subcommittee on International Economic Policy, 28 September 1981, 187.

39 On the Ford Motor Company and Michelin tire plan incidents, see C. Fred Bergsten, *The International Economic Policy of the United States* (Lexington: D.C. Heath, 1980), 217, 223, 255, 300-3. On the Ford Motor Company incident, see also *Canadian Annual Review 1978*, 257, and Robert S. Strauss to Senator John Glenn, 13 September 1978, in WHCF, Country box 14, folder: CO 28, 10/1/77-4/30/78, Carter Library. On the nationalization of the potash industry, see Jeanne Kirk Laux and Maureen Appel Molot, "Potash," in *Natural Resources in US-Canadian Relations*, 176-7.

40 Investment Policy Division, Office of International Investment, International Trade Administration, US Department of Commerce, *The Use of Incentives and Performance Requirements by Foreign Governments* (Washington: October 1981), 15.

41 Testimony of Harvey E. Bale of the Office of the US Trade Representative, Hearings before the Subcommittee on International Economic Policy, 28 September 1981, 187. Statement of Robert D. Hormats, Assistant Secretary for Economic and Business Affairs, State Department to the Hearings before the Subcommittee on International Economic Policy, 10 March 1982, 10, 12.

42 Hearings before the Subcommittee on International Economic Policy, 18 September 1981, 197, and 28 October 1981, 221; see also testimony by Marc E. Eland of the Department of the Treasury, 10 March 1982, 21.

43 Hearings before the Subcommittee on International Economic Policy, 10 March 1982, 25.

44 *Canadian News Facts*, 19 July 1983, 2909; *Canadian Annual Review 1982*, 111; *New York Times*, 14 July 1983. For a legal discussion of the American complaint to GATT, see Emily Carasco, "The Foreign Investment Review Agency (FIRA) and the General Agreement on Tariffs and Trade (GATT): Compatible?" *Georgia Journal of International and Comparative Law* 13, 2 (1983): 441-63.

45 Testimony by Marc E. Eland of the Department of the Treasury, Hearings before the Subcommittee on International Economic Policy, 10 March 1982, 21.

46 Edelgard Mahant, *Free Trade in American-Canadian Relations* (Melbourne: Krieger, 1993), 45 and 146-7; G. Bruce Doern and Brian W. Tomlin, *Faith and Fear: The Free Trade Story* (Toronto: Stoddart, 1991), 29.

47 For a summary of the investment provisions of the FTA, see A.E. Safarian, Harmonizing Investment Policies in Canada, the United States and Mexico: Is Liberalization Possible? Paper read to the Centre for International Studies Conference, How is Free Trade Progressing? University of Toronto, 18-19 November 1991.

48 US House of Representatives, Committee of Energy and Commerce, Hearings before the Subcommittee on Commerce, Consumer Protection and Competitiveness of the Committee on Energy and Commerce, 100th Congress, 2nd session, 23 February 1988 (Washington: US Government Printing Office, 1988), 197, 200; Doern and Tomlin, *Faith and Fear*, 191.

49 Michael Gestrin and Alan Rugman, "The NAFTA's Impact on the North American

Investment Regime," *C.D. Howe Institute Commentary* 42 (March 1993): 10; Safarian, Harmonizing, 3; Susan Liebeler and William Lash, "Exon-Florio: Harbinger of Economic Nationalism," *Regulation, the Cato Review of Business and Government* <http:www.cato.org.pubs/regulations/reg/Gnld.html, 1-7>.

50 Doern and Tomlin, *Faith and Fear,* 189-93.

51 Elizabeth Smythe, Unfinished Business: North American Free Trade and Canadian Foreign Investment Regime Change, Paper read to the Annual Meeting of the Canadian Political Science Association, 8 June 1993; Barry Appleton, *Navigating NAFTA: A Concise User's Guide to the North American Free Trade Agreement* (Toronto: Carswell, 1994), 79-85; Gestrin and Rugman, "The Nafta's Impact," 2-5 and 9-10; *Globe and Mail,* 21 and 26 March 1992.

52 Panel on the Future Design and Implementation of US National Security Export Controls, Committee on Science, Engineering and Public Policy, National Academy of Science, National Academy of Engineering, Institute of Medicine, *Finding Common Ground. US Export Controls in a Changed Global Environment* (Washington: National Academy Press, 1991). This book gives an excellent summary and critique of American export control legislation. The article by Mitchel Wallerstein and William Snyder, "The Evolution of US Export Control Policy: 1949-1989," in Appendix G (3908-320), is especially informative. Unless stated otherwise this and the next paragraph are based on this book.

53 On export controls generally, see also Vernon and Spar, *Beyond Globalism,* 119-21.

54 Lawrence Robert Aronsen, *American National Security and Economic Relations with Canada, 1945-1954* (Westport: Praeger, 1997), 61.

55 See for example the March 1962 document, Canada, State Department, Guidelines for Policy and Operations, which urges the US administration to avoid export controls and antitrust measures "which appear in Canadian eyes to infringe on Canadian sovereignty." RG 59. General Records of the Department of State, Records of the Policy Planning Staff 1962, box 213, folder Canada.

56 Various documents, *FRUS, 1955-1957,* X, 461-507.

57 The 371st Meeting of the National Security Council, memorandum of discussion, 3 July 1958; Assistant Secretary of Commerce (Kearns) to the Chairman of the Council on Foreign Economic Policy (Randall), memorandum, 7 July 1958; 393rd Meeting of the National Security Council, memorandum of discussion, 13 January 1959; Secretary of the Council on Foreign Economic Policy (Cullen) to the Council, memorandum, 19 January 1959, all in *FRUS, 1958-60,* IV, 718-25 and 755-9.

58 Memoranda of conversation, 20 February 1961 and 17 April 1962, both in *FRUS, 1961-63,* XIII, 1140-9 and 1170-1. US newspaper quotation from *Canadian Annual Review 1963,* 331, and *1962,* 80. Visit of Canadian Prime Minister Pearson, 21-22 January 1964, Talking Points Paper, NSF, Country File 1/21-22/64, box 167, LBJ.

59 Joint United States-Canadian Committee on Trade and Economic Affairs, Washington, communique, 4-6 March 1966, Papers of Henry Fowler, box 67; Embassy Ottawa to State Department, 2 January 1968, Canadian Centenary 1967; Celebration of Coronach, NSF, Country File: Canada, boxes 167-8; Administrative History of the Department of State (1968), I, ch. 3, Europe; Benjamin Head, memorandum for Walt W. Rostow, White House Staff, 22 September 1967, NSF, Country File: Canada, box 167-8; all from LBJ.

60 John H. Harper, memorandum for Secretary of the Treasury Simon, 7 January 1977; William E. Simon, Microfiche of Papers at Lafayette College, Fiche 47.

61 Jeff Sallot, *Globe and Mail,* 6 July 1993.

62 Secretary of State Rusk to President Johnson, memorandum, 12 December 1963, *FRUS, 1961-1963,* XIII, 1216-7.

63 Quotations from, in order, *Hearing before the Subcommittee,* 10 March 1982, 4; Ivan B. White, "American Business in Canada," in *Neighbors Taken for Granted* (New York: Frederick Praeger, 1966), 92; memorandum of conversation, 25 November 1966, Fowler Papers, no box number, LBJ Library.

64 Testimony of Stephen Canner, US Department of the Treasury, to the Committee on Banking, Housing and Urban Affairs, United States Senate, 20 May 1998, *The Banking Jurisdiction within the United States/Canada Free Trade Agreement* (Washington: US Government Printing Office, 1988), 10.

Chapter 7: Canada in American Trade Policy

1 For brief reviews of American trade policy before the Second World War, see E.E. Mahant, *Free Trade in American-Canadian Relations* (Melbourne: Krieger, 1993), 16-31; Richard Cooper, "Trade Policy as Foreign Policy," in *US Trade Policy in a Changing World Economy,* ed. Robert Stern (Cambridge: MIT Press, 1988), 290-321.

2 David Haglund, "Unbridled Constraint: The Macdonald Commission Volumes on Canada and the International Political Economy," *Canadian Journal of Political Science* 20 (1987): 607.

3 For the story of the abortive ITO, see Steve Dryden, *Trade Warriors: USTR and the American Crusade for Free Trade* (New York: Oxford University Press, 1995), 13-31; Judith Goldstein, *Ideas, Interests and American Trade Policy* (Ithaca: Cornell University Press, 1993), 158-63; on its burial, see Deputy Assistant Secretary of State for Economic Affairs (O'Hara) to the Secretary of State, memorandum, 10 November 1950, *FRUS, 1950,* I, 780-7.

4 On protectionist measures in the US Congress and on the history of "fast track," see Dryden, *Trade Warriors,* 117 and 183-4; on Section 301, see Anne Krueger, *American Trade Policy: A Tragedy in the Making* (Washington: The AEI Press, 1995), 38-40; on bilateral free trade, see Mahant, *Free Trade in Canadian-American Relations,* 41.

5 For a brief summary of each of the four acts, see David Haglund and Alex von Bredow, *US Trade Barriers and Canadian Minerals* (Kingston: Queen's University Centre for Resource Studies, 1990), 22-37.

6 Krueger, *American Trade Policy,* 67. For a detailed analysis of Section 301, see *Aggressive Unilateralism: America's 301 Trade Policy and the World Trading System,* eds. Jagdish Bhagwati and Hugh Patrick (Ann Arbor: University of Michigan Press, 1990); Stephen Cohen, *The Making of United States International Economic Policy* (New York: Praeger, 1988), 211. In 1985, a Canadian cabinet minister claimed that over the last "few years," over a thousand protectionist bills had been introduced in Congress; see Mahant, *Free Trade,* 46.

7 On the trend toward bilateral or regional trade agreements, see Robert Lawrence and Charles Schultze, "Evaluating the Options," and Rudinger Dornbusch, "Policy Options for Freer Trade: The Case for Bilateralism," both in *An American Trade Strategy: Options for the 1990s,* eds. Robert Lawrence and Charles Schultze (Washington: Brookings Institution, 1990), 106-41; and John Jackson, "Multilateral and Bilateral Negotiating Approaches for the Conduct of US Trade Policies," in Stern, *US Trade Policies,* 377-86.

8 Ann Krueger, "Free Trade Is the Best Policy," in *An American Trade Strategy,* 90-2.

9 Cohen, *The Making of United States International Economic Policy,* 209-18.

10 Krueger, *American Trade Policy,* 53-4.

11 The background to the preparatory conference is described in a large number of documents, dated from January to November 1946 and reproduced in *FRUS, 1946,* I, 1260-368.

12 On Australia and the wool issue, see Minutes of a Meeting of the United States Delegation, Geneva, Switzerland, 6 May 1947, and Minutes of a Meeting of the United States Delegation, Geneva, Switzerland, 4 August 1947, *FRUS, 1947,* I, 925-8 and 974.

13 On breaking the empire bloc, see Minutes of Meeting of the United States Delegation, Geneva, Switzerland, 5 May 1947, and Clair Wilcox to Representatives of the British Commonwealth, Geneva, Switzerland, statement 15 September 1947, *FRUS, 1947,* I, 920-3, 983; Lawrence Robert Aronsen, *American National Security and Economic Relations with Canada, 1945-1954* (Westport: Praeger, 1997), 41; and Michael Hart, "Almost But Not Quite: The 1947-48 Bilateral Canada-U.S. Negotiations," *American Review of Canadian Studies* 19 (1989): 32-3; on "good support," see Minutes of Meeting of the United States Delegation, Geneva, Switzerland, 2 July 1947, *FRUS, 1947,* I, 963.

14 On the bilateral Canadian-American negotiations, see Homer S. Fox, Member of the United States Delegation Staff, memorandum of conversation, 9 May 1947, *FRUS, 1947,* I, 933-7.

15 On the possibility of separate agreements, see Vice Chairman of the United States Delegation (Wilcox) to the Chairman of the United States Delegation (Clayton), memorandum, 6 August 1947, *FRUS, 1947,* I, 975. On the completion of the tariff negotiations, see The Consul General at Geneva (Troutman) to the Secretary of State, Geneva, 2 October 1947, and Director of the Office of International Trade Policy (Wilcox) to the Under Secretary of State for Economic Affairs (Clayton), memorandum, 5 October 1947, both in

FRUS, 1947, I, 1006-9; on the attempt to make Canada give up the preferences, see Chairman of the Committee on Trade Agreements (Brown) to President Truman, memorandum, 17 October 1947, *FRUS, 1947,* I, 1015. On the implementation of the GATT, see Chairman of the Committee on Trade Agreements (Brown) to President Truman, memorandum, 17 October 1947, *FRUS, 1947,* I, 1016-25.

16 Hart, "Almost But Not Quite," 31-2.

17 Ibid., 38-40; Ambassador in Canada (Atherton) to the Secretary of State, *FRUS, 1947,* III, 127-8; Director of the Policy Planning Staff (Kennan), memorandum, 4 September 1947, *FRUS, 1947,* III, 405; Summary of U.S.-Canada Financial Discussions October 28-31, Washington, 1 November 1947, *Documents on Canadian External Relations, 1947,* XIII (Ottawa: Minister of Supply and Services, 1993), 1435-40; Aronsen, *American National Security,* 56. For an excellent summary of Canadian moves and motivations, see Thomas Thong, "Postwar Canadian Trade Policy 1945-1948," an essay submitted to Laurentian University, 1996, esp. 27-34, 40-2.

18 Hart, "Almost But Not Quite," 40-1.

19 Ibid., 43-9; for State Department plans and a summary of the proposed agreement, see Assistant Secretary of State for Economic Affairs (Thorp) to the Under-Secretary of State (Lovett), memorandum, 8 March 1948, and the following documents in *FRUS, 1948,* IX, 406-11.

20 Chief of the Division of Commercial Policy (Willoughby), memorandum, 2 February 1949, and Assistant Chief of the Division of British Commonwealth Affairs (Snow) to the Director of the Executive Secretariat (Humelsine), memorandum, *FRUS, 1949,* II, 393-4, 396-400.

21 Wilfred Malenbaum to Allen Evans, 19 January 1948, Records of the Policy Planning Staff, Assistance to Foreign Countries, RG 59, box 5, folder 13, NARA.

22 Secretary of State to the President, memorandum, 20 November 1950, *FRUS, 1950,* I, 782-4.

23 William Sanders, Special Assistant to the Assistant Secretary of State for United Nations Affairs (Hickerson), memorandum, 27 April 1950; Secretary of State to the Acting Secretary of State, 16 May 1950; United States Delegation at the Tripartite Preparatory Meeting to the Secretary of State, London, 28 April 1950; Preparatory Meetings of the United States and France, London, 27 April 1950; Head of the United States Delegation at the Tripartite Preparatory Meetings (Jessup) to the Secretary of State, London, 5 May 1950; United States Delegation at the Tripartite Foreign Ministers Meeting to the Acting Secretary of State, 10 May 1950, and 16 May 1950, *FRUS, 1950,* III, 76, 105, 115, 846, 894, 912, 1024, and 1070.

24 Goldstein, *Ideas,* esp. ch. 1; Acting Chairman of the United States Delegation to the Torquay Conference (Cose) to the Secretary of State, Torquay, 17 March 1951, and Temporary Acting Chairman of the United States Delegation to the Torquay Conference (Phelps) to the Secretary of State, 3 February 1951, *FRUS, 1951,* I, 1278, 1282, 1338.

25 On the 1953 and 1957 proposals, see Donald Barry, "Eisenhower, St. Laurent and Free Trade, 1953," *International Perspectives* (March/April 1987): 8-10; Hart, "Almost But Not Quite," 49-51; United States Minutes of the Second Meeting Between President Eisenhower and Prime Minister St. Laurent, White House, 8 May 1953, 3:00 PM, *FRUS, 1953,* VI, 2088-90; President's Special Assistant (Randall) to the Secretary of State, Washington, letter, 1 April 1957, and Secretary of State to the Chairman of the Council on Foreign Economic Policy (Randall), Washington, letter, 25 July 1957, *FRUS, 1953-1957,* XXVII, 883-5, 902.

26 The same poll found that 74 percent favoured further restrictions on American takeovers of Canadian firms! Peter C. Newman, "The US and Us," *Maclean's,* 6 June 1964, 16, 33.

27 Livingston Merchant and A.D.P. Heeney, "Canada and the United States: Principles for Partnership," *Atlantic Community Quarterly* 3 (Winter 1965): 388.

28 US State Department, Canada, State Department Guidelines for Policy and Operations, General Records of the Policy Planning Staff 1962, RG 59, box 213, folder Canada, NARA.

29 R.J. Wonnacott and P. Wonnacott, *Free Trade between the United States and Canada: The Potential Economic Effects* (Cambridge: Harvard University Press, 1967); W.W. Butterworth

to State Department, 2 January 1968, and 4 September 1968, both in NSF, Country File, Canada, boxes 166-8, LBJ Library.

30 *Canadian Annual Review of Politics and Public Affairs, 1971,* 241-5, 326, 329-30, and *1973,* 231-5.

31 United States Public Law 1993-619; Congressional Record, Senate, 13 December 1974, 39757; "Legislative History. Trade Act of 1974," *United States Code: Congressional and Administrative News,* 93rd Congress, 2nd Session, 1974, IV, 7363-4.

32 "Legislative History: Trade Agreements Act of 1919," *United States Code: Congressional and Administrative News,* 96th Congress, First Session, 1979, 645-6. See also *Congressional Record, Senate,* 5 April 1979, 7490, 21 May 1979, 11897-8, and 17 November 1979, 32295, and House of Representatives, 11 June 1979, 14240-1.

33 Mahant, *Free Trade,* 41-2; *New York Times,* 14 November 1979.

34 United States House of Representatives, Committee on Ways and Means, Subcommittee on Trade, 26 June 1980, 125; Hearings before the Subcommittee on International Economic Policy of the Committee on Foreign Relations, United States Senate, 97th Congress, 28 October 1981 (Washington: US Government Printing Office, 1982), 242-3.

35 Dryden, *Trade Warriors,* 255-77; World Demand/Supply Trends and Prospects – Grains (1974-85), Council of Economic Advisors, box 68, Gary L. Seeders File, GFA.

36 Peyton Lyon, *Canada-United States Free Trade and Canadian Independence* (Ottawa: Economic Council of Canada, 1975); Denis Stairs, "North American Continentalism: Perspectives and Policies in Canada," in *Regionalism and Supranationalism,* ed. David Cameron (Montreal: Institute for Research on Public Policy, 1981), 102-3; Donald Barry, *Calgary Herald,* 13 September 1979; John Holmes, *Life with Uncle* (Toronto: University of Toronto Press, 1981), 100.

37 For a good brief introduction to the 1965 Autopact, see Paul Wonnacott, *The United States and Canada: The Quest for Free Trade* (Washington: Institute for International Economics, 1987), 72-8.

38 Visit of Canadian Prime Minister, 21-22 January 1964, NSF, Country File: Canada, 1/21-22/64; Under-Secretary of State, Washington, memorandum for the president, 14 September 1964, NSF, Country File: Canada, LBJ/Pearson Meeting, 9/16/64, both in box 167, LBJ Library. Dean Rusk, memorandum for the president, 18 September 1964; Henry Ford to the President, letter, 16 September 1964, NSF, Country File: Europe and USSR, Canada Cables, I, 12/63-7/64, part 2, boxes 162-5, LBJ Library. On Senator Hartke, see *Congressional Record-Senate,* 22 November 1974, 37086-7 and 13 December 1974, 39836-8.

39 Douglas Dillon, memorandum for the president, 15 September 1964, NSF, Country File: Europe and USSR, Canada Cables, I, 12/63-7/64, part 2, boxes 162-5, LBJ Library; George Ball, memorandum for the president, 16 September 1964, NSF, Country File: Canada, LBJ/Pearson Meeting, 9/16/64, box 167, LBJ Library. See also, John Kirton and Robert Bothwell, "A Proud and Powerful Country: American Attitudes toward Canada, 1963-1976," *Queen's Quarterly* 92, 1 (1985): 113-4.

40 McGeorge Bundy, memorandum for the president, 27 November 1964, NSF, Country File: Europe and USSR, Canada Cables, I, 12/63-7/64, part 2, boxes 162-5, LBJ.

41 McGeorge Bundy, memorandum to the president, 27 November 1964, NSF, Country File: Europe and USSR, Canada Cables, I, 12/63-7/64, part 2, boxes 162-5, LBJ.

42 Sources of statistics: Ambassador Butterworth to State Department, 4 September 1968, NSF, Country File: Canada, V, box 166, LBJ Library; *Canadian Annual Review 1972,* 261; Paul Wonnacott, *The United States and Canada: The Quest for Free Trade* (Washington: Institute for International Economics, 1987), 76.

43 J.L. Granatstein and Robert Bothwell, *Pirouette: Pierre Trudeau and Canadian Foreign Policy* (Toronto: University of Toronto Press, 1990), 64-5.

44 On Reagan and Brock, see Dryden, *Trade Warriors,* 266, 271, and Ronald Reagan, *An American Life* (New York: Simon and Schuster, 1990), 242; on the trend toward bilateral agreements, see Krueger, *American Trade Policy,* 7, 30.

45 To say that the Reagan administration welcomed a Canadian initiative is not to say that it orchestrated it. Much later, the American ambassador to Canada, Paul Robinson, tried to take credit for the free trade initiative. Mel Hurtig, *The Betrayal of Canada* (Toronto: Stoddart, 1991), 177-8.

46 Unless indicated otherwise, this section is based on Mahant, *Free Trade*, 43-53, 136-47. A number of interviews one of the authors conducted with American officials (in 1991) confirmed the importance the American side attached to the initiative coming from Canada.

47 Joe Clark, "Towards Closer Co-operation with the United States," *Statements and Speeches* (Canada, Department of External Affairs), 84/1, 15 October 1984.

48 The Quebec Summit, 17-18 March 1985, a collection of press releases provided by the Office of the Prime Minister, The Rt. Honourable Brian Mulroney; for a summary of American aims during the Uruguay Round, see Jeffrey Schott, *The Uruguay Round: An Assessment* (Washington: Institute for International Economics, 1994), 8.

49 Text of Report by US Representative Clayton Yeutter to the President on Bilateral Trade with Canada, included in an untitled, unnumbered Sessional Paper submitted to the House of Commons by Prime Minister Mulroney, 26 September 1985. The report by Yeutter is on pp. 70-2.

50 *Economic Report of the President*, transmitted to Congress, February 1985 (Washington: United States Government Printing Office, 1985), 126; Jeffrey Schott, *More Free Trade Areas?* (Washington: Institute for International Economics, 1989), 2. See also, G. Bruce Doern and Brian W. Tomlin, *Faith and Fear: The Free Trade Story* (Toronto: Stoddart, 1991), 157.

51 Doern and Tomlin, *Faith and Fear*, 157-8.

52 On Murphy, see *Trade Warriors*, 340-3. Information on the size of the negotiating teams is from William Merkins, the deputy American negotiator, Washington, 12 March 1991. On the organization of the two negotiating teams, see Doern and Tomlin, *Faith and Fear*, 163-7.

53 Michael Hart, Bill Dymond, and Colin Robertson, *Decision at Midnight: Inside the Canada-US Free Trade Negotiations* (Vancouver: UBC Press, 1994), 155-366; Doern and Tomlin, *Faith and Fear*, 152-201.

54 In early September, Prime Minister Mulroney's chief of staff, Derek Burney, had written the chief of the White House staff, Howard Baker, to request negotiations to break the FTA impasse. Baker told Burney to speak to Treasury Secretary James Baker, who technically was in charge of international tariff negotiations. Doern and Tomlin, *Faith and Fear*, 175.

55 The text of the agreement was published by both governments separately. The Canadian version is *The Canada-US Free Trade Agreement* (Ottawa: External Affairs, 1987). A detailed analysis of the FTA's provisions in non-legal language can be found in Marc Gold and David Leyton-Brown, eds., *Trade-Offs on Free Trade: The Canada-United States Free Trade Agreement* (Toronto: Carswell, 1988). A shorter summary is found in Mahant, *Free Trade*, 56-65.

56 Technically, the Free Trade Agreement is not a treaty but an intergovernmental agreement to pass concurrent and complementary legislation.

57 Donald Barry, "The Road to NAFTA," in Donald Barry, ed., *Toward a North American Community: Canada, the United States and Mexico* (Boulder, CO: Westview Press, 1995), 3-4.

58 Ibid., 5.

59 *Washington Post*, 28 June 1990.

60 [President Reagan] State of the Union Address, Congressional Record, 26 January 1988, Proceedings and Debates of the 100th Congress, 2nd Session; interview with State Department official, 14 March 1991; Paul Krugman, "The Uncomfortable Truth about NAFTA," *Foreign Affairs* 72, 5 (1993): 18-9; Ambassador Edward Ney, Free Trade Revisited: Mexico and the GATT, Remarks to the Canada-US Business Association, 4 December 1990; George Bush, "Remarks Announcing the Completion of Negotiations on the North American Free Trade Agreement, 12 August 1992," *Public Papers of the Presidents*, Administration of George Bush 1992, II, 1340-1. On American enthusiasm for Mexican economic reforms, see also "Fact Sheet: US-Mexico Economic Relations," *US Department of State Dispatch*, 26 November 1990, 293.

61 A New Framework for Global Growth in the 1990s, Hearings before the Subcommittee on International Economic Policy and Trade of the Committee on Foreign Affairs, House of Representatives, 100th Congress, 2nd Session, 19 September 1988, 273; *Washington Post*, 21 April 1990.

62 "Commitment to Reach North American Free Trade Agreement," *Department of State Dispatch* 3, 29 (20 July 1992): 565.

63 On the Caribbean Basin Initiative and the NAFTA, see Krueger, *American Trade Policy*, 90.
64 *Free Trade Observer*, June 1990, 109; *Globe and Mail*, 14 June 1990; "Commitment to Reach North American Free Trade Agreement," 565.
65 Transcript of Press Conference: President George Bush, 5 February 1991, The White House, Federal Information Systems Corporation; *Globe and Mail*, 12 January and 7 February 1991; *Toronto Star*, 7 February 1992.
66 *Globe and Mail*, 4 September 1992.
67 Though the Canadian Parliament had voted on NAFTA before the 1993 elections, the formal legal ratification did not take place until after the Americans and Mexicans had completed their domestic ratification requirements.
68 "Commitment to Reach North American Free Trade Agreement," 567; "Gist: North American Free Trade Agreement," *Department of State Dispatch*, 24 June 1991, 454; Overview. The North American Free Trade Agreement, Washington: Office of the US Trade Representative, August 1992.
69 Overview, August 1992.
70 A brief tabular comparison of the NAFTA and the FTA can be found in *Globe and Mail*, 13 August 1992. A longer, more detailed comparison is that in Richard Lipsey, Daniel Schwanen, and Ronald Wonnacott, *The NAFTA: What's In, What's Out, What's Next* (Toronto: C.D. Howe Institute, 1994).
71 A good summary of the NAFTA in language more comprehensible than the original text is that by Barry Appleton, *Navigating NAFTA: A Concise User's Guide to the North American Free Trade Agreement* (Toronto: Carswell, 1994).
72 On the Autopact in the FTA, see "The Automotive Industry," 265-8, and Paul Wonnacott, "Autos and the Free Trade Agreement: Toward a More Secure Trading Relationship," 269-75, both in Gold and Leyton-Brown, *Trade-Offs*.
73 *Globe and Mail*, 5 and 15 August 1990, 14 February 1992, 9 and 14 March 1992, and 14 July 1992; "Estranged Partners," *Maclean's*, 16 March 1992, 34-5; *Toronto Star*, 17 August 1989.
74 On the automotive industry provisions of the NAFTA, see Description of the Proposed North American Free Trade Agreement Prepared by the Governments of Canada, the United Mexican States and the United States of America, 12 August 1992 [no place of publication], 7-9; NAFTA, Annex 300-A, from gopher://wiretap.spies.com:70/001/Clov/NAFTA/03.markets, website prepared by the University of Texas and Texas A&M University; Lipsey, *The NAFTA*, 53-5; Peter Morici, "NAFTA Rules of Origin and Automotive Content," in *Assessing NAFTA: A Trinational Analysis*, eds. Steven Globerman and Michael Walker (Vancouver: Fraser Institute, 1993), 226-50. On the Mexican auto industry, see also *Globe and Mail*, 5 May 1992; *Toronto Star*, 14 August 1991; *New York Times*, 14 November 1993.

Chapter 8: Conclusions
1 Lawrence Aronsen, *American National Security and Economic Relations with Canada, 1945-1954* (Westport: Praeger, 1997), 154-5.
2 Ibid., 53 and 170.
3 On the 1951 review, see ibid., xvi.
4 The trade example is taken from ibid., 40-3.
5 Ibid., 192.
6 Edelgard Mahant and Graeme Mount, *An Introduction to Canadian-American Relations* (Toronto: Nelson, 1989), 244-5.
7 John Holmes, *Life with Uncle: The Canadian-American Relationship* (Toronto: University of Toronto Press, 1981), 73.
8 Literally dozens of studies bring together the contributions of various parts of the American administration to either specific foreign policy decisions or to more general policies. The following brief list thus provides examples only. Three pioneers in the field are: Glenn D. Paige, *The Korean Decision* (New York: Free Press, 1968); C. Snyder, H.W. Bruck, and Barton Sapin, eds., *Foreign Policy Decision-Making* (New York: Free Press, 1962; and Graham Allison, *Essence of Decision* (Boston: Little Brown, 1971). Morton Halperin, "The

Decision to Deploy the ABM," *World Politics* (October 1972), 62-95, deals with defence policy. Irving Janis, *Victims of Groupthink* (Boston: Houghton Mifflin, 1972) discusses the Marshall Plan, Cuba, and Vietnam.

9 The following constitute only a small sampling of the many theoretical studies of foreign policies produced in those years: W.F. Hanrieder, ed., *Comparative Foreign Policy in Perspective* (New York: McKay, 1971); Charles Kegley, *A General Empirical Typology of Foreign Policy Behavior* (Beverly Hills: Sage, 1973); Charles Kegley, *International Events and the Comparative Analysis of Foreign Policy* (Columbia: University of South Carolina, 1975); John P. Lovell, *Foreign Policy in Perspective: Strategy – Adaptation – Decision-Making* (New York: Holt, Rinehart and Winston, 1970); Patrick McGowan, *Comparative Study of Foreign Policy* (Beverly Hills: Sage Library of Social Research, 1973); James Rosenau, ed., *Linkage Politics* (New York: Free Press, 1969); James Rosenau, *The Scientific Study of Foreign Policy* (Don Mills: Collier-Macmillan, 1971). There is at least one recent study on the concept of foreign policy: Laura Neack, Jeanne Hey, and Patrick Haney, *Foreign Policy Analysis: Continuity and Change in Its Second Generation* (Englewood Cliffs: Prentice Hall, 1995).

10 Judith Goldstein, *Ideas, Interests and American Trade Policy* (Ithaca: Cornell University Press, 1993); Alastair Smith, "Diversionary Foreign Policy in Democratic Systems," *International Studies Quarterly* 40 (1996): 133-53. Another interesting recent study that tries to go beyond the material basis of foreign policy is Kjell Goldmann, *Change and Stability in Foreign Policy* (Princeton: Princeton University Press, 1988).

Index